The Good Work of Non-Christians, Empowerment, and the New Creation

The Good Work of Non-Christians, Empowerment, and the New Creation

The Efficacy of the Holy Spirit's Empowering for Ordinary Work

STUART C. WEIR

Foreword by John C. McDowell

◦PICKWICK *Publications* • Eugene, Oregon

THE GOOD WORK OF NON-CHRISTIANS, EMPOWERMENT, AND THE NEW CREATION
The Efficacy of the Holy Spirit's Empowering for Ordinary Work

Copyright © 2016 Stuart C. Weir. All rights reserved. Except for brief quotations in critical publications or reviews, no part of this book may be reproduced in any manner without prior written permission from the publisher. Write: Permissions, Wipf and Stock Publishers, 199 W. 8th Ave., Suite 3, Eugene, OR 97401.

Pickwick Publications
An Imprint of Wipf and Stock Publishers
199 W. 8th Ave., Suite 3
Eugene, OR 97401

www.wipfandstock.com

PAPERBACK ISBN 13: 978-1-62032-810-1
HARDCOVER ISBN 13: 978-1-4982-8857-6

Cataloguing-in-Publication data:

Weir, Stuart C.

The good work of non-Christians, empowerment, and the new creation : the efficacy of the Holy Spirit's empowering for ordinary work / Stuart C. Weir ; foreword by John C. McDowell.

xvi + 242 pp. ; 23 cm. Includes bibliographical references.

ISBN: 978-1-62032-810-1 (PAPERBACK) | ISBN: 978-1-4982-8857-6 (HARDCOVER)

1. Employees—Religious life. 2. 3. I. McDowell, John. C. II. Title.

BV4593 .W45 2016

Manufactured in the U.S.A.   04/22/2016

New Revised Standard Version Bible: Catholic Edition, copyright 1989, 1993, Division of Christian Education of the National Council of the Churches of Christ in the United States of America. Used by permission. All rights reserved.

To Esther and Elia

Contents

Foreword by John C. McDowell | ix
Acknowledgments | xv
Introduction | xvii

1 **Francis Schaeffer** (1912–84) and **John Stott** (1921–2011): The Epistemological Problem of the Good Work of Non-Christians in Twentieth- and Twenty-First-Century Evangelical Theology | 1

2 **Thomas Chalmers** (1780–1847): The Ingratitude of Sinners' Work as Earthly and Heavenly Impediments | 41

3 **Richard Baxter** (1615–91): The Work of Infidels and their Noetic Obstacle to the *Vita Contemplativa* | 75

4 **John Calvin** (1509–64): Peculiar Grace as Unsalvific, Pneumatological Empowerment for the Work of the Impious | 112

5 **John Wesley** (1703–91) : Co-operative Heathen Conscience with Prevenient Grace | 147

6 **An Evangelical Re-reading of the Sheep and the Goats**: The Grace-Empowered and Eternal Efficacy of Good Work by Non-Christians | 186

Bibliography | 213

Foreword

THE WESTERN IMAGINATION FOR some time now has been dominated by questions concerning agency and the agent that assume something of a disjunction from each other. Images of the autonomy of the agent have taken shape in, among other things, the cultural pervasiveness of ideologies of *choice* undergirded by an account of the agent's *will*. The implications for a theology of the work of agents has been pronounced.[1] However, while the theological disrepair of certain construals of agent-and-agency will take many forms, one of the most enduring has been the alienation of the Christian agent from her work when faith topples into the mode of consolation. Much British evangelicalism has capitulated too neatly to just such a mood of faith-in-the-mode-of-comfort, thereby subverting the discomfort necessitated by Christian faith's iconoclastic or interrogative mood in its work of offering critical challenge and suggesting ways for reparative change. Stuart Weir's analysis does not take that form. According to it, many of the binary oppositions are inappropriate to a well ordered theology, and the selection of conversation partners proves to be judicious in this critical enterprise. Even so, to tackle Schaeffer and Stott alongside the likes of Calvin would appear to offer substantial intellectual inequitability. However, the voices of each are attended to by the study with a just and sensitive ear informed by the Spirit of God's grace.

The theological resource that the book's typology finds most helpful is pneumatological. There is sense in this, especially since it offers considerably more promise as a theologically reparative lens than that which emerges from essentialised readings of creation or the *imago dei*, or at least if that creationist imagery is not reinterpreted eschatologically.[2] The Spirit

---

1. See L. Gregory Jones, "Beliefs, Desires, Practices, and the Ends of Theological Education," in *Practicing Theology: Beliefs and Practices in Christian Life* , ed. Miroslav Volf and Dorothy C. Bass (Grand Rapids: Eerdmans, 2002) 185–205.

2. It is this christological loss that dogs so-called "natural theology" and its apologetic expression, disappearing under the force of epistemologies separated from critical

is spoken of in the New Testament under images such as *freedom* (Gal. 5), and God's uncontrollability (Jn. 3:8). Yet the Spirit has more often than not been constrained and domesticated by forms of ecclesial control, so that pneumatology becomes little more than an extension of the modes of scriptural reading by the believer or the believing community, of the self-extension of 'spiritual' feeling, or of sacramental distribution. Accordingly, the Spirit becomes an *instrument* of human work rather than its ground, occasion and ongoing renovation. It is here that the temptations to theologically order identity in a Donatistic mold loom large. This mold provides a politics of purity for the Spirit-possessing person/people which is now set over against the impious 'other', an 'other' increasingly alienated from regard for the divine resources for well-being. This accords with what John Milbank calls "crypto-fascism": that is, a form of thought that while imagining that it knows what the common good looks like from which to generate supportive theological models, operates as an act of arbitrary self-assertion on the part of desire.[3] Recovery of testimony to the dangerous, troubling and traumatic presence in the Spirit is necessary for the flourishing of transformative practices in, with and under God's disruptively redeeming work.

The control of an instrumentalising trajectory has been much in evidence in the philosophies that have accompanied and undergirded the industrial age. However, to reduce things, especially persons as workers or consumers, to an instrumental rationality is to alienate that which should not be alienated. With the growth of leisure activities and the sentiment of Romantic 'feeling' the alienation becomes complete (it is here that another binary, that of public/private, particularly takes shape). As Brad Evans and Henry Giroux admit, "The utopian promise of the Enlightenment thus contained within it the violence and brutalities embedded in the logic of instrumental rationality and the unchecked appeal to progress and ideological purity."[4] It is here that what Deuleuzian inspired Daniel Bell calls the capitalist technology of desire emerges and spreads in the violent, competitive and instrumentalising form of "savage capitalism" that is sustained by "cancerous consumption," and is reducible to the self-perpetuating nihilism of ungrounded desire.[5] Such a move results in state terror, the terror of the

---

consideration of the politics of "rationality". Much evangelical theology, for instance, has been steeped in imaging that epistemic issues are primary and that conscience is a natural moral guide.

3. John Milbank, *The Word Made Strange: Theology, Language, Culture* (Malden and Oxford: Blackwell, 1997) 262.

4. Brad Evans and Henry A. Giroux, *Disposable Futures: The Seduction of Violence in the Age of Spectacle* (San Francisco: City Lights, 2015) 13.

5. Daniel M. Bell, Jr., *Liberation Theology After the End of History: The Refusal to*

market which leads powerful states into military invasion; of quelling dissent at home; and of the market's making lives 'disposable'. Post-industrial societies may have liquefied the solid forms of alienation, but the alienations have, if anything, intensified as well as diversified. Narratives of progress slip silently into the night, even if they had operated only through a fog hindering their moral accountability. As Theodor Adorno once observed, "It would be advisable to think of progress in the crudest, most basic terms: that no one should go hungry anymore, that there should be no more torture, no more Auschwitz. Only then will the idea of progress be free from lies."[6] Liquid- or late- modernity generates conditions that render employment insecure, workers' rights increasingly fragile, relations temporary, locations mobile as the corporatisation of power becomes unhindered by local borders and markets, and a "human being as a mere statistical unit."[7] Lives become disposably wasted. They become collateral damage to a system which serves sheer profit, which provides the leisure time to enjoy earnings, and which dismantles the forms of welfare protection required to protect the vulnerable.[8] As Zygmunt Bauman catchily announces, "A consumerist attitude may lubricate the wheels of the economy; [but] it sprinkles sand into the bearings of morality."[9]

To speak critically in this way is to challenge theology to recall that its pneumatology is informed by the Spirit of the *crucified* Christ. The 'Spirit' who is 'Holy' is not a signifier floating freely on linguistic winds uninformed by its theological operations within the theo-grammatical rule of the indivisibly singular work of God. The Spirit is not an *individual* within the outworking of God's own life, even if the manner of God's presence in the Spirit takes a particular and individuated form appropriate to the nature of

---

Cease Suffering (London and New York: Routledge, 2001) 10, 85. The concept of "savage capitalism" is developed by Bell from Franz Hinkelammert. Cf. Bell, *The Economy of Desire: Christianity and Capitalism in a Postmodern World* (Grand Rapids: Baker Academic, 2012).

6. Theodor Adorno, cited by Detlev Claussen, *Theodor W. Adorno: One Last Genius* (Cambridge: Harvard University Press, 2008) 338.

7. Leonidas Donskis, in Zygmunt Bauman and Leonidas Donskis, *Moral Blindness: The Loss of Sensitivity in Liquid Modernity* (Cambridge and Malden: Polity, 2013) 52.

8. Even those of us engaged in higher education increasingly recognise the sting of a bureaucracy driven less and less by matters of moral accountability than the formal pressure of accountability to market forces and destructive forms of competition.

9. Zygmunt Bauman, in Zygmunt Bauman and Leonidas Donskis, *Moral Blindness: The Loss of Sensitivity in Liquid Modernity* (Cambridge and Malden: Polity, 2013) 15. Cf. Henry A. Giroux, *Zombie Politics and Culture in the Age of Casino Capitalism*, 2nd ed. (New York, Bern, Frankfurt, Berlin, Brussels, Vienna, Oxford, Warsaw: Peter Lang, 2014) ch. 10.

the Spirit.[10] It is here in the pneumatic making of all things new that disruptive possibilities lie which are so sorely needed to feature in any conception of the actuality of the eschatological embrace of the creature. God, through God's Spirit, takes up in consummating healing all the works of God's hands. Not only does this mean that in a certain sense nothing is ontologically 'trivial' or 'mundane' or 'secular' where those terms are constructed in a purely negative contrast with 'meaningful' or 'significant' or 'sacred', since all will be remembered (even if forgiven) in God.[11] It also indicates that the works of God are *gifts*, given in order to cultivate creaturely well-being in participation in the abundance of God's own eternally rich life.[12]

This takes us back to the notion of the agent and agency, the worker and her work. By embracing the ecology of all work in the plenitudinousness of the transfigurative power of God's Spirit of the crucified and risen Christ a lens (or a prism) is provided for conceiving of human work as lifted up (or gifted) into mutual responsibility and celebration, hospitality and gratitude. Life in humble, kenotic and responsive *poesis* provides a witness to the God who works to make all things new, and therefore to the contingent conditions of making a life together without end even in what may appear to us as the very strangest of places. This is the context for being given eyes to see and ears to hear the signs of the healing workings of God's Self-presenting to all God's creatures. Here Weir's study offers a timely claim concerning the need for embodying repair at the level of the theological imagination itself, and that that this occurs within a better ordered biblical account of the sacramentality of the works of God's justice which makes covenantal hospitality in and through the healing of the workers. Such a testimony is badly needed in cultures prone to commodify and instrumentalise life and dehumanise workers. After all, "We live at a time in which instrumental rationality," particularly well expressed in the biopolitics of the 'free' market,

---

10. This is to say that there are not two teleologically *different* works of God in the Spirit and in the Son, and this needs to be factored into imagery of the end of God's work lest there be two different graces being given in God's salvific favour.

11. Unpacking this eschatological hope would be a speculative step too far. The eschatological imagination requires a certain hesitancy to be built into its dogmatic account of the eschatologically provisional conditioning of perception, while providing criteriological conditions for making provisional judgments in the *hic et nunc*.

12. This theo-ontology should be deeply troubled by claims that Christian works, for example, are motivated by fear of eschatological punishment or hope of eternal reward. This is a politics of self-interest run amok rather than the kenotic care. The 'Good Samaritan' even more than the sheep and the goats may prove to be particularly instructive.

"appears increasingly divorced from the community-building values of democracy, public life, and education."[13]

Such an account of all workers within the redemptive activity of God would involve considerably more than the provision of "a more comprehensive understanding of the meaning of human work."[14] It would crucially help provide conditions for "changing the myths we live by."[15]

Professor John C. McDowell
Director of Research
University of Divinity
Melbourne, Australia

---

13. Evans and Giroux, *Disposable Futures*, 63.

14. Weir, "Introduction."

15. Rowan Williams, *Faith in the Public Square* (London and New York: Bloomsbury, 2012) 175. This is considerably more, then, than imagining that the Gospel's primary moral function is *motivational*. It is not merely inspirational but transformative and regulating.

Acknowledgments

ANYONE WHO IS ACQUAINTED with the process of writing understands that it is by no means a task which takes place in complete isolation, and is therefore in one sense, written by many. Consequently, I wish to express my thanks to those who have in one way or another been instrumental in shaping this piece of writing. I would like to thank first and foremost my wife Esther who has given me the opportunity and freedom to research that which this thesis contains. Her unending love and support has coasted me through. My parents also deserve many thanks, particularly for their spiritual and financial undergirding of me throughout this project. My proofreaders require especial gratitude—my mum, in particular, who has spent endless months helping me; Ash Cocksworth, who read my final draft; Brodie McGregor, who commented on several chapters; Jeremy Kidwell, who influenced my Wesley and final chapters, and Paul Ede. All have performed an immeasurable task in honing this final draft. Their dedication in this task will not be forgotten.

I would also like to thank my PhD supervisor, Michael Northcott, who helped me to appreciate the necessity of doing theology within one's own tradition, and who has done much to improve my writing. Professor Northcott's "lab," as we called it, was crucial to the exchange of ideas contained in this thesis. Thus, I also wish to thank Jeremy Kidwell, Chad Rimmer, Daniel Miller, Alistair Macindoe, Jamie Pitts and Becky Artinian-Kaiser for their insights and friendship within the bounds of academic scrutiny and safety. I also wish to thank my initial doctoral supervisor John McDowell for his encouragement at the start of this doctoral process, and for his friendship. Although this thesis has taken quite a different trajectory to that which was initially envisioned, I am grateful for all John's expertise at the front end of this big project. Thanks, too, must go to Esther Reed for commenting on my Wesley chapter, and to David Fergusson for his remarks on my Calvin chapter. Oliver O'Donovan and Paul Nimmo too helped shape this piece broadly with their thoughts at my first year board. Projects like this do not spring from nowhere, and this one is no exception. In view of this I must thank my friend Darrell Cosden for illuminating the theological reality that everyday work can be of great significance to God. As my introduction will reveal, this project in some ways has its genesis in the reading and thinking done in those early years of study.

My friend Andy Fearon is to be thanked as he kept me on the narrow path of following Jesus throughout. I would also like to thank St. Silas Episcopal Church in Glasgow, to which Esther, Elia and I belong, for this thesis has been written in this ecclesial context. They have been supportive and have protected me from over-committing my energies into extra tasks in church life.

Lastly, but most importantly, the triune God is to be praised and glorified for all his grace and help through the Holy Spirit via the aforementioned persons to complete this humble offering. I hope and pray it is as pleasing to Him as Abel's offerings.

Soli Deo Gloria

Introduction

Unless the Lord builds the house, those who build it labor in vain. (Ps 127:1a)[16]

THE LAST TWO DECADES have seen a large increase in evangelical theologies of work, as has also been the case in other Christian traditions. Numerous different angles and perspectives on the subject have been unfolded so as to provide a more comprehensive understanding of the meaning of human work. Prominent themes have included work as a means towards sanctification;[17] work as a means towards effective proclamation of the gospel;[18] work that enables a fuller expression of worship to God;[19] work as a means towards serving one's neighbors,[20] and even work that might transfer from this age into the new creation as part of humanity's salvation in Christ.[21]

THE PROBLEM

This thesis will provide in a thoroughgoing manner that which has not yet been dealt with in evangelical theology—an examination of the work of those who are not Christian as it pertains to the new creation. That is, this project will examine whether there is any connection between earthly work performed by those who are not Christian, and the kingdom of

---

16. I will exclusively employ the NRSV translation throughout unless scripture is imbedded within an existing quotation.
17. Stevens and Ung, *Taking Your Soul to Work*.
18. Rundle and Steffen, *Great Commission*.
19. Jensen, *Responsive Labor*.
20. DeKoster, *Work*.
21. Cosden, *Theology of Work*; Cosden, *Heavenly Good*.

heaven. Protestant theologies (e.g., William Perkins,[22] Emil Brunner,[23] Karl Barth,[24] Lee Hardy,[25] together with each theological figure of this study) almost exclusively rule that such a connection lies beyond the margins of orthodoxy. Miroslav Volf, however, following in the theological footsteps of Jürgen Moltmann, briefly suggests the importance of such a connection in his *Work in the Spirit* in an attempt to assemble a framework for a synthetic vision of work. This passing mention by Volf has been the initial idea and point of departure for this study. And since Volf has welcomed others to develop his structures further into something more robust, I will do so as it pertains to the good work of non-Christians and the eschaton.[26] Although I will seldom revisit Volf's contribution to the theology of work in the subsequent chapters, it is an appropriate launching point for this study and has made a formative impact upon this project's inception.

Volf fleetingly considers the meaning of the work of Christians in light of the future transformation of the world (*transformatio mundi*).[27] He claims that the potential continuance of the work of Christians into the new creation stems from their co-operation with God in their work. This hope for the eternal redemption of work provides a Christian's work with its greatest significance, he argues.[28] Given that God wishes to retain and redeem some work by Christians for the new creation, might not he do the same for non-Christians? Might there be such a connection between the work of non-Christians and the new creation?

Volf asserts that if the good work of non-Christians correlates with the new creation, this must also become a pneumatological investigation, for it requires a discussion "on how we conceive of the relationship between the Spirit of God and the non-Christians." To support this move, Volf outlines a theology of charisms as the means by which his pneumatological proposal functions, and he ponders whether this could and should also be applied to those who are not Christian.

There are three theological areas which require careful attention, according to Volf, to illuminate whether this trajectory of thinking has any

---

22.. Perkins, "A Treatise of the Vocations," 473–76.

23.. Brunner, *Divine Imperative*, 397–98.

24.. Barth, *Church Dogmatics* III/4, 53.

25. Hardy, *Fabric of This World*, 79.

26. Volf, *Work*, ix, viii.

27. A point a large majority of evangelicals would disagree with as my chapters will demonstrate.

28. Volf, *Work*, 117.

merit: *(a) the Lordship of Christ, (b) the interplay between the Holy Spirit and human culture, and (c) the eschatological nature of the Holy Spirit.*

(a) The Lordship of Christ

The Lordship of Christ reigns over all humanity, not simply over his overt followers. And so if the Spirit of Christ rules in power throughout creation, can it not be asserted that he is active in some manner in and through all humanity, even among those who are not Christian? In fleeting support of this, Volf cites Basil of Caeserea who observes that "creation possesses nothing—no power, no motivation, or ingenuity needed for work—that it did not receive from the Spirit of God."[29] Thus Volf believes there is a need to investigate how the Lordship of Christ relates to the Spirit's presence in creation at large. However, that the Lordship of Christ here is only considered with respect to humanity, and not all creation, appears to create a tautology between this point and the one following.

(b) Human Culture[30]

The Holy Spirit is present in human culture as well as in the church. Even though the Spirit is present in an especial way through redemption and sanctification as the first-fruits of the kingdom of God, He is simultaneously present in a providential manner in the world of culture. What is key to this latter point, Volf believes, is "the nature of the receptivity of human beings" to the Spirit's movements and influence in culture.[31] Volf's succeeding theological hunch is that a pneumatological understanding of human culture must be unpacked *eschatologically* to make sense of this participation with the Spirit through work.

(c) The Eschatological Spirit

"[T]he goal of the Holy Spirit in the church and in the world is the same," Volf suggests, for "the Spirit strives to lead both the realm of nature (*regnum*

---

29. Ibid., 118.

30. The noun "culture" is a complicated one. I am not referring exclusively to "high cultural" activities such as opera, poetry, and philosophy, as the noun can often convey. Rather, "culture" should refer more broadly to beneficial human work regardless of class status activities. Gorringe, *Furthering*, 5–7.

31. Volf, *Work*, 118–19.

naturæ) and the realm of grace (*regnum gratiæ*) toward their final glorification in the new creation (*regnum gloriæ*)."³² Given that Volf's project was admittedly "a rough draft" he did not take time to develop the correlation between the work of non-Christians and the new creation, thus it remains an "[in]sufficiently investigated subject."³³ However, he has fleetingly acknowledged the possibility of the work of non-Christians participating with God's plans, but given that there is not yet a *thoroughgoing pneumatological* account of *how* the work of those who are not Christian interrelates with the new creation, this project will hitherto attempt to rectify this lacuna.³⁴

Volf's eschatological project for work also suggests that the good work of non-Christians might even continue into the new creation, meaning that some work by non-Christians will be redeemed and present in the new creation, but ontologically separated from its agents because of their lack of faith in Christ. This eschatological continuity will not be specifically dealt with here as Richard Mouw and Darrell Cosden have already fulfilled this.³⁵ Mouw asserts in this regard that even the fleet of ships deployed by the evil seafaring merchants of Tarshish will be redeemed and be honed *for* the new Jerusalem, although he does not make his case for this pneumatologically.

METHODOLOGY

To examine the proposed theological area, this thesis will provide from a British evangelical perspective, a robust theology of the good work of non-Christians. This is not to say that all work by non-Christians is inherently good; I am arguing nothing of the sort. Rather, I am simply wishing to forge a theological account of good work by non-Christians whenever such occurs in the world.

It will be shown that Francis Schaeffer, John Stott, Thomas Chalmers, Richard Baxter, John Calvin, and John Wesley argue that because of their lack of faith in Christ, the good work of non-Christians must be restricted to temporal ends. This is argued despite claims of divine empowerment infusing their work. Such a wholesale restriction of good work by non-Christians to temporality by British evangelicals is curious, and I intend to investigate such a grand claim. In reparation, this thesis will present a novel reading

---

32. Ibid., 119.

33. Ibid., viii. In correspondence and conversation with Volf, he intimated that he is still unaware of such a study having been produced as a derivative of his pneumatology of work—March 2009 (personal email) and May 2010 (personal conversation).

34. Ibid., 91–102.

35. Mouw, *When the Kings*, 20–37; Cosden, *Heavenly Good*, 140–41.

of the parable of the sheep and the goats that will claim a direct correlation between the good work of some non-Christians in this age and the new creation, justifying Volf's coupling of the two.

Contrary to British evangelical theology, it will be argued that this eschatological outcome will take place precisely because of the Holy Spirit's inspiration in good work by non-Christians, not because of their lack of Christian faith. I will assume as correct Volf's identification of the Holy Spirit as the crucial link between the good work of non-Christians and the new creation. I propose to build upon Volf's pneumatology of work by fleshing out his initial sketch in my own way. My intention is not to theologically evaluate Volf's pneumatology; there is not space for this here nor is this my purpose.[36]

This thesis also raises the question of categories. How are those who do not consider themselves Christian best described? I will not use the term *secular* to describe these workers as I do not wish to infer a sacred/secular dichotomy within created reality. Neither is the more contemporary use of *secular* helpful (denoting anyone who is strictly irreligious, and distanced from any association with spirituality) because this excludes all religious groups who are not Christian. Most evangelical theologians would adopt the term *non-Christian* (so Volf) or *non-believer* (so Darrell Cosden), thus I too will adopt the category non-Christian when developing my own thoughts as this is the most common denomination by British evangelicals.

The category *humanity* also needs mention. From chapter 1 through to 5 I will follow the chapter interlocutor's plural use of *man* or *men* in order to genuinely represent their categories with accuracy. There is no misogynism intended here, simply an attention to original categories. In the final chapter, I will employ contemporary convention of *humanity* or *humankind*.

A word must also be said about the meaning of the term *evangelical* or *British evangelical* for its expressions are multifarious, and its history complicated.[37] *Evangelical* will not be used as a synonym for *Protestant* in accordance with the German *evangelische*. This classical understanding was the old Reformation notion where sacraments and worship were stressed as *signs* and *seals* of grace. This definition of *evangelical* in Britain was supplanted in many circles by the eighteenth century British revival movement, and its doctrine, as exemplified by the Methodists.[38] This alternative understanding of *evangelical* originates from the younger Westminster confessional Puritans who were key antecedents to revivalist evangelicals, and

36. Preece has already accomplished this in, *The Viability of the Vocation Tradition*, chapter 6.

37. Noll, *Introduction to Modern Protestantism*, 261.

38. Bebbington, *Evangelicalism*, 1.

who emphasized sacraments and worship as *badges of faith* rather than signs and seals of grace.[39] Despite this, the Westminster tradition claims to follow authentically Reformation theology, but understood in a distinctive way.

Today, British evangelicals, according to the Westminster tradition's understanding of the term *evangelical*, are not always identifiable by their church affiliation but sometimes only by specific theological convictions. Church historian David Bebbington encapsulates these theological convictions which give the movement its shape:

> There are four qualities that have been the special marks of Evangelical religion: *conversionism*, the belief that lives need to be changed; *activism*, the expression of the gospel in effort; *biblicism*, a particular regard for the Bible; and what may be called *crucicentrism*, a stress on the sacrifice of Christ on the cross. Together they form a quadrilateral of priorities that is the basis of Evangelicalism.[40]

Geoffrey Grogan's recent volume *The Faith Once Entrusted to the Saints?* defines *evangelical* entirely through a high view of scripture (or "biblicism" to use Bebbington's designation[41]) which is abridged by the propositional kernels of UCCF's (Universities and Colleges Christian Fellowship) statement of faith.[42] Nevertheless, I will adhere to Bebbington's definition throughout this project as his summation has become the best possible consensus among evangelicals.[43] Furthermore, as the Westminster tradition's interpretation of the term *evangelical* is the tradition to which I belong, this thesis will interact with thinkers who pertain to this strand of evangelical theologies.

It must also be acknowledged that there is a generous overlap of influence between British evangelical theology, and its larger partner in North America. That said, the latter differs from its British counterpart at times in that *evangelical* can denote a party political association. Nevertheless, both North American and British evangelical theology do closely relate, even if British tradition has not shown the same eagerness to address the theological subject of work like that of its larger counterpart.[44] Accordingly, I will

---

39. Torrance, *Scottish Theology*, 233.

40. Bebbington, *Evangelicalism*, 15.

41. "Biblicism" in Bebbington's sense, however, does not necessarily indicate a literalist hermeneutic of scripture.

42. Grogan, *The Faith*, 14–18.

43. Tidball, *Who Are The Evangelicals?*, 14.

44. Grogan, *Faith*, 16. Work became a subject in its own right through nineteenth century political economists like Karl Marx (1818–83). Hughes, *The End of Work*, 7.

draw upon North American evangelical contributions where they have made a significant impact upon British evangelical theologies of work, and where they aid my argument. This will be the case in chapter 1 particularly as I analyze Francis Schaeffer.

WORK OR WORKS?

It is also essential to discuss the issue of whether *work* and *works* are synonymous or differentiated in British evangelical thinking. Such a distinction between *work* and *works* has its roots in early Christian monastic interpretations of the Apostle Paul's notion of *calling*. These interpretations argue that because Christians are cognizant of their calling to a heavenly "supermundane hope" they must confirm this, and take advantage of working *for* God, despite many being ignorant of such an impetus. Thus a rift was forged between a fulfilled vocation through faith (works) and mundane work without reference to God (work).[45]

The manner of the evangelical debate on *work/works* simultaneously discloses the same tendency by spiritually ordering *work* below *works*. Evangelicals classify works that are enacted from a seedbed of faith in Christ as *evangelical works*, whereas all other manner of human agency is simply rendered *work*. By so doing, evangelicals ensure that any agency found in scripture which appears dangerously meritorious can simply be asserted as *evangelical works*. This will be exemplified chiefly by each interlocutor of this thesis.

These terms should not be, however, strictly differentiated from each other as numerous contemporary scholars seem content with the interchangeable nature of *work/works* in scripture and theology.[46] Moreover, the biblical Greek term *ergon* is used in this same interchangeable manner throughout scripture so that both *work* and *works* simply reveal a singular and plural usage where appropriate, thus *works* is not restricted to compassionate *evangelical* acts of faith as something distinct from, e.g., bricklaying.[47]

Historically, the notion of *work* has developed from the sixteenth century to the current day, coupled with works and work's differentiation.

45.. Holl, "History of the Word," 127. Rom 11:29; Phil 3:14; 2 Thess 1:11; Eph 1:18, 4:1, 4:4; Heb 3:1; 2 Tim 1:9; 2 Pet 1:10 are the biblical texts appealed to for such a conviction.

46. Bertram, *Theological Dictionary*, 635–55; Reid, *Evangelical Dictionary*, 1295; Osterhaven, *Evangelical Dictionary*, 1295–97.

47. Thanks to Oliver O'Donovan who encouraged me to investigate this.

As previously mentioned, I will subsume work and works together in my criticism of each thinker. However, because work did not actually become a subject until just after Chalmers (at the time of Karl Marx) I will acknowledge the differences of both while assuming that each thinker is reflecting upon what they considered to be work.

My view of work is defined by a threefold dynamic of instrumentality, relationality and ontology. Both the instrumentality and relationality of work relates to workers and others' needs being fulfilled; the sanctification of Christians; workers conveying their humanness, and developing their natural, social and cultural environments, henceforth preserving the integrity of the earth. These are all areas of work in which my understanding of it will happily cohere with my engagement partners.

However, the ontology of work is a relatively novel perspective on work that will differ from each of this thesis' thinkers. The eschatological and teleological dimensions of work, however, stem from an ontology of work, something my interlocutors rarely, if ever, consider.[48] Evangelical definitions of work are typically developed via analyzes of figures such as Luther and Calvin, and those following them. Accordingly, this thesis will rigorously engage those who succeed the current day so as to inform and shape that which will be proposed. As such, this thesis' definition of work is both something which is novel to my interlocutors while also being recognizable through its instrumentality and relationality.

STRUCTURE AND STAGES OF THE ARGUMENT

The chapters are intentionally unchronological in their order. Not because I wish to ignore history; on the contrary, I wish to set up an *intellectual geography* that will allow me to analyze and criticize British evangelical theologies of the good work of non-Christians. In so doing, each century of British evangelical theology will be considered in the form of a seminal figure, including the two preceding centuries of Protestant thought, thus giving historical credence to this project.

I investigate Schaeffer and Stott in chapter 1 as an initial foray into both the meaning of the work of non-Christians in twenty and twenty-first century evangelical thinking to discover whether there is any correlation between work and the new creation present in their theology. My intention in doing so is to reveal what contemporary British evangelical thinking has concluded about good work by non-Christians, and its potential connection with the new creation. In this way, this study sets out where evangelicals

---

48. I am relying upon Cosden's definition of work in, *Work*, 178–79.

are currently located on the matter. This will be something of a launch pad to introduce the subject to the reader, and from where I can then return to evangelical history.

Onwards from Thomas Chalmers in chapter 2, each theological figure demonstrates an incremental increase in credit given to the good work of non-Christians, and to God's part in it. Thus, Thomas Chalmers is selected in chapter 2 because he gives the *least* significance to the good work of *sinners*, and therefore to God (the Holy Spirit in particular) as the progenitor of their work. It will be seen in each chapter a sharing of the conviction that good work by non-Christians has no relation to the eschaton regardless of its moral merits.

A large percentage of each chapter will be allocated to how each theologian understands *the empowerment* which infuses non-Christians to work for good. This is important for the identification of British evangelicals who might be augmented in the final chapter towards a robust theology of work of non-Christians. Furthermore, in discovering how each figure understands the empowerment of good work by non-Christians, additional theological convictions significantly emerge that reveal the *scope* and *efficacy* of such empowered work (i.e., theological anthropology, hamartiology, theologies of the state, *ordo salutis*, ecclesiology).

In seeking to discover the nature of empowerment in each theology of work presented, this project will eventually turn to pneumatology through John Calvin and John Wesley. This connects Volf to the British Evangelical tradition by selecting pneumatology as the prism to understanding the potency of work, albeit Calvin and Wesley ruling out the connection between work and the eschaton which Volf proposes.

What is my purpose in employing *pneumatology* for a theology of the good work of non-Christians? It is because in my final chapter it will be argued that as the Holy Spirit is the key agent influencing good work in non-Christians (albeit unrecognized by non-Christian co-agents, a link that *Lumen Gentium* also made at Vatican II[49]) both in work's inspiration and empowerment, such work should be understood as worthy of divine recognition for entry into the new creation. In this ultimate sense then, it will be argued that 'unless the Lord builds the house, those who build it labor in vain' (Ps 127:1a).

In order to demonstrate the eschatological potency of the Spirit's work in human culture more broadly, each chapter will include an interpretation of the parable of the sheep and the goats (Matt 25:31–46) according to the theologian concerned. The only exception to this is in chapter 1 where I will

---

49. "*Lumen Gentium*" in Flannery, *Vatican Council II*, 366–67.

employ John Stott's reflections on Matt 25:31–46, as Francis Schaeffer did not comment on the parable. As somewhat of a climax, I will offer my own reading of the parable in the final chapter in repair of the examined British evangelical theologies of work, and in so doing, argue for an intrinsic connection between the good work of non-Christians and the eschaton.

The British evangelical tradition will be shown to be obstinate towards the parable of the sheep and the goats as it confronts its already settled theological beliefs. It is hoped that this fresh interpretation of the parable will provide an openness to the inclusion of some non-Christians in the new creation because of their good work.

What will become apparent is that my selected figures' evangelical systems are more sacrosanct to them than some teachings in scripture itself. Resultantly, this thesis will become a heuristic that illuminates the inability of British evangelical theologies to appropriate key stories in the biblical narrative for a theology of work. This study, then, will exemplify a corrective to British evangelical theologies in its use of scripture in and for the theology of work.

My justification for employing this parable has a threefold rationale. First, using scripture to shape theology and ethics is to hold the Bible as an authority, as the primary source for all theology. Evangelical Stanley Grenz rightly suggests that, "[a]s Christians, we acknowledge the Bible as scripture in that the sovereign Spirit has bound authoritative, divine speaking to this text. We believe that the Spirit has chosen, now chooses, and will continue to choose to speak with authority through the biblical texts."[50] The Apostle Paul had this very much in mind when utilizing the term 'God-breathed' (*theopneustos*) with respect to scripture (2 Tim 3:16). As such, it is incumbent upon readers of scripture to "identify and clarify [its] claim[s] as it confronts" them.[51] It is the claim of Jesus' teaching in the parable of the sheep and the goats which readers will be confronted with here.

Second, in light of this biblical authority, and its primary place for shaping theology, the parable of the sheep and the goats has been selected as a scriptural solution to Volf's identification of the direct correlation between human agency and the final state. It will be argued that there is no more clear and suitable episode in the biblical narrative to address the interrelation between work and the eschaton.

Third, I am employing this parable in light of British evangelical tradition which can be said to have a horizontal and vertical structure. Each *direction* of the structure is polarized. On one hand, following David Kelsey's

---

50.. Grenz and Franke, *Beyond Foundationalism*, 65.

51.. O'Donovan, 'Towards an Interpretation of Biblical Ethics,' 71.

articulation of it, it might be said that this tradition stems from "a community of people who understand their communal and personal identities to be shaped by the fact that they live "before God." On the other hand, the presence of God in and through a set of common forms of speech (homiletical, creedal, doxological, and simply "pious"), common liturgical actions and uses of biblical writings are all related in some way to the life, death and resurrection of Jesus of Nazareth."[52] British evangelical forms of speech will be analyzed in this thesis as they discuss the empowerment of the work of non-Christians, and the parable of the sheep and the goats. The speech of British evangelical theology claims to always be rooted in talk of the Bible.

JUSTIFICATION OF SOURCES

On what basis have I selected this study's theological figures? Francis Schaeffer and John Stott between them have made a seminal impact upon twenty and twenty-first-century North American and British evangelical theologies through their theological reflection on human work. Schaeffer was an American evangelical who had a noteworthy impact upon British evangelical theology. Not only were his books considerably influential in Britain, but in 1958 the establishment of a L'Abri community (community "study centers . . . where individuals have the opportunity to seek answers to honest questions about God and the significance of human life"[53]) in England compounded his influence, combined with his visiting lectures to British universities.[54] The stated purpose of the L'Abri centers, which Schaeffer devoted much of his life to, is "[t]o show forth by demonstration, in our life and work, the existence of God."[55] In other words, the work of Schaeffer through L'Abri was apologetic and evangelistic in nature. Although he considered himself an evangelist, and not a theologian, Schaeffer frequently found himself invited by academics and students to lecture in European and American universities.[56] Theologians have thus engaged his thought in the academy, and Ronald Ruegsegger believes that his academic scrutiny "raise[s] fairly high expectations"[57] of him as a thinker.

52. Kelsey, *The Uses of Scripture*, 174.

53. http://www.labri.org/.

54. Catherwood, *Five Evangelical Leaders*, 142. Of course, the English L'Abri followed the well-established Swiss original.

55. Schaeffer, *L'Abri*, 15–16. Francis Schaeffer says in the foreword to this text: "This book and my books form a unity."

56.. Pierard, *Reflections*, 207; Hurley, *Reflections*, 274.

57.. Ruegsegger, *Reflections*, 27.

Schaeffer's early public ministry began in England, although his initial impact subsequently waned, due in no small part to the perception that Schaeffer was "too clear, too fundamentalist, too outspoken, too confusing, too simple, too demanding, too confrontational."[58] Nevertheless, Schaeffer's influence on British evangelicals was further manifest through his friendship with the London-based Welsh preacher, Martyn Lloyd-Jones, not least because their adherents saw them as doctrinal bedfellows.[59] Moreover, Christopher Catherwood claims that the five most influential evangelicals of the twentieth century include Schaeffer, Lloyd-Jones, Billy Graham, J. I. Packer and John Stott.[60]

Schaeffer's significance as an evangelical is further revealed by the part he played in *The Lausanne Congress on World Evangelization* of 1974, this congress contributing towards the resurrection of evangelical social thought from obscurity.[61] Schaeffer was included at Lausanne, not only because of his clear commitment to evangelism, but also because of his dedicated interaction with philosophy, the arts, science, politics, pollution, ecology, and theology more generally. His engagement with human culture is of particular value to evangelical theology because prior to Schaeffer few twentieth century evangelicals had attempted such an interaction. One exception is his former teacher Carl Henry (1913–2003).[62]

Why am I interacting with an American evangelical at the beginning of this thesis? Simply because there is no outstanding twentieth century British evangelical from whom to draw out the significance of the good work of non-Christians.

If Schaeffer was influential among British evangelicals, John Stott, too, was a seminal British evangelical. In fact, Stott has been called "one of the most influential figures in the Christian world,"[63] such that his opinion was sought-after on almost all theological matters by evangelicals.[64]

Stott followed Schaeffer in discussing evangelical social ethics after the social gospel movement, and also specifically addressed the issue of work.[65]

58.. Macauly, *Francis Schaeffer*, 57, 55.

59. Catherwood, *Five*, 114, 143–44.

60. Ibid., 9–11. Some would wish to include C. S. Lewis in this list.

61. See the following link for the script of Schaeffer's address at Lausanne: http://www.lausanne.org/documents/lau1docs/0368.pdf.

62. Henry, *The Christian Mindset*; *A Plea for Evangelical Demonstration*; *Christian Personal Ethics*; *The Uneasy Conscience*; *The God Who Shows Himself*. The name of this last title is tellingly akin to Schaeffer's later title *He is There*.

63. Hastings, *A History of British Christianity*, 455.

64. Bebbington, *Evangelicalism*, 261.

65. Stott, *Issues*, 135–60, 217–68.

Consequently, following *the Lausanne Congress on World Evangelization* of 1974 Stott's brainchild emerged—*The London Institute of Contemporary Christianity (LICC)*—in 1982 in order to "relate the truth to life."[66] His concern was that "one of the major reasons why people reject the Gospel today is not because they perceive it to be false but because they perceive it to be trivial."[67] *LICC* was his call from God to remedy such a misperception.[68] Stott's analysis of the parable of the sheep and the goats is what will be focused upon here.

Thomas Chalmers' theology of the work of *sinners* will be examined in chapter 2. It will be shown that he suggests *natural conscience* as the basis for good work by *sinners*. It is imperative to state that Chalmers was a theologian of seminal nature shown by the national impact he made through his public writings and preaching from 1810 onwards.[69] In this vein Hugh Miller says: "Chalmers, like all the truly great, may be said rather to have created than to have belonged to an era."[70] Furthermore, Henry Cockburn, a keen student of Chalmers, ranked him alongside Dugald Stewart, Walter Scott and Francis Jeffrey in terms of the significance he made upon Scottish culture and thought. Alongside these three, Cockburn claims that Chalmers "made Scotland illustrious."[71]

Chalmers developed an evangelical theology of work that sought to baptize the "political economy into Christianity, this being the main thing needful to bring about its regeneration."[72] By the 1830s and 1840s he was renowned for social reform in his Glasgow parishes (the Tron from 1815–19, and St. Johns from 1819–23), which was informed by his political economic theory, and made a prominent contribution to the Christian praxis of work.[73] Thus, his contribution to work will be evaluated here.

The seventeenth-century Puritan theology of Richard Baxter will be evaluated in chapter 3. His theology deeply shaped the evangelical tradition's negative understanding of the work of *infidels*. His notion of "a godly commonwealth" will advance past Chalmers with only a modicum of improvement. Richard Baxter is one of British evangelical theology's primary

---

66. Dudley-Smith, *John Stott*, 338.
67. http://www.licc.org.uk/about-licc.
68. Dudley-Smith, *John Stott*, 260.
69. McCaffrey, *The Practical*, 31.
70. Quoted in Anderson, *Reminiscences*, 401.
71. Cockburn, *Journal*, 258.
72. Laylor, *Money*, xvii.
73. McCaffrey, "The Life of Thomas Chalmers," 31.

antecedents on the issue of work.⁷⁴ There was no one among English seventeenth-century nonconformist Puritans who provided such comprehensive instruction on ordinary work as Baxter. In this regard R. H. Tawney exaggerates only a little when he states:

> If the inward and spiritual grace of Puritanism eludes the historian, its outward and visible signs meet him at every turn, and not less in marketplace and counting-house and camp, than in the student's chamber and the gathering of the elect for prayer. For to the Puritan, a contemner of the vain shows of sacramentalism, mundane toil becomes itself a kind of sacrament.⁷⁵

Chapter 4 will investigate John Calvin's account of *peculiar grace* that provides a more sophisticated approach than the previous three accounts of the good work of the *impious* by identifying *pneumatology* as the interpretive key for all good work. Having said that, Calvin's theology of work is not interacted with by secondary sources to the extent one might expect, particularly concerning the work of the *impious*.

Calvin is the second critically important antecedent to British evangelical theologies of work whom I will investigate. He is an important figure to consider because he, more directly and prominently than Luther, has formed British evangelical minds with his reformation thinking. As such, his emphasis on the renewal of all areas of life made a considerable impact upon Britain's shores and, arguably, Calvin is still the most influential theological figure in several streams of British evangelical thinking to date.⁷⁶

Chapter 5 provides a reading of John Wesley's theology of *prevenient grace* which offers an alternative, but similar and improved pneumatological explanation to Calvin. This analysis will reveal a definite unity of interpretation with Reformation and British evangelical thinking from the fifteenth to the twenty-first century. Some of his critics believe he is the last of the great Reformation thinkers—whether or not this is true is debatable—but the seminal nature of Wesley's theological contribution to the evangelical tradition is not.⁷⁷ Even though Wesley is not employed by contemporary theolo-

---

74. Tidball, *Evangelicals?*, 34, 176. It is not insignificant, for instance, that noteworthy British evangelical Jim Packer did his doctoral work on Richard Baxter: *The Redemption and Restoration of Man*. The other Puritan figure that might have been considered in Baxter's stead is William Perkins (1558—1602), but he has had significantly less influence upon contemporary British evangelical theology and belonged to the sixteenth century where John Calvin's theology of work must take precedence.

75. Tawney, *Religion*, 199.

76.. Reid, *Evangelical Dictionary*, 201.

77.. Cobb, *Grace*, 21; Collins, *Theology of John Wesley*, 82.

gies of work as a subject, I will rectify this by making use of his doctrine of grace as it is understood to empower *heathen* man towards advantageous action. The issue of moral agency's source is essential toward discussions of work's correlation from the present age to the eschaton.

Wesley has argued vigorously for a robust understanding of works, and it would be easy to assume, given the lack of attention to Wesley in Max Weber's famous thesis, that Wesley has little or nothing significant to contribute to the subject of work. Weber claims that Wesley did little more than emphasize the notion that grace should evidence itself in people's lives through good works.[78] Likewise, in R. H. Tawney's thesis, Wesley only merits one mention and even then it is simply a passing mention of his sermon *The Use of Money*.[79]

These famous accounts have omitted much of Wesley's intention, for he wished to amplify industriousness in his Methodism.[80] Indeed, such was Wesley's stress on the importance of everyday work that he could cite many instances of families who had been transported from the gutter into working life due to Methodism's emphasis upon it. In this sense, Methodists were often self-made and modest in their upward mobility.[81]

CONTRIBUTION TO ITS FIELD

This thesis will add a unique contribution both to *(a) the theology of work*, and *(b) British evangelical theologies*. Both these two points will intersect.

(a) Theology of Work

As it stands, there is no thoroughgoing exploration of the ultimate scope of good work by non-Christians in any of burgeoning literature in the theology of work. There is certainly no devoted study to this topic. Currently, there exists only fleeting mention of good work by non-Christians as theologians attempt to comprehensively treat the subject of work. I will attempt here to provide a rigorous account of good work by non-Christians, and its scope for the new creation. Moreover, no one yet has wholeheartedly developed a pneumatological theology of work *from* Volf's synthetic framework. This project intends to be the first.

78.. Weber, *The Protestant Ethic*, 90.
79.. Tawney, *Religion*, 194.
80. Walsh, "'The Bane of Industry?,'" 224.
81. Ibid., 225.

(b) British Evangelical Theologies

Further, this study is unique in British evangelical theologies precisely because I will argue that the *scope* of some good work by some non-Christians is linked directly with the new creation. Good work by non-Christians, until now, has always been restricted by British evangelicals to temporality, thus giving it no significance for heaven. This thesis will challenge this unilaterally held conviction by re-examining the eschatological dimensions of pneumatology for good work enacted by anyone. In so doing, it is acknowledged that this study will run against the grain of British evangelical thinking entirely. Moreover, this raises a point of uniqueness about this project: there is not yet a British evangelical theology of work which analyzes *(a)* the *pneumatological* empowerment of good work by non-Christians, and therefore, *(b)* recognizes the inspiration of the Holy Spirit as the basis for such work as its direct correlation with the eschaton.

In what sense, then, is this thesis still evangelical? This thesis is thoroughly evangelical in the sense that it is in keeping with British evangelicals who originally clung to the Reformation principle "reformed but always reforming" (*reformata semper reformanda*). If improved interpretations of the bible goad established evangelical theologies, then this is right and good. Evangelical theologies should heed any such challenges from the Bible. The words of evangelical Charles Simeon of Cambridge (1759–1836) express this clearly:

> My endeavour is to bring out of Scripture what is there and not to thrust in what I think might be there . . . I never wish to find any particular truth in any particular passage. I am willing that every part of God's blessed word should speak exactly what it was intended to speak, without adding any single iota to it, or taking from it the smallest particle of its legitimate import.[82]

Indeed, if Simeon is representative of the manner in which British evangelicals should seek to interpret the bible, then the theology which the parable of the sheep and the goats implies will be a critique to already settled evangelical beliefs about the nature and scope of good work by non-Christians. It will be revealed that the interlocutors selected for this thesis do exactly what Simeon sought to avoid doing—deflect a message that is uncomfortable and incompatible with presumed airtight British evangelical thinking.

I will argue that good work by some non-Christians has an intrinsic correlation to the new creation by virtue of its empowerment by the Holy

---

82. Quoted from Tidball, *Evangelicals?*, 81.

Spirit (that which is *good* will be shown to be any work which co-operates with the Spirit). Because of the prior instigation of God the Spirit, the good work of non-Christians, inspired by the prevenient grace of the Spirit, should not be deemed temporal in nature as British evangelical theologies of work insist.[83] I will argue that the efficacy of the Spirit's co-agency in the work of non-Christians provides the basis of its eschatological connection to the new creation. I will offer both an account of how such work can be good, while simultaneously explaining the eschatological potency of the Spirit's work in human culture more broadly.

Why does this thesis matter? British evangelical theologies are too quick to exclude non-Christians and their work from the life to come, consequently making too neat a binary outcome of the great judgment of humankind. This thesis will attempt to argue for more fluidity to this argument because of the vision of work shown in the parable of the sheep and the goats. It is hoped that evangelicals may adopt less certain lines between Christians and non-Christians in their work as it pertains to their entry to heaven.

---

83. Some streams of evangelical thought would find *prevenient grace* controversial and thus inappropriate for use here, but I will show in my chapter on John Wesley that such a doctrine is both wholly evangelical and entirely suited for the conclusions which I will propose.

1

Francis Schaeffer (1912–84) and John Stott (1921–2011)

The Epistemological Problem of the Good Work of Non-Christians in Twentieth- and Twenty-First-Century Evangelical Theology

I BEGIN MY INVESTIGATION with the thoughts of Francis Schaeffer and John Stott, who between them made a seminal impact upon North American and British evangelical theology through their theological reflections on human work in the twentieth and twenty-first centuries. This first chapter will provide an initial foray into both the meaning of the work of non-Christians in evangelical thinking, and whether there is any correlation between work and the new creation.

I will evaluate Francis Schaeffer's account of good work by non-Christians as there are some who believe he was the first to activate and politicize evangelicals in the twentieth century.[1] Even if this claim is exaggerated, there is no debating the thoroughgoing nature of Schaeffer's engagement with human civilization, and therefore with those who have shaped culture in opposition to the Christian God. Perhaps Karl Barth (1886–1968) is the only competing alternative, but Barth does not belong to the Westminster strand of evangelical theology that this thesis is operating within.

Because of the depth of theological analysis that Schaeffer has devoted towards the cultural tasks of non-Christians, he is the best possible

---

1. Budziszewski, *Evangelicals*, 73–74.

interlocutor to evaluate within twentieth-century evangelical theology. Specifically, I will investigate Schaeffer's doctrine of creation, his theological anthropology, man's epistemological problem, and his understanding of important areas of culture as a consequence of this problem. My intention in doing so is to reveal how much esteem good work by non-Christians is granted by him.

I will then engage John Stott's eschatological reflections on the parable of the sheep and the goats, providing a picture of an accepted interpretation of the work of non-Christians, and its relevance to the new creation in British evangelical theology. Stott is not only trusted in the British evangelical tradition, but in evangelical theology more broadly. He is considered an authority of evangelical dogma among British evangelicals, and is being introduced here because Schaeffer did not comment upon the sheep and the goats in his writings or sermons.

This will be a much shorter section than the space allocated to Schaeffer due to the relatively brief nature of Stott's comments on the sheep and the goats. Nonetheless, his interpretation is significant for the purposes of showing the disconnect between the work of non-Christians and the eschaton. The brevity of these comments should not belittle the importance of Stott's place in this chapter in any way.

Before Schaeffer, evangelicals had been at odds over issues of culture and work ever since they clashed with the social gospel movement in the late nineteenth and early twentieth centuries. In his assessment of the social gospel movement, a movement identified primarily with the figure of Walter Rauschenbusch (1861–1918), John Stott claims the *true* gospel had been betrayed.[2] In fact, the social gospel has its original ground in the evangelical movement,[3] but despite this, Stott claims that the betrayal of the true gospel is manifest in Rauschenbusch's rationale: "We have a social gospel. We need a systematic theology large enough to match it and vital enough to back it." Further, Rauschenbusch deemed it necessary to "furnish an adequate intellectual basis for the social gospel."[4]

For Stott, the social gospel is essentially a philanthropic project that requires theological justification as an afterthought for credibility's sake.[5] Coupled with this was Rauschenbusch's open rejection of a penal substitutionary understanding of the atonement, and his suspicion of biblical accounts of the miraculous. By contrast, penal substitutionary interpretations

---

2. Stott, *Issues*, 7.
3. Bebbington, *Evangelicalism*, 211.
4. Rauschenbusch, *A Theology*, 1.
5. Stott, *Issues*, 7.

of the atonement had become quasi-orthodox in evangelical theology.[6] Accordingly, the social gospel created evangelical anxiety over its perceived scriptural inaccuracy, and thus its Christian inauthenticity. Bebbington summarizes this well:

> The liberals were rightly perceived at the time to be innovators. They wished to modify received theology and churchmanship in the light of current thought. Inevitably their ideas were swept along by the Romantic currents that had already been flowing powerfully in the later nineteenth century. Biblical inspiration, for example, was reinterpreted as of a piece with the uplifting power of the arts.[7]

Consequently, by association, the social gospel's societal responsibility and focus on work suffered a deliberate neglect in evangelical circles from the late nineteenth century onwards.[8] Decades later Schaeffer took up the necessary task of engaging culture in his theology, which included an analysis of the work of non-Christians through his doctrine of creation.

FRANCIS SCHAEFFER

While visiting a bookshop at the age of seventeen, Schaeffer came across a book on Greek philosophy. As he read, he discovered that Greek philosophers were asking many questions about the human condition to which they had no answers. "In God's providence," his wife Edith remarks, "reading this book on Greek philosophy set his mind on fire."[9]

At that time he was attending what he called a *liberal church*, and he listened to one final sermon there before never returning, realizing that this form of Christianity also did not offer answers to man's basic problems. Schaeffer considered dispensing with the Bible before realizing that he had never actually read it. For whatever reason, he decided to read Ovid and the Bible simultaneously to see what he thought of both. Shortly afterwards Schaeffer put Ovid aside, and began reading the Bible seriously, beginning with Genesis.

The Bible slowly revealed to Schaeffer answers to man's basic problems and set his imagination alight. Edith Schaeffer relates her husband's revelation in the following way: "He thought he had discovered something no one

---

6. Erickson, *Christian Theology*, 2:815; Paul, *Atonement*, 109.
7. Bebbington, *Evangelicalism*, 183.
8. Ibid., 264.
9. Schaeffer, *Tapestry*, 51–52.

else knew about. He thought what he had found was unique, and that he alone had found it."[10] This discovery changed the way Schaeffer worked at school, and his perception of the world. "The flow of biblical history" in its creation, fall and redemption, provided Schaeffer with satisfying answers to his questions about life.

Subsequently, he went on to study at Hampden-Sydney College, Virginia, and in 1935 attended Westminster Theological Seminary, Philadelphia, where he absorbed the biblical foundations of Geerhardus Vos. Vos' theological influence on Schaeffer can be clearly seen from statements from Vos which resemble Schaeffer's comments on the Bible that "[it is] the study of the actual self-disclosures of God in time and space."[11] From there Schaeffer ventured into pastoral ministry in the 1940s, and eventually Edith and he felt called to move to Switzerland in 1948.[12]

It is highly significant that Schaeffer lived through the Wall Street crash of 1929, a cataclysmic event which badly affected the everyday lives of Americans, and which in Schaeffer's mind, shattered any utopian dreams of capitalism and hope for the world through anthropocentric means. It might be argued that Schaeffer saw all work through the prism of this tragic event of 1929, thus work was in desperate need of redemption. In light of this, it is essential that Schaeffer's perceived "flow of biblical history" is unpacked and his theology of work inherent within it.

THE WORK OF NON-CHRISTIANS IN VIEW OF A THEOLOGY OF CREATION

For Schaeffer, God's creation *ex nihilo* is a work which took place in space-time history; it is not a mythical episode. He cites Psalm 136's account of creation to support his case:

> O give thanks to the LORD, for he is good . . .
> who spread out the earth above the waters;
>   for his steadfast love endures forever;
> who made the great lights,
>   for his steadfast love endures forever;
> the sun to rule over the day,
>   for his steadfast love endures forever;
> the moon and stars to rule over the night,
>   for his steadfast love endures forever;

---

10. Ibid.
11. Vos, *Biblical Theology*, 13.
12. Barrs, "Francis Schaeffer: The Man," 2.

> who struck Egypt through their firstborn,
>   for his steadfast love endures forever;
> and brought Israel out from among them,
>   for his steadfast love endures forever ... (vv. 1, 6–11)

Schaeffer argues from the psalmist that the primeval creation by God was an indubitably historical act, precisely because of its connection with another historical event—the exodus:

> So Psalm 136 brings us fact to face with the biblical concept of creation as a fact of space-time history, for we find here a complete parallel between creation and other points of history: the space-timeness of history at the time of the Jewish captivity in Egypt, of the particular time in which the psalm itself was written and of our own time as we read the psalm today.... The early chapters of Genesis are to be viewed completely as history—just as much so, let us say, as records concerning Abraham, David, Solomon or Jesus Christ.[13]

Schaeffer then discusses the meaning of the phrase "in the beginning," as it is disclosed in the Genesis narrative, to discover when history began. He reasons that if "in the beginning" means anything, it cannot mean that time and history began before this "beginning," otherwise why call it such? So with what categories is before "the beginning" to be discussed? Schaeffer adopts the term "sequence" so as to avoid confusion with the word *time*. Thus, Schaeffer argues that when God created *ex nihilo*, space and time began, but prior to this God was in "sequence." The significance of this is that "something existed before creation and that something was personal and not static; the Father loved the Son; there was a plan; there was communication; and promises were made prior to the creation of the heavens and the earth. This whole conception is rooted in the reality of the Trinity."[14]

Furthermore, this sequence is "personal" because an impersonal explanation of the universe leaves man with too many unanswerable questions about his identity. Rather, by understanding the universe in the way briefly explained, some obvious facts are manifest:

> Man has a mannishness. You find it wherever you find man—not only in the men who live today, but in the artifacts of history. The assumption of an impersonal beginning can never adequately explain the personal beings we see around us, and

---

13. Schaeffer, *Genesis*, 15.
14. Ibid., 18.

when men try to explain man on the basis of an original impersonal, man soon disappears.[15]

In contradistinction to an impersonal explanation, Schaeffer argues, the Christian tradition answers the question *Who am I?* in light of "a personal beginning on the high order of the Trinity. That is, before "in the beginning" the personal was already there. Love, thought and communication existed prior to the creation of the heavens and the earth."[16]

The modern non-Christian responds to this Christian answer with a further question: *Where do love and communication come from?* Non-Christians attempt to answer this question by singing, writing, and painting in a manner which desperately attempts to resolve such a mystery. The humanist non-Christian then is ontologically confused about human reality.[17] But for Schaeffer "the biblical answer is quite otherwise: Something was there before creation. God was there; love and communication were there; and therefore, prior even to Genesis 1:1, love and communication are intrinsic to what always has been."[18]

This is the foundational apologetic of Schaeffer's project. Whereas non-Christians occasionally cry out because they cannot answer the second question, *where do love and communication come from?* Schaeffer points out that Christians can provide the answer. Hence, Schaeffer concludes, "It is either not knowing or denying the createdness of things that is at the root of the blackness of modern man's difficulties."[19]

Even if the non-Christian does not know why nature exists (despite his exuberant investigation of the same), nature is a reality precisely because the triune God created it out of nothing (*ex nihilo*).[20] Schaeffer goes on to emphasize that in a Christian theology of creation there is an ontological distinction between God and all created things because of God's "infinity" and his "person[hood]." In the same way that God brings into being that which had never existed, man is also able to bring certain things into being. However, the two creators must be starkly differentiated, according to Schaeffer, for God brought materials into being which had never before existed, whereas man is limited to making from that which already exists: "The artist reaches over and uses his brush and his pigments. The engineer uses steel and pre-pressed concrete for his bridge. Or the flower arranger

15. Ibid., 21.
16. Ibid.
17. Budziszewski, *Evangelicals*, 75.
18. Schaeffer, *Genesis*, 22.
19. Ibid., 30.
20. Schaeffer, *Pollution*, 27–28.

uses the flowers, the moss and the rocks and the pebbles that were already there. God is quite different."[21]

Man, too, should be understood as ontologically distinct from inanimate creation and "machines," as only he was made in the image of God (*imago Dei*). Granted, man should not be so distinguished from inanimate creation as to deny the creatureliness of all things, but man should "humbly" and "reverently" view himself as "personality," distinguishable from inanimate creation and machines.[22] In this vein, Schaeffer criticizes Albert Schweitzer for only having an account of man with other created beings; for example, talking of man in equal relation to a hippopotamus because of their common creatureliness without a sufficient account of man's relationship to God, will not do.[23]

The importance of such a fundamental Christian distinction provides an explanation for creation's "common origin," such that the evolutionist or "modern man" struggles to grasp. For Schaeffer, the Bible reveals that all people stem from the same origin, but then is quick to nuance that among men there are in actual fact *two* humanities. One stands in revolt against God, while the other seeks to lay down its autonomy in order to live according to God's purposes. "The members of this second group, having believed on Christ, have cast themselves upon God and have become the sons of God."[24] Since sin has entered the world, the first humanity fails to perceive or believe that created reality came into being, exists, is sustained, and will be redeemed by this God, so treating inanimate creation and machines contemptuously.

This is most evident from the narrative of Cain and Abel. The narrator does not explain why Cain's offering was not pleasing to God, while Abel's was. However, the acceptance of one, and the rejection of the other, is an early indication of two humanities, argues Schaeffer. Schaeffer's wife Edith also comments upon this but with much more conviction about God's distaste at Cain's offering: "Cain came in defiance, saying something of this sort: 'My fruits are good enough, *I* have raised them. God must accept me because of those very good works I've brought to Him.'"[25]

Moreover, Schaeffer describes Cain's progeny building cities, and becoming civilized:

21. Schaeffer, *Genesis*, 28.
22. Schaeffer, *Pollution*, 29.
23. See Schweitzer, *Philosophy*, 309–27.
24. Schaeffer, *Pollution*, 30.
25. Schaeffer, *L'Abri*, 178.

> Genesis 4:11–24 tells of the gradually developing culture of the ungodly line. For man is still really man, and he can bring forth culture. But it is a culture with a mark upon it, a culture without God. . . . Here is humanistic culture without God. It is egoism and pride centered in man; this culture has lost the concept not only of God but of man as one who loves his brother.[26]

Without a *theological* prism through which to view creation, treating created things with "integrity" and taking note of their æsthetic beauty is overlooked and neglected. "[W]e should treat each thing," Schaeffer insists, "with integrity because it is the way God has made it." Schaeffer adds, "The value of the things is not in themselves autonomously, but that God made them—and thus they deserve to be treated with high respect."[27] This vantage point, though, does not exist among non-Christians, because even though they may sometimes treat creation with integrity, they do not do so because God commands it. This branch of "humanity says there is no God, or it makes gods in its own imagination, or it tries to come to the true God in its own way. The other humanity comes to the true God in God's way. There is no neutral ground."[28]

Schaeffer stresses that because God treats creation with integrity, so man ought to follow suit. Accordingly, Christian workers can say, "[B]ecause I love God—I love the One who has made it!"[29] This can be so despite man's dealing with created matter often being "mechanical" in nature; it does not come naturally to him to deal rightly with material objects. Schaeffer highlights the architect in this regard. Although probably more adept in relating to numerous materials than other workers, an architect must become accustomed to particular materials, and the environment, in order to treat the "material honestly." Mankind is able to get into this non-pantheistic frame of mind with created materials "since they are made in the image of God, even if they do not know it."[30] This speaks of the working ability of non-Christians. On the other hand, Christians have "a special understanding" of the material world due to "their special relationship with God." In other words, even though they are oblivious to this, non-Christians can relate well to non-human creation because they have been made in God's image (*imago Dei*). Nonetheless, the capability of the non-Christian is only ever at an

26. Schaeffer, *Genesis*, 114.
27. Schaeffer, *Pollution*, 32.
28. Schaeffer, *Genesis*, 115.
29. Schaeffer, *Pollution*, 33.
30. Ibid., 34.

intermediate level because he "has set himself at the center of the universe," argues Schaeffer.[31]

Schaeffer favorably quotes Lynn White's famous essay *The Historical Roots of our Ecological Existence* in support of this point, which states, "What people do about their ecology depends on what they think about themselves in relation to things around them."[32] Schaeffer afterwards distances himself from White as he appears to have proposed a pantheistic solution to man's destruction of creation. Nevertheless, they are both agreed that a skewed worldview affects the way man interacts with creation.

Schaeffer's understanding of man's relationship to the rest of creation implies that work can be done well, and appropriately, irrespective of whether someone has faith in Christ or not. However, *the motivation* for relating to creation must be crowned with faith in Christ for it to fulfill the heights to which work was intended. *In other words, the autonomy of man from God must be surrendered to God's sovereignty for work to become as fruitful as God originally intended.* Thus, both the work plus its intent have their importance in Schaeffer's mind. It might be said then that "the man without the Bible" (a synonym used by Schaeffer for non-Christians) is under God's judgment because of his unchristian view of creation.

THE SIGNIFICANCE OF MAN

Man is in a dilemma because of this unchristian view of creation. That is, he has "deliberately turned away" from God so as to exert his autonomy, thus leaving him in complete isolation.[33] But this isolation says something highly important about man: "he can really influence significant history." Despite the fact that sin has brought tragic ruin to him, "that does not mean he is nothing." To be pejorative against man by labeling him a sinner is to overstep the mark, according to Schaeffer, because he is made in God's image. Hence, man must be viewed as a creature who can "influence history for this life and the life to come, for himself and for others."[34] That man is capable of such grand responsibility equates to him being a "wonderful" and "tremendous" creature, according to Schaeffer. This outlook expresses the dignity and respect with which God views man despite his rebellion.[35]

31. Ibid., 41.
32. Quoted in ibid., 6.
33. Schaeffer, *Death in the City*, 68.
34. Ibid., 69.
35. Harper, "Francis A. Schaeffer," 135.

Because non-Christian man cannot answer the question *Who am I?*, this presents a window of opportunity for Christians to provide an answer—man is made in the image of God, and this God is the God who is there. However, according to Schaeffer, the non-Christian "in his own naturalistic theories, with the uniformity of cause and effect in a closed system, with an evolutionary concept of a mechanical, chance parade from the atom to man . . . has lost his unique identity. As he looks out upon the world, as he faces the machine, he cannot tell himself from what he faces. He cannot distinguish himself from other things."[36]

This lack of self-awareness, and loss of identity, leads to non-Christian ignorance of the imperative to responsibly rule the earth. Schaeffer says further: "We have been given a dominion which puts a moral responsibility on us. We don't need to succumb therefore to the ethics of the Marquis de Sade, where might or whatever is, is right."[37] Even though the Fall of man devastated him, resulting in work being administered badly, man is still required to have responsible dominion over the earth.[38] Because man has been set the task of ruling creation, his sin has necessarily caused the world around him to change also. Schaeffer states,

> So now the earth itself is abnormal. We read, for example, in Genesis 5:29, which speaks of the world before the flood: "And he [Noah's father] called his name Noah, saying, This same shall comfort us concerning our work and toil of our hands, because of the ground which the LORD hath cursed" . . .
>
> Why is it like this? Because, one might say, you, O unprogrammed and significant Adam, have revolted. Nature has been under your dominion (in this sense it is as an extension of himself, as a king's empire is an extension of himself). Therefore, when you changed, God changed the objective, external world. It as well as you is now abnormal.[39]

Schaeffer bases these anthropological convictions partly upon Rom 1:21–2 which reveals that non-Christian man is without excuse, "for though they knew God, they did not honor him as God or give thanks to him, but they became futile in their thinking, and their senseless minds were darkened. Claiming to be wise, they became fools." Man is therefore responsible for all that he is and does; his choices shape history for good or bad. "Even

---

36. Schaeffer, *Genesis*, 46.
37. Ibid., 48.
38. Ibid., 50.
39. Ibid., 95–96.

sin," claims Schaeffer, "is not nothingness," thus man is "great" because he has the freedom to rule and subdue the earth in whichever way he wishes.[40]

Because many are "without the Bible" and are morally responsible, non-Christians are seen as those who "suppress the truth" (Rom 1:18). This is critical to Schaeffer's theological system, for "the man without the Bible" is "contrary to the moral law of the universe and as a result he is morally and legally guilty. Because man is guilty before the Lawgiver of the universe, doing what is contrary to His character, his sin is significant and he is morally significant in a significant history. Man has a true moral guilt."[41]

Without a subjective response to Christ, and the belief that the Bible is the whole and only truth, non-Christians do not and cannot operate in the world with the fullness to which they were divinely called.[42] The phrase "the man without the Bible" is also telling of Schaeffer's theological education in this regard, for without the Bible man cannot know God for himself because therein lies revelation of the triune God in the person of Jesus Christ. Schaeffer thus allies himself with the Reformers as he wishes that "the man without the Bible" would simply read it for himself.[43] Such is the vision of the L'Abri centers, that "the man without the Bible" would read the Bible for themselves so as to discover the God who is there.

Schaeffer's emphasis on the Bible reflects the influence of his teacher Carl Henry (Fuller Theological Seminary) who stressed the inerrancy of the Bible, and held a classically foundationalist theological position.[44] This account of inerrancy propagated the nature of scripture as "historical and propositional revelation, plenary inspiration, and verbal inerrancy."[45] Henry understood scripture in this way because it provides the foundations for a Christian worldview,[46] and this foundationalist position was largely a reaction against nineteenth-century liberal theology (e.g., Friedrich Schleiermacher) and philosophy.[47] Schaeffer adopts Henry's bibliology wholeheartedly.

Even though the non-Christian is "the man without the Bible," because he is made in God's image he retains his "moral nature." Schaeffer employs Rom 2:15 to illustrate this: "They [non-Christians] show that what the law

40. Schaeffer, *Death*, 70.
41. Schaeffer, *The God Who is There*, 115.
42. Barrs, "Francis Schaeffer: His Legacy," 81–82.
43. Ibid., 33.
44. Henry, *God, Revelation and Authority*, 103–219.
45. Henry, *Frontiers*, 134–35.
46. Grenz, *Renewing the Center*, 97.
47. Grenz and Franke, *Beyond Foundationalism*, 33–34.

requires is written on their hearts, to which their own conscience also bears witness; and their conflicting thoughts will accuse or perhaps excuse them." Schaeffer comments on this text: "Despite what a man may say in theory, he cannot escape being a moral creature. The man who says morals do not exist is not amoral in the sense that he has no moral motions."[48]

Furthermore, non-Christians suppress the truth because "they refuse to bow to the God who is there and because they hold to their presuppositions as an implicit faith—hold some of the truth about themselves and about the universe, but they do not carry these things to their logical conclusions because they contradict their presuppositions."[49]

The contradiction of non-Christian presuppositions comes from what Schaeffer calls the "antithesis." Admitting that God is there will always clash with those who deny such a claim, and where there is denial, God is "really blasphemed, discredited and dishonored."[50] Schaeffer's stance relies upon the premise that either Christianity is completely true and realistic, and thus there is hope for the world, or it is nothing at all.[51]

Returning to Rom 1:21–22, Schaeffer identifies that non-Christians have become "futile in their thinking" and thus their minds need altering in order to know and accept the truth, which leads to right living.[52] Non-Christian man is therefore under God's judgment precisely because God values him, and is "significant" to him. Divine indifference to man might indicate a lack of commitment to his wellbeing, but this is not the case. That non-Christian man is under divine judgment reveals God's keen interest in him, hence "[t]he world is what it is, not as a result of the cruelty of God to man, but of the cruelty of man to man."[53] The cruelty of man to God, man to inanimate creation, and man to himself, are further omissions which should also be included here.

Schaeffer continues, "[i]t's because men turn away from God that moral problems arise."[54] This assertion stems from Schaeffer's continued attention to the Apostle Paul's argument in Romans 1. On three occasions Schaeffer notes that "non-Christians" have "exchanged the glory of God for images" (v. 23), "exchanged the truth of God for a lie" (v. 25), and "they did not see fit to acknowledge God" (v. 28). Consequently, God "gave them up"

---

48. Schaeffer, *Death*, 84.
49. Ibid., 90–91.
50. Schaeffer, *The God Who Is There*, 47.
51. Ibid., 46.
52. Schaeffer, *Death*, 91.
53. Ibid., 91.
54. Ibid., 92.

(vv. 24, 26, 28) to their false inclinations and desires. This "giving up" is the nature of God's judgment upon them.

THE EPISTEMOLOGICAL NECESSITY: THE NON-CHRISTIAN PROBLEM

So what are non-Christian presuppositions which Schaeffer spoke of earlier? For "unless our epistemology is right," states Schaeffer, "everything is going to be wrong."[55] Schaeffer attempts to show that without a Christian view of metaphysics, morals, and epistemology, any non-Christian worldview is completely unsatisfactory. In fact, having taken much time to explore non-Christian worldviews he concludes that in actuality there are really only *two* worldviews, one of which is true. It is here that he returns to the concept of two humanities: "[M]an, beginning with himself, can define the philosophical problem of existence, but he cannot generate from himself the answer to the problem. The answer to the problem of existence is that the infinite-personal, triune God is there, and that infinite-personal, triune God is not silent."[56]

Concerning his epistemology, Schaeffer believes that a thoroughgoing analysis of culture is worthwhile, indicating his indebtedness to Cornelius Van Til (1895–1987), a former teacher from Westminster Theological Seminary.[57] Van Til is a Dutch Calvinist heavily influenced by Abraham Kuyper (1837–1920) who set the trend for Calvinist political engagement in the late nineteenth and early twentieth centuries. It was Hans Rookmaaker (1922–77) who introduced Schaeffer to Kuyper's thought and other Dutch Reformed theologies (Groen Van Prinsterer and Herman Dooyeweerd), linking Schaeffer to Calvin, albeit via the Dutch Reformed tradition.[58]

By extension, British evangelical theologies were introduced to Kuyperian theology via Schaeffer, which is curious because British evangelical theologies have not taken up Kuyperian theology in any significant way.[59] The reason for this, perhaps, is because Schaeffer did not adopt Kuyper's theology in its pure form. Van Til's North American adaptation of it was that which Schaeffer inherited.

---

55. Schaeffer, *He is There*, 275.
56. Ibid., 290.
57. Schaeffer, "A Review of a Review," 7–9.
58. Duriez, *Francis Schaeffer*, 79.
59. Two exceptions to this are: Oliver O'Donovan (who received Princeton Theological Seminary's 2008 Kuyper Prize for Excellence in Reformed Theology and Public Life) and Heslam, *Creating a Christian Worldview*.

Van Til, a *presuppositionalist*, influenced Schaeffer, who in turn became "an inconsistent presuppositionalist."[60] In other words, "for Schaeffer, as with Van Til, there *are* two humanities. However, Schaeffer believes there is a common ground which both Christians and non-Christians share—something Van Til would deny."[61]

This divergence from Van Til identifies something important about Schaeffer's understanding of non-Christian work: no man is *entirely* inconsistent in applying his presuppositions, meaning Schaeffer believes that non-Christians possess a degree of philosophical and practical coherence. Furthermore, non-Christians share a level of understanding with Christians and Schaeffer puts this down to *common grace*, the *imago Dei* present among all men. This common grace enables communication between both "humanities," which reveals the overall motivation underlying Schaeffer's evangelistic apologetic.[62]

In light of this view of the Bible, and the "man without the Bible," Schaeffer avers that society is on sure ground when it is founded upon biblical principles, a view influenced by Carl Henry. Thus, Schaeffer appeals to the Reformation as the exemplary movement that attempted this. He says, "So the Reformation's preaching of the gospel brought forth two things which were secondary to the central message of the gospel but nonetheless were important: an interest in culture and a true basis for form and freedom in society and government."[63]

An implication of society being founded upon biblical principles, Schaeffer argues, is that "the private citizen" in a minority group can stand up against majority opinion on biblical grounds and be heard. In Northern Europe, this resulted in the establishment of political systems with checks and balances, not that this was a novel political idea.[64] Calvin, influenced by Martin Bucer (1491–1551), saw the need for checks and balances given the sinfulness of man, proving that Calvin was not the authoritarian figure in Geneva he is accused of being, Schaeffer argues; rather, his influence had more of an "informal" and "moral" tone, both ecclesiastically and politically.[65] Because Calvin "did not lose contact with daily life the biblical insistence on the responsibility of people—even of monarchs—to God's law

---

60. A philosophical approach to theology which insists that all epistemologies are based upon postulations that cannot be proved about God, man, and reality.

61. Harper, "Francis A. Schaeffer," 138.

62. For Van Til's notion of two humanities, see Van Til, *The Defense of the Faith*, 90–95.

63. Schaeffer, *How Should We Then Live?*, 139.

64. Ibid.

65. Ibid., 140.

turned the political tide in those countries where the Reformation emphasis on the Bible as the only final authority took root."[66]

Calvin's influence spread to England where Presbyterianism sought to play a "creative role in trimming the power of the English kings," but more significant in Schaeffer's mind was Scotland's *Lex Rex*, penned by Samuel Rutherford (1600–1661).[67] Schaeffer lauds Rutherford's approach that societies established upon the sole authority of the Bible are indeed greater and considerably less sinful. In light of such an exemplary Reformation, Schaeffer interacts with several large areas of human culture, although his survey of culture is conditioned by his awareness of "the line of despair." His text *The God Who Is There* is devoted to tracing how widely this despair has pervaded Western culture.[68]

Living above "the line of despair" were those who held romantic notions of absolutes that had no logical basis, and who maintained a unified view of the world. Such views were held prior to 1890 in Europe, and prior to 1935 in America, according to Schaeffer.[69] Early modern scientists believed the world was created reasonably by a reasonable God, thus man could by his reason discover Him. In short, "God stood as an epistemological Guarantor for man."[70] Before these dates "'non-Christians' had no right to act on the presuppositions they acted on. That is true. They were being romantic in accepting optimistic answers without a sufficient base. Nevertheless they went on thinking and acting as if these presuppositions were true."[71]

After these dates a seismic shift in the way man understood truth took place both epistemologically and methodologically,[72] and Schaeffer believes that this shift pushed man below "the line of despair" for no longer did he romantically assume absolutes, but instead viewed truth subjectively because "it has no point of reference outside oneself."[73] A rudimentary understanding of the presuppositions below "the line of despair" revealed that there is one ruling belief: there is an infinite, personal God. Stemming from this are two corollaries: (1) the universe has a personal origin as shown by its creation, and (2) nature must be viewed as being an open

---

66. Ibid., 137.

67. Ibid., 139.

68. Harper, "Francis A. Schaeffer," 134.

69. 1935 is given as a date for the seismic shift in American thought because of WWI and also the devastating effects of the Wall Street crash.

70. Morris, *Francis Schaeffer's Apologetics*, 40.

71. Schaeffer, *The God Who Is There*, 6.

72. Ibid., 6, 8.

73. Harper, "Francis A. Schaeffer," 132.

causal system. "By contrast, the non-Christian holds the negation of these three presuppositions."[74]

Above "the line of despair" Schaeffer talks of the "upper story" which refers to the non-logical and non-rational, whereas below "the line of despair" a "lower story" of rationality and logic is present. These two stories never meet: "In other words, in the lower story, on the basis of all reason, man as man is dead. You have simply mathematics, particulars, mechanics. Man has no meaning, no purpose, no significance. There is only pessimism concerning man as man."[75]

The "upper story" requires a non-rational, unreasonable leap of faith so as to infuse man with vacuous optimism. Ruegsegger correctly sums this up by saying, "After," 1890 in Europe, and 1935 in America, "Christians continued to maintain that truth is absolute, but non-Christians accepted the notion that truth is relative."[76] With this, Ruegsegger believes that Schaeffer does not make one theological move, but two. First of all, he talks of crossing "the line of relativism," and secondly, a crossing of "the line of despair" occurs, and it is by crossing from absolutism to relativism in the first instance that "the line of despair" is then traversed.[77]

It must also be noted that below "the line of despair" is a continual descent of despair, beginning with the excursus into philosophy which winds its way into art, music, general culture, and finally theology.[78] It is this point of despair which is so critical to Schaeffer's apologetics, for if the non-Christian comes to a point of despair to the extent that he understands the illogical and unjustified nature of his presuppositions, it can then be shown to "him that he must give up that which he loves the most if he is to remain rational," and this is absolutely essential for Schaeffer in being able to share the gospel.[79]

It has been critical to first of all understand how significant the doctrine of creation and theological anthropology are to Schaeffer's discussion of non-Christian epistemology. Without these undergirding assumptions, Schaeffer's conception of non-Christian work is meaningless. Beginning at the top of Schaeffer's cascading notion of despair I will now outline his understanding of scientific and philosophical presuppositions.

74. Ruegsegger, "Schaeffer's System of Thought," 33.
75. Schaeffer, *Escape from Reason*, 238.
76. Ruegsegger, "Schaeffer's System of Thought," 30.
77. Ibid.
78. Schaeffer, *The God Who Is There*, 8. I will not engage Schaeffer's critique of modern theology as this does not pertain to the work of non-Christians.
79. Ibid., section 4, chapter 1.

NON-CHRISTIAN CULTURE

1. Science and Philosophy

"Epistemology," states Schaeffer, "is the central problem of our generation."[80] Even at the time of Plato (424/3–348/7 BC) the problem of knowing was fiercely debated. "The Greek philosophers, and especially Plato, were seeking for universals that would make the particulars meaningful."[81] Thomas Aquinas (1225–74), Schaeffer argues, took up this problem but came to different conclusions because he elevated particulars by analyzing nature. Artists like Cimabue (1240–1302) and writers like Dante (1265–1321) were deeply influenced by Aquinas' stress upon nature, which was "re-established and re-emphasized in men's thinking; [but] there is that which was destructive. They were making the particulars autonomous and thus losing the universal that gave the particulars meaning.... [I]f nature or the particulars are autonomous from God, then nature begins to eat up grace."[82]

The result of this, according to Schaeffer, is that man becomes morally and epistemologically bankrupt because there is no longer any room for grace to shape him. Leonardo da Vinci (1452–1519), as a mathematician, saw this problem and argued that if man begins and ends knowledge with himself then he will always end up "with only mathematics and particulars and would end up with only mechanics. In other words, he was so far ahead of his time that he really understood that everything was going to end up only as a machine, and there were not going to be any universals or meaning at all."[83]

Schaeffer believes that da Vinci was a key thinker for such humanistic epistemology. The questions of the Renaissance and Reformation were basically the same, Schaeffer argues, but the way they were answered was quite different. Schaeffer recalls Aquinas' argument that when sin entered the world man's *will* fell but his *mind* did not. The implication of this, Schaeffer postulates, is that man is capable of *reasoning* all the world's great questions from an anthropological starting point.[84]

On the other hand, the Reformers, Schaeffer believes, followed Augustine of Hippo's biblical views. By doing this, Schaeffer deems their theology more orthodox than renaissance thinkers because the Reformers' stress on the pervasiveness of sin in man prevented theology beginning

---

80. Schaeffer, *He is There*, 303.
81. Ibid., 304.
82. Ibid., 306.
83. Ibid., 307.
84. A point Reinhold Niebuhr also discerns from Aquinas in, *Love and Justice*, 47.

from anthropology.[85] Indeed, Schaeffer specifically concurs with Calvin's unromantic understanding of anthropology.[86] By siding with Reformation theology in this way discloses Schaeffer's belief that the Reformation was *the* "pivotal event" in the history of Western culture.[87]

"At its core, therefore, the Reformation was the removing of the humanistic distortions which had entered the church."[88] This shift of emphasis was significant because "the Renaissance centered in autonomous man, while the Reformation centered in the infinite-personal God who had spoken in the Bible."[89] Schaeffer continues:

> It is important that the Bible sets forth true knowledge about mankind. The biblical teaching gives meaning to all particulars, but this is especially so in regard to that particular which is the most important to man, namely, the individual himself or herself. It gives a reason for the individual being great. The ironic fact here is that humanism, which began with Man's being central, eventually had no real meaning for people. On the other hand, if one begins with the Bible's position that a person is created by God and created in the image of God, there is a basis for that person's dignity. People, the Bible teaches, are made in the image of God—they are nonprogrammed. Each is thus Man with dignity.[90]

After the Renaissance and the Reformation, however, (at the time of Immanuel Kant 1724–1804 and acknowledging the many figures who preceded Kant) a sense of the autonomous had become well developed. Schaeffer says, "Whereas previously men had spoken of nature and grace, by the eighteenth century there was no idea of grace—the word did not fit any longer."[91] Rationalism was now in full flow, and the concept of revelation was long since lost. No longer was *nature/grace* the appropriate dichotomy as advocated by Aquinas and the Reformers, but *nature/freedom* had become the new watchword in an age of increasing secularization. This move stemmed from Jean-Jacques Rousseau (1712–78) who propagated an account of "absolute freedom."[92] Schaeffer sums up this period's tenor

---

85. Schaeffer, *How Should We Then Live?*, 121.
86. Ibid., 140.
87. Pierard, "Schaeffer on History," 203.
88. Schaeffer, *How Should We Then Live?*, 121–22.
89. Ibid., 123.
90. Ibid., 124.
91. Schaeffer, *Escape from Reason*, 227.
92. Schaeffer, *He is There*, 308.

once more, "[n]ature has totally devoured grace, and what is left in its place "upstairs" is the word *freedom*."[93] What is autonomous freedom according to Schaeffer? "It means a freedom in which the individual is the center of the universe. Autonomous freedom is a freedom that is without restraint. Therefore, as man begins to feel the weight of the machine pressing upon him . . . It merely hopes and tries to will that the finite individual man will be free—and that which is left is the individual *self-expression*."[94]

In three texts, according to Schaeffer, *Critique of Pure Reason* (1781), *Critique of Practical Reason* (1788), and *Critique of Judgment* (1790), Kant sought to bring together the noumenal world (the concepts of meaning and value) and the "phenomenal world" (the world which can be weighed and measured). Schaeffer believes Kant never fulfilled this. Ultimately, there was no presentation of a unified knowledge given, but a splitting apart of two matters which were not adequately reconciled.[95] Kant concludes, according to Schaeffer, that the cosmos can engage with nature, but no longer with God through grace.

The German philosopher Georg Wilhelm Friedrich Hegel (1770–1831), too, sought to marry the "noumenal world" with the "phenomenal world," but his attempts to do so were opaque and indecipherable, claims Schaeffer.[96] By Hegel's time, science had solidified into a naturalistic philosophy, meaning that science was understood as natural causes taking place in a *closed* system.[97] Eventually, Schaeffer argues, Hegel proposed a new solution of practicing philosophy by altering both epistemology and methodology. Rather than antithesis, he proposed that people think in terms of thesis/antithesis, "with the answer always being synthesis."[98] What this did, according to Schaeffer, was to relativize all things, and this shift in thinking was not something which was desirable, other than a way of moving past rationalistic thought which had already failed.

In short, this was a new way of discovering truth as a result of a changed methodology.[99] Hegel, then, according to Schaeffer, fostered the notion that man is at the center of his own universe and should never relinquish

---

93. Schaeffer, *Escape from Reason*, 227.
94. Ibid., 228.
95. Schaeffer, *How Should We Then Live?*, 177–78.
96. Ibid., 178.
97. Schaeffer, *Escape from Reason*, 229–30.
98. Ibid., 233.
99. Ibid., 233.

his rebellion against God or his rationalism. This is what it means to be autonomous.[100]

Søren Kierkegaard (1813–55), in reaction to Hegel, put away thoughts of a unified knowledge (nature/grace or nature/freedom) for a fresh dichotomy: *faith/rationality*. With this, Kierkegaard ensured that there would be no unity between universals and nature, but cemented "the line of despair."[101] From Kierkegaard, argues Schaeffer, stem two differing forms of existentialism: "secular" and "religious" existentialism: secular existentialism finding its expression in French (Sartre, Camus) and German (Heidegger, Jaspers) philosophy; religious existentialism being manifest in the theology of Karl Barth. For Schaeffer, both were equally detrimental to man and brought him far below "the line of despair." Schaeffer says of Sartre, Camus, Heidegger, Jaspers, Kierkegaard and Barth, "To these men as rationalists the knowledge we can know with our reason is only a mathematical formula in which man is only a machine. Instead of reason they hope to find some sort of mystical experience 'upstairs,' apart from reason, to provide a universal. . . . Man hopes to find something in his head because he cannot know certainly that anything is 'out there.'"[102]

Finding no hope in these thinkers in his analysis of non-Christian culture, Schaeffer then moves from science and philosophy into the sphere of art.

2. Art

On the cascading descent beneath the "line of despair," philosophy only pervaded a limited group of people. Art, believes Schaeffer, touched considerably more. Art is also a "doorway" of descent below "the line of despair" as exemplified by the post-Impressionists. Schaeffer summarizes the experience of Post-Impressionist art to the onlooker: "The viewer comes to the painting and in one way sees what the artist pictures, but in another way asks himself, 'Is there any meaning to what I am looking at?' The art had become sterile."[103]

For Schaeffer, Vincent Van Gogh (1853–90) and Paul Gauguin (1846–1903) stand out as two key figureheads of the movement. They both sought to claw a way back to reality by expressing universals latent in natural things, but despite determined attempts to retrieve these absolutes,

---

100. Ibid.
101. Ibid., 237.
102. Schaeffer, *He is There*, 310.
103. Schaeffer, *How Should We Then Live?*, 196.

according to Schaeffer, they ultimately failed.[104] "The fragmentation shown in post-Impressionist paintings was parallel to the loss of a hope for a unity of knowledge in philosophy."[105]

Van Gogh's letters reveal a depth of feeling which is much admired, but Schaeffer argues that this admiration concomitantly "became the vehicle for modern man's view of the fragmentation of truth and life."[106] His paintings fostered a feeling of deep depression and morbidity that reflected his suicidal tendencies due to mental illness which followed Gauguin's relationship with a woman Van Gogh liked. This darkness was compounded by a raging disagreement with Gauguin which saw them go their separate ways artistically, and in turn led to Van Gogh's eventual suicide.[107]

Schaeffer continues his insight into "the line of despair" in non-Christian art through the post-Impressionist Paul Gauguin, who similarly to Van Gogh, sought for universals. This is demonstrated clearly in his painting entitled *What? Whence? Whither?*, a painting Rookmaaker believes is the standout painting stemming from Gauguin's philosophy, and the most mature fruit of his ability.[108] Gauguin moved to Tahiti in order to live out the philosophy of Jean-Jacques Rousseau (1712–78), being particularly moved by his notion of the noble savage. This savage was understood as a pure state of nature, full of virtue and uncorrupted by civilization. Thus, Gauguin, by rooting himself in the noble savage, "the child of the race," believed he could begin to discover the universal. He began painting nude women in an attempt to realize this:

> So what we have is destructive freedom not only in morals (though it shows itself very quickly in morals, especially quickly perhaps in sexual activity), but in the area of knowledge as well. In metaphysics, in the area of Being, as well as morals, we are supposed to have absolute freedom. But then the dilemma comes; how do you know and how do you know you know?[109]

But his *What? Whence? Whither?* Schaeffer argues, speaks volumes of the depths of despair Gauguin reached in his quest.[110] In the top left corner is written the title of the painting and instructions to view it from right to left. On the right is a beautiful woman, reminiscent of his famous works,

---

104. Ibid., 196.
105. Ibid., 197.
106. Ibid.
107. Schaeffer, *The God Who Is There*, 28.
108. Rookmaaker, *Gauguin*, 192.
109. Schaeffer, *He is There*, 309.
110. Schaeffer, *The God Who Is There*, 28.

which is juxtaposed with three other figures. One is a Tahitian beauty standing beside a dying old woman who is being observed by a disturbing bird. "There is the same exotic symbolism, the same appeal to the sensuous in the concept of the noble savage,"[111] says Schaeffer. Gauguin himself comments: "I have finished a philosophical work on this theme, comparable to the gospel. A figure lifts up its arms into the air and, astonished, looks at these two personages who dare to think of their destination." Further, Gauguin says, "Whither? Close to the death of an old woman, a strange, stupid bird concludes: What? The eternal problem that punishes our pride. O Sorrow, thou are my master. Fate, how cruel thou art, and always vanquished, I revolt."[112]

Schaeffer concludes his thoughts on Gauguin's quest for the universal with the contention that Gauguin's universal was humanistic and thus it was inevitable that he attempted to end his life in suicidal despair.[113] Gauguin's art:

> is only a step, really from . . . the hippie culture of the 1960s, and as a matter of fact, to the whole modern culture. In a certain sense there is a parenthesis in time from Rousseau until the birth of the hippie culture and the whole modern culture which is founded on the view that there are no universals anywhere—that man is totally, hedonistically free, that the individual is totally, hedonistically free, not only morally but also in the area of knowledge. We can easily see the moral confusion that has resulted from this, but the epistemological confusion is worse. If there are no universals, how do we know reality from nonreality?[114]

Both Van Gogh and Gauguin, Schaeffer insists, are classic examples of trying to live autonomously without a *divine* universal, and it was also the Gauguins of this world who would often come to the L'Abri centers "seeking the answers to the basic questions which bother any thinking person."[115]

3. Music

Like philosophy, science, and art before it, music also provides an alternative "doorway" below the descending "line of despair." The Beatles, for example,

---

111. Ibid., 28.
112. Rookmaaker, *Synthetist*, notes n, p, aa, af in chapter 9.
113. Schaeffer, *The God Who Is There*, 29.
114. Schaeffer, *He is There*, 309.
115. Schaeffer, *L'Abri*, 13.

produced their *Revolver, Strawberry Fields Forever, Penny Lane* and *Sergeant Pepper's Lonely Hearts Club Band* albums at a time when experimenting with the psychedelic genre. Their lyrics at this time reveal the message of drug taking as a means of finding religious answers to life's anxieties and woes. Schaeffer explains: "The religious form was the same vague pantheism which predominates much of the new mystical thought today. One indeed does not have to understand in a clear way the modern monolithic thought in order to be infiltrated by it."[116]

Schaeffer did not limit his argument to popular twentieth-century music however. Following on from Ludwig van Beethoven (1770–1827) and Wilhelm Richard Wagner (1813–83), Gustav Mahler (1860–1911) offered his enormous symphonic and orchestral sound to the European world, and Schaeffer quotes Leonard Bernstein extensively to comment upon Mahler's music:

> Ours is the century of death and Mahler is its musical prophet. . . . If Mahler knew this [personal death, death of tonality, and the death of culture as it had been] and his message is so clear, how do we, knowing it too, manage to survive? Why are we still here, struggling to go on? We are now face to face with the truly ultimate ambiguity, which is the human spirit—the most fascinating ambiguity of all. . . . We learn to accept our mortality; yet we persist in our search for immortality. . . . All this ultimate ambiguity is to be heard in the finale of Mahler's Ninth.[117]

Schaeffer adds that Mahler's ninth symphony speaks of Friedrich Nietzsche's (1844–1900) philosophy which is best rendered by the words of an inscribed poem found on a plaque of a great Swiss rock:

> Oh man! Take heed
>   of what the dark midnight says:
> I slept, I slept—from deep dreams I awoke:
> The world is deep—and more profound than day
>   would have thought.
> Profound in her pain—
> Pleasure—more profound than pain of heart,
> Woe speaks; pass on.
> But all pleasure seeks eternity—
>   a deep and profound eternity.[118]

---

116. Schaeffer, *The God Who Is There*, 41.
117. Schaeffer, *How Should We Then Live?*, 200–201.
118. Ibid., 193–94. Translated by Udo Middelmann.

As Schaeffer comments: "This is modern man's position. He has come to a position of the death of man in his own mind, but he cannot live with it, for it does not describe what he is."[119] Music, like other forms of human culture which are adrift from the triune God and his glory, lead below 'the line of despair.' The increased secularization of Western society has fueled this shift, argues Schaeffer, and thus it has permeated society in its entirety. Even theology has been susceptible to its far-reaching tentacles.

The overriding problem with non-Christian work then, according to Schaeffer, is its performance without any reference to God. The early Ludwig Wittgenstein (1889–1951) encapsulates this epistemological dilemma when he concludes that in the realm of reason all man can rely upon is facts. Thus, man only has the propositions of natural science at his disposal for language. Schaeffer concludes from this that "[t]his is the limit of language and the limit of logic."[120]

Mathematical formulations are the distillation of language restricted to reason that leaves man once again in the place of nature without grace. Schaeffer claims therefore that

> positivism is dead, and what is left is cynicism or some mystical leap as to knowing. That is where modern man is, whether the individual man knows it or not. Those who have been raised in the last couple of decades stand right here in the area of epistemology. The really great problem is not, for example, drugs or amorality. The problem is knowing. . . .
>
> Man, made in the image of God and intended to be in vertical communication with the One who is there and who is not silent, and meant to have horizontal communication with his own kind, has, because of his proud rationalism, making himself autonomous, come to this place.[121]

Non-Christian man has an epistemological problem: he has become autonomous from God; therefore, he cannot know or work aright. Consequently, his work must be judged. This is the theological basis for splicing apart *evangelical works*; works done through Christian faith and ordinary work performed by the "man without the Bible." An accurate epistemology is critical for ordinary work to become works which are significant to God.

---

119. Ibid., 201.
120. Schaeffer, *He is There*, 314.
121. Ibid., 319.

THE ESCHATOLOGICAL JUDGMENT OF NON-CHRISTIANS

So "[h]ow is the man without the Bible to be judged by God?"[122] In answering this question Schaeffer returns to his evaluation of Rom 2:15–16: "They ['non-Christian' Gentiles] show that what the law requires is written on their hearts, to which their own conscience [*suneidēseōs*] also bears witness; and their conflicting thought will accuse [*katēgorountōn*] or perhaps excuse [*apologoumenōn*] them on the day when, according to my gospel, God, through Jesus Christ, will judge the secret thoughts of all." It is highly significant, Schaeffer argues, that in the letter to the Romans the Apostle Paul addresses the man *without* the Bible prior to the man *with* the Bible, and this manifests the fact that non-Christian man remains significant to God.

The law written on the hearts of non-Christians can either accuse (*katēgorountōn*) or excuse (*apologoumenōn*). The right living of non-Christians is capable of excusing them from God's judgment, which again indicates the significance of man to God, but how will this divine judgment take place? Schaeffer imagines that every newborn baby in history has a tape recorder hung around its neck that automatically records "when moral judgments are being made."[123] Curiously, according to Schaeffer, "æsthetic judgments" do not necessitate recording. Finally, when the fearsome judgment day arrives God will play back every recorded moral judgment to each non-Christian in order to remind them where their ethics were at fault. Schaeffer imagines further that as

> thousands of moral judgments pour forth, and God simply turns and says, "On the basis of your own words, have *you* kept you own moral standards?" And each man is silent. No person in all the world has kept the moral standards with which he has tried to bind others. Consequently, God says, "I will judge you upon your own moral statements (those judgments upon which you have bound and condemned others), even if they are lower than moral statements should be. Are you guilty or not guilty?" No one will be able to raise his voice.[124]

Schaeffer interprets that any non-Christian can *excuse* himself through his obedience to conscience. However, the possibility of perfect moral judgment cannot be consistently maintained throughout life, thus,

---

122. Schaeffer, *Death*, 97.
123. Ibid., 98.
124. Ibid.

divine judgment will eventually come: "I tell you, on the day of judgment you will have to give an account for every careless word you utter; for by your words you will be justified [*dikaiōthēsē*], and by your words you will be condemned [*katadikasthēsē*]" (Matt 12:36).[125] Jesus' words here indicate the same freedom which the letter to the Romans conveys, that man can liberate or condemn himself. This is a responsibility, says Schaeffer, that God has left with all men, but man will never meet the grade which excuses him from condemnation.

Man will be judged according to his words but he will also be judged according to his *works*. Schaeffer appeals to Rev 20:12 in support of this view: "And the dead were judged according to their works [*ta erga*], as recorded in the books."[126] Schaeffer says, "I have known evangelicals who have been somewhat embarrassed by this, and say that this passage really means that people will not be judged on whether they have accepted Christ as Saviour or not."[127]

Nevertheless, content that he is on safe biblical ground, Schaeffer presses the point that in the process of producing work, non-Christians will make faulty moral judgments that will condemn them in the age to come.[128] The connection between the work of non-Christians and the eschaton is severed when considered from the perspective of the ability of non-Christians themselves. In no way, Schaeffer avers, can they work their way to heaven because they have either no conception or a false conception of the God who is there. Right epistemology is critical for work to be considered good.

ANALYSIS OF SCHAEFFER

What should be made of Schaeffer's interpretation of the work of non-Christians? First of all, Schaeffer's elevation of man's significance rightly identifies his ability to affect activities and projects in the world for good or ill. His theological anthropology is predicated upon the imperative for all men to have faith in the triune God as the only entry point to fulfilled meaning for all creaturely questions. Schaeffer is also correct to have recognized that the good in man is because he is God's image despite sin's pervasiveness.

---

125. Ibid., 99.

126. The judgment of works is also found in: Matt 16:27, 25:31–46; John 5:29; Rom 2:6; 1 Cor 3:8; 2 Cor 5:10; Rev 22:12. This is a consistent biblical voice, not an exception.

127. Schaeffer, *Death*, 100.

128. Ibid.

Second, Schaeffer's survey and analysis of history is dubious to say the least.[129] Most of his references are to his own work, with the exception of Jeremy Jackson, who himself was a follower of Schaeffer's thought.[130] For example, his characterization of the modern scientific worldview as a cause-and-effect system is more befitting of eighteenth-century not twentieth-century science.[131]

Also, "Schaeffer's handling of medieval thought has made Christian scholars of that era nervous."[132] For example, Reformed evangelical and philosopher Arvin Vos has questioned Schaeffer's interpretation of Aquinas, and moreover, his portrayal of Reformation history being often narrow and misrepresentative.[133] Anabaptism, Lutheranism after Luther, coupled with the Reformation movements of southern and Eastern Europe, are not considered with equal weight by Calvin and Calvinist Reformed movements, thus leaving Schaeffer's account of the Reformation highly selective.

Third, there are questions, too, as to whether Schaeffer has accurately assessed philosophy. Ronald Ruegsegger shows that Schaeffer mistakenly claims that relativism has its origins in Hegel's synthesis and, therefore, contending that there is no absolute truth whatsoever in Hegel's synthesis.[134] Furthermore, Schaeffer was highly critical of Kierkegaard because of his notion of "the Absurd" paradox that leads to the leap of faith, his argument being that Kierkegaard is rationally *inconsistent* and thus *contradictory*. That Kierkegaard insists faith in God is paradoxical and not rational leaves him vulnerable to Schaeffer's scathing critique. Applying Schaeffer's logic strictly, however, would render belief in the incarnation and the resurrection null and void, for example, as such events do not follow rational logic either.[135]

Fourth, Schaeffer's comments on art have not escaped criticism either. Harold Best is one such critic, observing Schaeffer's analysis of the "deep personal psychological problems" of seminal post-Impressionists, concluding that "one can assume a plethora of lines of despair all through art history, based simply on the emotional conditions of any number of creative people." If by seeking to establish a universal inevitably drags an artist below "the line of despair," Best argues, "then all great artists despair," if indeed

129. Pierard, "Schaeffer on History," 209.

130. Daane, "A Review," 923; Giacumakis and Tiffin, "Francis Schaeffer's," 57; Reid, "John Knox," 381.

131. Rogers, "Francis Schaeffer," 28:16.

132. Pierard, "Schaeffer on History," 215.

133. Vos, *Aquinas, Calvin*; Marchant, "Review of He is There," 63.

134. Ruegsegger, "Francis Schaeffer on Philosophy," 116–17.

135. Evans, *Kierkegaard's "Fragments,"* 214–19.

"universal" here refers to a fully-fledged absolute that is realized in a piece of art. However, if universal means *universalizing*, then it is possible that all artists can succeed in bringing about that universal irrespective of their despair. "Universalizing in this sense is another word for integration, synthesis, and interrelationship."[136] This means that art can refer to multifarious strands of suggestion and subtle allusion, a point which Schaeffer seems not to have accounted for. Best correctly concludes that because Van Gogh is made in God's image it is entirely feasible that he was creatively inspirational in his work, despite his emotional struggles, without affronting God by it.[137]

Fifth, why is it that æsthetic judgments will be excluded from divine judgment, according to Schaeffer? What Schaeffer is arguing is that æsthetics themselves are amoral, and a conduit for man *"without the Bible"* to make moral judgments. Æsthetics are a means towards an end. Eventually, non-Christians will falter in their moral ability, which renders them guilty before God. Schaeffer, however, should have included æsthetic judgments as moral in nature because they are not only a means to moral judgment but can be moral in and of themselves.

For example, environmental psychologist Roger Ulrich has provided empirical research that reveals post-surgery hospital patients have a more speedy and wholesome recovery when in wards with windows that have views out to the natural environment. He also argues that a light-filled environment, complemented with appropriate wooden window and door facings, rather than cold concrete or steel, and combined with a color scheme which enhances the wood and light, encourages health at a pace and depth which current NHS (the British health service) design does not.[138]

Despite Schaeffer's dismissal of Leonardo da Vinci's approach to science, mathematics and art, da Vinci is correct to assert in this context that, "The power of meditation can be ten times greater under violet light falling through the stained glass window of a quiet church."[139] Thus, when architectural design is æsthetically pleasing it benefits human well-being rather than creating arbitrary and irresponsible spaces, that hinder health.[140] Put differently, thoughtless and utilitarian design can sin (sometimes unwittingly) against fellow men and nature if æsthetic design principles are ignored. The unwitting occurrences of this are the reason why Schaeffer incorrectly

---

136. Best, "Schaeffer on Art and Music," 136.

137. Ibid.

138. Nasar, *Environmental Æsthetics*, 9, 138. I have arbitrarily used the NHS as an example of his thought here.

139. Quoted from Venolia, *Healing Environments*, 58.

140. See the following as an example of the negative side of poor design toward human ill-health: Jencks, "A View From the Front Line," 21.

classes æsthetic judgments only as a means towards moral judgments, not moral in and of themselves.

Had Schaeffer included in his theology of eschatological judgment the good intentions and beneficial outcomes for the earth of non-Christian work, then the ramifications of certain work decisions would not be dependent upon whether someone's worldview is theologically correct or not. These implications for work do far more justice to biblical narratives such as Ruth the Moabite who selflessly served her mother-in-law despite both being widowed, and therefore having no future prospects. Nevertheless, Ruth declares to Naomi: "Where you go, I will go; where you lodge, I will lodge" (Ruth 1:16). The compassionate and faithful impulse of Ruth to devote herself to such a task, despite her non-Israelite heritage, manifests the kind of dedicated mercy the God of Israel expected from his people. This commitment takes place prior to Ruth declaring "your people shall be my people, and your God my God" (Ruth 1:16), which in turn spurs her diligent gleaning in Boaz's fields to support Naomi and herself.

Of greater import than all these criticisms of Schaeffer's engagement with non-Christian culture, however, is his notion that it all has fallen below "the line of despair." This descent is based upon Schaeffer's overriding principle regarding any culture-making at the hand of non-Christians—"What one believes shows in what one makes."[141] There is some truth to this because right epistemology is critical to good work, but to assert that non-Christians cannot do anything of worth in creation prior to having faith in Christ, is to be shut off from reality. Schaeffer has been at great pains to argue that non-Christians have contributed to civilization in a way that manifests life apart from "the God who is there." In other words, "the man without the Bible" will always work in such a manner so as to create out of a sense of hopelessness, not with contentedness and satisfaction in life. Schaeffer believes that because non-Christians are without the Bible they do not have knowledge of the truth to fulfill God's image to the extent which Christian workers can. There is profound truth to this conviction.

That Schaeffer's notion of common grace, too, only extends so far as to be the means by which non-Christians can be persuaded of the "God who is there" in dialogue with Christians, is shortsighted. This truncated understanding of common grace among non-Christians shows an evangelical tendency to relativize all non-Christian endeavor, irrespective of its obvious earthly benefits. Schaeffer's general principle, as Harold Best sees it, "What one believes shows in what one makes," dictates his highly subjective and selective interpretation of much of Western philosophy, art and music. A

---

141. Best, "Schaeffer on Art and Music," 134.

lack of faith in Christ, according to Schaeffer then, is that which determines whether work falls below "the line of despair," and thus amounts to limited importance. This is unsurprising given that much of evangelical theology views the earth *as a means* of getting to heaven. Thus, that the earth itself is of great import to God struggles to take hold. What is of most consequence to Schaeffer, rather, is the possession of an accurate Christian worldview in order that men make morally without blaspheming God.

Although Schaeffer's apologetic offering is unique in its form, the underlying principle that non-Christians cannot work in such a way as to benefit the world discloses an evangelical impulse to segregate the work of non-Christians (ordinary work) from the work of Christians (evangelical works). This impulse provides the impetus for proclamation of the gospel to non-Christians.

This is an evangelical tendency that I will both ascertain and criticize in each of my successive theological partners so as to repair it in chapter 6. Such a perspective overlooks much of that which is clearly good for the earth, whether for the environment or man. Examples that could be identified include humanist compassion, ecological wisdom, societal concern and personal well-being, all adrift from Christian faith. Yet Schaeffer is not able to account for such clear examples of good work by non-Christians and this is problematic. He is content to create a binary picture of those who work aright pitted against those who work adrift from God. There is no intermediary view of non-Christians being able to offer beneficial working efforts for the world while simultaneously being separated from God. His truncated reworking of *common grace* illuminates this—that grace is only available to non-Christians as they exchange ideas within the context of Christian witness. By collapsing the doctrine of common grace into the exchange that takes place in Christian witness Schaeffer unnecessarily extracts much goodness in the work of non-Christians.

A further reason for this is that evangelical theology has a low view of work in general, failing to recognize that work necessarily fits men for heaven in an important way. As such, the other related question which this thesis seeks to address is whether non-Christian work has any eschatological value. That is, in twenty and twenty-first century evangelical theologies, does good work by non-Christians have any correlation to the new creation? In order to examine this, I will turn to my second theological partner, John Stott, as Schaeffer does not deal with Matt 25:31–46 in his vast corpus.

JOHN STOTT

John Stott's life was immense in its impact and variety. He was an Anglican clergyman who enjoyed as much influence from the pulpit as he did in print. Committed to exegetical and theological issues as he was to missiological matters, Stott did not shy away from cultural engagement. This was so despite his conservative bent on theological matters and the charismatic movement.[142] Once his ecclesiastical ministry was formally concluded, he augmented *The London Institute of Contemporary Christianity* in 1982. This endeavor was birthed to address how the message of the Christian gospel interacts with culture at the coalface of mission.

At the 1974 Lausanne Congress on World Evangelization Stott stepped up to the role of facilitator in the debate between the American delegation and the Latin American and African voices, making a surprisingly groundbreaking impact upon the congress.[143] In the Latin American context, the revolution of Liberation theology had emerged in reaction to the Western Roman Catholic Church, which by means of cross-pollination at the Lausanne Congress meant that British evangelicals were exposed to a serious examination of Marx's critique of capitalism.[144] Subsequently, many British evangelicals engaged with Marx's philosophy of work.[145] In fact, under his chairmanship, Stott invited José Miguez Bonino to lecture the first series of "London Lectures in Contemporary Christianity" in 1974. These were eventually published in the book *Christians and Marxists: The Mutual Challenge to Revolution*.

Compounding this, Stott attempted in 1984 to deal with issues of work concerning industrial disputes which took place in the late 1970s and early 1980s. Hence, in his *Issues Facing Christians Today*, Stott attempts to define a theological meaning of work while simultaneously seeking to reflect theologically and practically on the trials of industrial labor.[146] Furthermore, his patient dialogue with liberal David Edwards over many theological questions exemplified the extent to which Stott was willing to listen and compassionately exchange convictions with those from different perspectives.[147]

---

142. Callahan, "John R. W. Stott," 1151.

143. Smith, *Transforming*, 91.

144. Ibid., 112–3.

145. Lyon, *Karl Marx*; Bockmuehl, *The Challenge of Marxism*; Miller, *Christian Significance*. Also, Croatian evangelical Volf did his doctoral studies on Marx's philosophy of work: *Zukunft der Arbeit—Arbeit der Zukunft: Der Arbeitsbegrif bei Karl Marx und seine theologische Wertung*.

146. Stott, *Issues*.

147. Edwards and Stott, *Essentials*.

As a result of Billy Graham's worldwide evangelistic efforts, and prior to his retirement from *All Souls*, Stott was at the heart of a global evangelical attempt to clarify the issue of mission at the Lausanne Congress on World Evangelization in 1974, the congress distilling their deliberations into several covenant statements. Stott's role was "active and significant"[148] in that he diplomatically facilitated discussion between those from the Southern Hemisphere and American evangelicals over their concerns for the future of evangelical missiology.[149]

Stott's involvement in the Lausanne movement also saw him engage the question of how eschatology impinges upon evangelical social ethics. As such, Stott initiated an exploration of whether human work will continue into, or be discontinued from, the new creation. He is the only one of my chosen theological partners to discuss work eschatologically in this manner; the others simply assume the discontinuation of earthly work for the new creation. Stott, however, wishes to dip his toes into the debate, and significantly, this discussion pertains directly to the final chapter of this thesis. Stott's evaluation of this subject is limited however to one paper which means that the extent of its scope is far from thoroughgoing.

It might be expected that as Curate, Rector (1970–82) and Rector Emeritus of All Souls Langham Place, London for fifty years that Stott would have some sermon material on the sheep and the goats which this thesis could analyze. Surprisingly, there is not one sermon on this parable in the *All Souls* database to which this thesis can turn. Perhaps this is telling of the discomfort this parable creates upon Stott, or, at the very least, this omission speaks of Stott's demotion of Matt 25:31–46's importance for the formation of his congregation. Nevertheless, Stott's lead in the twenty-first Lausanne Occasional Paper (hereafter *LOP 21*) will allow me to introduce concepts surrounding work which might pertain to the eschaton through his reflection on Matt 25:31–46. Stott's cultural awareness is important here because he simultaneously understands that this directly impinges upon biblical hermeneutics, something British evangelicals have continually overlooked throughout the twentieth century: "The first step towards the recovery of our own Christian integrity will be the humble recognition that our own culture blinds, deafens and dopes us. We neither see what we ought to see in Scripture, nor hear God's Word as we should."[150]

It is now time to discover just how Stott perceives culture's effect on hermeneutics in Matt 25:31–46.

---

148. Dudley-Smith, *Stott*, 204.
149. Smith, *Transforming*, 91.
150. Stott quoted in: France and McGrath, *Evangelical Anglicans*, 33, 42, 53.

NON-CHRISTIAN WORK AND THE NEW CREATION

Does any human work correlate with the new creation? Stott broadly considers this question as the chair and European representative of *LOP 21*, and the views that follow represent Stott's convictions as chair of this commission.[151] The focus of the *LOP 21* is the interface between evangelism and social responsibility. Ordinary work is not its specific focus, but it would not be stretching the scope of the paper to suggest that work is included under the breadth of *social responsibility*, especially given that in another place Stott has made a strong case that one of the main aims of human work is to serve one's neighbor.[152]

Stott turns to the parable of the sheep and the goats (Matt 25:31–46) in his foray into eschatological considerations for social ethics, and the scene is set with the introduction of the Son of Man on his throne, who has come near to mankind with a company of angels; all nations are gathered before this ruler so that he can divide them into two distinct camps: the sheep and the goats. The story continues (vv. 34–40):

> Then the king will say to those at his right hand, "Come, you that are blessed by my Father, inherit the kingdom prepared for you from the foundation of the world; for I was hungry and you gave me food, I was thirsty and you gave me something to drink, I was a stranger and you welcomed me, I was naked and you gave me clothing, I was sick and you took care of me, I was in prison and you visited me." Then the righteous will answer him, "Lord, when was it that we saw you hungry and gave you food, or thirsty and gave you something to drink? And when was it that we saw you a stranger and welcomed you, or naked and gave you clothing? And when was it that we saw you sick or in prison and visited you?" And the king will answer them, "Truly I tell you, just as you did it to one of the least of these who are members of my family, you did it to me."

Turning to address the goats, the Son of Man condemns them to "the eternal fire" (v. 46) that is fit for the devil and his followers, because they did not grasp opportunities to serve those in need throughout their lives. Like the former group, the goats did not recognize the fact that they were, by association, encountering the Son of Man among the needy. This is crucial towards their destiny after judgment as the ruling Son relates: "just as you

---

151. The other contributors were Osei-Mensah (African representative), Rin Ro (Asian representative), Wells (American representative), and Olson (Latin American representative). http://www.lausanne.org/all-documents/lop-21.html.

152. Stott, *The Cross of Christ*, 289–94.

did not do it to the least of these, you did not do it to me" (v. 45). Consequently, because the goats did not aid those in need, and by association the Son of Man, he will put them away "into eternal punishment," whereas the sheep are to be granted "eternal life" as "the righteous" (v. 46).

Immediately, readers of Stott's interpretation of this parable are struck by the fact that he automatically identifies "the righteous"/the sheep as Christians who have faith in Christ. He says, quoting the Apostle Paul first of all,

> "Knowing the fear of the Lord," he wrote, "we persuade men." "Men-persuading" is a clear reference to his evangelistic methods, as we know from the Acts, and "the fear of the Lord" to appearing before Christ's judgment seat, of which he has written in the previous verse (2 Cor 5:10, 11). The same motivation can sustain us in our works of philanthropy, as is evident from the sheep and the goats passage which we studied together one morning.[153]

Stott claims that a wholesome fear of judgment day motivates the sheep to serve the poor appropriately, which he identifies specifically as *philanthropic* work, and without such an eschatological spur, work which identifies and helps "the least of these" (v. 40) would not take place. This philanthropy should also be understood as *evangelical works*; that which is acted out of an already established Christian faith. The quote above reveals that Stott understands the sheep as Christians, without any warrant for such a claim, and so he interprets the parable accordingly: "As the rest of the New Testament teaches, the dead will be judged "by what they have done" (e.g., Rev 20:13), and our deeds will include either the loving service of those in need or a scandalous indifference to their plight. These will be an acid test whether we are true believers, or unbelievers."[154]

Stott never considers the interpretation that those who will be included because of their good acts might not be identifiable Christians. Nevertheless, Stott does briefly consider broader interpretations of the identity of the sheep: "Whether Christ's 'brethren' are his followers in general, as other passages seem to indicate (e.g., Matt 12:46–50; Heb 2:10–18), or in particular his messengers, as may be suggested by the 'cup of cold water' passage (Matt 10:9–15, 40–42), or may include the rest of needy humankind with whom Christ humbly identifies himself, the principal message is the same."[155]

---

153. Lausanne Occasional Paper 21, 6.C.
154. Ibid.
155. Ibid.

The term "brethren" which Stott refers to is the rendering of *adelphōn* (v. 40) from the King James Version translation. Why does he use this translation here? For Stott, the term "brethren" has particular force in indicating who belongs to God and thus governs how he interprets the entire parable. Because "the principle message remains the same"—that works will be the "acid test" of whether one is a Christian or not—Stott is confident that the loving acts of the sheep are indeed acts of faith performed by genuine Christians. "Brethren" as a term, then, proves to Stott that the sheep refer to no one other than Christians. Matthean biblical scholar Ulrich Luz concurs with this point because "the few references from the church's tradition to 'brothers of Jesus' point in the same direction." For example, in the Easter narrative, the post-resurrection Jesus refers to his disciples as "my brothers" (Gk. *adelphois mou*—Matt 28:10) and the inference of such reasoning is that in no way will non-Christians accidentally be found as sheep.[156]

Also, Stott recognizes the biblical voice of God's eschatological reward of human work, albeit without explicating the nature of these rewards.[157] But this notion must not be interpreted as salvation *by* works, Stott caveats, for this would undo the notion of salvation by grace through faith. Rather, this parable highlights that

> neither of these two passages [the other being (Matt 10.9–15, 40–42)] of Scripture can possibly mean that we can gain entry to heaven by our good works. To interpret them in this way would be to turn the gospel upside down. What they are emphasizing is that though we are justified by grace alone through faith alone, we shall be judged by those good works of love through which our secret faith is made public.[158]

Without referring to him specifically, "secret faith is made public" is clearly a reference to Calvin's theology of the "invisible Church."[159] Stott also connects his eschatology of reward with his definition of work as *service*, as the parable of the sheep and the goats helpfully illustrates: "All work needs to be seen as being, at least to some degree, public service. This principle throws light on the discussion about the purpose(s) of business."[160]

Work as relational service to our fellow creatures and God has eschatological value insofar as it reveals those who are genuine Christians. Work reveals, then, whether a person has faith in Christ and that conversely, said

---

156. Luz, *Matthew*, 279–80.
157. Chester, *Mission*, 123.
158. LOP 21, 6.C.
159. Calvin, *Institutes*, IV.1.2 n. 6.
160. Stott, *Issues*, 222.

faith, will inspire good work. This follows Martin Luther's (1483–1546) logic, "faith also must be in all works the master workman and captain, or they are nothing at all."[161] It is here that the question of the empowerment of good work enters the discussion. Stott argues that it is only Christians who are empowered to work in such a way that reveals their faith and serves in a way that recognizes Christ incognito. The reward for work, that is enabled by a prior faith in Christ, reveals divine empowerment to perform these works.

What Stott's interpretation of the parable of the sheep and the goats discloses is how the link between human agency and the eschaton theologically harmonizes with a doctrine of justification by faith. In true Protestant form, Stott elevates justification by faith as the most prominent locus around which all other doctrines must fit, and so when assessing Matt 25:31–46, he must assume that the sheep in this Matthean parable are Christians acting out of loving faith, so as to resist conveying justification by works in any way. Moreover, it is essential for Stott that the sheep are understood as Christians, because otherwise the parable would be teaching that anyone, even non-Christians, are able to work themselves into heaven without the grace of Christ. In order to do this without conveying works-salvation, he must interpret that "righteous" works are done from a seedbed of faith in Christ, i.e., evangelical works. In this sense, then, evangelical or righteous works are those which flow out of a heart of prior faith.

This is not an uncommon interpretation of this parable in evangelical theology for the reasons just stated. In what ensues in the subsequent chapters, however, I will show that Stott has inherited a tradition of interpretation of this parable so as to vociferously defend the Pauline doctrine of justification by faith. This inheritance is that which firmly believes that if certain parts of scripture contradict others then one's original interpretation must be amiss. This is a generally accepted evangelical hermeneutic with its own internal logic. In reaction to liberal theology, Stott wishes to guard against the notion that there is no inherent unity among the sixty-six books of the Bible; that there may even be multifarious theologies in scripture.[162]

The fact that Stott feels compelled to interpret the sheep and the goats through the Apostle Paul's doctrine of justification by faith divulges Stott's discomfort with the message of the parable. It is clear that he does not wish to conclude that which the parable itself so readily communicates. This wish to skew the parable slightly so as to detract from its clear message should alert readers of Stott to his unwillingness to deal with portions of the biblical

161. Luther, *A Treatise*, XIII.
162. Stott, "Theology," 4.

narrative which do not neatly fit with his evangelical theological system. Stott is therefore amiss in interpreting the sheep and the goats in this manner. This caginess is ironic considering that Stott himself criticizes others who lower their theological standards in doing such a thing: "The . . . danger is that systematic theologians may become so enamored of their construct that, if God were to cause fresh truth and light 'to break forth out of his holy Word' (as John Robinson put it to the Mayflower Pilgrims in 1620), they are tempted to trim the truth to fit the system instead of adapting the system to absorb the truth."[163]

As I have shown, Stott ventures into this danger himself. I will demonstrate in the ensuing chapters that my other interlocutors have also "trim[med] the truth to fit the system" of evangelical truth. Stott's reticence to interrelate work with the eschaton concerning those outwith Christian faith is further manifest when he considers the possibility that "the final kingdom [might] enjoy some continuity with its present manifestation, or will the future be discontinuous with the present, so that nothing will survive the judgment except those who by God's sheer grace are the heirs of his kingdom?"[164]

In answer to this question he does not initially commit himself to a position, but in light of his conclusions of the sheep and the goats the eschatological continuity of social responsibility must be highly doubtful for Stott. For supposing that some human work continues from this age in the new creation creates in him a nervousness despite quoting many of the supporting biblical texts for work's continuance into the new creation:[165]

> We are on more uncertain ground, however, when we ask how many of our present works will be carried over into eternity. Certainly evangelism has eternal consequences, since converts receive God's free gift of eternal life. So does our teaching, if we build with "gold, silver and precious stones" upon the foundation of Christ (1 Cor. 3:10–15). But what about our social activity? We are told of those who "die in the Lord" that "their deeds follow them" (Rev. 14:13; cf. 1 Cor. 13:13). We also are told that the kings of the earth will "bring their glory" into the New Jerusalem, and that they will "bring into it the glory and the honour of the nations," while what will be excluded is everything "unclean" (Rev 21:24–27). This has seemed to many to teach that whatever is beautiful, true and good in human cultures, once

163. Ibid., 9.
164. LOP 21, 6.E.
165. See Marshall's support of the continuance of work into the new creation from the book of Revelation: "Culture and the New Testament," *Down to Earth*, 17–31.

purged of everything which defiles, will be consummated in the final kingdom. Those who have the assurance of this continuity find in it a strong incentive to social and cultural involvement.[166]

Even though Stott has left himself open on this issue, Darrell Cosden has provided the robust and positive evangelical account of works' continuance in the new creation which Stott withholds himself from advocating.[167] More recently, however, in fleeting response to Miroslav Volf's synthetic framework for work as revealed in my introduction, Stott has clarified his thoughts about the good work of non-Christians. This clarification comes in light of Stott's updated views on work; no longer are there discussions of industrial debates, but interaction with contemporary issues in British workplaces. Significantly, the one criticism Stott elects to bring to the door of Volf's proposal is to his views of the work of non-Christians:

> Although indeed the Holy Spirit is at work in the world, and although the nations will bring their "splendour" into the New Jerusalem (Rev 21:24, 26), does Paul's vision of the charismata really embrace the work of non-Christians? And can humans really cooperate with God in the eschatological transformation of the world? Is the kingdom of God, both in its present reality and in its future perfection, not a gift of God, rather than a human achievement?[168]

The kingdom cannot come (even partially) through the agency of men according to Stott. It must only arrive via the power of God. This is indeed indicative of Stott's estimation of man's ability since the Fall and a commitment to monergism—that it is God alone who accomplishes such grand tasks apart from man. This is a problematic conclusion on Stott's part for clearly Revelation 21 shows that "the God revealed by the New Testament writers surely has in mind the conservation and transformation of human culture and human society in the world to come."[169] Of one thing Stott is certain—the works that may continue into the new creation cannot be of non-Christian agency, as his interpretation of the sheep and the goats has shown, but rather of the positive success of evangelistic efforts.

---

166. LOP 21, 6.E.
167. Cosden, *Theology*; Cosden, *Heavenly*.
168. Stott, *Issues*, 224.
169. Marshall, "Culture," 31.

CONCLUSION

This chapter has shown and evaluated the most important twentieth-century account of work by non-Christians in evangelical theology. The basis upon which non-Christian work is discussed comes under Schaeffer's overall apologetic program that man has an epistemological problem. The problem is that he has no means to perceive, accurately, meaning in the world because grace has been suppressed by cultural humanism and rationalism. Work by non-Christians is thus performed amid confusion and anxiety over the mystery of this earth's meaning and one's own identity. In short, nature has eaten up grace.

Schaeffer interprets this skewed understanding pervading history from the Renaissance onwards into all areas of culture, and consequently, work and culture are performed without reference to God. Although unique in his engagement with human culture, Schaeffer's theology of the work of non-Christians discloses that it is not highly esteemed before God or man, but this does not render non-Christian man completely insignificant to God.

However, with the realization that the triune God is personal and that meaning, love and communication all stem from Him, non-Christian man can do *evangelical works* aright once more through faith. By coming to the realization that their perception of the world is amiss, non-Christians can acknowledge the great honor bestowed on them by God that they are made in God's image through faith in Christ. Only in this way can work regain its true meaning and the epistemological problem resolved. Schaeffer's binary conclusions, however, lack adequate nuance. He is right to acknowledge that epistemology is highly significant to this discussion, but to discount good work performed by non-Christians in the manner he does is far from a satisfying conclusion.

In continuity with Schaeffer's theology, my analysis of John Stott's interpretation of the parable of the sheep and the goats reveals the hermeneutical moves required to maintain that the sheep are Christians and that their *evangelical works* stem from a prior faith in Christ. To admit that unwitting non-Christians can work their way to a heavenly salvation is a conviction that is beyond the pale for British evangelical theology, let alone the possibility of the eschatological continuation of their works into heaven.

As I will show, Stott's hermeneutic here is problematically representative of historical evangelical interpretations of the sheep and the goats; there is no eschatological bliss in store for non-Christians, or their work, because it is just that—mundane work reserved for temporality. Given that evangelical theology has landed where it has with regard the good work of non-Christians, a start is required to show how it theologically and historically arrived in this form.

This will be done as I evaluate the work of *sinners* in the theology of Thomas Chalmers. I will probe whether in his estimation there is any causation between sinners' good work and the eschaton.

2

Thomas Chalmers (1780–1847)
The Ingratitude of Sinners' Work as Earthly and Heavenly Impediments

IN THE PREVIOUS CHAPTER I showed that Schaeffer views all work by non-Christians as beset by the epistemological problem of viewing creation from a non-theological perspective. Consequently, their work is malpracticed because of their unanswered questions of meaning for the world. This drives non-Christians to work from a despairing disposition, otherwise known as *work* not *evangelical works*. Moreover, concerning the work of non-Christians, and its connection to the eschaton, Stott is reluctant to commit himself to viewing any work that has eschatological value other than the Church's positive fruits of evangelism. Thus, the good work of non-Christians is left with no connection with the final state whatsoever. Their work only pertains to this age because it is a mundane performance with no reference to God.

"In the nineteenth century," on the other hand, "the doctrine that work was a sacred duty incumbent upon everyone reached its apotheosis."[1] The most important British evangelical example of this is found in Thomas Chalmers' perspective on work, albeit his theology has strong influences from eighteenth-century thought.[2]

During Chalmers' lifetime, urbanization was rapidly on the increase. Scotland was making a break with much of eighteenth-century industry, following the lead of countries such as England, Wales, Belgium, northern

1. An editorial subtitle by Thomas, *Oxford Book of Work*, 112.
2. McCaffrey, "The Life of Thomas Chalmers," 34.

Italy, and the Netherlands in their quest to form a new social order. But unlike its European counterparts, Scotland only took a few decades to make this transition.[3]

A mass shift in food production was necessary in order to supply these new emerging urban centers. Hence, rural communities became much more stable as the demand for food poured in from the cities. From 1750 to 1820 the output of corn and vegetables had doubled in Scotland, while animal foods exploded in growth to a sixfold multiplication. Consequently, there was a greater need for commercial, legal and financial facilities in Scottish towns. Further, Scottish industrialization gave much easier access to the dense concentration of producers and consumers.

This had two resulting factors: "Scotland was in a superb geographical position to take advantage of the changing direction of international trade towards the Atlantic world." It is no surprise then that places such as Greenock, and others in the Clyde basin, were the fastest growing towns in Scotland. "Commercial success was bound to foster urban expansion."[4]

The other outcome was the inevitable expansion of manufacturing industry which became essential for nineteenth-century urbanization. The advantages gained in industrial concentration in towns were that manufacturers were able to reap from *eternal* economies. Firms cut costs by not having to provide accommodation for workers because of the proximity between the home and the workplace, guaranteeing a huge pool of labor and transport costs between sources of supply, finishing trades and repair shops were markedly reduced. This was all compounded by steam propulsion technology and the construction of new roads and canals, such as the Caledonian Canal.[5]

It was into this great cultural shift in the nature of work that Chalmers proposed one of two major economic models of the day (the other being Ricardian).[6] Chalmers' economic model was free-trade orientated, retributive, static, nationalist and physiocratic.[7] Naturally, this chapter will focus upon Chalmers' *evangelical* rather than his earlier liberal writings; the latter he veered away from as a consequence of a life-threatening illness.[8]

In this chapter I will analyze Chalmers' account of the good work of sinners. I will raise the issue of whether sinners are capable of doing good

3. Devine, *Scottish Nation*, 153.
4. Ibid., 156.
5. Ibid, 156–57.
6. Ricardo, *Works*, 49–51, 126–27.
7. Hilton, *The Practical*, 142–43.
8. Rice, "Natural Theology and the Scottish Philosophy," 34 n. 1.

work at all, and how Chalmers is torn over this issue.⁹ Chalmers employs numerous terms to denote non-Christians who work: "the irreligious," "the ungodly," "the children of wrath," "the wicked," and "the unregenerate." But there is no more frequently employed term by Chalmers than the term *sinners*, hence I will restrict my use in this chapter to *sinners* work because of its frequency.

He gives credit where credit is due to good work performed by sinners but ends up concluding that their depravity, stemming from a lack of faith in Christ, ensures that work performed with sinful ingratitude is ultimately of no import to God. In other words, sinners can only offer "mundane work" not "evangelical works," the latter of which is only of interest to God. Nevertheless, his use of *conscience* as a category for accurately depicting the good work of sinners must be evaluated, and this will be revealed as evidence of the presence of divine sovereignty in good work. For without an adequate explanation of *how* good work is enacted, such is an account without any substantiation of its goodness.

The second focus, like that of my analysis of Stott, is to assess whether any good work performed by sinners has any correlation to the final state. If some work performed by sinners is *good*, might there be any correspondence between it and the new creation in light of Chalmers' interpretation of the parable of the sheep and the goats (Matt 25:31–46)? Chalmers' theology of the work of sinners will be evaluated against this question.

SINNERS AND THE MERCHANT WORLD

Chalmers' identification of how Christian faith enhances and liberates work will help infer a significant and initial foray into sinners' work. He quotes the Apostle Paul to augment this: "The one who . . . serves Christ is acceptable to God and has human approval" (Rom 14:18). If this statement holds true, those who live apart from God in Christ, on the other hand, must be "utterly devoid of piety, [and] they go to aggravate the reproach of his ingratitude; and to prove that of all the men upon earth who are far from God, he stands at the widest distance."¹⁰

For Christians, there is an entirely unique prospect for their work because following Jesus is not restricted to the pardon of sins. Rather, "[i]t takes all those who accept of its overtures under its supreme and exclusive direction." In other words, once acquiescing to the sovereignty of Christ,

---

9. This discussion is taken up by Luther and many since, *Good Works*, I.

10. Chalmers, *Discourses*, 37.

Christ teaches his followers to work according to his purposes.[11] Chalmers elaborates:

> In what way shall we establish the authority of God over all the concerns of a man's history? Should not the solemnity of religious obligation be made to overspread the whole field and compass of human affairs?—and if it be not so is not this deposing God from the supremacy which belongs to Him? Is it not saying that there are places and occasions in which we will not have Him to reign over us? Is it not disowning His right of having all things done to His glory? And those hearers who love to be told of what they owe to God on the Sabbath and in the holy days of sacrament and prayer—but who love not to be told of what they own Him in their shops and in their market places and in their every-day employments[?][12]

Dissolving any notion of a secular/sacred divide under Christ, Chalmers perceives all life under the surveillance of Christ's lordship, and this extends to the realm of work as it does religious finery kept for Sundays. During Chalmers' lifetime some forms of work were deemed superior by some Christians; gathered church-based rites were viewed as more spiritually valuable than everyday work, hence the seventh day predominated and was spiritually elevated over the other six. Chalmers swipes at the academics of his day on this point because "they have made their Christianity one thing, and their civil business another."[13] He clearly denounces such segregation in light of the pervasiveness of Christ's sovereignty which should seep its way into all areas of life.

Grounding this more specifically, Chalmers points to the fourth ("Remember the sabbath day, and keep it holy. Six days you shall labor and do all your work" [Exod 20:8–9]) and eighth ("You shall not steal" [Exod 20:15]) commandments as key nodes which will help Christians "feel the religiousness" of work's relevance to God.[14] Both commands exist to guard Christians against detrimental work ethics, and Chalmers insists that their chronological position in the Decalogue does not belittle them.[15] In the act of stealing, for example, one forgets how to give in a way which mirrors God's great gift of Christ to man.[16] An additional spur towards wholehearted obedience to

11. Chalmers, "The Influence of Christianity," 39.
12. Chalmers, *Discourses*, 302.
13. Chalmers, "On the Moral Influence," 325.
14. Ibid, 303.
15. Ibid.
16. Ibid., 305.

these commandments is the threat of "an awful day of reckoning" where a slackness of hand or mind, coupled with habitual thieving, will be dealt with severely at the final judgment because such unethical living cannot inherit the kingdom of God.[17] Chalmers explains: "The aggravations which we have just now spoken of will tell on the awful sentence of the great day. The discerner of the thoughts and intents of the ear sees and judges of every one of them; and when the time cometh that the secrets of all hearts shall be laid open, the low pilferments of the farm, of the family, and of the workshop, will appear to the shame and condemnation of the guilty."[18]

This warning shows the eschatological consequences that evangelicals tend to emphasize in light of ethical living, but why does Chalmers make such a particular fuss of stealing? Because the entrance of sin into the world came through *stolen* fruit in man's original sphere of work: "The master he stole it from was the Lord of Heaven and of Earth—to whom belongs the cattle on a thousand hills, and who sits surrounded with the wealth of innumerable worlds."[19]

God's original intention for man was to work in harmony with Him by His sapient parameters for life but this was squandered early on with a wayward act. The plucking of the forbidden fruit is deemed stealing because God is the world's Great Proprietor and Landlord, and if anything is wrongly taken from the earth, in opposition to work's original order, such a pilferer is guilty and at odds with the divine Landlord. Put simply, Chalmers says, "It is not in the magnitude of the thing done, that the chief magnitude of the offense lies. It is the state of mind implied by the doing of it."[20]

In light of such a Reformed theological anthropology, the work of sinners has little or no value to God. Those with no Christian belief, such as practical atheists and the ignorant, do their work according to their beliefs (or lack thereof) and thus do not rely upon the Christian God in so doing. Therefore, these workers could never perform *good* work or *evangelical works*.

"SINFUL" BUT PERIODICALLY VIRTUOUS MERCHANTS

Can the work of sinners ever be considered *good* in Chalmers' theology? Chalmers deploys *conscience* as the key category to soften what I have just revealed of his theological anthropology. From the outset he makes no

17. Ibid., 304.
18. Ibid., 309.
19. Ibid., 312.
20. Ibid., 313.

mistake in identifying the origins of a *natural conscience* operating among all men. This is located in his essay "The Supremacy of Conscience":[21] "Virtue is not a creation of the Divine will, but has had everlasting residence in the nature of the Godhead. The mind of man is a creation; and therefore indicates, by its characteristics, the character of Him, to the fiat and the forthgoing of whose will it owes its existence."[22]

In other words, the divine will is the basis and progenitor of human virtue, and it is God's ineffable character spawning purity of virtue which shapes human virtue. Chalmers pays little attention to God's triunity in his theology, and in this respect he has much in common with Friedrich Schleiermacher.[23] Chalmers is uninterested in shaping a Scottish moral theory with the concept "natural conscience." Rather, he is attempting to ground an account of human responsibility as an alternative to Calvin's divine decree.[24]

Notwithstanding the deliberate departure from Calvin here, natural conscience provides man with the moral antenna by which virtue can be honed, and just as God is personal, so man is to mirror His flawless character in becoming virtuous. Even if sinners respond positively to the moral indicators of conscience, they cannot be viewed as "naturally moral." Instead, the affirmation of a moral sense in sinners only exists to prove that morality is "grounded in the nature of conscience."[25] By identifying conscience as the key category to analyze the work of sinners, Chalmers reveals the influence of Anglican Bishop Joseph Butler (1692–1752) upon his thinking.[26]

This may explain the origin of conscience, but what about the nature of its operation? Butler moved Chalmers from the *a posteriori* of "the felt experience of a judge within the breast to the inference of a Judge above and over us, who planted it there."[27] Butler reveals,

> That which renders Beings capable of moral Government, is their having a moral Nature, and moral Faculties of Perception and of Action. Brute Creatures are impressed and actuated by various Instincts and Propensions; so also are We. But additional to this, We have a Capacity of reflecting upon Actions and Characters, and making them an Object to our Thought: And on doing this,

---

21. At the end of his life, after evaluating German philosophy in more detail, Chalmers concluded that his notion of the supremacy of conscience was mirrored in Kant's "Categorical Imperative." Hilton, *The Age of Atonement*, 183 n. 78.

22. Chalmers, *Natural Theology*, 1:306.

23. Voges, *The Practical*, 159.

24. Rice, "Natural Theology," 41.

25. Ibid., 41.

26. Ibid., 35.

27. Chalmers, *Modern Philosophy*, 6:311.

we naturally and unavoidably approve some Actions, under the peculiar View of their being virtuous and of Good-desert, and condemn Others, as vitious and of Ill-desert.[28]

The moral philosopher Francis Hutcheson (1694–1746) is also detectable in Chalmers' notion of conscience. Demonstrating thoughts that a later Lord Shaftsbury (1801–85) would propound against the views of Thomas Hobbes (1588–1679), Hutcheson says,

> Another important determination or sense of the soul we may call the *sympathetic*, different from all the external sense; by which, when we apprehend the state of others, our hearts naturally have a fellow-feeling for them. When we see or know the pain, distress, or misery of any kind which another suffers, and turn our thoughts to it, we feel a strong sense of pity, and a great proneness to relieve, where no contrary passion withholds us. And this without any artful views of advantage to accrue to us from giving relief, or of loss we shall sustain by these sufferings. We see this principle strongly working in children, where there are the fewest distant views of interest; so strongly sometimes, even in some not of the softest mould, at cruel executions, as to occasion fainting and sickness. This principle continues generally during all our lives.[29]

This ability to discern good or ill is the general presence of natural conscience in man. However, conscience is not understood here as a form of "Natural Theism"[30] where the relationship between man and God is discerned through natural reason,[31] rather, Chalmers argues that natural conscience is "the rightful Sovereign in man."[32] As virtue originates then in the transcendent divine, natural conscience is the means by which virtue can be formed in man. Therefore, natural conscience is the immanent presence of divine sovereignty in all men, Chalmers argues, irrespective of total depravity. This explains how morality is "grounded in the nature of conscience," for by portraying natural conscience as "the rightful Sovereign in man," Chalmers allows for the honing of virtue in *all* men ensuring the transcendent immanence of God's inspiration.

Chalmers' understanding of God's sovereignty in man's conscience is more akin to a transcendental deism rather than the triunity of God which

---

28. Butler, *The Analogy*, 309.
29. Quoted in Robinson, *The Story of Scottish Philosophy*, 35.
30. Chalmers, "On the Supremacy of Conscience," 308.
31. Rice, "Natural Theology," 35.
32. Chalmers, "On the Supremacy of Conscience," 312.

is a hangover from Chalmers' liberal past, a past which promoted God (according to William Paley's distant clockmaker) as inaugurating creation and then remotely detaching himself from it. Nevertheless, the ethical *ought* is always present in Chalmers' view of natural conscience and therefore an awareness of the divine command is present in everyone through conscience. When this command of conscience is adhered to, God's sovereignty *de jure* is honored, even if it is not present in its eschatological completion.

Chalmers was willing to forego any commitment to the doctrine of limited election with his conviction that *all men* can act according to natural conscience. This is an illuminating caveat given his theology in the previous subsection. Nevertheless, Chalmers states that "there is not a human creature under heaven, from whom the offers of this said gospel ought to be withheld; and it is on the undoubted truth of this position that we have founded at least one reply to a question put, and sometimes in the form of a charge or complaint against the equity of the Divine administration, Why the blessings of Christianity should be so limited in point of extent."[33]

Limited election, on the other hand, problematically circumvents the requirement of the gospel's *universal proclamation* which was an inherent and unresolved tension in British evangelical Calvinism throughout the eighteenth and nineteenth centuries.[34] T. F. Torrance distills this inherent evangelical tension: "Regarded from the end result, therefore, the penal satisfaction offered by Christ in his sacrificial death was held to be actually and finally effectual only for *particular* people. . . . The question had to be asked, therefore, as indeed it was by Thomas Chalmers, *what kind of God does this imply?*"[35]

With this skepticism in mind, it is unsurprising that Chalmers does not subscribe to all the hallmarks of Westminster theology or scholastic Calvinism[36], and yet, Chalmers is hugely influenced by the scholastic Richard Baxter, albeit bypassing Baxter's scholastic commitments to exclusively focus on his concept of the "holy commonwealth."[37]

In contradistinction to five-point Calvinism then, Chalmers' missionary verve promoted the *universality* of the gospel offer, and therefore universality to natural conscience as it confronted the doctrine of total

33. Chalmers, "Lectures on the Epistle."
34. Chalmers, "On the Universality," 395.
35. Torrance, *Scottish*, 262.
36. Roxborogh, *The Practical*, 174.
37. The influence of Richard Baxter upon Chalmers was evident through his recasting of Baxter's "Holy Commonwealth" for nineteenth-century Scotland. This influence is further established by Chalmers' impulse to reprint Baxter's *A Call to the Unconverted to Turn and Live*.

depravity.[38] The catalyst for this move was the biblical injunction: "God . . . now commands *all people everywhere* to repent" (Acts 17:30), coupled with the inspirational influence of Baptist William Carey (1761–1834) who rejected limited atonement and a strict doctrine of God's sovereignty in order to fulfill Jesus' Great Commission.[39] Hence, Chalmers and his friend John Erskine (1721–1803) spread Carey's resistance against this form of hyper-Calvinism through their influence at the General Assembly of the Church of Scotland.[40]

Theological *systems* in general—like Calvin's—Chalmers found suspicious as his approach to theology was unsystematic[41] (this is the case even though Chalmers in other places draws heavily upon the magisterial Reformer[42]). For example, in March 1812 Chalmers began reading Calvin's *Institutes* in Latin, followed by the English version.[43] A year later he had finished book three, and while beginning book four, he admits that he found it "heavy and uninteresting" and gave up.[44] This tension is further revealed when he notes, "My Christianity approaches nearer, I think, to Calvinism than to any of the *isms* of Church History: but . . . I feel the influence of these systems to be most unfortunate in the pulpit. . . . Is not this scrupulous orthodoxy of Calvin a principle altogether foreign and subsequent to the native influence of divine truth on the heart?"[45]

This unsystematized approach is a "difficulty" in Chalmers' theological method according to Voges,[46] but by advocating natural conscience thus far conceived, allows Chalmers to contend that all men are responsible and capable of good work irrespective of faith in Christ. The *universality* of natural conscience reveals the influence of Thomas Robert Malthus (1766–1834) upon Chalmers. For "[o]ne of the reasons that Chalmers found Malthus' 'preventative check' compelling was its implication that *all* men, including the lowest, possess a moral sense."[47] Malthus' "preventative check" was the notion that famine, disease and mortality continually and conveniently cull the population as a means of perfecting it. In other words, Malthus

---

38. Torrance, *Scottish*, 229.
39. Roxborogh, "Chalmers' Theology of Mission," 179 (my emphasis in Acts 17:30).
40. Torrance, *Scottish*, 250.
41. Roxborogh, "Chalmers' Theology of Mission," 175.
42. Rice, "Natural Theology," 34 n. 1.
43. Chalmers, *Memoirs of the Life and Writings*.
44. Ibid., 22, March 1813.
45. Letter to J. Anderson, 2 November 1811, in ibid., 1, 241f.
46. Voges, "Chalmers' Thinking Habits," 159.
47. Hilton, *Age*, 184.

articulated an anthropology which sought to justify a God who promotes the creation of wealth while being at odds with human survival,[48] revealing the keen nineteenth-century awareness of human finitude.[49] Thus in classical antiquity and modern business practice, Chalmers reasons, even sinners can act in a characteristically moral manner because all men are enabled to discern how to live and work morally. This understanding of the abilities of all men should "be applauded,"[50] for when sinners pay attention to their conscience, Chalmers argues, "the desire of acting virtuously, which is a desire consequent on our sense of right and wrong, may not be of equal strength with the desire of some criminal indulgence—and so, practically, the evil may preponderate over the good. And thus it is that the system of the inner man, from the weakness of that which claims to be the ascendant principle of our nature maybe thrown into a state of turbulence and disorder."[51]

This "turbulence" is more commonly the case with sinners than with Christians. Such is the consistent capability of Christians over sinners, due in no small way to the fact that Christians have been "crucified with [Christ] so that the body of sin might be destroyed and no longer be enslaved to sin" (Rom 6:6). Sinners, however, "let sin exercise dominion in [their] mortal bodies" (6:12) without much restraint, and what this means for the transcendent immanence of sovereignty in man's conscience is that when virtuous acts are left undone, God's sovereignty is ignored and thus dishonored. For, Chalmers adds, "it is not that every man obeys her [conscience's] dictates, but that every man feels he ought to obey them."[52]

VIRTUOUS WORK

What then is the final goal of the "rightful sovereign in man" through natural conscience? Chalmers answers, "Believe that Christ's righteousness is your righteousness; and His graces will become your graces. Believe that you are a pardoned creature; and this will issue in your becoming a purified creature."[53]

Real virtue is fostered, according to Chalmers, via acquiescing completely to Christ's Lordship, a point I will discuss in more depth in the

---

48. Malthus, *An Essay*, 200–217.
49. Milbank, *Theology*, 46.
50. Roxborough, "Chalmers' Theology of Mission," 176.
51. Chalmers, "On the Supremacy of Conscience," 313.
52. Ibid., 314.
53. Chalmers, *Select Works*, 165.

following subsection. But how does this character formation take place among sinners, if it does at all? Chalmers states, "For tracing forward man's moral history, or the changes which take place in his moral state, it is necessary that we should advert to the influence of habit. Yet it is not properly the philosophy of habit wherewith our argument is concerned, but with the leading facts of its practical operation. . . . [And] the effects of Habit, in as far as these effects serve to indicate the design or character of Him who is the author of our mental constitution."[54]

Natural conscience witnesses to a distant God who is simultaneously immanent in man when man chooses to act morally and righteously. In Aristotelian fashion, Chalmers promotes that virtue, particularly in work, can be honed through continual, repetitive practice; this goes for vice as well as virtue. Aristotle advises workers "to become just by performing just acts, temperate by performing temperate ones, brave by performing brave ones . . . Men will become good builders as a result as a result of building well, and bad ones as a result of building badly."[55]

For those who are repeatedly degenerate in their behavior, an eventual numbing of moral instinct materializes, not coming about immediately, but through the continual choice of immoral action.[56] Chalmers elaborates, "At each repetition, would he find it more difficult to break this order, or to lay an arrest upon it—till at length, as the fruit of this wretched regimen, its unhappy patient is lorded over by a power of moral evil, which possesses the whole man, and wields an irresistible or rather an unresisted ascendancy over him."[57]

The same pitfalls exist for Christians as they do for sinners in the development of vice over virtue, but contrariwise, "virtue is augmented" through repetition enacted by the will[58] and it is possible to resist the draw of vices: "The man whose thoughts, with the purposes and doing to which they lead, are at the bidding of conscience, will, by frequent repetition, at length describe the same track almost spontaneously—even as in physical education, things laboriously learned at the first, come to be done at last without the feeling of an effort."[59]

Each virtuous act perpetuates positive momentum which eventually becomes instinctive. Thus, "the acts of virtue ripen into habits; and the

54. Chalmers, "The Power and Operation," 384, 390.
55. Aristotle, *Nicomachean Ethics*, book II, 1.
56. Chalmers, "The Power and Operation of Habit," 392.
57. Ibid., 393.
58. Ibid., 394–95.
59. Ibid., 395.

goodly and permanent result is, the formation or establishment of a virtuous character."[60]

For Christians, this virtuous character is God's will for them as he cajoles them along the path of obedience which leads to the hope of "collect[ing] the character of Him who hath ordained it."[61] This is something the sinner is either disinterested in or oblivious to, according to Chalmers. Yet sinful man can only ever inconsistently act with virtue. This inconsistency, however, can be fully redeemed if faith in Christ takes place in the agent concerned. Despite his elucidation in this direction, Chalmers does not attribute this thinking to Aristotle.

Comprehending the meaning of this virtuous formation is fraught with misunderstanding until the end arrives, Chalmers admits: "Had there been no death, the mystery of our present state might have been somewhat alleviated."[62] Nevertheless, the righteousness that is formed as a consequence of virtue, Chalmers argues, is a reward in and of itself, just as wickedness brings with it the bitterness of life.[63] This is true for both sinners and Christians, for even though the path to a righteous character among Christians takes a lifetime,[64] the necessity of familiarizing themselves with the ways of heaven informs them prior to a *de facto* righteousness in the final state.[65] For sinners, however, this virtue can only be set in motion once a base level of education has been imparted to them.

EDUCATING THE SINFUL POOR

In order to deal with the problem of pauperism which was epidemic in nineteenth-century Scottish urban centers, Chalmers identified *education* as the solution, for "[o]n no other subject does Christianity more evince its immense importance to the well-being of society."[66] Consequently, Chalmers ardently prayed for his political and philosophical leaders to be converted to Christ so legislation and philosophical thought could be Christianized. By this method the leaven of Christ's gospel would pervade Scotland, Chalmers believed.[67]

60. Chalmers, "The Power," 396.
61. Ibid., 397.
62. Ibid., 397–98.
63. Ibid., 399.
64. Ibid.
65. Ibid., 404.
66. Chalmers, *Political Economy*, 10.
67. Roxborough, "Chalmers' Theology of Mission," 181.

The French Revolution (which took place during Chalmers' lifetime), Chalmers claims, did not exist to coerce sinners to follow Christ or help them work morally in the world more consistently or qualitatively, nor was the Revolution's purpose a limitation of political power or property. For Chalmers, none of these at any rate is capable of affecting a change great enough to convert the sinful masses.[68] Instead, Chalmers' conservative tendencies curbed any personal interest in the radical French Revolution.[69]

Education had to take primacy of place in order to solve the epidemic proportions of pauperism. There was a more pertinent reason why education was of importance to a sinful society, according to Chalmers; the goal of educating the poor is not so that the educator can "purchase a reputation," or for the alleviation of the poor's plight, but to spread abroad the Christian gospel.[70] This is essential because education is the most suitable "machinery" to immerse sinners with the religion of Christ,[71] for "it is to prepare them for immortality; yet, in the single-hearted prosecution of this object, he becomes the all-powerful, though, perhaps, the unconscious instrument of those secondary, those subordinate blessings, which form the only ones that a mere worldly philanthropist cares for."[72]

Although some objected to this "civilizing" process of education,[73] Chalmers' spiritual order of things should be noted: the elevation of the eternal salvation of the poor above physical needs is disclosed because Chalmers "count[s] the salvation of a single soul of more value than the deliverance of a whole empire from pauperism."[74] In uncharitable fashion, Chalmers postulates that the motivating factor for any disciple of Jesus, in view of the New Testament, cannot be debates of pity for the poor[75] because without the civilizing of sinners through education the gospel remains hindered and unheard.[76] I will discuss this in more detail later as it pertains to Chalmers' interpretation of the parable of the sheep and the goats.

68. Chalmers, *Discourses*, 254. "Lower Orders" here is originally a Malthusian designation which encourages those who belong to lower classes to strive towards a middle region, thus resisting complacency to poverty. Malthus, *Principles*, 206–7.

69. Rice, "Natural Theology," 26.

70. Chalmers, "On the Christian Education of the People," 10.

71. Chalmers, *Memoirs of the Life and Writings*, 1:35.

72. Chalmers, "On the Christian Education of the People," 10–11.

73. Duncan, *Edinburgh*, 484–87.

74. "Letter to James Brown, 30th Jan 1819," in Chalmers, *Memoirs of the Life and Writings*, 2:341ff.

75. Chalmers, "On the Christian Education of the People," 11.

76. Inglis, *The Grounds of Christian Hope*, 12; Roxborogh, *Thomas Chalmers*, 191–92.

Only that which pertains to eternity, in this case the salvation of sinners, is that which should be given priority in this age, and even though there are important "subordinate blessings" to be addressed throughout this fleeting existence, "spiritual and eternal things, still adheres to him."[77] "Spiritual" here refers to that which does not pertain to this earth. The earth, as far as work is concerned, is nothing more than a theatre for obedience and even this is a secondary task to the superior mandate of making disciples.[78] This emphasis, too, originally stems from Malthus.[79] What impact did Chalmers foresee this process of Christianizing education having? He says,

> It is thus that Christianity has elevated the general standard of morals; and so spread a beneficent influence, far and wide, among the many, beyond the limit of its own proper and peculiar influence upon the few. It is this which gives it the property of a purifying and preserving salt in every community of human beings; *and that, not merely in respect of those virtues which enter into the moral character, but also in respect of those virtues which are essential to the economic well-being of a people.*[80]

As an example of the leavening principle of Christianity, Chalmers appeals to the Abrahamic narrative of Gen 18:16–33. In this story Abraham responds to God with strong prayers because of God's intention to eradicate Sodom's depraved inhabitants. Abraham contends, "standing before the LORD," "'Will you indeed sweep away the righteous with the wicked? . . . Suppose ten [righteous Sodomites] are found there.' He [the LORD] answered, 'For the sake of ten I will not destroy it.'" Chalmers likens these ten righteous Sodomites, who prevent the city's annihilation, to the representative and pervasive influence of his parishioners among the sinful poor. For this representation to make a proper impact, Chalmers envisions a gradual dissolving of the "compulsory provision for indigence" which England and Ireland were actively fostering. Because of continual handouts to the poor, Chalmers argued, pauperism perpetuates,[81] and what he proposes as an alternative, is that

> [t]he clergyman . . . may reclaim hundreds to principle and sobriety, who shall form a wholesome and better class of peasantry.

---

77. Chalmers, "On the Christian Education of the People," 11.

78. For contemporary evangelical thinkers that contend both *the cultural mandate* (Gen 1 and 2) and *the Great Commission* (Matt 28:16–20) are equally binding, see Stevens, *Other Six Days*, 89–104; Macaulay, *Christianity*, 39–50.

79. Malthus, *Principles*, 200–208.

80. Chalmers, "On the Christian Education of the People," 14 (my emphasis).

81. Ibid., 16.

> But the parish vestry... remains an attractive nucleus, around which there will gather and settle, in every little district of the land, a depraved and improvident class, whom the temptation of this legal charity has called into being, and who will bid inveterate defiance to all the moral energy which might be brought to bear upon them.[82]

In other words, the Scottish poor laws, advocates of retrenchment, colonization or any political expediency, cannot be a substitute for a *genuine* moral transformation of the poor.[83] The state, Chalmers challenges, is simply unable to bring about authentic transformation among the poor because it does not carry the moral capability to effect change. The Church of Scotland on the other hand, as a "religious establishment, is of no value other than an instrument of Christian good."[84] There is no other force potent enough to reform the poor other than "Christian instructors [who] will be its only saviours. These reformers of our national morality will be the only reformers that will do us good. . . . it is with the Christianity of our towns and parishes that the country is to stand or fall."[85]

In his published writings, Chalmers did not take a specific interest in the Highland clearances, but what he achieved in the various parishes in the central belt of Scotland must generally be applied to the equivalent in the north. Chalmers argues that the relief of poverty, or at least the administration of such a task, should be at the behest of the Kirk Session, in the same manner as the maintenance of parish schools. Relying upon statutory assessments, rather than parish-based voluntary giving, fosters a slavish dependence of the poor upon the state, coupled with the suspicion of donors.[86] Chalmers states,

> The more that you generalize the administration for the poor, the more does it stand before you the eye of the population in the imposing characters of power and of magnitude; and the delusive confidence which they are thus led to place in its resources, is one of the main feeders of pauperism. And again, the more also in this way do you widen the distance between the dispensers and the recipients of charity, adding thereby to the

---

82. Ibid., 17.

83. The Scottish poor laws (1579–1929) differed from the English poor laws in that parishes were responsible for their own poor without any organized help from central government.

84. Chalmers, "On the Christian Education of the People," 20. Obviously, this statement took place prior to the Disruption of 1843.

85. Ibid., 21.

86. Paton, *The Clergy*, 130.

helplessness of the former, and giving for more advantageous scope and license to the dexterity of the latter.[87]

Even though Chalmers' approach to dealing with pauperism was far from the most convenient model, he believed that it would lead to the effective Christianization of a Godly Commonwealth, which was his motive in aiding the poor and this explains his continual rallying of the Christian charity of the rich.[88]

Chalmers also relies upon Edmund Burke's (1729–97) conservative political philosophy in much of this approach. Burke proposed that "[a] state without the means of some change is without the means of its conservation"[89], and this means of change, in Chalmers' mind, was the parish Church. Burke was interested in the functioning of organic communities without imposition and Chalmers adopted these transformative views, but with his own Presbyterian twist of Christian piety and benevolence. Chalmers says of Burke, "His was the wisdom of intuition, so that, without formal development, or the aid of any logical process, he often, by a single glance, made the discovery of a great principle; and, by a single word, memorably and felicitously expressed it. That education is the cheap defence of nations, is one of the weightiest of those sentences, or oracular sayings, which have ever fallen from any of the seers or sages of our land."[90]

Chalmers' parishes were motivated by the spirit of charity so as to improve the lives of the poor through their conversion and by following Burke and stressing poverty as a *moral disease*, Chalmers sought to reinvigorate the communal tradition of Fife's Covenanters to challenge the patronizing and legalistic attitudes of the wealthy towards poverty.[91]

Despite the eventual failure of Chalmers' social programs to create a Godly Commonwealth, (it buckled under the great famine of 1846–47, and as a result, stalled the interest of Scottish philanthropists[92]) his activist spirit was unquenched in attempting to Christianize the poor. Through education provided in parishes, the poor were helped to help themselves back into work and thus the gospel message spread widely. The benefits of

---

87. Chalmers, "Speech Delivered on the 24th May 1822, before the General Assembly of the Church of Scotland, explanatory of the measures which have been successfully pursued in St. John's Parish, Glasgow for the extinction of its compulsory pauperism," printed as an appendix to his *Christian and Economic Polity of a Nation*, London 1856.

88. Paton, *Clergy*, 131.

89. Burke, *Reflections*, 21.

90. Chalmers, "On the Christian Education of the People," 32–33.

91. Brown, *Chalmers*, 67.

92. Ibid., 369 and 366.

this were eternally significant, but what if sinners resist the gospel? Of what significance is their work in this case? In answer to this, I will return to Chalmers' understanding of natural conscience among sinful workers.

THE BENEFITS OF WORKING WITH NATURAL CONSCIENCE

When poor, sinful workers positively respond to the inner voice of the sovereignty of God, pleasure is derived as virtue is formed: "[r]ectitude is thus its own reward." Contrariwise, when natural conscience is ignored, sin becomes its punishment. This doctrine grew in popularity among evangelicals at this time and was a prevalent view among nineteenth-century moralists,[93] and again, this view discloses Butler's influence upon Chalmers.[94] Such thinking proposes that in God's economy, rewards and punishment for acting in accordance with natural conscience or sinning respectively belong to natural providence. "Eternal damnation merely mirrors sublunary misfortunes," and is meant to deter sinners from going against their conscience.[95] Chalmers remarks that divine justice is done "when intemperance is followed up by disease; and these eventual pains or chastisements are often far greater than the immediate enjoyment, as when the disgrace of a whole lifetime results from the indulgence, which lasts but for a moment, of some ungovernable passion."[96]

Going against natural conscience, as Chalmers describes it, brings about slow moral death, even if temporal punishments are unjustly absent. At the very least, each person will reap what they have sown in this lifetime at the inauguration of the next, for there must be an "equitable adjustment in a future state" for those missed opportunities to work virtuously.[97] William Cobbett (1763–1835) originally employed the economic term "equitable adjustment" with reference to the collection of debts and contracts in moral discussions thus highlighting the eschatological implications of working with or against natural conscience. This antecedent of social Darwinist thought at work in Chalmers' political economy demonstrates unchristian harshness for those who fall foul of disease, poverty and "equitable adjustment" of unjust fortunes in this age.

---

93. Hilton, *Age*, 185.
94. Butler, *Analogy*, part 1 chapter 2.
95. Hilton, *Age*, 184.
96. Chalmers, *Posthumous Works*, 9:15–6.
97. Hilton, *Age*, 184 n. 82.

What was God's original aim for natural conscience prior to the Fall? That both the inward desires of man, concomitant with outward action, cohere and are actualized according to what Chalmers calls "our moral affections." With both the interior and exterior aspects of life subordinated to God as "governor," natural conscience's superiority is satisfied. Contrariwise, "if this superiority be denied to it, there is a felt violence done to the whole economy of man."[98]

Without converting to Christ, sinners have not crowned natural conscience with evangelical works and thus have robbed God. Nevertheless, natural conscience remains operational in all and for all to orientate lives to the glory of God.[99] Using nineteenth-century mechanical grammar to convey his point, Chalmers says that by working according to conscience rather than obstinately resisting it, "every man is led, by the very make and mechanism of his internal economy, to feel that this is as it ought to be."[100]

Natural conscience is not one faculty of man among a plethora of feelings and emotions, Chalmers insists, but rather a "guide" or "governor" to lead man aright because divine sovereignty itself is present as the natural conscience of man in the form of a "monitor" or "law."[101] Moreover, natural conscience should "regulate" all inclinations to "sacred . . . authority," which directs conscience back to its Maker.[102] Chalmers exclaims while quoting Bishop Butler extensively,

> The conclusion on the whole is—that 'man cannot be considered as a creature left by his Maker to act at random, and live at large up to the extent of his natural power, as passion, human willfulness, happen to carry him; which is the condition brute creatures are in; But that from his make, constitution, or nature, he is, in the strictest and most proper sense, a law to himself. He hath the rule of right within: What is wanting is only that he honestly attend to it.' Now it is in these phenomena of Conscience that Nature offers to us, far her strongest argument, for the moral character of God.[103]

For sinners, according to Chalmers, natural conscience is nothing more than an "instantaneous feeling" within themselves, something that is unseen and misunderstood. For example, even the most heathen nations

---

98. Chalmers, "On the Supremacy of Conscience," 317.
99. Ibid., 316.
100. Ibid., 318.
101. Ibid., 321.
102. Ibid., 322.
103. Ibid., 323.

have accounts of truth and reason which the civilizations of Greece and Rome exemplified by their contradictory brutalism juxtaposed with their practice of jurisprudence; their justice system, according to Chalmers, was a partial imprint of transcendent immanence upon their cultures through natural conscience.[104] But when faith in Christ emerges in sinners "there is instant transition made" into cognizant awareness of a "living Sovereign" which enables faith-living.[105] The subjective difference between sinners and Christians then is *cognizance* of transcendence through faith, which necessarily leads to a greater profundity and consistency of ethical living, hence, Chalmers' Baxterian education of the poor towards conversion.

By being model examples of fidelity in the workplace, Christians must "adorn the doctrine of God our Saviour in all things."[106] But the present state of sin still lingers in working efforts and requires liberation from ill-effects, and without faith in Christ emblazoning sinners' hearts with "every feeling of confidence," "affection," and "esteem," such characteristics remain dormant in sinful workers.[107] Christ's continual teaching of his followers leads to "kindness and civility" in their neighborhood, "faithfulness" and "responsibility" in their workplace, "wisdom" and "gentleness" in their family life, crowned with "keepership" (stewardship) in the service of their lives. It is surprising that Chalmers claims the exclusivity of these traits to Christians, for clearly sinners can be civil, kind, trustworthy, gentle, and can steward with wisdom, though perhaps not to the illumined degree which Chalmers describes among Christians. Sinners are nonetheless able to demonstrate these same characteristics in their work as the half-caste heterodox Samaritan exemplifies (Luke 10:25–37).

At best, sinners' work might be said to be materially significant, but because Christ is not subjectively "honoured," they cannot demonstrate Christlikeness in their work so it is of little importance. In short, "evangelical works" are not enacted and thus their work remains mundane and shackled to their own self-centeredness.

In seeming contradiction, however, in his essay titled "On the Mercantile Virtues Which May Exist Without the Influence of Christianity," Chalmers examines how the virtues of Phil 4:8 are occasionally present among sinners. It reads, "Finally, beloved, whatever is true, whatever is honorable, whatever is just, whatever is pure, whatever is pleasing, whatever is commendable, if there is any excellence and if there is anything worthy of

---

104. Ibid., 333.
105. Ibid., 331–32.
106. Chalmers, *Discourses*, 305.
107. Chalmers, "On the Moral Influence," 325.

praise, think about these things." Chalmers explains this in light of the good work of sinners:

> There are certain phases, and certain exhibitions of this nature which are more lovely than others—certain traits of character, not due to the operation of Christianity at all, and yet calling forth our admiration and our tenderness—certain varieties of moral complexion, far more fair and more engaging than certain other varieties; and to prove that the gospel may have had no share in the formation of them, they in fact stood out to the notice and respect of the world, before the gospel was ever heard of.[108]

By the powers of honest observation, Chalmers notes that those without faith in Christ can manifest virtue in their working lives à la Phil 4:8. In this regard Chalmers muses once again how it was that Greek and Roman civilizations exhibited aspects of "heathenism" and "moral abominations" juxtaposed with "gathered things which are pure, and lovely, and true, and just, and honest, and of good report."[109] How can the doctrine of total depravity and the clear manifestation of virtue co-exist in sinners?[110] Chalmers responds,

> Might not a sense of honour elevate that heart which is totally unfurnished with a sense of God? Might not an impulse of compassionate feeling be sent into that bosom which is never once visited by a movement of duteous loyalty towards the Lawgiver in heaven? Might not occasions of intercourse with the beings around us, develop whatever there is in our nature of generosity, and friendship, and integrity, and patriotism; and yet the unseen Being, who placed us in this theatre, be neither loved, nor obeyed, nor listened to? Amid the manifold varieties of human character, and the number of constitutional principles which enter into its composition, might there not be an individual in whom the constitutional virtues so blaze forth and have the ascendancy, as to give a general effect of gracefulness to the whole of this moral exhibition; and yet may not that individual be as unmindful of his God, as if the principles of this constitution had been mixed up in such a different proportion, as to make him an odious and a revolting spectacle?[111]

---

108. Chalmers, *Discourses*, 16.
109. Chalmers, "On the Mercantile Virtues," 16.
110. Ibid., 17.
111. Ibid., 17–18.

Chalmers seeks to reconcile his existential experience with his theological anthropology to explicate these virtuous characteristics in sinners by recognizing their necessary tension. It is entirely feasible to behave and work well in the world in such a way which impresses upon any onlooker and yet simultaneously be far from God and ignorant of the imperative to convert to Christ. In other words, works of some description are performed but they are not *evangelical works*, only these having spiritual significance. Chalmers illuminates this thought further when alluding to Phil 2:13: "Only grant, that we have nothing either in the constitution of our spirits, or in the structure of our bodies, which we did not receive; and that mind, with all its varieties, is as much the product of a creating hand, as matter in all its modifications; and then on the face of human society, do we witness all the gradations of a moral scenery, which may be directly referred to the operation of Him who worketh all in all."[112]

Moral characteristics, then, do manifest themselves among sinners, according to Chalmers, because natural conscience "whisper[s] in the ear of his inner man the claims of an unseen Legislator."[113] This is evidence of progression of thought in Chalmers' theology, for that which was shown at the beginning of this chapter demonstrates a binary harshness towards the ethical ability of sinners in their work.

Chalmers' argument thus far is not aimed at unraveling the doctrine of total depravity. Far from it. Rather, he wishes to hold total depravity and the good work of sinners empowered by God's sovereignty in tension, but eventually, though, the agency of sinners is disclosed by Chalmers as encapsulating no merit. He insists that any hint of meritorious work "charge[s] him [the sinful worker] direct with his utter disloyalty to God and to convict him of treason against the majesty of heaven. It is to press home upon him the impiety of not caring about God."[114]

Unsurprisingly, in light of his commitment to total depravity, Chalmers argues that good work by sinners does not merit any acknowledgment from God, nor does it make a way to heaven. Despite any beneficial efforts which sinners contribute to the earth, or any sign of virtue, sinners are ultimately viewed by God as those who have "revolted against that Being who has done so much to beautify and exalt her."[115] It is not that God pays no heed to character development and its impact upon the workplace, but this must be viewed through the prism of union with Christ. As Chalmers puts

---

112. Chalmers, "The Influence," 36.
113. Chalmers, "On the Mercantile Virtues," 19.
114. Ibid., 21.
115. Ibid., 22.

it, "God's controversy with our species is not, that the glow of honour or of humanity is never felt among them. It is, that none of them understandeth, and none of them seeketh after God."[116]

Being estranged from God, the work of sinners is disregarded outright because they work "as if there was no presiding Divinity at all."[117] This is a constituting principle in all Reformation theology, and in Chalmers' thought this is no exception. Because sinners "rebel" against God by their lack of faith in Christ, their virtuous work is only "seen from afar" by God because of the gulf that separates them.[118]

Chalmers comes full circle after considering the good work of sinners by arriving back at his original principle: "The one who . . . serves Christ is acceptable to God and has human approval" (Rom 14:18). The clear inference is that all those who do not serve Christ are unacceptable to him for they do not perform *evangelical works* of faith as Christians do. And yet Chalmers still wishes to show a measure of esteem to the virtuous work of sinners because virtue is not entirely absent from them through natural conscience. Indeed, he states above that sinners "may blazon the character of him who stands against it" and the term "blazon" here does more than imply that sinners can occasionally manifest the character of God. If sinners happen to work unwittingly according to the will of the "Lawgiver," they do this not because of any knowledge or compulsion from the divine law, but according to their "own instinctive sensibilities."[119]

Chalmers admits that he has never experienced a sinful merchant who worked in such a manner as to be "unimpeachable."[120] But work in the commercial world without thought of God, while concomitantly displaying some degree of virtue, describes "a man of integrity, and yet he is a man of ungodliness."[121] This is a helpful distinction for it finally reveals how Chalmers marries total depravity with the good work of sinners. Good work enacted by sinners is acknowledged by God as *moral action*, but given the agent's salvific separation from God, his work cannot be taken seriously in an *ultimate sense*. In other words, the work of sinners always remains ontologically connected to its agents, for without showing due gratitude to

---

116. Ibid., 23.
117. Ibid.
118. Ibid., 23–24.
119. Ibid., 26.
120. Ibid., 27.
121. Ibid., 29.

God, sinful workers are in constant threat of an eternity of hell; this threat hangs over all who are oblivious or cognizant of this terrifying fact.[122]

ANALYSIS OF CHALMERS

How sufficient is Chalmers' use of "the rightful Sovereign in man" through natural conscience as the source of power for the good work of sinners? It is a theistic account at best. Closer to the truth, however, is that his account is deistic as his language befits that of Scottish enlightenment philosophy and liberal theology with his constant appeal to transcendentalism in his talk of natural conscience. In fairness, Chalmers employs this language but comprehends it through an evangelical interpretative grid. However, his account is certainly not a pneumatological one for christology and pneumatology generally are relegated to a smattering of appendices in Chalmers' corpus.[123] On a rare occasion when he speaks of work pneumatologically, he says, "Would even this imperfect but universal homage continue to be given, were it a wicked Being who presided over the great family of Nature, or breathed life and spirit and sentiment into the human framework?"[124]

The close of this quote echoes Gen 2:7, "then the LORD God . . . breathed into his nostrils *the breath of life*," and Ps 103:29b-30a, "when you take away *their breath*, they die and return to the dust. When you send forth *your spirit*, they are created." These echoes speak of the Holy Spirit's infusion of breath into created beings enabling life. As John V. Taylor puts it, "The Spirit of Life is ever at work in nature, in history and in human living."[125]

It is disappointing that Chalmers did not develop this isolated pneumatological vignette because allocating a particular triune person to natural conscience's operation would have been biblically advantageous and would have made his argument all the more convincing. Precisely because of the immanent ubiquity of his operations, the Holy Spirit lends himself to being the obvious operational influence of natural conscience and moral reason in man, for as the Father sits on his throne with his Son at his side, the Spirit's transcendent immanence enables people "to live and move and have [their] being" (Acts 17:28).

Armand Larive proposes a further reason why this trinitarian dynamic is often ignored in theologies of work: "This problem of making room for the Spirit occurs because the role of Christ as mediator, the one who reveals

---

122. Ibid., 30.
123. Roxborough, "Chalmers' Theology of Mission," 174–75.
124. Chalmers, "On the Supremacy of Conscience," 329.
125. Taylor, *The Go-Between God*, 27.

the Father, our *Abba*, to the world, seems to leave nothing left for the Holy Spirit to do."[126] Such logic is typical of nineteenth- and twentieth-century Western theologies; the Holy Spirit is often resigned to mere sanctifying duties and so there often is no room for a second structural tier of divine mediatorial presence alongside Christ for ethics.[127] Having said that, if the Spirit's role in sanctifying human beings is extended to mundane life to ethically effect change in and for this world, then the Spirit's broader operation as sanctifier could be more readily embraced.[128] But to have considered this in the way just described would have been alien to Chalmers' *Sitz im Leben*.

Chalmers' account of Aristotelian ethical momentum, both moral and immoral, is to be admired for it accurately portrays the stimulus that urges moral behavior onwards while also the constraint of immoral behavior from breaking its negative trend.

Although Chalmers does occasionally approve the good work of sinners when he rightly says, "There are certain phases, and certain exhibitions of this nature which are more lovely than others—certain traits of character, not due to the operation of Christianity at all," he cannot envision that their good work is granted ultimate divine commendation because their unsalvific state before God is too great an impediment to overcome.[129] In resolute commitment to Reformation principles, Chalmers views the good work of sinners through the prism of *sola fide*, that extracts the worth of sinners' work entirely. In other words, their lack of faith is an impediment to their work being viewed as "good" or "virtuous." Thus, total depravity is too all-pervading for the good work of sinners to penetrate the eternal heart of God; no *evangelical works* can be enacted. However, this is doctrinally problematic because if man is as *totally* depraved as maintained, surely he would not know himself to be such.[130]

Even so, Chalmers gives some temporal credit to the obvious occasions where sinners virtuously contribute to the world, but this must be rapidly quashed in the following breath to be true to *sola fide*. What the latter point enables, though, is prime motivation to Christianize Scotland through the proclamation of the gospel. But herein lies an old evangelical problem. The sinful poor are aided in their physical wants only *as a means* to convince them of Christ. Of course, it is not denied that helping the poor

---

126. Larive, *After Sunday*, 108.
127. Williams, *On Christian Theology*, 114–15.
128. Stackhouse, *The Gospel-Driven Church*, 180–81.
129. Chalmers, "On the Mercantile Virtues," 16.
130. Lewis, *The Problem of Pain*, 54–55.

out of their poverty and into employment are "subordinate blessings," but they cannot compare to the *real* work of the salvation of souls.

As I will show in the following subsection, even though Chalmers' impact among the poor was momentous, to relegate the alleviation of the poor's material requirements to a secondary level of importance is to miss the primary place Jesus gives such work entirely in his teaching and example.

THE FINAL STATE OF SINFUL MERCHANTS AND THEIR MERCHANDISE

The second focus of this chapter assesses whether any good work performed by sinners has any correlation to the final state. If some work performed by sinners can be *good*, might there be any correlation between it and the new creation, according to the parable of the sheep and the goats (Matt 25:31–46)? Chalmers's theology of the work of sinners will be evaluated against this question.

In view of this sobering parable Chalmers meekly hopes for the best: "I pray for the preparation of the inner man—for the spirit in my heart to sustain the faith and the faithfulness of a true disciple. . . . O that the uncertainty of the time of our final summons would put us on the constant outlook, and in the attitude of leaning upon Christ—abiding in Him, that He may abide in us, and cause us ever to abound in much fruit."[131]

Challenged by the parable's austere message, Chalmers prays for the ability to work faithfully for Christ in light of his fickle heart. The neglect of fruitful work, despite faith in Christ, is enough to make any Christian question their spiritual condition and this insecurity is no more evident when Chalmers expresses, "I have much very much wherewith to reproach myself. Under the impulse of a constitutional delight in activity I may have done something—but how little on the principle of the glory of God, he alone knoweth. Blot out, O Lord, the fearful account of debt and deficiency which Thou has against me. Enable me to consecrate all I have, and all I am able for to Thy service here—that I may be prepared for the high services of eternity hereafter."[132]

Understanding the vacillation of his own heart to incline towards God the Father, Chalmers passionately petitions God to make restitution for any ethical inconsistency which has not fallen in line with divine purposes. The sharp goad of this parable has had the desired effect upon Chalmers, but what is noticeable is that he assumes there are actions he is unconscious of

131. Chalmers, *Posthumous*, 4:41.
132. Ibid., 42.

that may put him in a dangerous predicament with God. In other words, there could be occasions, Chalmers is convinced, where the ability to perceive sinful actions is stultified, therefore causing anxiety that there are unresolved sinful works not dealt with before God. However, with *sola fide* on his mind, Chalmers exclaims further, "Save me, O God, from the delusion, that by a negation of the good and the useful in my life, I shall only fall short of a reward."[133]

It is surely fantasy to conclude that by omitting works that ought to be have been identified and performed, ultimate salvation will be withheld, Chalmers says warily. Clearly, once salvation through faith in Christ is solidified through faith it cannot be surrendered; it is indelible. Disregarded works, then, are not crucial to the abrogation of salvation according to Chalmers.

Notwithstanding this conclusion, the sheep and the goats propels the imperative to act and not rest on antinomian laurels of *sola fide*, but to compound faith with its definitive demonstration. Concerning the sheep who ask the Son of Man why their work prompts the generous grant of "eternal life" (vv. 37–9), Chalmers says, "I have sometimes felt relieved by the question of the righteous to their Judge, as implying an unconsciousness of what they had nevertheless done and were rewarded for. I am very unconscious of aught which can give me a part in their reward."[134]

With this, Chalmers admits the plausibility of serving the divine Son of Man unwittingly. The sheep's obliviousness to the Son of Man's generous gift administers salve on Chalmers' anxiety over his possible unperformed works.

This unawareness of righteous work also demonstrates Chalmers' assumption that the work of the sheep is performed by those with faith in Christ. Furthermore, he assumes himself to be a sheep and takes great comfort from the sheep's ignorance of their own doings; never at any juncture does he assume himself to be a goat. This is telling of Chalmers' convictions about the basis of the eschatological judgment of Christians and sinners, for Chalmers recalls, "while I rejoice in being justified by faith, let me forget not that I am judged by works."[135]

Integrating a Pauline theology of justification by faith with this parable, Chalmers recognizes the message of the parable as instructive for that which men should *do* in this life, as secondarily mandatory for a heavenly reward. Chalmers understands that justification is a status of faith which

---

133. Ibid., 42–43.
134. Ibid., 43.
135. Ibid.

is irrevocable and that consequently the day of judgment will only be an analysis of works performed. Ultimately, however, a lack of works cannot discount the sheep from ultimate salvation, although this parable does make Chalmers fleetingly waver on this point.

As such, Chalmers means to implore God to judge him with mercy on the day of judgment, despite mistakes made. As long as there is no deliberate neglect of those in need, but merely an obliviousness to that which is required, "not on evil-doing but on the want of well-doing," the dread of the Son of Man's sentence will be tempered. Thus, in the interim Chalmers implores his divine judge to enable him to "do good unto all men, specially to the household of faith—to those whom Christ calls His brethren."[136] He is referring to Matt 25:40 where the Son of Man states, "Truly I tell you, just as you did it to one of the least of these my brothers, you did it to me." The term "brothers" (Gk. *Adelphōn*) for Chalmers, refers to Christians, for who else would Jesus refer to as sheep? "[B]rothers" is interpreted this way because of an imposed assumption that they are Jesus' disciples. This is the very same move Stott makes later in the twentieth century.

The parable of the sheep and the goats also compounds the message of an earlier Matthean teaching of Jesus:[137] "Not everyone who says to me, 'Lord, Lord,' will enter the kingdom of heaven, *but only the one who does the will of my Father in heaven.* On that day many will say to me, 'Lord, Lord,' did we not prophesy in your name, and cast out demons in your name, and do many deeds of power in your name?' Then I will declare to them, 'I never knew you; go away from me, you evildoers'" (7:21–23, my emphasis).

As with the sheep and the goats, Chalmers acknowledges that Jesus' teaching in Matthew 7 emphasizes that his true followers will be obvious because of their exemplary ethical living. In view of this Chalmers exclaims, "O God, put the right principle within me, that I may be rooted and grounded in the faith—forgetting not that while justified by faith I am judged by works."[138]

Here Chalmers reveals that it will be according to works that Christians will be judged ultimately, "grounded" by their irrevocable faith. The implied faith of Christian sheep, insists Chalmers, means that judgment day will take place because of an *a priori* position of divine approval which will still probe for right intentions, behavior and work. He is correct to acknowledge that the judgment of the sheep and the goats is based upon works. Once again Chalmers manifests the Pauline stress of saving faith, but in

---

136. Ibid.
137. Luz, *Matthew*, 282.
138. Chalmers, *Posthumous*, 12.

conjunction with works shown in Matt 7:21–23. Curiously, however, neither the parable of the sheep and the goats nor Matt 7:21–23 indicates that faith is necessary for Jesus' ultimate acceptance of their work for eternal life, but simply their right action.

In this same regard, Ulrich Luz candidly remarks upon Matt 7:21–23 and the sheep and the goats that "important are works, not one's confession or charismata."[139] Yet this entire interpretation hinges on Chalmers' *a priori* identification of the sheep as *bona fide* followers of Christ and yet in these two Matthean passages Christ never discusses Chalmers' Reformation point that one must have faith in order for work to be divinely acclaimed for the eschaton.

Despite the discordant nature of the parable of the sheep and the goats with Chalmers' theology of the good work of sinners, virtuous work empowered by "natural conscience" is akin to Jesus' condemnation of the Pharisees' self-righteous spirituality, according to Chalmers: "So whenever you give alms, do not sound a trumpet before you, as the hypocrites do in the synagogues and in the streets, so that they may be praised by others. *Truly I tell you, they have received their reward*" (Matt 6:2; my emphasis). The Pharisees' reward was praise from their impressed onlookers, but sinners' work, argues Chalmers, merits Jesus' scathing condemnation of the Pharisees' motive in their giving. For "when disjoined from a sense of God, it [work] is of no religious estimation whatever; nor will it lead to any religious blessings, either in time or in eternity."[140]

Neither in temporality nor when the kingdom comes in all its fullness will the work of sinners be worthy of any divine reward or acknowledgment. It is both an earthly and heavenly impediment to God, as it is nothing short of "spiritual idolatry" because of its faulty intention. Chalmers insists instead that work must be orientated to God's service through faith (*evangelical works*) so as to fulfill and crown it.[141] Philippians 4:8, therefore, takes on a renewed understanding for work in light of faith in Christ: "Whenever the religious principle has taken possession of the mind, it animates these virtues with a new spirit; and when so animated, all such things as are pure, and lovely, and just, and true, and honest, and of good report, have a religious importance and character belonging to them."[142]

In evaluating the connection between work and the eschaton, Chalmers offers the following comment: "There is no one topic on which the Bible,

---

139. Luz, *Matthew*, 283.
140. Chalmers, "On the Mercantile Virtues," 31.
141. Ibid., 31.
142. Ibid., 32.

throughout the variety of its separate compositions, maintains a more lucid and entire consistency of sentiment, than the superiority of moral over all physical and all external distinctions."[143] He emphasizes these dualities again when he states,

> There is a predominance given in both to worth, and to wisdom, and to principle, which leads us to understand, that within the compass of human attainment, there is an object placed before us of a higher and more estimable character than all the objects of a common-place ambition . . . this is quite akin with the superiority which the Bible every where ascribes to the soul over the body, and to eternity over time, and to the Supreme Author of Being over all that is subordinate and created.[144]

Chalmers reveals an *anthropological duality* here which elevates the soul over the body because of the soul's perceived incorporeal superiority. Second, Chalmers speaks of an *eschatological duality* where this earthly age is viewed as distinctly inferior from the coming new creation.[145] This is conveyed in terms of time versus timelessness. The implication of Chalmers' *anthropological duality* is that the physicality of work and works' physical objects are diminished unless they serve as *a means* towards the preaching of the gospel and the sanctification of the interior, ethereal soul. Philip Blair articulates well the kind of duality Chalmers is arguing, "The kingdom which Jesus was calling upon men to enter was therefore not to be an outward or political kingdom. It was a kingdom which was to exist solely in the hearts of its members. It was, in other words, to be a spiritual kingdom."[146] "Spiritual" here should read "immaterial" or "incorporeal." The vast bulk of human work, following Chalmers' logic, is of little to no value in and of itself because the *materiality* of work poses a problem in view of an immaterial heaven.[147] Chalmers admits such when he says,

> Commerce may flourish, or may fail—and amid the ruin of her many fluctuations, may elevate a few of the more fortunate of her sons to the affluence of princes. Thy merchants may be princes, and thy traffickers be the honourable of the earth. But if there be truth in our text, there may, on the very basis of human society, *and by a silent process of education, materials be formed, which*

---

143. Chalmers, "On the Advantage," 249.
144. Ibid., 249–50.
145. This typology of dualities is outlined in Wright, *The New Testament*, 253–54.
146. Blair, *What on Earth?*, 57–58.
147. For a critique of Lutheran, Liberation and Pentecostal versions of this same argument, see Volf, "Materiality of Salvation.".

> *far outweigh in cost and true dignity, all the blazing pinnacles that glitter upon its summit*—and it is indeed a cheering thought to the heart of a philanthropist, that near him lies a territory so ample, on which he may expiate—where for all his pains, and all his sacrifices, he is sure of a repayment more substantial, than was ever wafted by richly laden flotilla to our shores—*where the return comes to him, not in that which superficially decks the man, but in a solid increment of values fixed and perpetuated on the man himself—additions to the worth of the soul form the proceeds of his productive operation*—and where, when he reckons up the profits of his enterprise, he finds them to consist of that, which, on the highest of all authorities, he is assured to be more than meat, of that which is greatly more than raiment.[148]

Profits, innovations, food and shelter are the products of work that pertain to the body and thus to the corporeality of life on earth prior to the eschaton. Such ends for human work are inferior to the "silent process of education," Chalmers argues, that shore up "the worth of the soul." In other words, the sanctifying work of the Holy Spirit in the lives of Christian workers is intangible but has a superior quality that fits believing workers for heaven and this reveals the interconnection between Chalmers' anthropological and eschatological dualities.[149] For Chalmers, this age is distinct from the age to come precisely because this age is corporeal and the next will be incorporeal. Because this age's corporeality is understood as inferior to incorporeality, precisely because of its materiality, this means that this age is ordered below that of the one to come. This emphasis was not to be at the expense of the earthly usefulness of work however, as "the business of . . . sanctification" required a "daily and hourly and ever-doing business."[150] Being useful in serving one's neighbor is a means toward such "values fixed and perpetuated on the man"!

As each generation is born, Christian families are exhorted by Chalmers to "train the footsteps of his children in the way that leads to" heaven[151] for by so doing these young Christians will develop a "moral respectability" which is "far beyond the reach of any present calculation."[152] In other words, only the incorporeal qualities of heaven that shape interior souls can be formed in Christians by working virtuously. This limits the eschatological potential of earthly work solely to Christians and even the poverty of

148. Chalmers, "On the Advantage," 251–52 (my emphases).
149. Roxborough, "Chalmers' Theology of Mission," 178.
150. Chalmers, quoted in ibid., 178.
151. Chalmers, "On the Advantage," 252.
152. Ibid., 253.

the poor is a superior spiritual condition compared with the industrious, wealthy sinner, if faith in Christ is present. This is so, argues Chalmers, because "we must look to the calculation of eternity" above all other factors.[153] Put differently, in the case of sinful workers, irrespective of work's skill and success, such will "pass away; how soon death will strip the one of his rags, and the other of his pageantry, and send them, in utter nakedness, to the dust; how soon judgment will summon them from their graves, and place them in outward equality before the great disposer of their future lot, and their future place."[154]

Because the agents concerned are sinners, there is no chance their work will be deemed important or worthy of transformation for heaven. It does not matter that through their conscience they periodically participate in the world virtuously or that transcendence can influence their decision-making at work to benefit the world. Because the agents concerned are sinners they cannot perform *evangelical works* through faith. This clouds any good and virtuous work performed and Chalmers argues that at that great day of judgment "when examined by the secrets of the inner man, and the deeds done in their body, the treasure of heaven shall be adjudged only to him whose heart was set upon it in this world."[155]

Workers without a Christian family, therefore, begin life with a moral and social disadvantage compared to Christians who have an informed perspective of the importance of the ethereal soul for work. To counter this imbalance, Chalmers avers that education of the poor should be the means of effectively Christianizing Scotland. With such a strategy, not only can Christian families work morally, but sinners can be incorporated through Christian faith.

ANALYSIS OF CHALMERS' INTERPRETATION OF THE SHEEP AND THE GOATS

Stott and Chalmers make the same hermeneutical move by identifying the sheep as followers of Christ as they employ *adelphōn* to support their case. Chalmers makes this move because no one other than followers of Christ can be saved for heaven, therefore, he assumes that the sheep must be Christians with a prior faith in Christ. But both Matt 25:31–46 and 7:21–3 say nothing of a prior faith in Christ as their accession to eternal life. These agents are accepted by Christ because of the demonstration of a lived life.

153. Ibid., 255.
154. Ibid.
155. Ibid.

Even though Chalmers is unsubstantiated in imposing the identity of the sheep as Christians, he at least recognizes that the sheep and goats teach that judgment will take place according to works. Consequently, Chalmers must find a way of harmonizing the prior faith of followers of Christ with the judgment of works. His synthesis is conclusively unsatisfying because the latter point is spoiled and warped by his imposition of an *a priori* faith in Christ among the sheep, a point he never justifies.

The judgment of works causes Chalmers personal anguish because of potential works ignored and omitted. However, he finds relief in the fact that the sheep were ignorant of their good works by which they enter eternal life. The distinction, however, between good works which the saints are oblivious to, and those deliberately ignored, is important to him. Nonetheless, the salve that Chalmers finds to soothe his concern about the judgment of works is predicated upon the assumption that he is a sheep by virtue of being a follower of Christ, an assumption which the text itself does not advocate. The parable's message has the desired effect on Chalmers, but his distinction between deliberate neglect and genuine omission of works may be on very shaky ground when viewed in light of the sheep and the goats. It seems that both animals deserve their respective ends because neither group knew what they had done or omitted.

The reason for Chalmers' imposition of justification by faith upon the sheep and goats is because earthly work is problematic due to its corporeality. The anthropological duality between the body and the soul informs his eschatological duality of a corporeal earthly reality and an incorporeal heaven to come. As such, the corporeal and societal benefits of work have a "subordinated" place in light of that which orientates the incorporeal soul to Christ, for only that which is immaterial can pertain to an ethereal heaven. If Chalmers were really to take this seriously he would have recognized that working according to the way of the sheep, which was a corporeal service to those in need, is by extension serving a heavenly Son of Man (Matt 25:31) thus intrinsically linking the earth with heaven. The way these dualities are framed into a dichotomy between material/immateriality is problematic, for not only must the resurrection of the body be endangered in Chalmers' theology, but the hope of the kingdom's fulfilled arrival and being done "on earth as it is in heaven" (Matt 6:10) must also be by-passed. It is little wonder then for Chalmers that almost all work is devalurized because of its corporeality.

CONCLUSION

In this chapter I have shown in Chalmers' theology of the good work of sinners a reliance upon the sovereignty of God in all men through natural conscience. Through his societal reform of educating the poor, Chalmers believes that this primes its recipients to receive the gospel and through this analysis I have demonstrated that Chalmers believes only the fruits of the church's evangelization will continue into heaven from this current age. Any other human endeavors, even those of Christians, have no eternal value other than the potential for virtue to be formed in Christian agents.

Analyzing Chalmers' candid response to the sheep and goats, two things are disclosed: (1) the sheep are interpreted as Christians, and (2) he acknowledges that the final judgment will be according to works performed, whereas justification by faith is something that irrevocably takes place in this age. The parable also forces Chalmers to assess himself before God to ensure that he has not omitted the fruits of a true disciple. His interpretation of the identity of the sheep, however, is incorrectly assumed.

Even though sinners can perform good work, because their relationship with the Father of Jesus Christ is non-existent, their work can never be viewed with any ultimate divine favor. In other words, the work of sinners is wholeheartedly connected in an ontological sense with the sinful agent's lack of Christian faith or other religious faith, and it is this which automatically discredits all their work from any eschatological significance for heaven. In short, sinners cannot perform *evangelical works* through faith.

What this chapter has demonstrated, in similar fashion to Schaeffer and Stott, is that Chalmers' designation of *sinners* is entirely indicative of his theology of their work; their sinful status before God cannot be overcome by good work or by a character of integrity. Sinners' unwillingness or ambivalence towards God is an insurmountable impediment to the benevolence or quality of their work for the world. Unlike Schaeffer, Chalmers uses his Scottish transcendental categories, intermixed with Reformed language, to convey this theological point. As such, Chalmers improves only a little upon Schaeffer and Stott, despite having a valuable account of how sinners can simultaneously be workers of integrity.

In the following chapter I will evaluate Richard Baxter's theology of the work of *infidels* to discover whether he believes they can enact good work. Furthermore, can Baxter envision any eschatological connection between the good work of infidels and heaven? His interpretation of the sheep and the goats will be assessed in order to answer this question.

3

Richard Baxter (1615–91)
The Work of Infidels and their Noetic Obstacle to the *Vita Contemplativa*

IN THE PREVIOUS CHAPTER I demonstrated that Thomas Chalmers provides a modicum of esteem to good work performed by sinners through the category *natural conscience*. However, even this work, despite its regular or irregular habits is worth nothing to God without converting to Christ. Thus the good but mundane work of sinners is always understood as temporal in nature as opposed to *evangelical works*. The parable of the sheep and the goats is resultantly perceived as a portrayal of good work performed by Christians and a subsequent judgment of works at the final judgment.

I have shown thus far the low esteem in which the work of non-Christians is held in British evangelical theology. I have demonstrated this through Francis Schaeffer, John Stott, and Thomas Chalmers. By now shifting to the seventeenth century I will be able to clearly identify how Schaeffer, Stott, and Chalmers' conclusions generally reflect that of Richard Baxter's theology of the work of infidels.

In this chapter I will ask two questions of Baxter's theology of work: (1) is the good work of infidels noted by God in any sense, and (2) does their good work have any eschatological connection with the new creation? It will be shown that Baxter's theology of work reveals a series of deeply imbedded dualities that undermine the corporeality of work and its significance for the earth because the earth is to be valued loosely because of its temporality. The result of all that is made holy in this life is its presence in a future heaven; all that is material on earth is therefore relegated to temporal insignificance. As such, Baxter provides a clear example of the type of theology I wish to repair.

His strand of Puritanism had reached its zenith in Britain during his lifetime.[1] Puritanism was the party within the established Church of England that wished for a far deeper Reformation than actually took place. The Church, according to Baxter, was still too Roman, and so he pressed for a more deeply distinctive Protestant ecclesiastical life.[2] Also, Baxter resisted the spirit of the Renaissance with its affiliation to Elizabethan and Stuart literature, as well as its governmental policy and feudal economics, and consequently, the makeshift Elizabethan settlement of 1559 saw increasing Puritan disillusionment within the established Church.[3] This resulted in vocal dissension over the state of ecclesiastical ministry, the imposition of ritual, and current leadership structure.[4] Because of his opposition, Baxter's stripe of Puritanism became *nonconformist* in churchmanship as a result of its subsequent expulsion from the state Church. As such, it can be confidently said that Baxter is without doubt an exemplar of his particular strand of Puritanism.[5]

Instead of preaching, Baxter's theological writing became his vocation and because he and many other Puritans sought a second Reformation (which demanded the rigorous transformation of everyday life) the Church would require *discipline* to effect true change.[6] It is unsurprising, therefore, in light of the watchword of *discipline* that the issue of work was taken up wholeheartedly as a critical aspect of Christian spirituality in Baxter's corpus.[7] Yet, simultaneously, despite the revolutionary will of Baxter, the nature of this notion of reformation was politically conservative[8] and what

---

1. Tulloch, *English Puritanism*, 281; Cragg, *The Church*, 66.
2. Fuller, *Church History*, 474; Marshall, *Kind of Life*, 38.
3. Troeltsch, *Social Teaching*, 2:679. George Yule contends against the claim that the Puritans were the originators of ecclesiastical reform for he believes that the Archbishop of Canterbury William Laud (1633–45) was the "innovator" who guided the Church's restructuring to something akin to modern British evangelical standards rather than its anglo-Catholic form. Yule, *Puritans*, 13.
4. Packer, *Redemption*, 17.
5. Troeltsch, *Social*, 678. Weber, Tawney and Troeltsch's renowned theses will be three secondary sources for this chapter because of the scarcity of theological analysis on Baxter's theology of work. Although these sources are socially scientific in nature, they do still provide invaluable insight into Baxter's theology of work.
6. Martin, *Puritanism*, 127; Yule, *Puritans*, 115.
7. Troeltsch, *Social*, 678.
8. Tawney, *Religion*, 224.

emerges in Baxter's theology, therefore, is a two-sided coin: *revolution* and *transformation* towards *political conservatism*.⁹

Baxter lived during a time when the Puritan spirit burned in the hearts of all classes of men to the extent that those of lower social grade were as inspired to work for the glory of God as were the gentry. However, it was obvious that there were certain conditions that the Puritan spirit thrived under more than others. Those of a particular economic independence who enjoyed a good education, boasted in their status, spurned their earthly superiors and who held the weak of character in contempt, were those who had most earthly success. "Such," says Tawney, "above all, were the trading classes of the towns, and of those rural districts which had been affected by the partially industrialized by the decentralization of the textile and iron industries."¹⁰ Work, as a result, was gradually moving away from the influence of feudal society.

Politics and work coincided to reveal the particular expression of creed that each one committed to. For example, in the clothing towns of Lancashire, or "the Genevas of Lancashire" as some coined it, emerged significantly stark pockets of Puritanism surrounded by the dominance of Roman Catholicism. This Puritan textile industry spread to towns such as Bradford, Leeds, Halifax, Birmingham, Leicester, Gloucester, Taunton, Exeter, and of course, Baxter's Kidderminster. "The identification of the industrial and commercial classes with religious radicalism was, indeed, a constant theme of Anglicans and Royalists, who found in the vices of each an additional reason for distrusting both."¹¹

DIRECTIONS TO GRACELESS SINNERS

It was during this industrial expansion that Baxter wrote his most voluminous text (amounting to more than one million words), *A Christian Directory* (1673). This is the most essential of his texts for my initial step, as it addresses the subject of work most thoroughly.¹² This volume divides the subject of work into (1) Christian ethics, (2) Christian economics, (3) Christian ecclesiastics, and (4) Christian politics, a structure akin to Luther's orders of creation (Church, state, household).

9. Ibid., 212.
10. Ibid., 202.
11. Ibid., 203–4.
12. Packer, *A Man for All Ministries*, 4. Another text concerning "graceless sinners" is Baxter's *A Call to the Unconverted* (1658), but this treatise is not as specific to ethics and work as *A Christian Directory*.

From the outset, Baxter addresses those he refers to as "sinners," "unbelievers," "the ungodly," and most commonly, "infidels," by trying to convince them of the reasonable nature of becoming godly through faith in Christ. I will restrict myself to Baxter's term *infidel* in this chapter because he majors on the category *infidel*, despite also utilizing *sinner* and the *impious* periodically.

Baxter's opening move in his account of Christian ethics is to convince his infidel readership of the plausibility and necessity of becoming a saint, and if successful, to move to Christian catechesis to which the rest of *A Christian Directory* is directed. This is an unsurprising move by Baxter as he is hugely motivated by the task of converting sinners from their darkness into Christian light. Early on Baxter discloses with clarity his understanding of the potential of the work of infidels:

> While you are unsanctified, you are impotent, and dead to any holy, acceptable work: when you should redeem your time, and prepare for eternity, and try your states, or pray, or meditate, or do good to others, you have no heart to any such spiritual works: your minds are biased against them, Rom. Viii.7. And it is not the excusable impotency of such, as would do good, but cannot: but it is the malicious impotency of the voiced, (the same with that of devils,) that cannot do good, because they will not; and will not, because they have blind, malicious, and ungodly hearts, which makes their sin so much the greater, Titus i.16.[13]

Two things are clearly revealed by Baxter in this passage. First, infidels are identified as those who are unfaithful to God and his way of salvation. They are morally "impotent" and their work is incapable of being "acceptable" to God as a consequence. Baxter refers to Rom 8:7 which says: "For this reason the mind that is set on the flesh is hostile to God; it does not submit to God's law—indeed it cannot," as evidence that infidels could never produce or perform any work significant enough for God. *Infidels, per se,* are to be understood as those of "the flesh," as the Apostle Paul refers to them, because those of "the flesh" (Gk. *sarx*) demonstrate a weakness of perception. Romans 6:19, too, emphasizes this deficiency: "For just as you once presented your members as slaves to impurity and to greater and greater iniquity..."[14] With such a noetic obstacle to God, infidel work could never please him.

Second, such moral "impotency" to work according to a godly pattern is inexcusable before God, Baxter reasons, because infidel hearts are

---

13. Baxter, *A Christian Directory*, 20.
14. Schweizer, *Theological Dictionary*, 7:125.

polluted with evil equivalent to the devil himself, thus there was never hope for infidel work amounting to any significance. Confusingly, Baxter also makes comments to the contrary elsewhere: "A natural power of freely determining itself, both to the choice of God and spiritual good remains in the will of the unregenerate. For the sinner is free from a fatal predetermination to evil, and from the dominion of created causes over his will, and from the necessity of sinning, imposed in any other way."[15] And again he says, "Both habitual and dispositive and actual willingness or unwillingness is not called usually *strength* or power, but will; the will itself hath its proper power to will, for it is a natural faculty; but its habits and acts are better known by the name of willingness or unwillingness than of power."[16]

The confusion between these contrary thoughts in Baxter, Fisher reveals, is Baxter's use of the term 'will' which is used by his contemporaries and some medievals "to denote not only the power of choice but also the tendencies or involuntary inclinations that influence the mind in choosing."[17] Even though sin has had a crippling effect on man, avers Baxter, infidel impotence is not total, "but [simply a] weakness of power." He says further, "But by means of sin, the active powers may be languid, and the intellect ill-disposed to perceive higher things, and the will disposed or inclined, by evil habits against spiritual and toward sensual good."[18] So *natural powers* exist in infidel man even if his former *spiritual powers* are hamstrung by sin.

Baxter also employs the term "habit" here in the sense of a practice that is second nature and this implies, says Fisher, "a greater likelihood of the act than the term *moral power*." Baxter adds that prior to the formation of a "holy habit" the mind involuntarily inclines towards God and holiness through the "natural power to do right."[19] This seems to contradict all that Baxter boldly claims in that which I first revealed from *A Christian Directory*. So is there a governing position for the empowerment of infidels to do good?

Where men are given gracious help to enable them to perform acts they do not instinctively incline towards, Baxter refers to such as man's *moral ability* to act. All men have the mental faculties present to repent and believe through *natural power* (not a power independent from God) but if

---

15. Baxter, *Methodus*, 215.
16. Baxter, *Catholick Theologie*, pt. 2, 98.
17. Fisher, "Theology of Richard Baxter," 151.
18. Baxter, *Methodus*, pt. 1, 215, 216.
19. Fisher, "The Theology of Richard Baxter," 152.

they co-operate with the moral power of God's grace they might be able to reach conversion and salvation.[20]

Moreover, Baxter uses the term "faculty" in such a way to describe the functional powers of man, a power not entirely disabled. Hence, when talking of infidels who accomplish something good, this must be viewed as human agency performed by "a previous agency of God." *Infidels* can perform good work by virtue of co-operating with divine agency through their *natural power* just as the saints do similarly by the empowerment of God's grace, "for both nature and grace, and the powers of both, are totally from God."[21] This comment descends from Calvin. To identify which of Baxter's conflicting thoughts about the good work of infidels takes precedence is manifest in the following statements: "the more power a creature hath, the more he glorifieth the power of God." "To deny or extenuate any power given of God, is to dishonor him in his works."[22]

Because infidels continually dishonor God due to their refusal and inability to surrender themselves to Christ's covenants of grace (a point which I will discuss shortly) they will only ever operate from their *natural power*, never from grace. *Natural power* lacks any moral impetus to perform acts because there is a lack of regeneration present.[23] Baxter says, "The moral power given by grace, consisting in the right disposition of the will, is not of the same kind with the natural power or faculty, and the words can and cannot used of both sorts, have not the same signification, but are equivocal; otherwise sin and grace should change man's species."[24] With added caveats he remarks, "The word moral power signifieth, first, sometimes a power to moral actions, and so natural power in man is also moral in some degree; secondly, sometimes a holy disposition, especially in the will to such holy moral actions; which is the rectitude of our natural powers, or the health of them in a saving degree or sort, and is the gift of grace, since sin departed."[25]

Moral power is to "some degree" present in man, even an occasional "holy disposition" in *natural power*, but this moral ability is mainly dormant, unpronounced and not awakened in infidel workers. Thus, their ability to work for the good of the commonwealth is handicapped and incapacitated. The "promptitude" and "facility" to perform "holy habits" is

20. Ibid., 152.
21. Anonymous, "Richard Baxter's 'End of Controversy,'" 357–58.
22. Baxter, quoted in ibid., 358.
23. Ibid.
24. Ibid.
25. Baxter, quoted in ibid., 360.

otherwise described by Baxter as the "sufficient or effectual grace" of God helping men. To a minor extent this is plausible.

Having said all that, Baxter deploys an overarching maxim that infiltrates all such thinking about infidel work: "To deny or extenuate any power given of God, is to dishonor him in his works." Baxter ensures there is no ambiguity over the scope of the work of infidels before God which reveals his influence upon Chalmers. What then is the nature of *sufficient* or *effectual* grace according to Baxter?

SUFFICIENT OR EFFECTUAL GRACE

So what of the grace that empowers infidel work to a certain moral degree? Baxter says, "By sufficient grace is meant that without which, the thing could not occur, and with which, it could be done. It is what is necessary and sufficient to produce the act; but not sufficient to render the event actually necessary or certain."[26]

The last clause above shows Baxter's resistance to any form of determinism, but his main point is nonetheless that all men are empowered to fulfill their duty as men (in theory at least).[27] To what degree, then, is this ability realized among infidels? When an infidel is given unhindered ability to be able to do a holy or good work by the persuasion of God (which s/he is free to resist), *effectual grace* is also said to be operative. However, when God allows the infidel to use an "unbiased decision," this is understood as *sufficient grace*. Baxter is uncertain if any truly good or holy action can be enacted without *effectual grace*, yet he wishes to leave the door open to the suggestion that good acts might be possible by *sufficient grace*.[28] The difference, too, between a *good* and *holy* act is very confusing in Baxter's writings. In comparison with prelapsarian Adam, even the "best unregenerate man" who co-operates expertly with *sufficient grace*, cannot reach the heights of divine co-operation like that of the unspoiled Adam.[29]

This moral handicap illuminates the grave situation which infidels find themselves in and from which Baxter wishes to persuade them to exit. In order to comprehend this, it is essential to understand the *state* which hinders infidels. Concerning this *state*, Baxter's *covenant theology* must be investigated.

---

26. Baxter, *Methodus*, pt. 3, 265.
27. Fisher, "The Theology of Richard Baxter," 162.
28. Anonymous, "Richard Baxter's 'End of Controversy,'" 361.
29. Baxter, quoted in ibid., 361.

BAXTER'S COVENANT THEOLOGY

Baxter is a "federal" (*fœdus*) or "covenant" theologian, a seventeenth-century stream of Calvinism partially disclosed by the Westminster Confession. His theology is undergirded by his deep reading of medieval and Renaissance scholastics, such as:[30] Duns Scotus, William of Ockam, Juan Luis Vives, Richard Hutton, Julius Caesar Scaliger, Desiderius Erasmus, Thomas Aquinas, Guillaume Durandus, Isaac Casaubon and Thomas Bradwardine.[31]

Baxter should be understood as a *Protestant scholastic*, his knowledge of this strain of thought being incomparable in seventeenth-century England.[32] The basic orientation of Baxter's metaphysics in light of his scholastic theology is Aristotelian, but not in the traditional sense as Baxter's fellow Puritan theologian John Owen manifests. Instead, Baxter is influenced by Tommaso Campanella's revision of Aristotle and this form of scholasticism links much of Puritan covenant theology with portions of the Westminster Confession.[33]

In the spirit of Westminster covenant theology, Baxter asserts that there are four covenants initiated by God primevally:[34]

(i) *the covenant* that God made with man primordially was *the covenant of innocency*. This prelapsarian covenant contained a "promise of blessedness to Adam" on condition of him remaining pure and undefiled.[35] This covenant, as described by Packer, "with its promise of life and its penal sanctions, was intended both to animate Adam to his duty of free, deliberate, constant love for God as the highest good and, with this, to deepen his appreciation of the Love which made him and set before him such a glorious hope."[36]

Because this first covenant was abrogated due to man's rebellion against God, an alternative was required. In view of this, George Fisher accurately points out that Baxter's hamartiology is the locus around which most of his other doctrines orbit.[37]

---

30. Trueman, *Protestant Scholasticism*, 184.
31. Loane, *Makers of Religious Freedom*, 167.
32. Trueman, "A Small Step," 184.
33. Ibid., 186, 188, 190.
34. Fourfold covenant theology is a construction reminiscent of Scottish theologian Thomas Boston's *Human Nature*.
35. Anonymous, "Richard Baxter's 'End of Controversy,'" 369.
36. Packer, *Redemption*, 135.
37. Fisher, "Writings of Richard Baxter," 311.

(ii) The second covenant is *the covenant of mediation made with Christ incarnate.* As unusual as this covenant is in covenant theology generally, Baxter maintains this second covenant was manifest throughout the times of the Old Testament in the foretelling of the coming Messiah. He says, "Therefore, all the descriptions of it in the Old Testament are but prophecies and promises containing the terms of the *future* covenant; as we call a form of prayer, a *prayer*, though it be but matter fitted to be a prayer when it hath the formal act."[38]

In other words, this second covenant is a proleptic anticipation of the third covenant which anticipates Christ's future incarnation as "his entire righteousness, his complete performance of duty" so as to fulfill the law of this covenant.[39]

(iii) The third covenant God made with man was *the covenant of grace, first edition*. This covenant applies to all men, like the first covenant, and its condition was that all repent of their sin and subjectively accept the *truth* as revealed to them. The reward for this covenant's acceptance through obedience, is heaven; resisting it, results in hell. "This law of grace is in force over the heathen world" and has a curious afterword, as God addressing Abraham and his seed discloses.[40] Abraham and his family were called to be a 'peculiar people' which was manifest by the outward sign of circumcision; this was the condition of the third covenant at this particular historical stage. With Moses, the condition was "made still fuller" with the introduction of the law's stipulations. This was a renewal of God's covenant with his people, and with the ceremonial and moral laws this covenant became when combined with the Abrahamic equivalent, a "covenant of peculiarity."[41] "It is this *operous* law of Moses which Paul meant usually by the law of works, and the old or former covenant."[42] In other words, this covenant is not merely a covenant of works or nature, but a moral law, a law or covenant of grace.

For Baxter, the covenant of grace is also, in a certain sense, a covenant of works.[43] "Grace was given," says Gavin McGrath, "for this

---

38. Baxter quoted in, Anonymous, "Richard Baxter's 'End of Controversy,'" 369–70.

39. Ibid., 370.

40. Ibid., 371.

41. Ibid., 372.

42. Baxter, quoted in ibid., 372.

43. Packer, *Redemption*, 133–34.

purpose; the Spirit was bestowed in order to move men and women into further growth in the way of grace and sanctification."[44] The maturity that emerges from the reception of the grace of Christ manifests itself in work. Grace is not based on work, but work is nonetheless essential to man's response to God's grace.[45]

When the Apostle Paul later interpreted the meaning of the Mosaic law in accordance with the infidel, according to Baxter he meant that "he that will heartily observe all the burdensome ceremonies of the Mosaic law shall live. This is the *peculiar* command of that law; the *peculiar* condition of that covenant. When Paul declares, that none can be justified by the works of the law, he means, that none can be justified by 'the mere *body* of Moses's law separated from the law of grace which is its *soul*;' he cannot be justified 'by the written political law and its externals—put in opposition to Christ.'"[46]

(iv) *The fourth covenant* God made with man was *the covenant of grace, final edition*. This is the gospel of Jesus Christ. Faith in Christ's atoning work on the cross and cognition of the fulness of the New Testament message is a prerequisite for entry into this covenant. Baxter says, "The law is magnified by Christ as man hath an intellect, and will, and an executive power, and the Gospel is to work on all, so the [Apostle's] creed is the summary of our belief, and Lord's prayer of our desire, and the Christian Decalogue and institutions of our practice, as expounding what baptism generally expresseth."[47][/NL 1–4]

The gospel is deemed a law, and to partake in this covenant is to come under the law of Christ. This law does not require subsequent moral perfection necessarily, but it does require fulfilled duty "to as much perfection of duty as we are naturally capable of performing at that time."[48] In these four covenants, Baxter states, "though the word (*Law*) do principally signifie the regulating Imposition of our Duty, and the word *Covenant* doth principally signifie a *mutual Contract*; yet it is the same *Divine Instrument*, which is meant oft and usually in Scripture, by both these names . . . It is called a *Law* in one respect, and a *Covenant* in another . . ."[49] Baxter shows

44. McGrath, *Grace*, 12.
45. Ibid., 13.
46. Baxter, quoted in Anonymous, "Richard Baxter's 'End of Controversy,'" 372.
47. Baxter, quoted in ibid., 372–73.
48. Baxter, quoted in ibid., 373.
49. Baxter, *An End of Doctrinal Controversies*, 99.

his indebtedness to Hugo Grotius' governmental influence in his theology here.[50]

In Augustinian fashion, then, Baxter elevates man in his original innocence for Adam was pure in this original state; he lived and worked according to the laws of nature: "Indeed the whole sensible world and all things in it, is some way or other a sign of God's will: especially the nature of man himself, with the nature of all creatures about him, and the order in which he standeth to them; which is therefore called, The Law of Nature."[51]

Through the unspoiled covenant of innocency God activated three faculties in humanity: (1) *Vital Active Power*—under which two further faculties stem; if there is no life (*vita*) the subsequent two cannot function.[52] The ability and inclination to be active is intrinsic to mankind and from this vitality stems the (2) *Intellect*—that enables the senses, the ability to think and utilize conscience. The power to cognitively and morally discern external circumstances, while also being able to inwardly self-reflect, is given by God. Lastly, and also flowing from vital life is (3) *the Will*—that can act promptly with moral certainty and is subsequently activated when the intellect discerns the means of action.[53] These three character traits originate from God's nature as revealed in his dealings with creation and that correspond to fundamental attributes in man as his mirror in creation.[54]

Packer reveals that for Baxter the natural *Will* is an attraction towards an object when denominating it, which has Greek and mediaeval origins, not Calvinistic ones.[55] Regarding these three faculties, Baxter avers: "So the soul is *inclined* or *propense* (and not only *able*) to *Activity* as such, to *Intellection* as such, to *Volition* as such; and objectively to *Truth* as such and to *Natural Good* and *felicity* as such."[56] This was the ability which innocent man was initially endowed with.

Holmes Rolston III has rightly pointed out that the merits of man's work, not ability itself, were not *intrinsic* but *ex pacto* (without agreement) to the original covenant of innocency. Even though Calvin understood the Mosaic covenant *ex pacto*, Baxter's notion of work's merits were applied to all in Adam according to the covenant of innocency. Consequently, this

---

50. Grotius, *Annotationes*, preface.

51. Baxter as quoted in Packer, *Redemption*, 134.

52. Ibid., 106.

53. Baxter, *Catholick*, 10:202.

54. Baxter believed that the Trinity's "external works" accurately disclosed "his internal being" (Trueman, "A Small Step Towards Rationalism," 190–92).

55. Packer, *Redemption*, 108.

56. Baxter, *Catholick*, 10:201 (original emphases).

understanding did not view God drawing near to primal humanity by his grace, as in Calvin; instead, man enacted his work in the covenant of innocency by the laws of nature in the unspoiled creation.[57] Holmes correctly concludes that this covenant "is connected, moreover, with the law of nature written on man's heart so that man naturally, and apart from revelation, can know this covenant."[58] Holmes sums up this line of thought well: "Originally and ideally man lives in a relationship to God where he by his own works justifies his own existence. This is paradise as it was intended to be."[59] With sin's entrance into the world, man was rendered incapable of living and working by these laws of nature. Baxter describes, "When the soul is depraved by sin, there is no virtue left in nature to rectify that by generation, and hinder the propagation of the pravity."[60]

There is not one shard of goodness which remains in man postlapsarianly. In this, Baxter follows Calvin, yet without developing or emphasizing this in the same manner. Baxter does, however, loosely follow the Westminster Confession: "Man, by his fall, having made himself incapable of life by that covenant, the Lord was pleased to make a second, commonly called the covenant of grace."[61] Packer is incorrect to assert here that the postlapsarian covenants run on a parallel track with the covenant of grace in Baxter's theology;[62] the essence of the covenant of innocency is that it becomes *a necessary pre-condition* to the covenant of grace: "God demonstrates his grace to man only after man is unable to provide his own works."[63] Grace comes into the picture only when man's initial ability goes awry, for grace is the solution to a problem, "a second resort."[64] In other words, innocent man initially existed without any necessary requirement of God's grace, but now man must be saved by the grace of God in Christ because he could not operate, live effectively or save himself through the original covenant. Hence, grace is required because man is corrupt before God. Baxter says, "No man of brains denyeth that man hath a will that's Naturally free . . . But it is not free from evil Dispositions. It is Habitually averse to God. . . . It is

---

57. Rolston, "Responsible," 134.

58. Ibid., 134.

59. Ibid., 136–37.

60. Baxter, *Two Disputations of Original Sin*, 113. "Pravity" here refers to both guilt and pravity according to Reformed theology's understanding of original sin, meaning the punishment because of guilt. Packer, *Redemption*, 141 n. 34.

61. The Westminster Confession of Faith, http://www.reformed.org/documents/wcf_with_proofs/index.html.

62. Packer, *Redemption*, 292.

63. Rolston, "Responsible," 136.

64. Ibid.

enslaved by a sinful byas . . . You have not this Spiritual Moral Free-will, which is but your right Inclinations . . . If you had a will that were freed from wicked Inclinations, I had no need to write such Books as this."[65]

Because man is deeply contorted by sin, Baxter postulates that man requires divine redemption to fulfill his purpose upon the earth. This is reminiscent of Plato (as Calvin follows his thought) who asserts that man sins only out of ignorance because in the act of sinning man's mind is unable to existentially recognize his immorality so as to refrain from it. Calvin says, "Man is so indulgent toward himself that when he commits evil he readily averts his mind, as much as he can, from the feeling of sin. This is why Plato seems to have been compelled to consider (in his *Protagoras*) that we sin only out of ignorance."[66]

With man's abrogation of the laws of nature, he will require grace in order to work according to the common good. With this, Baxter has come full circle and revisits the issue of empowerment of infidels: "This is to be granted of all *de re*, that *Unbelievers* want not that *Natural Power* or *faculty*, which *can Believe* and *Repent* if duly *suscitated* and *disposed*: But through an *Ill Disposition* and contrary course of *action*, and want of due excitation, that Power *will not Act*, without God's special Grace."[67]

Baxter differentiates between those who have accepted Christ's special grace with those who have not, which couches the discussion of agency into the dichotomy between nature and grace. Baxter must differentiate between those who are enabled to work according to the common good (those who belong to the covenant of grace, final edition) and those who do not, because only postlapsarian work that stems from the covenants of grace can truly be *good* work. *Good* work is that which is inspired and empowered by the Holy Spirit indwelling the saints that regenerates their work. Conversely, those who cannot act uprightly manifest a lack of the indwelling Spirit. Baxter states, "It is for action that God maintaineth us and our abilities: work is the moral as well as the natural end of power. It is the act by the power that is commanded us. It is action that God is most served and honored by: not so much by our being able to do good, but by our doing it. Who will keep a servant that is able to work and will not? Will his mere ability answer your expectation? The public welfare, or the good of the many, is to be valued above our own."[68]

---

65. Baxter, *A Call*, preface.
66. Calvin, *Institutes*, II.2.22; Plato, *Protagoras*, 357.
67. Baxter, *Catholick*, 10:204 (original emphases).
68. Baxter, *Christian*, 376.

In this, Baxter explicitly relies upon Augustine's discussion of causality in human agency.[69] Augustine says, "Now the Lord Himself not only shows us what evil we should shun, and what good we should do, which is all that the letter of the law is able to effect; but He moreover helps us that we may shun evil and do good, which none can do without the Spirit of grace."[70]

God the Spirit himself is the primary cause of all moral agency which is only a secondary cause of God's agency, thus infidels do not and cannot act morally for the common good, and are not endowed with such ability unless the special grace of Christ which comes through faith and repentance, is subjectively received.

Philip Edgcumbe Hughes rightly shows that such virtue stemmed from an understanding of the sanctifying work of the Holy Spirit as part of the ongoing salvation of the saints. Only by means of the indwelling Holy Spirit can the saints enact works of virtue or can such works be brought into line with the sovereign purposes of God, honoring God according to his command. This is why the saints will be ultimately called to account for their work.[71]

Moreover, co-operation with Christ in everyday work, according to Hughes, should not be viewed as *activism*, despite the active nature of human agency, so as to guard against possible human ostentation which would negate the sanctified essence of such works.[72] It can be confidently said, then, that infidels cannot beneficially and morally contribute to the common good because they are completely disabled from doing so. Baxter's cleavage between nature and grace means that only those of the covenant of grace can truly shape the commonwealth for God's glory.

Strikingly, Baxter claims that "the Promoting of this Holy Theocratical Government is the point of Reformation that we are called to desire, by them that now plead for the Reign of Christ and the Saints."[73] Baxter dreamt of a Christianized commonwealth that would emerge first and foremost through conversions to Christ. Here it is observed how much Chalmers relied upon Baxter's holy commonwealth. Any other method of creating a "happy" commonwealth would surely fall short, for "it is no meer frame or mode of Government, Whether Monarchy, Aristocracy, Democracy, or mixt, whether the Roman, Spartan, Venetian, or any other Mode, that will make happy a Common-wealth in the hands of imprudent, *impious men*,

---

69. Baxter, *Catholick*, 10:204 ff.
70. Augustine of Hippo, "On Rebuke and Grace," 5:2.
71. Hughes, *Theology of the English Reformers*, 87–88.
72. Ibid., 89.
73. Baxter, *The Holy Commonwealth*, 223.

so much as one of the other forms; supposed worse, will do in the hands of men of prudence, and the fear of God."[74]

THEOCRACY

It is no surprise then that Baxter proposed a theocratic form of government for England in his Christian Politics because without the enforcement of God's law upon society the realization of such a dream could never take place. In Baxter's 192nd thesis of *The Holy Commonwealth*, he summarizes, "The more Theocratical, or truly Divine any Government is, the better it is."[75] Because no human version of government can compete with God's perfect rule, God's law is deemed a superior form of politics for mankind. Baxter reasons, "None can deny this, that denyeth not God: if he have more Authority than man, and be wiser and better, and more Powerful to defend his subjects, and repress his enemies, and do Justice in the execution of his Laws, then as no man should dare to compare with God, so no Government with his."[76]

He continues: "that God be King, is essential to a Theocracie. If any Infidel say that God will not condescend to be our King, and therefore this supposition deludeth us, and lifteth us up too high; I answer that he contradicteth not only the stream of Scripture that calleth God our King, but the clearest Light of Nature, which from his Creation and sole capacity, shews that by necessary Resultancy, he must Rule."[77]

Two reasons undergird Baxter's rationale for an English theocracy: (1) the reality that *God is king over all his creation* regardless of the unbelief of some. Anyone who does not acknowledge such is considered an infidel. That scripture reveals God as creator of all is appealed to without warrant and as unquestionable proof for infidels to reverse their perspective. A theocratic government also manifests (2) the *natural revelation* of God. Since God is evident to all by the works of his hands, that he is also king of creation, Baxter assumes, infidels should necessarily concede permission to rule over them by way of a Christian ruler. Consequently, Baxter argues caustically at the expense of infidels who choose to ignore such rationale. But if the two reasons above become the bedrock of society, Baxter claims the "happiest" possible society can be born.

74. Ibid., 224 (my emphasis). The nomenclature "impious men," as I will show, is the term Calvin uses of "infidels."
75. Ibid., 209.
76. Ibid.
77. Ibid., 210.

Within this divine commonwealth it is assumed that all people are God's subjects *de jure* (by right). However, this must also become a *de facto* reality, thus all are obliged to respond subjectively and positively to Jesus Christ in faith. Given that some will resist such a demand, "only the voluntary subjects of God should be the proper *Cives* or free subjects of a Divine Commonwealth; and only Christians of a Christian Commonwealth."[78] What of involuntary subjects? This is of little concern to Baxter, for "the commonest way of Constituting forms of Government is by a forced consent, (as it is commonly called); when a Conquerour, or a person of greatest strength doth constrain the weaker to consent, to escape a greater mischief."[79]

This "greater mischief" is none other than the eternal misery of hell. It is far worse, in Baxter's mind, to end up eternally bound in torment due to poor earthly decisions than being coerced to follow Christ.[80]

"A long life was to teach him [Baxter] in old age that it was not by means of Charles I nor Charles II but by the stern hand and iron rule of Cromwell that England was likely to have become 'a land of saints and a pattern of holiness to all the world.'"[81] At the end of the day Baxter's *holy commonwealth* was unrealized due to society's lack of confidence in the military credentials of Richard Cromwell who was overthrown by a coup despite being Lord Protector of the Commonwealth. Baxter, however, despite his projects' failures, proposed how vocation benefits the common good.

VOCATION FOR THE COMMON GOOD

Max Weber was accurate when he claimed that in Baxter's schema the whole world has a vocation to work for God's glory.[82] Baxter postulates, "the public welfare, or the good of the many, is to be valued above our own. Every man therefore is bound to do all the good he can to others, especially for the church and commonwealth."[83]

Working for the good of the commonwealth is no mean feat, however, because a righteous character is required and such character, Baxter insists,

---

78. Ibid., 211.

79. Ibid., 182.

80. Baxter struggled emotionally with the notion of "hell" but felt compelled to preach the threat of it nonetheless because he could not explain it away from scripture. He defined hell as "a rational torment by conscience, according to the nature of the rational subject" (Loane, *Makers*, 186).

81. Thomas, *Autobiography of Richard Baxter*, 84.

82. Weber, *Protestant*, 106.

83. Quoted by Ryken from Baxter's *Christian* in, *Worldly Saints*, 30.

can only be brought about by the indwelling of the Holy Spirit among the saints: "Uprightness of heart and life is a certain fruit of the Spirit of grace, and consequently a mark of our union with Christ, and a proof of our acceptableness with God."[84] What Baxter means here is that when good work is performed by those of impeccable character, such must be interpreted as work empowered by the subjective reception of Christ's grace. Scriptural warrants are given to demonstrate this:

> O LORD, who may abide in your tent? Who may dwell in your holy hill? Those who walk blamelessly, and do what is right, and speak the truth from their heart. (Ps 15:1–2). Those who walk righteously and speak uprightly, who despise the gain of oppression, who wave away a bribe instead of accepting it, who stop their ears from hearing of bloodshed and shut their eyes from looking on evil, they will live on the heights; their refuge will be the fortress of rocks; their food will be supplied, their water assured. (Isa 33:15–6)

Baxter comments on these biblical voices: "The upright are the pillars of human society, that keep up truth and justice in the world: without whom it would be but a company of liars, deceivers, robbers, and enemies, that live in constant rapine and hostility. There were no trust to be put in one another, further than self-interest did oblige men."[85]

As a consequence of this ethos of personal discipline and the spirit of community (which included virtues such as selflessness and mutual concern), rigor and commitment became the means of achieving the common good. Thus the poor were not dealt handouts which perpetuated their poverty, for such prolongs societal abuses, says Baxter. Instead, he advocated an alternative form of social conscience which cared for the poor by providing them with meaningful work, otherwise they remained a social menace. He did this by ensuring there were no fraudulent cases or charlatans taking unfair advantage.[86] For instance, Baxter undertook a successful program of equipping the poor for work in the Kidderminster clothing industry and this provided a deeper and more sustained approach to looking after the poor. He believed that while ensuring the former poor could themselves contribute to the commonwealth through their societal integration.[87]

---

84. Baxter, *Christian*, 737.
85. Ibid., 738.
86. Hill, *Puritanism*, 222.
87. Ibid., 138.

INFIDEL WORK AND THE *VITA CONTEMPLATIVA*

Having taken time to consider that which underpins Baxter's interpretation of infidels and their work, I shall return to his directions for graceless sinners.

Baxter appeals to infidels, some of whom believe they are true saints, but who Baxter claims otherwise due to evidence that they are not "in a penitent, pardoned state."[88] His denial of their election is further postulated with eighteen points of supposition followed by twenty directives for them to consider. One supposition goes as follows:

> You see that a religious, holy life, is every man's duty, not only as they owe it to God as their Creator, their Owner, Governor, and Benefactor; but also because as lovers of ourselves, our reason commanded us to have ten thousandfold more regard of a probable or possible joy and torment which are endless, than of any that is small and of short continuance. . . . For if it be but man's duty to manage this life, by the hopes and fears of another life, then I must follow, that either there is such a life to come, or else that God hath made it man's duty to hope, and fear, and care, and labor, and live in vain.[89]

As he arduously pens page after page of suppositions, Baxter believes that he can persuade his fellow men of the compunction to honor Christ in their work. Moreover, his general assumption is that infidels understand his theological grammar and its potency for their lives, thus indicating that he is not referring to Muslims, but those among whom he lives.[90] Baxter's reasoning often relies upon, as in the example above, subjective experience through which he might convince infidels. This is unsurprising given that Puritan spirituality was that which appealed to the things of the inward heart, as Tawney rightly summarizes: "Like an iceberg, which can awe the traveller by its towering majesty only because sustained by a vaster mass which escapes his eye, the revolution which Puritanism wrought in Church and State was less than that which it worked in *men's souls*."[91]

Once completing his suppositions Baxter offers twenty directives to infidels, an example of which goes as follows:

> If it be a matter of as great concernment to know how to do your worldly business, and to trade and gather worldly wealth,

---

88. Baxter, *Christian*, 8.
89. Ibid., 8.
90. Incidentally, when Baxter refers to Muslims he clearly calls them "the Turk."
91. Tawney, *Religion*, 199 (emphases mine).

and to understand the laws, and to maintain your honor, as it is to know how to be reconciled unto God, to be pardoned and justified, to please your Creator, to prepare in time for death and judgment, and an endless life, then let worldly wisdom have the pre-eminence. But if all earthly things be dreams and shadows, and valuable only as they serve us in the way to heaven, then surely the heavenly wisdom is the best. Alas, how far is that man from being wise, that is acquainted with all the punctilios of the law, that is excellent in the knowledge of all the languages, sciences, and arts, and yet knoweth not how to live to God, to mortify the flesh, to conquer sin, to deny himself, nor to answer in judgment for his fleshly life, nor to escape damnation! As far is such a learned man from being wise, as he is from being happy.[92]

This direction discloses Baxter's understanding of the work of infidels clearly. First, Baxter's entire outlook on work is governed by an *eschatological duality*, that which distinguishes between the present age and an eschatological age to come, "reckoning the present age as evil and the age to come as good."[93] As such, anything done on earth, in Baxter's estimation, is merely "dreams and shadows," for earthly things are "valuable only as they serve us in the way to heaven." "The world" or "the earth" in its authority and glory is viewed as having "been given over to" Satan (Luke 4:6), who is also known as "the ruler of *this world*" (John 16:11). Human culture is marred by sin and is destructively swayed by demonic impulses. Thus, the Apostle John remarks that "the world" is defined by "the desire of the flesh, the desire of the eyes, the pride of riches," which consequently ensures that "*the world and its desire are passing away*" (1 John 2:16–17). When understood in this sense, "the world" is contrary to the kingdom of God, therefore, "the world" is to be resisted while simultaneously lived within.

Second, and connected with the previous point, the worldly business of infidels is interpreted to be wholly corrupt because of its lack of reference to the triune God. Without a godly attitude to business and work, which necessitates the justifying and sanctifying powers of God, work is of absolutely no import to God. Faith is critical to work's significance in God's eyes, and even then its significance is only of instrumental value, as Baxter himself reveals: "all earthly things be dreams and shadows, and *valuable only as they serve us in the way to heaven*." Hence, because infidels cannot attract God's notice due to their lack of justifying faith, they could never serve the purposes of heaven with their work either.

92. Baxter, *Christian*, 11–12.
93. Wright, *New Testament*, 253.

Again, this reveals how great an influence Baxter was on Chalmers' theology of the good work of sinners. There are two sorts of infidel who exhibit this "damning ignorance": (1) the poor of Kidderminster who have been born into poverty and have not had the opportunity to read scripture for themselves because of their illiteracy,[94] and (2) "sensuous gentlemen, and scholars" who demonstrate an ignorance of the godly life which God will not overlook. Despite the fortunes of their upbringing, these infidels "never knew the nature, truth, and goodness of the things they speak of." Indeed, they have not taken up the opportunity to discover "the nature of faith."[95] Baxter concludes his depiction of these two types of infidel with the following: "Well, gentlemen or poor men, whoever you be that savour not the things of the Spirit, Rom viii.5–7, 13, but live in ignorance of the mysteries of salvation, be it known to you, that heavenly truth and holiness are works of light, and never prosper in the dark; and that your best understanding should be used for God and your salvation, if for anything at all."[96]

Instead of laboring without godliness, Baxter appeals to infidels to "labour first to understand the true nature of a state of sin and a state of grace."[97] The shift here is from a labor of the hands to the labor of comprehension of the true nature of their state before God. They must transfer from "pleasures, or profits, or hours of this world" to "the favour of God and the happiness of the world to come" in order for their ordinary labor to have elevated significance.[98]

Notable is Baxter's emphasis on the essential transfer required from rebellion to the covenant of grace final edition, for the infidel can only transfer by "making his [God's] favour, and everlasting happiness in heaven, our end, and Jesus Christ our way, and referring all things in the world unto that end, and making this the scope, design, and business of our lives."[99] This requirement originates with universal human reason, for it is *reason* which must be exercized in order to consider the "matters of salvation." Without the awakening of reason, "the truth is, though sinners are exceeding blind and erroneous about the things of God, yet all God's precepts are so reasonable, and tend so clearly to our joy and happiness, that if the devil did not win most souls by silencing reason, and laying it asleep, or drowning its

---

94. Ibid., 12.
95. Ibid.
96. Ibid., 13.
97. Ibid.
98. Ibid., 14.
99. Ibid.

voice with the noise and crowd of worldly business, hell would not have so many sad inhabitants."[100]

This is why Baxter appeals to the subjective experience of infidels in his long list of suppositions in *A Christian Directory*. According to Baxter, work itself, if reason is not appropriated, distracts infidels from perceiving and being able to respond to the salvation God offers in the covenant of grace. Worldly business also diverts the infidel from being able to ruminate over "the end of thy life." The difficulty of focusing on these "serious thoughts" in the "main business of our lives" is that the devil seeks to "procure" infidels to damnation by side-tracking them from the "remembrance of spiritual and eternal things."[101]

In other words, if infidels concentrate fully on worldly business for the duration of their lives, irrespective of how moral or momentous their achievements become, it is a victory for the devil because he has succeeded in averting their attention from future heavenly bliss due to the frantic nature of everyday work. Addressing those with a slavish dependence upon the needs of the world, Baxter argues, "if you seek not first God's kingdom, and the righteousness thereof; and if your hearts be not in heaven, and your affections set on the things that are above; and you prefer not your hopes of life eternal before all the pleasures and prosperity of this world, it is a certain sign that you are but worldly and ungodly men."[102]

God's kingdom here refers to an ethereal heaven. This reveals the *vita contemplativa*.

WORK AS A MEANS TOWARDS THE *VITA CONTEMPLATIVA*

I wish to focus now upon a second aspect of Baxter's theology of work: his vision for the *eschatological* ends of work. To do this I will examine how another of Baxter's seminal works, *The Saints' Everlasting Rest*, manifests the ultimate potential of the work of infidels. With particular eschatological ends in view, Baxter approaches the issue of the work of infidels in the same manner he does with its temporal meaning and I will show this through Baxter's reflections upon the parable of the sheep and the goats.

Although the benefits of work for the commonwealth take center stage in Baxter's theology of work, as I have shown thus far, Baxter also echoes Augustine's *City of God*, Cyprian's *Epistle to Donatus*, Jean Gerson's nine

100. Ibid., 15.
101. Ibid., 16.
102. Ibid., 18.

considerations, plus the moralism of both Seneca and Clement of Alexandria in his reflections upon the eschatological ends of work.[103] Recognizing the moral depravity and narcissism of the world, Baxter reverberates the sense of these seminal thinkers when emphasizing that the physical world is not the goal of human existence:[104]

> I require thee, reader, as ever thou hopest for a part in this [heavenly] glory, that thou presently take thy heart to task, chide it for its wilful strangeness to God, turn thy thoughts from the pursuit of vanity, bend thy soul to study eternity, busy it about the life to come, habituate thyself to such contemplations, and let not those thoughts be seldom and cursory, but bathe thy soul in heaven's delights; and if thy backward soul begin to flag and thy thoughts to scatter, call them back, hold them to their work, bear not with their laziness, nor connive at one neglect.[105]

In light of such a belief, Baxter recommended between thirty minutes to an hour of scheduled heavenly contemplation each day[106], and the reason for this emphasis on the *vita contemplativa*, Hugh Martin conjectures, is that Baxter wrote *The Saints' Everlasting Rest* in the naivety of his youth.[107] This claim is left unsubstantiated, and so it should, for although this early work of Baxter is seminal and has had numerous reprints, it is too convenient to reduce its contemplative content to youthful naivety, thus sidelining its importance.

When accurately interpreting *Saints' Everlasting Rest* it must be recalled that Baxter's ongoing ailments left him expecting his life to be cut short. Suffering from a serious breakdown at the age of thirty-two while serving as a parliamentary army chaplain, Baxter's health was so poor that during a five month illness he was "sentenced to death by the physicians." Hence, Baxter's reflections on the meaning of earthly life were radically minimized due to the perception of heaven's close proximity.[108] Marcus Loane describes the knock-on effect of this aptly: "But he did not return from the gates of death until with long look and rapt gaze he had viewed the land where is the rest that remains for the people of God. He had no books but his Bible

---

103. See these lengthy treatments in ibid., parts 2 and 4.
104. Packer, *Redemption*, 386–87.
105. Baxter, *The Saints,'* XI.
106. Packer, *Redemption*, 384.
107. Martin, *Puritanism*, 128.
108. Ibid., 127.

and concordance, but his heart burned within him as he mused on that theme."[109] Baxter's new emphasis was the *vita contemplativa* as he reveals:

> Thesis 198.5. In a Divine Common-wealth the Honour and Pleasing of God, and the salvation of the people are the Principal Ends, and their corporal welfare but subordinate to these. For it is much denominated *à termino vel fine*: that which is but for earthly Ends, is but an earthly Society: The Body that is not for the *soul* and subject to it, is not the Body of a man, but of a bruit: And the Kingdom that subjecteth not corporal felicity to spiritual, and temporal to eternal, and looketh not to that, is but a bruitish sensual Kingdom.[110]

A number of dualities are disclosed here and which, for Baxter, are intrinsically linked. An *anthropological duality* is revealed first; if the body is ordered above the soul, according to Baxter, the human being is reduced to a "bruit." Following Aristotle, Baxter demotes corporeality below the immaterial intellect. For example, Aristotle states, "For contemplation is both the highest form of activity (since the intellect is the highest thing in us, and the objects that it apprehends are the highest things that can be known)."[111] Why is the intellect elevated so? Because if the intellect is "divine compared with man" then the life of the intellect must be "divine compared with the life of a human being." Moreover, Aristotle asserts that the intellect is deemed "the true self" of the individual, which makes it the "authoritative and better part of him."[112] Hence, the intellect was elevated as the highest part in man, the true self, because it was concealed from all corporeal baseness, and as such, the practice of contemplation fostered this ethereal aspect of the individual. It was this faculty of man which mattered most, which mattered ultimately. Work's low value in Greek society at this time is indeed reflected by its lack of terminology for it, thus work's materiality took second place to leisurely reflection. In Aristotle's thought, heavenly contemplation through leisure demotes the material world, not least the working body. Materiality and corporeality become problematic.[113]

Secondly, following Augustine, Baxter demotes temporal life below a heavenly existence in an *eschatological duality*. Augustine remarks,

---

109. Loane, *Makers*, 173.
110. Baxter, *Commonwealth*, 212.
111. Aristotle, *Politics*, X.vii.270.
112. Ibid., X.vii.272.
113. Marshall, *Calling*, 3.

> What wonderful—*one might say stupefying*—advances has human industry made in the arts of weaving and building, of agriculture and navigation! With what endless variety are designs in pottery, painting, and sculpture produced, and with what skill executed! . . . *Who could tell the thought that has been spent upon nature, even though, despairing of recounting it in detail,* he endeavored only to give a general view of it? In fine, even the defense of errors and misapprehensions, which has illustrated the genius of heretics and philosophers, cannot be sufficiently declared. *For at present it is the nature of the human mind which adorns this mortal life which we are extolling, and not the faith and the way of truth which lead to immortality.*[114]

"Stupefying" is the term employed to describe time "spent upon nature" and its development, Augustine exclaims with feeling, because these things are merely "adorn[ing] this mortal life" and not that which leads to "immortality." Only that which directly pertains to God's grace, as opposed to nature, has any eschatological potential and worth, for only that which pertains to "immortality" or "the Kingdom" is considered the highest end. Notable in the above paragraph is Augustine's use of the term "adorns" when referring to the things of this fleeting world. With this term he intends to warn sternly against the love and worship of "the world," a sinful system, which opposes the great City of God (i.e., heaven): "that which is but for earthly Ends, is but an earthly Society."

All things that are material are automatically viewed as *temporal realities* which do not have an eschatological future for only ethereal realities which pertain to the immaterial kingdom of God can continue unblemished from earthly life to a heavenly future.[115] Because physical and material entities are so marred by sin's pervasiveness, only the soul or intellect (which is deemed the only human faculty worth redemption) can continue into heaven. This *eschatological duality* belittles much of work's own value because if corporeality and human work are solely a means to convert the masses to the glory of God, work itself is only of instrumental value, albeit the making of souls will eschatologically continue into the kingdom. Loane rightly summarizes this duality, "The woes of earth are but a foil for the joys of heaven, and hope kindles into rapture at the thought of the rest of the saints in glory."[116]

---

114. Augustine, *City of God*, 2:503 (my emphases).
115. Wright, *New Testament*, 253.
116. Loane, *Makers*, 174.

Third, a *cosmological duality* is also revealed in Baxter's thinking above when he says, "And the Kingdom that subjecteth not corporal felicity to spiritual, and temporal to eternal, and looketh not to that, is but a bruitish sensual Kingdom." Just as the soul is ordered above the body for ultimate salvation, so the kingdom of God is not viewed as an earthly or material reality but a incorporeal, ethereal one. All Baxter's reflections on materiality clearly show the physical world to be irredeemably tarnished by sin and selfishness.

The heavy overlap of Baxter's dualities of anthropology, eschatology and cosmology manifest themselves here clearly and disclose that if it is solely the human soul which is to be fostered for heaven, corporeality itself is denigrated; if corporeality is denigrated an otherworldly heaven is elevated above earthly reality; and if a heavenly destination is to be ultimately sought after, this current creation does not amount to any import in and of itself. Work therefore becomes a task simply to keep man busy until such times.

WORK'S ESCHATOLOGICAL END

> And as for minding the "affairs of the church and the state;" so far as they illustrate the providence of God, and tend to the settling of the Gospel and the government of Christ, and consequently to *the saving of our own souls* and those of our posterity, they are well worth our diligent observation; *but these are only their relations to eternity*. Even all our dealings in the world, our buying and selling, our eating and drinking, our building and marrying, our peace and war, *so far as they relate not to the life to come*, but tend only to the pleasing of the flesh, are not worthy the frequent thoughts of a Christian. *And now, doth not thy conscience say that there is nothing but heaven, and the way to it, that is worth thy minding?*[117]

The materiality of work is of no heavenly importance for Baxter but is merely instrumental in focusing Christian workers' praise to God so as to sanctify them. In deductive fashion then, the work of infidels is superfluous because its agents are not justified by faith, hence, infidel agents do not and cannot work for heavenly ends. The work of caring for the earth is not unimportant for Baxter, as seen by his commitment to the earth's stewardship through his doctrine of vocation and the common good. Here he follows in the tradition of Thomas Adams and the Puritan tradition more generally

---

117. Baxter, *Saints*, 11:12 (my emphases).

in asserting that Christians can make use of any object in creation to the glory of God.[118] But again, creation, and by that he means pristine creation unspoiled by man, is merely an instrument to focus one's praise upon its creator.[119]

Creation, then, exists precisely to enable people to look beyond it; it is a spiritual gym to train the saints to be heavenly minded while remaining of earthly use; earthly work is an activity designed to discipline the soul in order to dwell upon the God of *the heavens*. Baxter explains, "Every creature hath the name of God and of our final Rest written upon it; which a considerate believer may as truly discern, as he can read upon a post or hand in a cross way, the name of the Town or City which it points to. The spiritual use of creatures and providences, is Gods great End in bestowing them on man; And he that overlooks this End, must needs rob God of his chiefest praise, and deny him the greatest part of his thanks."[120]

If workers set their countenance away from God in their work, God is slighted and not given his due; in this theological tradition Schaeffer and Chalmers follow Baxter. Baxter clearly affirms that the worship of God is the ultimate end of human works; this leaves infidel workers with insignificant eschatological ends to their work. *Infidels can* produce *some* earthly ends to their work which only provides the Church with ample motivation to seek their conversion. Those outwith the covenant of grace cannot work for the common good let alone any eschatological ends, but nonetheless, the provision of sustenance for living, worker satisfaction and social interaction are not to be scoffed at as lesser ends of infidels' work. But without work's direct, cognizant link with heaven, there is no eternal hope for work. Thus, all that ultimately matters to God is whether workers use their work as a means to contemplative praise of God. Tawney rightly states, "Overwhelmed by a sense of his 'Ultimate End,' the Puritan cannot rest, nevertheless, in reflection upon it. *The contemplation of God, which the greatest of the Schoolmen described as the supreme blessedness, is a blessedness too great for sinners, who must not only contemplate God, but glorify him by their work in a world give over to the powers of darkness.*"[121]

Work as a utility for contemplation of God, in Baxter's formulation, is similar to Plato's cave simile (except for Baxter's estimation of the usefulness of earthly work). Plato presents his readers with a simile of an underground cave that has numerous prisoners who have lived there since birth, shackled

---

118. Keeble, *Baxter*, 110.
119. Ibid., 112.
120. Unreferenced Baxter quote in ibid., 108.
121. Tawney, *Religion*, 200 (my emphasis).

in a particular spot in the gloomy passage with their heads secured in a fixed position towards the cave entrance, a long distance ahead of them. A considerable way behind the shackled group, stretching into the subterranean bowels, shines a fire. Between the fire and the prisoners there is a short partition behind which other people carry strange artifacts and because of the fire project strange images upon the walls ahead of the prisoners. These odd silhouettes are the only reality which the prisoners know, and the small shaft of light in the distance coming in from above ground is the sole focus of the prisoners and they set their minds on getting above ground for the first time, despite the disturbing, shadowy silhouettes. Plato avers that the prisoners outdoor focal point is akin to the mind's ascent to the heavenly realm which is the source of truth and knowledge. The prisoners are so focused on the bliss above ground that they ignore their present reality altogether; it numbs them to the dastardliness of their present reality. Plato postulates that those who engage in heavenly and otherworldly contemplation "don't want to engage in human business: there's nowhere else their minds would ever rather be than in the upper region."[122]

Plato's account reveals an extreme asceticism because the prisoners take no interest or account of what is happening around them; their immediate frustrations only compel them to reflect more ardently upon the hope of eventually being above ground. In like manner, for Baxter, work becomes spiritual when it enables the worker to focus on heaven. Of course, this does not include the work of immoral trades; a trade must contribute to the common good for heavenly contemplation to count as legitimate;[123] for example, Baxter strictly forbade economic exploitation.[124] When work destroys and sins against the material world, while simultaneously contemplating heavenly rest, such contemplation is nullified because of the immorality of such outward work. When work is unrelated to celestial reflection in this way, it is demoted to insignificant material work.[125]

Infidels, then, perform work which is solely temporal by virtue of the fact that their sinful state does not allow them to focus on the realms of heaven. In fact, as Baxter's reflections demonstrate here, work which does not act as a means to contemplation of the divine is not limited to infidels. Contemplative work (*vita contemplativa*) is something that the Church of

---

122. Plato, *Republic*, 240–45.
123. Weber, *Protestant*, 108.
124. Coffey, *Cambridge Companion*, 329.
125. It is Northcott's contention that Conservative Christianity (and by this he means North American evangelicals) does not conserve the earth because it is viewed as a temporal, spoiled reality which will eschatologically pass away. Northcott, "BP, the Blowout and the Bible Belt."

the day also struggled to live up to as Baxter's incessant teaching on this point suggests. However, a major trap awaits those who fail to focus their attention upon the joy of heaven in their work—the idolatry of money. This trap also illuminates the eschatological discontinuity of the spoils of this life:

> O unreasonable, deluded men! will mirth and pleasure stay by you? will gold and worldly glory prove fast friends to you in the time of your greatest need? Will they hear your cries in the day of your calamity? At the hour of your death will they either answer or relieve you? Will they go along with you to the other world, and bribe the Judge and bring you off clear, or purchase you a place among the blessed? Why then did the rich man want "a drop of water to cool his tongue"? Or are the sweet morsels of present delight and honor of more worth than eternal rest?[126]

Infidels can turn their work towards worshipful contemplation if they choose to convert to Christ, thus fulfilling the goal of the covenant of grace. Until then, they enact their work with a lack of transcendent connection which is automatically inferior because of its un-theological focus. Those who do not devote themselves to such heavenly reflection in and through their work are to be soberly reminded of the consequences of such:

> I here charge thee, *before God, and the Lord Jesus Christ, who shall judge the quick and the dead at his appearing, and his Kingdom*, that thou make haste, and get alone, and let thy self sadly to ponder on these things: Ask thy heart. Is this true, or is it not? Is there such a day? and must I see it? . . . but then, when mens rebellious ways are charged on their souls to death; || O that thou couldst rid thy hands of it! O that thou couldst say, Lord, it was not I! Then Lord, when saw we thee hungry, naked, imprisoned? How fain would they put it off? Then sin will be sin indeed; and Grace will be Grace indeed.[127]

After quoting 2 Tim 4:1 (original and italicized part of the quote) which refers to the great eschatological judgment day, Baxter implores his readers (whether failing Christian or infidel) to prepare themselves for eternal bliss rather than the horror of being ultimately rejected. In fact, at the || symbol in the margin of the 1654 edition of *The Saints' Everlasting Rest*, Baxter indicates that he is addressing the "heathen." This sober preparation will ensure that the incognito Christ will not be overlooked as he is present among "the least of these" in the parable in the sheep and the goats. This

---

126. Baxter, *Saints*, VII.
127. Baxter, *The Saints*, 1654, Pt. 1, 64–65.

is telling, for Baxter automatically assumes that those who recognize and respond positively to Christ hidden in the poor, are those who are already Christian. Baxter continues with his reflections on the sheep and the goats when indicating that anyone who has prepared themselves well for heaven

> will be glad of anything like Grace: and if they can but produce any external familiarity with Christ, or Common gifts, how glad are they? Lord, we have eat and drunk in thy presence, *Prophesied in thy name, cast␣our Devils, done many wonderful works,* we have been baptized, heard Sermons, professed Christianity: but alas, this will not serve the turn; *He will profess to them, I never knew you: Depart from me, ye workers of iniquity.* Oh dead-hearted sinner! Is all this nothing to thee? As sure as Christ is true, this is true. Take it in his own words: Matt 25:31. *When the Son of man shall come in his Glory: and before him shall be gathered all Nations: and he shall separate them one from another as a shepheard divideth his sheep from the goats: and he shall set the sheep on the right hand, and the goats on the left*[.][128]

Baxter uses, in the same way as Chalmers does after him, another Matthean text (Matt 7:21–23) which links work and the eschaton. Baxter seeks to warn even the lukewarm saint who goes through the motions, with all the correct outward finery of Christian practice, to check his own spiritual temperature so as to attend to a wavering faith. Both the parable of the sheep and the goats and Matt 7:21–23 serve to point out that those who do not truly belong to Christ in their hearts are in danger of being eschatologically denied by him and all this will take place regardless of the Christian accuracy of outward works and practices.

Making this point abundantly clear, Baxter maintains that "neither are works a certaine Medium or evidence whereby the world can know us to be righteous, for the outward part an hypocrite may performe, and the inward part, Principles and ends of the worke they cannot discern."[129] *Inward sincerity is of utmost significance* therefore for Baxter, because work itself is insufficient to disclose its import to Christ; all work that does not stem from a righteous heart in Christ holds no weight before him. Baxter explains further: "But the great loss of the damned, will be their loss of God, they shall have no comfortable relation to him: Nor any of the Saints communion with them; As they did not like to retain God in knowledge; but bid him, Depart from us, we desire not the knowledge of they waies; so God will abhor to

---

128. Ibid., pt. 1, 65–66. "Shepheard" is Baxter's spelling of the same.
129. Baxter quoted in Crandon, *Mr. Baxters Aphorisms*, 127.

retain them in his household, or to give them entertainment in his Fellowship and Glory."[130]

Again, appealing to Matt 7:21–23 as it connects with the message of Matt 25:31–46, Baxter explains why the goats are understood as infidels:

> Now these men dare belye the Lord, if not blaspheme, in calling him by the title of *Their Father*; How boldly and confidently do they daily approach him with their lips, and indeed reproach him in their formal prayers, with that appellation, *Our Father*? as if God would father the devils children; or as if the sleighters of Christ, the pleasers of the flesh, the friends of the World, the haters of Godliness, or any that trade in sin, and delight in iniquity, were the Offspring of Heaven! They are ready now in the height of their presumption to lay as confident claim to Christ and Heaven, as if they were sincere believing Saints.[131]

In the end the goats will discover that "God is not their Father, but their resolved foe" because they chose to live a double life "in their negligence and wickedness." Consequently, those that even ate and drank in Christ's presence on earth might be excluded from his presence forever and will have to "endure the torments prepared for them."[132] This latter quote is direct from Matt 25:41 where Jesus describes the eternal destination of the goats due to their willful ignorance him.

THE JUDGMENT OF WORKS

Further reflection by Baxter upon the sheep and goats raises the issue of the basis of the final judgment; is it based upon human work or faith distinct from work? Baxter says: "Justification at the great Judgment will be according to our works, and according to what we have done in the Flesh, whether good or evil."[133] Again, he remarks that the sheep must be "Evangelically qualified" for their justification to count ultimately. As such, "If this be Justification by Works, I am for it."[134] How could it be otherwise, Baxter exclaims, when so many instances in scripture clearly relate this (Gen 7:1; 22:16–18; 2 Chr 34:26–27; Ps 91:9, 14; Matt 25:21, 23, 34–35, 40, 46; Mark 7:29; Luke 19:17, 27; John 3:22–23; 16:27; 1 John 3:22–23; Rev 3:4, 10; 7:1–5)? Hans

---

130. Baxter, *The Saints*, 1654, pt. 3, 9.
131. Ibid., 1654, pt.3, 9.
132. Ibid., 1654, pt. 3, 9.
133. Baxter quoted in, Crandon, *Mr. Baxters*, 124.
134. Baxter, *Of the Imputation of Christ's Righteousness*, 163.

Boersma adds, "Baxter appeals to various texts from Scripture which seem to grant a causality to man's actions," and indeed, the sheep and the goats is a primary example of such a biblical stress.[135]

Schaeffer and Chalmers' accounts of the judgment by works relay their reliance upon Baxter's position here, and as will be revealed, Wesley's account also. As shown earlier, Baxter states that work itself does not necessarily convey the goodness of the acts, for unless work originates from true faith in Christ, it is to be skeptically treated.

However, Baxter adds, "Justification in the last day must passe by workes to declare to the World only the righteousness & obedience of the justified, but also the equity of the Justifier, and to stop every mouth from speaking against either."[136] John Crandon is scathing in his assessment of Baxter here for he claims that Baxter has been duped by Jesuit sophistry by asserting that the latter of the two statements about justification by works is intrinsically connected with the former. Sixteen other divines criticized Baxter's thinking on this issue also with William Eyre summarizing the issue that is always at stake: Baxter argued for a "Papist" view of justification by faith and works.[137]

Baxter believes, however, that he has resisted the conclusion that justification is purely by works with his latter statement (although he saw some "light" in the former claim via the wisdom of the Jesuits). Problematically for Crandon, though, is that Baxter has not only deigned to consider this "light" but he has adopted it so as to "prove it," thus arguing that work does ultimately become "a certaine Medium and evidence to manifest both [man's righteousness and Christ's equity] to the world."[138]

Baxter expands his meaning and in so doing seeks to clarify his position:

> Here I have these things to prove: 1. that the Justifying sentence shall passe according to works as well as Faiths. 2. That the Reason is, because they are parts of the condition. . . . And most plaine is that from the mouth of the judge himselfe describing the order of the processe of that day. Mat. 25.34,35. Come ye blessed inherit the Kingdom etc. [For] I was hungry etc.[139]
>
> Both [faith and works] justifie in the same kinde of causality, *viz.* as *Causæ sine quibus non*, or mediate and improper Causes;

---

135. Boersma, *Hot Pepper Corn*, 291 n. 229.
136. Baxter quoted in, Crandon, *Mr. Baxters*, 127.
137. Allison, *The Rise of Moralism*, 162, 167.
138. Baxter, quoted in Crandon, *Mr. Baxters*, 127.
139. Baxter, quoted in ibid., 128.

or as Dr *Twisse*) *Causæ dispositivæ:* but with this difference: Faith as the principal part; Obedience as the less principal. The like may be said of Love, which at least is a secondary part of the condition: and of others in the same station.[140]

Lay the blame then where it should lye, and speak the truth: say that I deny that Faith justifieth us as the Instrumental cause, and say that I give less to Faith, and so to man in Justification then others do; and do not say I give more to other acts, as Repentance, Love &c. When you know that others make them *sine qua non*, and necessary Conditions as well as I.[141]

In light of such a defense of his own position, Boersma argues that despite Baxter's understanding of the importance of works for the eschaton, he "insists that God justifies us *because* we are just," not suggesting a direct causality. "He only wants to say that Scripture uses words that seem to imply a causality when it speaks of the *conditio sine qua non*."[142] In other words, Baxter wishes to do justice to the plain meaning of scripture, in this case the sheep and the goats, but at the same time hedge against any Protestant attacks which undermine their understanding of the doctrine of the justification by faith. This theological dilemma makes more sense of why Baxter both appears confused in his lengthy argumentation over justification and why he is considered an Arminian or Roman Catholic by his Puritan brothers.

Crandon disputes Baxter's interpretation of Matt 25:34–35 by claiming that if he had read from the beginning of the parable, the fact that the Son of Man puts "the sheep" at his right hand, this divine naming of the sheep would have come more forcefully to the fore. Had he done this, Crandon argues, it would be more apparent that Christ's sheep are those who "know his voice" (John 10:4), thus stressing "the sheep" can only be viewed as saints.

This is compounded by further biblical proofs ("For the Lord himself, with a cry of command, with the archangel's call and with the sound of God's trumpet, will descend from heaven, and the dead in Christ will rise first" [1 Thess 4:16–7], and "Do you not know that the saints will judge the world?" [1 Cor 6:2a]). Crandon is seeking by all means to avoid concluding that the parable of the sheep and the goats advocates justification by works, thus he chides Baxter for placing so much weight upon the conjunction "for" (Gk. *gar*) in verse thirty-four where it says, "Come ye blessed inherit the Kingdom etc [for I was hungry etc.]" He concludes against Baxter that

---

140. Baxter, *Aphorismes*, 1:290 (185–86).
141. Baxter, *Rich: Baxter's Confession*, 301.
142. Boersma, *Hot Pepper Corn*, 291–92 n. 229.

"what the Lord Jesus addeth, for I was hungry etc and yea thus and thus ministered unto me; will Mr. Baxter because of the word *for*, conclude these offices to be the cause of their justification?"[143] With this criticism Crandon makes apparent why Baxter was branded an Arminian by many of his Calvinist foes.

Crandon wishes to make a distinction between a judgment of works that justifies and a judgment of works that is distinct from justification, otherwise "the sheep" (identified by him as true saints) save themselves by their works.[144] What Crandon fails to appreciate is Baxter's commitment to his covenant theology, for infidels who by default do not belong to the covenants of grace will be judged according to their work precisely because they are excluded from these covenants: "But the law does not rest on faith; on the contrary, "Whoever does the works of the law will live by them"" (Gal 3:12). Baxter states, "Even Enoch, the seventh from Adam, prophesied of this, saying, Behold, the Lord cometh with then thousand of his saints, toe execute judgment upon all, and to convince all that are ungodly among them, of all their ungodly deeds which they have ungodly committed, and of all their hard speeches which ungodly sinners have spoken against him."[145]

The saints will also have their works judged but only as viewed in light of the covenant of grace to which they belong. Their inclusion in this eternal blessedness is contingent upon the perseverance of the saints' "first justification," that is their earthly, subjective response to Christ, so as to seal and subscribe this "cordial covenant."[146] The "Ye blessed" of Matt 25:34 is indicative of the security of the destiny of these saints, according to Baxter, "for though the world hath accounted ourselves so, yet certainly those that he blesseth, are blessed, and those whom he curseth, only are cursed, and his blessing cannot be reversed."[147] If the sheep have been blessed they must be the saints, claims Baxter. If God has blessed the sheep and their destiny is eternal bliss, they must indeed be the saints because the rest of the New Testament witnesses to this effect, Baxter reasons.

ANALYSIS OF BAXTER

Baxter promotes a stark view of infidels and cannot attribute any good or moral quality to their work due to their exclusion from the covenant of

---

143. Baxter quoted in, Crandon, *Mr. Baxters*, 131.
144. Ibid., 132.
145. Baxter, *The Saints*, 1824, chp. 11, 25.
146. Ibid., 1824, chp. 1V, 51.
147. Ibid., 1824, chp. 11, 26.

grace. This exclusion includes no exceptions; all must belong to the covenant of grace for their work to have any import or significance before God. His view of the work of infidels propels the necessity of the Church's mission in order for a "holy commonwealth" to be realized, a motivating factor Schaeffer and Chalmers have also taken up. Without doubt, Baxter's covenantal system provides neat and tidy distinctions between Christian and infidel work, but in doing so he makes no allowances for biblical exceptions which counter his position.

His brief discussion of effectual and sufficient grace though, is heartening. Much more stress should have been laid upon this to elucidate the potential of infidels working for the good of the commonwealth. But this very point is something which Baxter did not wish to stress. The motivation, rather, was instilled in his congregation to convert depraved infidels because without a transference to the covenant of grace (final edition) they cannot work towards the common good. Therefore, effectual and sufficient grace are downplayed by Baxter.

For example, what of the instance of the Roman centurion Cornelius who was brought up short by the visitation of an angel? Despite his understandable terror, the benevolent messenger assures him all is well because of Cornelius' generous heart towards the poor and his prayers; indeed these acts are recognized by God the spectacular creature declares (Acts 10:2–5). It is unclear whether Cornelius had any prior knowledge of the God of Israel or his Son Jesus of Nazareth. This is highly unlikely since Peter was sent to explain the gospel to him and his family for this very purpose. Moreover, given his military credentials, it is safe to assume that he was a man of Roman religion, something which went hand-in-hand with Roman militarism.[148] The angel declares to Cornelius that he is acknowledged and honored in the sight of God *because* he has performed acts of worth. As God initiates this interaction it is striking that this takes place with a soldier of little or no link to Second Temple Judaism or "the Way," and prior to his explicit experience of the Spirit. In fact, this divine acknowledgement of Cornelius' acts may have taken place regardless of how he would later respond to the Spirit and the proclaimed gospel. He is an infidel and yet God reacts positively to this man because of his actions, and irrespective of his infidel state, God interprets this man's efforts as done unto him.[149]

Baxter makes no allowances for such narratives in his covenantal theology.

---

148. Kauppi, *Foreign*, 127.
149. Weir, "Unwitting Workers," 45.

Moreover, noticeable in Baxter's account of work is that the kingdom of God will be (1) a reality that will only be inaugurated at the *eschaton*, and (2) it will not be an earthly, corporeal reality. On the first point, and in light of late twentieth and early twenty-first century theology, it is shortsighted to conclude that the kingdom of God is only inaugurated at the eschaton. Conversely, C. H. Dodd rightly points out that in the Jewish understanding contemporaneous with the gospel writers, "we may distinguish two main ways in which the Kingdom of God is spoken of. . . . 'The Kingdom of God' is a present fact. But in another sense 'The Kingdom of God' is something yet to be revealed."[150] Jesus clearly ushered in the kingdom of God as he made known to Israel: "The time is fulfilled, and the kingdom of God has come near" (Mark 1:15), and "But if it is by the finger of God that I cast out the demons, then the kingdom of God has come to you" (Luke 11:20). Paul talks of the "not yet" of the kingdom when it reaches its crescendo, its completion: "Then comes the end, when he hands over the kingdom to God the Father" (1 Cor 15:24). If Baxter had realized this "Now-Not-Yet" kingdom dynamic in the biblical narrative he would have been less likely to mistakenly dualize the kingdom of God as an ethereal heaven opposed to a way of creational life before God in the Holy Spirit amidst corruption. This leads to the second point.

Baxter is silent on Jesus' prayer about God's kingdom coming to earth where His will shall be done "*on earth as it is in heaven*" (Matt 6:10). The earth is critical to God's kingdom purposes because the fulness of the kingdom of God will be a physical, earthly reality that manifests a healed and harmonious relationship between the Creator and his creation. To reject this is to ignore deliberately the earth's importance in light of a belief in its future annihilation (*annihilatio mundi*). In the same way that things on earth affect heaven (Cain's fratricide cries out to heaven from the earth [Gen 4:10–1], and "there will more be more joy in heaven over one sinner who repents" [Luke 15:7]), so God's wish for the earth is that heaven impacts and influences it.[151] "The world" as a category (which is primarily used in a positive sense in the biblical narrative, as the promised redemption of creation speaks of[152]) steadily began to disappear among biblical authors and was exchanged for the term "the kingdom of God."

Baxter did not ignore the earth in his theology of work entirely because God was still to be honored on earth through human work, however, his strong *eschatological duality* between the present age and the age to come

---

150. Dodd, *Parables*, 30.
151. Moltmann, *God in Creation*, 183 (hereafter *GiC*).
152. Barton, *The Gospel of John*, 8–9.

paints a binary picture of the future where heaven is finally eclipsed for the salvation of *souls*,[153] a point which Baxter is at pains to emphasize.

It is not insignificant either that Baxter, and those he debated with, interpreted "the sheep" from Matt 25:31–45 to be Christians for two main reasons. First, in no way could Baxter ever view the sheep as anyone other than those justified by faith because it is they who are granted eternal bliss. Asserting that anyone but the saints will enter heaven is theologically prohibited, thus, Baxter imposes the interpretation that the saints must be the sheep as he retrospectively deduces their identity from their predicted eternal destination.

Furthermore, and in connection with the previous point, by appealing to other theological and metaphorical language (i.e., sheep), Baxter, following Crandon, is able to show that the sheep of John's Gospel, for instance, is always in reference to Jesus' disciples. Again, if nineteenth- and twentieth-century historical/critical hermeneutical method is drawn in, just because the category *sheep* is used by the author of the Fourth Gospel does not and should not mean its use in conjunction with the Matthean Gospel follows the same meaning and emphasis. After all, in the Matthean Gospel the sheep of the parable of the sheep and the goats do not even know that Christ has been mysteriously present among the needy they have so marvelously served,[154] whereas the Johannine Gospel's sheep are much more discerning as they know their shepherd's voice. Does the ignorance of the Matthean sheep indicate an alternative identity more than Baxter is willing to admit? Disappointingly, he never discusses this possibility, but given his scholastic deductive methods, this is unsurprising.

Admirable, however, is Baxter's account of the judgment of works shown in the parable of the sheep and the goats. He correctly sees the causation between good works and the eschaton, but he has to work hard to convince his fellow Puritans that he is not a Roman Catholic who favors salvation by faith and works. Baxter's attempt to synthesize both the doctrine of justification by faith and the contents of this parable is commendable, but he often comes across confused as a result. Nevertheless, at least he honestly recognized the causality in the parable between good works and the eschaton.

Baxter relegates physicality below the immaterially spiritual in a cosmological duality. Even though Christians can lapse in their work by failing to attend to sacred reflection, by being in the covenant of grace they can swiftly rectify this. The work of infidels cannot contribute anything to the

---

153. Moltmann, *GiC*, 181.
154. Hauerwas, *Matthew*, 211.

world, according to Baxter, for they are disabled without special grace. Such thinking is not uncommon among British evangelical theologies today as Francis Schaeffer and John Stott's convictions put forward in the first chapter demonstrate.

CONCLUSION

This chapter has shown that according to Baxter, the work of infidels amounts to nothing before God. All men have been given a vocation by God, but each one must recognize and fulfill it by becoming a saint. Without becoming a saint, infidels are simply unable to contribute to the common good. Thus Baxter must segregate talk of work into nature and grace. Baxter acknowledges this with his brief appendage on effectual and sufficient grace. His enormous *A Christian Directory* is front-ended with an attempt to reason with infidels to become saints. The vast remainder of the directory is an extremely detailed catechesis for how to promote the common good for Christ, for it is through active work that God is most served by. Although the *vita activa* is strongly advocated by Baxter, it can only have meaning insofar as it is enacted for God's glory, thus only the saints can transform society into a "holy commonwealth" as only they are empowered by the Spirit so to do. Schaeffer and Chalmers' theologies of the good work of non-Christians strongly resemble Baxter's equivalent, even if Schaeffer and Chalmers use nineteenth- and twentieth-century theological method respectively to establish their case.

Given his negative outlook upon the work of infidels Baxter could never envision any eschatological place for their work. When asking eschatological questions of work at a different point in his life, the *vita contemplativa* takes precedence for Baxter, following Platonic and Aristotelian traditions, which further reveals his commitment to the superiority of spirit and soul over materiality and corporeality (*cosmological duality*). Thus work only has eschatological ends which pertain to the training of the ethereal soul and its salvation. Bodily life, and by extension, work, is merely instrumental in honing the rational soul; this can only be so if a worker comes under Christ's covenant of grace and perseveres to the end. This is brought to bear particularly in Baxter's analysis of the parable of the sheep and the goats where the sheep are necessarily understood as saints precisely because of their predicted eternal destination.

With this, Stott and Chalmers' views on the parable are understood as following Baxter's line of interpretation. What Baxter offers to that which has previously been examined is that he demonstrates a measure of sophistication in his theology which Chalmers fails to match despite being influenced by Baxter. His covenantal theology, his account of the common good and the holy commonwealth are particularly impressive. Indeed, unlike Chalmers, Baxter's account is beset by less of the philosophical baggage of his day. However, like Chalmers, Baxter at least acknowledges that the final judgment in the parable of the sheep and the goats is largely based upon works, something which Schaeffer would agree with, but which Stott would not. There is only a modicum of improvement made by Baxter upon Chalmers as his account is also governed by a Pauline theology of justification by faith. Consequently, according to Schaffer, Stott, Chalmers and Baxter, the expected outcome of the good work of non-Christians is notably consistent.

What is now required is analysis of a further account which gives more credit to the work of non-Christians. By assessing John Calvin in the next chapter, my second antecedent of British evangelical theologies of work will manifest some interesting conclusions.

4

John Calvin (1509–64)
Peculiar Grace as Unsalvific, Pneumatological Empowerment for the Work of the Impious

UNTIL NOW I HAVE shown that British evangelical accounts grant very little worth to the beneficent work of non-Christians. The "man without the Bible" who has an epistemological problem (so Schaeffer), the empowerment of natural conscience (so Chalmers), or the sufficient and effectual grace (so Baxter), have all been intriguing, but less than convincing. Moreover, each chapter's theological figure has ruled out any causal connection between the good work of non-Christians and the eschaton. As shown, this is because non-Christians can only enact mundane work, whereas Christians, because of their faith in Christ, enact *evangelical works*—that which stems from their faith. Perhaps John Calvin's pneumatological account will now enable this causal link between mundane work by non-Christians and the eschaton.

A Frenchman who trained as a humanist lawyer, Calvin's conversion to the burgeoning Protestant movement eventually led him to Geneva, resulting his expulsion from France.[1] From there he set out his theological agenda while reluctantly becoming the leader of the Protestants[2] with the aim of reforming all of society.[3] This was first of all apparent through Calvin and Heinrich Bullinger's (1504–75) ecclesiological reform of doc-

---

1. An exile who was based in Strasbourg where his close friend Bucer influenced much of his ecclesiastical theology and praxis. Duchrow, "Calvin's Understanding," 60.
2. Van Til, *Calvinistic Concept of Culture*, 89.
3. Biéler *Calvin's Economic and Social Thought*, 59.

trine and praxis which necessitated compromises of economic prosperity to preserve order and commit to fresh alliances, which was met with fury from magistrates.[4]

Robert Calhoun summarizes the nature of their task well: Calvin and his compatriots' "[a]ffirmation of the sole and total sovereignty of God and the common obligation of man carried over into a steady onslaught upon political as well as ecclesiastical autocracies."[5] This reformation of society was to filter through married couples, families, social hierarchies and the natural economic order as a whole, the result being that the permeation of Christian principles would seep through each of these spheres towards a true metamorphosis of the world.

Calvin himself practiced an extensive theology of work which stemmed from the notion that all earthly life is significant to God, not merely ecclesiastical activities.[6] Bruce Gordon rightly relates, "Calvin believed that he lived each day in the presence of God and that every activity, great and small, was consecrated to the Lord, to whom he would have to give account."[7] Calvin was nothing short of obsessed with his own work, which ultimately cost him his health.[8] This same work ethic has been reborn, according to the famous thesis of Max Weber (*The Protestant Ethic and the Spirit of Capitalism*), in all those Calvin influenced personally and in the theology which bears his name, as the strapline *the Protestant work ethic* illuminates.[9]

Just prior to his move to Geneva Calvin found himself surrounded by a change from church-centered to centrally organized welfare reform.[10] Unlike the feudal and medieaval social ethics of Luther, Calvin's understanding of work was shaped by the urban contexts of Strasbourg and Geneva. For the first time in the Christian tradition, Calvin, and those he influenced, argued for the necessity of capital, credit, banking, large-scale commerce and finance. No longer was the principle of "beyond what is necessary for subsistence" adhered to because it unfairly demonized middlemen and

---

4. Gordon, *Calvin*, 123.
5. Calhoun, *Work and Vocation*, 109.
6. Biéler, *Calvin's*, xxxv.
7. Gordon, *Calvin*, 144.
8. Ibid., 144.
9. Weber admits that his thesis does not closely follow Calvin's thoughts *per se*, but rather, Calvinists from the sixteenth and seventeenth centuries. Weber, *Protestant*, 56–80, 175 n. 7.
10. Olson, *Cambridge Companion*, 154.

usurers. "The profits of trade and finance . . . [were] on the same level of respectability as the earnings of the labourer and the rents of the landlord."[11]

Such a break from Christian tradition, and a desire to help encourage industrial and commercial endeavors, demanded that Calvin tease out the social ethics of the Church amidst such an economic revolution. Calvin wished to moralize this new commercial world with his Christian religion, and wholeheartedly interact with this new context. No longer is the economic world distrusted or looked upon suspiciously, but rather, Calvin's religious teaching is the first to "applaud the economic virtues."[12] Instead, the real enemy is the *misuse and abuse* of economic prosperity, not economic prosperity itself. It is the heart's ill-disposition towards money, not money itself which is the problem.

In this chapter I wish to analyze Calvin's doctrine of grace as it empowers benevolent human action in the world rather than focusing upon his doctrine of vocation or the details of how Geneva was designed and developed. However, it is important to admit that Calvin's theology was significantly formed by its Genevan *Sitz im Leben* as I have just shown. By making Calvin's notion of grace my focus, I wish to alert readers of my intention to enquire into *how* good work takes place by the impious, for the question of divine empowerment of the impious is a significant one, as suggesting that their good work originates with God raises questions of the efficacy and durability of such work. If God inspires certain work, regardless of the faith of any human agent involved, it is imperative to enquire as to the eschatological correlation of such work.

Like Chalmers and Baxter, Calvin has numerous interchangeable terms for those who are not Christian: "the wicked," "the ungodly," "the degenerate," "the unbelieving," and "the impious." There is no dominant term in his writings, but in passages which focus upon the empowerment of the work of those who are not Christian he marginally favors the term the *impious*, a term I will use exclusively throughout this chapter.

I will investigate Calvin's account of *peculiar grace* as it pertains to human agency, and will reveal its pneumatological ground. It will be shown that it is not insignificant that Calvin employs pneumatology in connection with the virtuous and beneficent work of the impious. Consequently, it will be demonstrated that Calvin vastly improves Schaeffer, Stott, Chalmers, and Baxter's theologies, precisely by appealing to pneumatology as the ground of good work by the impious. In light of this pneumatological basis I will explore the eschatological implications of such works in Calvin and I will do

11. Tawney, *Religion*, 113.
12. Ibid., 114.

this by analyzing his understanding of the parable of the sheep and goats, as has been my established pattern for each chapter thus far.

GRACE FOR WORK

When considering Calvin's theological anthropology, which is compulsory for a theology of work, his doctrine of grace comes to the fore. Early on in his *Institutes* he says, "the beauty of the universe (which we now perceive) owes its strength and preservation to the power of the Spirit."[13] Again Calvin claims that God's grace "not only . . . sustain[s] this universe (as he once founded it) by his boundless might, [but] regulate[s] it by his wisdom, [and] preserve[s] it by his goodness."[14]

Indeed, according to Calvin, it can be said the very existence of creation relies upon the *order* of grace. In other words, much of Calvin's theology of creation stems from an understanding of the generous emanation of God's grace.[15] Herman Kuiper describes Calvin's view of preserving grace as 'universal common grace'; grace that "touches absolutely all creatures, it involves little else than the preservation of the various creatures."[16] Many who claim to follow in Calvin's theological footsteps appeal to this overarching view of grace, but my task is not to focus exclusively on the breadth of grace, even though it undergirds that which aids my argument.[17]

More telling for my purposes is Calvin's assertion that, "Man's being is a dynamic existence grounded in God's continual communication of his own graciousness."[18] Kuiper correctly identifies this aspect of grace in Calvin as "general common grace." Grace, in this form, is a universally bestowed intelligence upon man, enabling a proclivity towards God's honor.[19] For example, Calvin says, "The fact remains that some seed of political order has been implanted in all men. And this is ample proof that in the arrangement of this life no man is without the light of reason."[20]

"Implanted" grace in man aids more than reason however. "Men of sound judgment will always be sure that a sense of divinity which can never

---

13. Calvin, *Institutes*, I.13.14.
14. Ibid., I.2.1.
15. Rolston, "Responsible," 137.
16. Kuiper, *Calvin*, 181.
17. For example, Weber, *Foundations*, 503ff.; Moltmann, *GiC*, 335 n. 31.
18. Rolston, "Responsible," 138.
19. Kuiper, *Calvin*, 183–84.
20. Calvin, *Institutes*, II.2.13.

be effaced is engraved upon men's minds."[21] The reason for this propensity among man is that he was created in God's image (*imago Dei*) to work and this involves, among other things, remaining "subject to God."[22] This designation of man means he was deemed a lord and master of the earth, otherwise known as "God's vice-regent in the government of the world."[23] With this great responsibility, man was to acknowledge that "God himself has demonstrated, by the very order of creation, that he made all things for the sake of man."[24] Thus, "[g]enerally the whole order of this world is arranged and established for the purpose of conducing to the comfort of men,"[25] which is why God made man for work. For example, "Moses now adds, that the earth was given to man, with this condition, that he should occupy himself in its cultivation. Whence it follows that men were created to employ themselves in some work, and not to lie down in inactivity and idleness. This labor, truly, was pleasant, and full of delight, entirely exempt from all trouble and weariness."[26]

Such was the carefree and pleasant way of work in a prelapsarian world.

THE NECESSITY OF GRACE FOR WORK

Because of man's misguided work in the garden, sin entered the world, and consequently the order of grace became *dis*ordered, confused and distorted. Nevertheless, God's plans for creation did not digress, according to Calvin, because without his incessant 'universal common grace' creation would simply cease to exist.[27] Man's response to God in his work because of sin, however, poses a potential problem for whereas man worked with an upright life of "rectitude" in unblemished relationship with God prior to sin, work became the toil of labor because of sin's curse.[28] Thus work now takes a "pedagogic" shape so as to awaken man to repentance, for if work awakens man to his skewed life without God it can become the task it was originally intended.[29] Calvin describes the rationale underpinning this pedagogy:

21. Ibid., I.3.3.
22. Calvin, *Genesis*, 2.16.
23. Ibid., 1.26.
24. Ibid., 1.26.
25. Calvin, *Commentary on Psalms*, 8.6.
26. Calvin, *Genesis*, 2.15.
27. Rolston, "Responsible Man," 139.
28. Calvin, *Institutes*, I.2.1.
29. Hart, "The Teaching of Luther and Calvin about Ordinary Work: 2. John Calvin," 122.

> It is, however, to be observed, that they who meekly submit to their sufferings, present to God an acceptable obedience, if, indeed, there be joined with this bearing of the cross, that knowledge of sin which may teach them to be humble. Truly it is faith alone which can offer such a sacrifice to God; but the faithful the more they labour in procuring a livelihood, with the greater advantage are they stimulated to repentance, and accustom themselves to the mortification of the flesh[.][30]

Not all workers are inclined to mortify the flesh in their work according to the sacrifices of Abel however. Some simply refuse to offer their work to God at all; some offer it to other religious gods and systems, while others still are ignorant of the need to orientate their active lives to God. In other words, these workers work without *Christian* faith. In light of this, Calvin provides a pedagogical template for rightly directed work in the *Geneva Catechism*:

> Q. What is the true method of rendering him [God] due honour?
>
> A. It is to put our whole trust in him; to serve him by obedience to his will, *all our life;* to call upon him in all our necessities, seeking in him salvation, and every good thing which can be desired; and finally, to acknowledge, both in the heart and with the mouth, that he is the sole author of all blessings.[31]

Note here four aspects which the active life requires: (1) faith, (2) obedience, (3) love and (4) gratitude. All four are regularly appealed to by Calvin with regard the potential of faith among the impious, yet without systematic analysis.[32] In view of those who inveigh against or are ignorant of the Genevan Catechesis, Calvin recasts a vision of God's grace and implores his readership to a godly reorientation of their lives. He employs Zech 12:10, a prophecy in which God declares, "And I will pour out a spirit of compassion and supplication on the house of David and the inhabitants of Jerusalem, so that, when they look on the one whom they have pierced, they shall mourn for him, as one mourns for an only child, and weep bitterly over him, as one weeps over a firstborn" (Zeph 12:10).

Commenting upon this, Calvin says, "God deals very bountifully with the unbelieving, but they are blind, and therefore he pours forth his grace without any benefit, as though he rained on flint or on arid rocks. However

---

30. Calvin, *Genesis*, 3.19.
31. Calvin, *The Catechism*, 10 (my emphasis).
32. Rolston, "Responsible," 143.

bountifully then God bestows his grace on the unbelieving, they yet render his favour useless, for they are like stones."[33]

This impious segment of man is continually inclined to utilize God's grace with ingratitude, and for evil ends, despite the fact that it gives his work impetus. As Rolston III aptly puts it, "Man from his side manufactures sin out of God's grace."[34] Work only reaches its full potential, in light of sin, when it is offered to God in recognition of his sovereign power over creation, for without the promotion of God's glorious name work performed by the impious is rendered spurious.[35] Calvin argues this point from Rom 1:21 ("for though they knew God, they did not honor him as God or give thanks to him, but they became futile in their thinking, and their senseless minds were darkened"):

> He [the Apostle Paul] plainly testifies here, that God has presented to the minds of all the means of knowing him, having so manifested himself by his works, that they must necessarily see what of themselves they seek not to know — that there is some God; for the world does not by chance exist, nor could it have proceeded from itself. But we must ever bear in mind the degree of knowledge in which they continued; and this appears from what follows.... Since men have not recognized these attributes in God, but have dreamt of him as though he were an empty phantom, they are justly said to have impiously robbed him of his own glory.[36]

Because not all men work with Christian faith, it might be easy to assume that Calvin segments this discussion into a dichotomy of nature and grace. However, Calvin chooses not to invoke Thomas Aquinas' (1225–74) dichotomy of nature/grace when discussing man's response to God in their lives.[37] Instead, he insists that God's "general common grace" empowers man as a whole despite sin's ubiquity, and this is a "non-saving grace" which does not regenerate persons.[38]

The breadth of this grace to empower man is emphasized further by Calvin when he says, "God may reveal his concern for the whole human race, but especially his vigilance in ruling the church, which he deigns to

---

33. Calvin, *Commentaries on the Twelve*, 12:10.
34. Rolston, "Responsible Man," 140.
35. Kuiper, *Calvin*, 183–84.
36. Calvin, *Commentaries on Romans*, 1:21.
37. Van Til, *Calvinistic*, 98.
38. Kuiper, *Calvin*, 190–91.

watch more closely."³⁹ Even though there is a subjective difference of faith status between the Church and the impious, God's "general common grace" remains ubiquitous in its operation.⁴⁰

PECULIAR GRACE

In light of God's generous grace for human agency, Calvin's account of the work of the impious or *common grace* describes the *inspiration* for virtuous work, albeit Calvin never uses this latter term. In actual fact, later Calvinists coined the term *common grace* even though it is often incorrectly attributed to Calvin.⁴¹ Instead, he uses the term *peculiar grace* to describe the empowerment of the beneficent work of the impious, which is not a systematically expounded topic in Calvin but one which is mentioned in a frequent but haphazard manner.⁴² I will concentrate my attention upon the impious who are inspired by *peculiar grace*, a dispensation of grace by which Christians are also empowered.

Calvin describes *peculiar grace* for the impious in the following manner:

> In every age there have been persons who, guided by nature, have striven toward virtue throughout life. I have nothing to say against them even if many lapses can be noted in their moral conduct. For they have by the very zeal of their honesty given proof that there was some purity in their nature . . . These examples, accordingly, seem to warn us against adjudging man's nature wholly corrupted, because some men have by its prompting not only excelled in remarkable deeds, but conducted themselves most honourably throughout life. But here it ought to occur to us that amid this corruption of nature there is some place for God's grace; not such grace as to cleanse it, but to restrain it inwardly.⁴³

---

39. Calvin, *Institutes*, I.17.1.
40. Biéler, *Calvin's*, 166.
41. Tellingly, Scottish Calvinist evangelicals, unlike Dutch Calvinists, have not historically adopted the doctrine of "common grace." The influence of Barth in Scotland somewhat prevented the deployment of such a concept. However, two exceptions are found: Murray (1898–1975), *Collected Writings of John Murray*, 2:93–122; and Rutherford House's first librarian: Needham, *Common Grace*.
42. Kuiper, *Calvin*, 177.
43. Calvin, *Institutes*, II.3.3.

Although Calvin latterly mentions the restraining qualities of this grace to prevent man from complete civic chaos, his emphasis is mainly upon *the beneficent ability* God graciously endows on those outside the Church. Here, Calvin honestly recognizes the deeds of virtue which the impious manifest, and which are frequently observed by society.

Calvin's comment on the unsalvific nature of this grace is also significant as this speaks first and foremost of Calvin's Reformation context. Calvin, like Luther, and despite his elevation of the meaning and significance of ordinary work (particularly through the abolition of the hierarchy of callings[44]), makes no mistake in ensuring that work itself is viewed unsalvifically.

Bavinck sums Calvin up well: "To the Romanist view he brings in principle the same objection that bears against the pagan conception: the doctrine of the meritoriousness of good works is a delusion."[45] This objection is put forward because Calvin believes the Roman tradition has minimized the depravity of the human condition, and has also circumvented his other concern, the potential for ostentation in work towards salvation. That man might interpret his good works in society as acts of his own conjured freewill was a notion Calvin wished to quash, thus *peculiar grace* empowering good work among the impious must correspond to an *unsalvific* account of grace because there must be no avenue made for salvation through work.

Because Reformers such as Calvin felt compelled to ensure the Roman Church understood the error of a faith and works-based salvation, the Counter Reformation at the Council of Trent (1545–63) sought, among other things, to deliberate over the Protestant contentions of Calvin and others about their doctrine of justification. Resisting Protestant critiques after some consideration, the Roman Church reiterated their original position on works as it relates to justification: "If anyone says that all works done before justification, in whatever manner they may be done, are truly sins, or merit the hatred of God; that the more earnestly one strives to dispose himself for grace, the more grievously he sins, let him be anathema."[46]

Given that the Roman Church had distorted the means of salvation, according to Calvin, it is no wonder he had such an aversion to the potential of human ostentation in work. Unsurprisingly therefore, Calvin draws upon Augustine (354–430) who in the following quotation wishes to counter pride in human agency, "It has been evidently explained, my brethren, where God would have us to be humble, where lofty. Humble, in

---

44. See: Stevens, *Other*, 3–49.
45. Bavinck, "Calvin," 120–21.
46. *The Canons and Decrees of the Council of Trent*, Canon VII.

order to provide against pride."[47] Augustine's passive virtues of submission, humility, patience, self-denial and cross-bearing, were deemed outstanding human virtues by Calvin in light of a God who empowers good works by grace.[48]

Indeed, Ian Hart goes as far to claim that Calvin's theology of work is founded upon self-denial,[49] whereas Bruce Gordon has contended that Calvin actually led a life of simplicity and tasteful style rather than one of austere urban asceticism.[50] Susan Hardman Moore confirms Gordon's view with respect the pleasure Calvin enjoyed in the arts, food and wine.[51]

Whichever view opted for here, the restraint of sin among the work of the impious is characteristic of Calvin's notion of *peculiar grace*, for without God's gracious restraint of man an unbridled selfish lust would dominate the earth without respite. Because of God's *peculiar grace*, however, man is kept in check so that he does not incessantly plunge towards a self-made hell. For example, God's gracious foiling of Egyptian wickedness and barbarism during Israel's exodus demonstrates the restraining element of peculiar grace:

> For it is the Lord who gives us favor, not alone among those who wish us well, but even 'in the eyes of the Egyptians' [Ex. 3.21]; indeed, he knows how to shatter the wickedness of our enemies in various ways. For sometimes he takes away their understanding so that they are unable to comprehend anything sane or sober, as when he sends forth Satan to fill mouths of all the prophets with falsehood in order to deceive Ahab [1 Kgs 22:22].[52]

Moreover, despite the risk of abusing God's grace in everyday work, *peculiar grace* is still universally available to man, and Calvin discusses this when commenting upon John 1:9 ("The true light, which enlightens everyone, was coming into the world"): "From this *light* the rays are diffused over all mankind, as I have already said. For we know that men have this peculiar excellence which raises them above other animals, that they are endued with reason and intelligence, and that they carry the distinction between

---

47. Augustine, "Exposition on Psalm 131," 5.
48. Bavinck, "Calvin," 121.
49. Hart, "Calvin," 121.
50. Gordon, *Calvin*, 147.
51. Hardman Moore, "Calvinism and the Arts," 75.
52. Calvin, *Institutes*, I.17.7.

right and wrong engraven on their conscience. There is no man, therefore, whom some perception of the eternal *light* does not reach."[53]

In this case Calvin talks of a "peculiar excellence" given to man to act morally in the world, and this excellence sets him apart from the animal world because man is able to reason and understand in a manner impossible to non-human mammals. Vincent Bacote rightly remarks, "Here Calvin describes the . . . means of human conscience but also the provision of reason and intelligence, which speaks to the issues of moral capacity and possibility of the study of nature, history, and society with benefits for all."[54]

Karl Barth (1886–1968), however, who stood in the tradition of Calvin, takes a contrary stance to Calvin's interpretation of John 1:9 as he believes this "light" should not be understood as a universal gift in man. If one takes Calvin's view, Barth posits, then one can claim that all mankind has some form of light implanted within him. Rather, only when a person subjectively and positively responds to the call to follow Jesus does this light (of which Jesus himself is the source) enable the agency of man. Barth concludes, "Only in this way and to this extent does he himself [Jesus] shed light so that others come to faith through him—only as he is illumined by this true and primary light."[55]

Barth's argument is insufficient here as he seeks to guard against any form or basis for natural theology, and by interpreting John 1:9 in this way he is successful in responding to his contextual and theological combatants (Nazism, Emil Brunner), but he surrenders biblical accuracy as a result. Having said that, Barth's argument appears to find initial support when the Apostle John states a little later in the same chapter: "But to all who received him, who believed in his name, he gave power to become children of God" (John 1:12). Despite Barth's insistence here, the inclusion of the phrase "children of God" does not exclude that "[t]he true light, which enlightens everyone" is a simultaneous universal bestowal upon man. In this regard, verse ten of the prologue to the Fourth Gospel states, "the world did not know him," thus revealing that although there is a universal illumination of man by the divine Word (or peculiar grace), this does not guarantee each and every person's co-operation with God through faith.

---

53. Calvin, *Commentary on John*, 1:9.
54. Bacote, *Spirit in Public*, 96.
55. Barth, *Witness*, 61–62.

THE GIFTS OF THE IMPIOUS

Man as a whole, then, receives such "peculiar excellence" or grace from God's Spirit for his work, but in order to excavate further how this grace functions among the work of the impious, Calvin's notion of nature and grace is eventually required. Only with the discussion of *gifts* to enable the work of the impious is it accurate to interpret Calvin's reliance upon Aquinas' conception of nature and grace. It was Aquinas who claimed:

> Now all virtues, intellectual and moral, that are acquired by our actions, arise from certain natural principles pre-existing in us, as above stated (1; 51, 1): instead of which natural principles, God bestows on us [the "pious"] the theological virtues, whereby we are directed to a supernatural end, as stated (62,1). Wherefore we need to receive from God other habits corresponding, in due proportion, to the theological virtues, which habits are to the theological virtues, what the moral and intellectual virtues are to the natural principles of virtue.[56]

Practical atheists, other religious adherents and ignorant workers, come under Calvin's designation of "nature." Calvin relies upon Aquinas' conception of nature and grace because it plays an enormous role in designating parallel ways of human manoeuvring before God.[57] This dichotomy of nature and grace, Aquinas remarks, reveals that on the nature side of this dichotomy "one is common, where He loves "all things that are" (Wisdom 11:25) and thereby gives things their natural being. But the second is a special love, whereby he draws the rational creature above the condition of its nature to a participation of the Divine good."[58]

What Aquinas states here is that both those in and outside the Church have their source for beneficent agency in God, but one is clearly empowered and loved more. What must also be identified here is that the nature/grace dichotomy is delineated into three further formulary subsets: (1) grace and providence—by which Aquinas outlines how those outwith God's special grace can perceive truth; (2) pristine nature and corrupt nature—"whether humans can do or will any good without God's grace";[59] and (3) the distinction between the natural and the supernatural—the difference between universal and especial giftings from God. Aspects 1 and 3 then are interwoven together to form a sophisticated conception of nature and

---

56. Aquinas, *Summa Theologica*, Prima Secundæ Partis, qu. 63, art. 3, obj. 3.
57. Mawson, "Understandings of Nature," 349.
58. Aquinas, *Summa*, I.II, 110.1.
59. Ibid., qu. I.II, 109.2.

grace, and it is this combination which Calvin draws upon in his theology of *charismata* for the impious. The roots of mundane work versus *evangelical works* emerges here in Aquinas. This is a very important differentiation, and one which clearly grades the agency of the impious as inferior.

In contrast to Augustine's account of the four virtues of love,[60] Aquinas constructed an upper "superstructure" of theological virtues and a lower order of "natural" virtues to account for pious and impious agency respectively.[61] What are considered *virtues* for Aquinas, however, Calvin reworks into *gifts*, and in so doing accounts for good works performed by the impious. The gifts of the impious in question are "apprehension," "reason," "rationality," "perception," "judgment" and "common sense." Calvin describes: "Hence, with good reason we are compelled to confess that its beginning is inborn in human nature. Therefore this evidence clearly testifies to a universal apprehension of reason and understanding by nature implanted in men. Yet so universal is this good that every man ought to recognize for himself in it the peculiar grace of God."[62]

These gifts are endowed in the impious despite their absence of relationship with God the Father, and consequently, they are solely understood as "natural gifts." Calvin explains his version of the dichotomy:

> The natural gifts were corrupted in man through sin, but that his supernatural gifts were stripped from him . . . Therefore, withdrawing from the Kingdom of God, he is at the same time deprived of spiritual gifts, with which he had been furnished for the hope of eternal salvation. From this it follows that he is so banished from the Kingdom of God that all qualities belonging to the blessed life of the soul have been extinguished in him, until he recovers them through the grace of regeneration ['. . . jusques à ce qu'estant regeneré par la grâce *du saint Esprit*' '. . . of the Holy Spirit'].[63]

60. See Augustine, *City of God*, chap. 15.
61. Ramsey, "Theory of Virtue," 181.
62. Calvin, *Institutes*, II.2.14.
63. Ibid., II.2.12 (emphasis mine). The Ford Lewis Battles' translation completely omits the direct attribution of good work performed by the "impious" to the Holy Spirit which I have included in brackets from the French version. This oversight of translation nullifies Calvin's intended pneumatological explanation entirely. I am highlighting the French rather than the Latin because other than his first edition of the *Institutes* in Latin (March 1536), Calvin's subsequent four editions were in French, a language which was rapidly growing in importance for both theology and philosophy at the time. It is thought that the first French edition was originally only six chapters and became a basic catechetical and apologetic text for France's King Francis I. Wright, "John Calvin" and Bebbington and Noll *Biographical Dictionary of Evangelicals*, 111–12.

Noted here is the fact that the grace of regeneration (special grace) does not empower the lives of the impious, disclosing that the form of grace which the pious receive is different in kind and degree from those who do not have faith in Christ. The supernatural gifts which were stripped from man because of sin are: faith, zeal for holiness, righteousness, charity towards one's neighbor, and love of God.

Consequently, the results of sin are such that man is no longer the mirror of God (*imago Dei*) for he could only be so while living and working in perfect obedience to him. As André Biéler puts it, "By removing himself from his Creator's authority, man loses the rights God conferred on him as a vassal over nature and the world."[64] In short, for the impious, work is no longer about the responsible stewardship of creation as God's servants, thus man's natural gifts of "soundness of mind" and "uprightness of heart" were corrupted within him. Leroy Nixon exaggerates when he says, "The prevailing state of mind of the impious is brutish oblivion."[65]

Hart recognizes Calvin's notion of pneumatologically empowered human agency here; whenever there is a beneficial skill disclosed by the impious, it should be recognized as "given to him by the Holy Spirit."[66] These skills should be understood as "good" and "free gift[s]" which stem from God's Spirit, "because it [grace] is bestowed indiscriminately upon pious and impious, it is rightly counted among natural gifts."[67] This indiscriminate impartation of the grace of God demonstrates that man is required to be an exhibition of God's natural gifts so as to benefit society.

Because of the handicapped ability of the impious, Richard Mouw warns that a hermeneutic of *caution* is required against giving unrestrained credit—or even worse—showing solidarity to the impious in their work. Not that he supports a hermeneutic of suspicion, but rather he believes there should be a critical openness to their efforts.[68] Mouw states, "we are nervous about giving the impression that there is something 'automatic' about the unregenerate person's ability to think good thoughts or to perform laudable deeds."[69]

However, Calvin argues that by the natural gifts of the impious beneficial scientific endeavors have been added to the world:

---

64. Biéler, *Calvin's*, 163.
65. Nixon, *John Calvin's Teachings*, 146.
66. Hart, "Ordinary Work: Calvin," 126.
67. Calvin, *Institutes*, II.2.14.
68. Mouw, *He Shines*, 93.
69. Ibid.

> Whenever we come upon these matters [of science] in secular writers, let that admirable light of truth shining in them teach us that the mind of man, though fallen and perverted from its wholeness, is nevertheless clothed and ornamented with God's excellent gifts [*ne laisse point toutesfois d'être ornée de beaucoup de dons de Dieu*]. If we regard the Spirit of God as the sole fountain of truth, we shall neither reject the truth itself, nor despise it however it shall appear, unless we wish to dishonour the Spirit of God. For by holding the gifts of the Spirit in slight esteem, we contemn and reproach the Spirit himself.[70]

Three points emerge from this passage: (1) the natural gifts given by God are understood as gifts of the Spirit—gifts that enable ordered societal living; (2) the Holy Spirit is revealed as the "Spirit of truth" as in Jesus' teaching (John 14:17). Such an indwelling of the Spirit in all mankind through natural gifts can periodically enable the impious to be "captivated by love of truth" by virtue of the Spirit's presence.[71] This love of truth is the very impulse which activates beneficial work for the world regardless of faith in Christ. (3) It is a matter of necessity that Calvin conceives these natural gifts of the impious pneumatologically, for to attempt otherwise is to flirt with blasphemy. From what other place should the source of goodness in man be located than in God's Spirit? Thus it can said that the impious can work in the Spirit by their natural gifts, unwitting of his presence. This thought is held in tension by Mouw, with Calvin's insistence that "unless we wish to dishonour the Spirit of God . . . by holding the gifts of the Spirit in slight esteem, we contemn and reproach the Spirit himself."[72] This is an important corrective to guard against a polemic skepticism of pneumatological human agency among the impious, a corrective Mouw struggles to uphold.

Attributing human abilities that benefit the common life to the Holy Spirit, deepens the potency of Calvin's overall argument, for attributing the good works of the impious to God himself heightens the salience of their earthly contribution. As a result, Calvin unfurls his pneumatological understanding of these natural gifts with optimistic language about the potential of the impious. Law, philosophy and mathematics are elevated as chief examples of this:

---

70. Calvin, *Institutes*, II.2.15. Notice that the French stresses the *abundance* rather than the *calibre* of God's gifts for the "impious" as the Ford Lewis Battles' translation does.

71. Ibid., II.2.12.

72. Ibid., II.2.15.

What then? Shall we deny that the truth shone upon the ancient jurists who established civic order and discipline with such great equity? Shall we say that the philosophers were blind in their fine observation and artful description of nature? Shall we say that those men were devoid of understanding who conceived the art of disputation and taught us to speak reasonably? Shall we say that they are insane who developed medicine, devoting their labour to our benefit? What shall we say of all the mathematical sciences [*autres disciplines*]?[73]

Moreover, the good works of the impious are manifest in other spheres of work: "If the Lord has willed that we be helped in physics, dialectic, mathematics, and other disciplines, by the work and ministry of the ungodly, let us use this assistance. For if we neglect God's gift freely offered in these arts, we ought to suffer just punishment for our sloths."[74]

Of the arts Calvin says, "The invention of the arts, and of other things which serve to the common use and convenience of life, is a gift of God by no means to be despised, and a faculty worthy of commendation."[75] Again, art is not a skill which emanates from man's innate abilities: "The poets are more correct who acknowledge that all which is suggested by nature ought comes from God; that all the arts emanate from him, and therefore ought to be accounted divine inventions."[76]

Further, Calvin saw art as a pedagological tool that proleptically anticipates the fulness of the kingdom but which is earthly in nature.[77] Abraham Kuyper rightly concurs with such an interpretation of Calvin. He states: "Calvin esteemed art, in all its ramifications, as a gift of God or more especially, as a gift of the Holy Ghost; that he fully grasped the profound effects worked by art upon the life of the emotions[.]"[78]

Calvin reveals this once more, "For, quite clearly, the mighty gifts with which we are endowed are hardly from ourselves; indeed, our very being is nothing but subsistence in the one God."[79] The "we" here is in reference to man generally, and unlike Mouw, Herman Kuiper acknowledges the voice of optimism in Calvin towards the impious without apology: "There are

---

73. Ibid., II.2.15.
74. Ibid., II.2.16.
75. Calvin, *Genesis*, 4.20.
76. Calvin, *Moses—Vol. 3*, Exodus 31.2.
77. Van Til, *Calvinistic*, 110.
78. Kuyper, *Calvinism*, 206.
79. Calvin, *Institutes*, I.1.1.

some who never taste one drop of saving grace and yet manage to conduct themselves honorably throughout the whole course of their life."[80]

In H. Richard Niebuhr's renowned text, *Christ and Culture*, Calvin is included within the Augustinian tradition in the chapter entitled "Christ the Transformer of Culture." Calvin rightly suggests the eventual redemption of creation where "the church and society will merge—everyone will have rediscovered their real goal: to live to the glory of God in communion with him and governed by him."[81]

According to Niebuhr, who is generally fair to Calvin in his brief excursus while also skirting past him too hastily, Calvin's view of the work of man "note[s] that it [sin] is deeply rooted in the human soul, that it pervades all man's work, and that there are no gradations of corruption, however various its symptoms. . . . Yet they believe also that such culture is under God's sovereign rule[.]"[82] In other words, the cultural mandate to "rule and subdue the earth" and to "tend and keep the garden" is still a binding mandate. In spite of a groaning creation alienation, and despite the loss of *imago Dei*, there remains the imperative to shape culturally the earth in obedience to Christ says Niebuhr of Calvin.

Calvin continues his investigation of those empowered by natural gifts by enquiring about those who deceive by the *appearance* of good works. Calvin asks, "Yet what if the mind had been wicked and crooked, and had followed anything but uprightness?"[83] Simply put, if evil underlies apparent good works, surely good cannot be attributed to such work. Calvin relates, "As for virtues that deceive us with their vain show, they shall have their praise in the political assembly and in common renown among men; but before the heavenly judgement seat they shall be of no value to acquire righteousness [*justice*]."[84]

Even though deception exists in some work of many impious men, it would be nonsensical to deny that all men periodically enact impressive works with right intentions. Modestly, man is at least able to abide by his own laws and thus can promote civil order because he has an aptitude for learning and transmitting both liberal and manual arts. Calvin says, "Then follow the arts, both liberal and manual. The power of human acuteness also appears in learning these because all of us have a certain aptitude. But

80. Kuiper, *Calvin*, 177.
81. Biéler, *Calvin's*, 235.
82. Niebuhr, *Christ*, 191.
83. Calvin, *Institutes*, II.3.4.
84. Ibid., II.3.4. Calvin uses the French term *justice* to describe the future hope of man in the judgment of such works. The Ford Lewis Battles' translation renders it *righteousness*, which is a synonym of *justice*.

although not all the arts are suitable for everyone to learn, yet it is a certain enough indication of the common energy that hardly anyone is to be found who does not manifest talent in some art."[85]

This ability to produce science, art and civilization by the power of the Spirit is performed in a tripartite manner, enabling Calvin to explain both the work of the Spirit in man generally and the pious/impious dichotomy effectively.

Calvin appeals in his commentary on Ephesians to the following scriptures as biblical warrant of the pneumatological empowerment of the impious: "You have granted me life and steadfast love, and your care has preserved my spirit [*ruach*]" (Job 10:12); "When you send forth your spirit [*ruach*], they are created" (Ps 104:30); "In him we live and move and have our being" (Acts 17:28).

In view of such scriptures, Alasdair Heron insists that what is common about such biblical quotations is that man exists "by his very nature in relation to God. *Ruach* (and "holy *ruach*") refer both to God acting upon man, and to the result of that action in man himself."[86] Kirsteen Kim concurs with Heron when she states the following: "*Ruach* can denote the life-force of an individual (e.g., Judg 15:19) or group (e.g., Num 16:22), but it is essentially from God."[87] In this sense, Calvin's appeal to these biblical texts is corroborated by Heron and Kim's depiction of the role of the Spirit (*ruach*), which essentially reveals Calvin's understanding of *peculiar grace*. However, in order to protect himself from getting too carried away, Calvin's biblical excursus concludes with an appeal to the Apostle Paul's words, "They [the impious Gentiles of Ephesus] are darkened in their understanding, alienated from the life of God because of their ignorance and hardness of heart" (Eph 4:18).

Calvin believes that according to the Apostle Paul only the pious cognizantly interact and are indwelt by the Holy Spirit to a superior degree in their work, a degree which the impious do not experience. This greater intensity of the Holy Spirit is the *eminence* of the life of God in the pious. *Peculiar grace* among the impious, on the other hand, is present but unsalvific by comparison because of the hardness of their unbelieving hearts. In reference to Old Testament occurrences of the Spirit of creation, the impious have a general ontological empowerment, not a radical pneumatological enhancement or seal of the Spirit which the pious experience through faith in Christ.

---

85. Ibid., II.2.14.
86. Heron, *The Holy Spirit*, 7.
87. Kim, *The Holy Spirit*, 11.

Nevertheless, the natural gifts among the impious provide them with some semblance of goodness for a particular purpose.

THE COMMON GOOD

Calvin's positive tone (which is unique in its positivity among the Reformers) towards the impious avers that work is "for the common good of mankind" and this is why the Holy Spirit "distributes to whomever he wills" his gifts to enable this.[88] Heard here are echoes of the Apostle Paul, who says, "To each is given the manifestation of the Spirit *for the common good* . . . All these are activated by one and the same Spirit who allots to each one individually just as the Spirit chooses" (1 Cor 12:7, 1; my emphasis). The Apostle Paul's audience in this text is clearly the Christian community in Corinth, not those *outside* the Church.[89]

Calvin quotes again from scripture, this time from Exodus, to provide another example of the Spirit allotting gifts to man for the common good, irrespective of faith. Puzzlingly, Calvin quotes from Exodus 31 and 35 where the subjects concerned are the people of God.[90] These passages do not refer to those outwith the Church, as Calvin mistakenly assumes, and this again is a weak argument for his case. Yet, Calvin still insists that, "It is no wonder, then, that the knowledge of all that is most excellent in human life is said to be communicated to us through the Spirit of God."[91] Calvin simply assumes that what applies to Christians with regard the Spirit's help to transform society, applies to the impious also, at least in these instances.

Calvin argues that earthly work performed with natural gifts by the impious exists to develop society: "we observe that there exist in all men's minds universal impressions of a certain civic fair dealing and order."[92] This universal ability to foster the best of human culture is due to the implanted seeds of civil order and obedience within all, and remarkable innovation and discoveries are some of their observable fruits. Calvin says, "Now the discovery or systematic transmission of the arts, or the inner and more excellent knowledge of them, which is characteristic of few, is not a sufficient proof of common discernment. Yet because it is bestowed indiscriminately upon pious and impious, it is rightly counted among natural gifts."[93]

88. Calvin, *Institutes*, II.2.16.
89. Hays, *First Corinthians*, 2:10.
90. Volf, *Work*, 113.
91. Calvin, *Institutes*, II.2.16.
92. Ibid., II.2.13.
93. Ibid., II.2.14.

Calvin's pnuematological account for work enables society to retain a degree of ordered cohesion. Calvin expands:

> Since reason, therefore, by which man distinguishes between good and evil, and by which he understands and judges, is a natural gift, it could not be completely wiped out; but it was partly weakened and partly corrupted, so that its misshapen ruins appear... [I]n man's perverted and degenerate nature some sparks still gleam. These show him to be a rational being, differing from brute beasts, because he is endowed with understanding. Yet, secondly, they show this light choked with dense ignorance, so that it cannot come forth effectively.[94]

Calvin portrays the abilities of the impious fairly here while also providing a realistic account of the effects of sin. Although, as Herman Bavinck insightfully remarks, it is "of even greater significance . . . that with Calvin reprobation does not mean the withholding of grace," and it is evident from the quotation above that Calvin perceives the sinfully impaired impious being unable to discern between good and evil.[95]

This discernment comes not from the will, but from *reason* and *intellect*, which are natural gifts. No beneficent work can be attributed to impious man in and of himself, but solely to the grace of the Holy Spirit working through natural gifts. With this move Calvin discloses the futility and depravity of man's *will* to live for the common good. Calvin says, "free will is not sufficient to enable man to do good works, unless he be helped by grace, indeed by special grace, which only the elect receive through regeneration."[96] There is absolutely no capacity for the will to make *free* choices prior to subjectively believing in Christ, thus gifts of *intellect* and *reason* among the impious protect them from becoming "brute beasts" of civic disorder:

> When we so condemn human understanding for its perpetual blindness as to leave it no perception of any object whatever, we not only go against God's Word, but also run counter to the experience of common sense. For we see implanted in human nature some sort of desire to search out the truth to which man would not at all aspire if he had not already savoured it. *Human understanding then possesses some power of perception*, since it is by nature captivated by love of truth.[97]

94. Ibid., II.2.12.
95. Bavinck, "Calvin," 117.
96. Calvin, *Institutes*, II.2.6.
97. Ibid., II.2.12 (my emphasis).

In view of this, general trade by the impious is something that is valuable in God's eyes. For example, Calvin remarks on Babylon's trading prowess as being something of spiritual value and worth, and the subsequent judgment of God upon these workers was not the result of trade itself, according to Calvin, but their haughty ostentation in carrying it out.[98] Furthermore, despite regular debate about the *minutiæ* of civil law, Calvin argues, man generally agrees with *equity* as a central motif for political life. "And this is ample proof," exclaims Calvin, "that in the arrangement of this life no man is without the light of *reason*."[99] Calvin goes even further when reflecting and exegeting Gen 4:20's portrayal of the development of civilization by the progeny of Cain, thus disclosing a contrary view to Schaeffer:

> But that there were, among the sons of Adam, industrious and skillful men, who exercised their diligence in the invention and cultivation of arts. Moses, however, expressly celebrates the remaining benediction of God on that race, which otherwise would have been deemed void and barren of all good. Let us then know, that the sons of Cain, though deprived of the Spirit of regeneration, were yet endued with gifts of no despicable kind; just as the experience of all ages teaches us how widely the rays of divine light have shone on unbelieving nations, for the benefit of the present life; and we see, at the present time, that the excellent gifts of the Spirit are diffused through the whole human race. Moreover, the liberal arts and sciences have descended to us from the heathen. We are, indeed, compelled to acknowledge that we have received astronomy, and the other parts of philosophy, medicines and the order of civil government, from them.[100]

Cain's family established culture for the common good through metallurgy, tool-making, tent-making, farming livestock and music making, and all of this was for the benefit of the common good. Calvin admits that this positive establishment of culture is to be recognized and lauded, but only to a limited extent, because this must be held in check by the *vocatio Dei*.[101]

---

98. Van Til, *Calvinistic*, 103.
99. Calvin, *Institutes*, II.2.13 (my emphasis).
100. Calvin, *Genesis*, 4.20.
101. Bavinck, "Calvin," 118.

VOCATIO DEI

Despite his general positivity concerning the Spirit's natural gifts among the impious, Calvin rhetorically asks,

> Nor is there reason for anyone to ask, What have the impious, who are utterly estranged from God, to do with his Spirit? We ought to understand the statement that the Spirit of God dwells only in believers [Rom 8:9] as referring to the Spirit of sanctification through whom we are consecrated as temples to God [1 Cor 3:16]. Nonetheless he fills, moves, and quickens all things by the power of the same Spirit, and does so according to the character that he bestowed upon each kind by the law of creation.[102]

A salient distinction must be made, Calvin insists, between those who are recipients of the grace of regeneration because of faith in Christ (Rom 8:9), and the inferior involvement of the Spirit in the impious. Yet, despite this distinction, "the God of creation and of regeneration is one," or again, the Spirit of creation and the Spirit of regeneration is one, just as the Apostle Paul states: "the Lord is the Spirit" (2 Cor 3:17), thus the Lord is mysteriously present in the impious.[103]

One of the main reasons in making this distinction is because the impious seldom (if at all) recognize natural gifts as being from God, and therefore do not give the gift-Giver his due glory (*vocatio Dei*). This is man's chief vocation for God in his work. Commenting upon Hos 9:10 ("Like grapes in the wilderness, I found Israel. Like the first fruit on the fig tree, in its first season, I saw your ancestors. But they came to Baal-peor, and consecrated themselves to a thing of shame, and became detestable like the thing they loved.") Calvin says,

> The first part then shows that God had great delight in this people. It is the same or similar sentence to that in Hosea 11, where he says, "When Ephraim was yet a child, I loved him," except that there is not there so much fervour and warmth of love expressed; but the same argument is there handled, and the object is the same, and it is to prove, that God anticipated his people by his love. There remained, in this case, less excuse, when men rejected God calling them, and responded not to his love. A perverseness like this would be hardly endured among men. Were any one to love me freely, and I to slight him, it would

---

102. Calvin, *Institutes*, II.2.16.
103. Bavinck, "Calvin," 127.

be an evidence of pride and rudeness: but when God himself gratuitously treats us with kindness, and when, not content with common love, he regards us as delectable fruit, does not the rejection of this love, does not the contempt of this favour, betray, on our part, the basest depravity?[104]

In his tainted state of unredeemed sin impious man cannot perceive his natural gifts as God-given, and thus makes defiled and inconsistent use of them. This point is critical, for Calvin insists that life must be acknowledged by those who are graciously bestowed it, and if some choose not to attest to God in their lives, the foundation of all moral action evaporates.[105]

Bavinck, therefore, accurately conveys Calvin when he avers that the "Christian life is always and everywhere a life in the presence of God, a walking before his face."[106] This move toward God is essential for full potential in moral ethical living. In everyday scenarios where people encounter dilemmas, the impious cannot be relied upon like Christians can, according to Calvin, even though they can interact unwittingly with the Holy Spirit through their natural gifts.

Nevertheless, Calvin was correct to have developed his theological anthropology pneumatologically because the biblical voice of the Spirit's immanence presence in creation is seldom employed with regard to the good work of the impious (Gen 1:2; Job 12:10, 27:3b, 32:8–10, 33:4, 34:14–5; Pss 104:29–30; 139:1–12; 146:4; Prov 8:22–31; Wis 11:24–12.1; Acts 17:25, 28; Rom 8:19–26). Calvin does not refer to or cite all of these biblical passages, but I have created a fuller list here to highlight the importance of this forgotten biblical voice.

Jürgen Moltmann is one of very few to have noticed this emphasis in Calvin and he has gone on to develop various offshoots of Calvin's pneumatological thinking, but not in the direction of work *per se*.[107]

This ignorance or refusal renders the impious beastly in status, according to Calvin, paring their humanity back so that they are almost unrecognizable as men. Their ingratitude to God proves the lack of comprehension of the pneumatological inspiration they receive. Calvin says, "Their ingratitude is also reproved as well as their contempt of the Law, because they served not God "with joyfulness and gladness of heart," when He had been so abundantly generous to them; for it is the fault of a corrupt and

---

104. Calvin, *Commentaries on the Twelve Minor Prophets*, Hosea 9:10.
105. Bavinck, "Calvin," 124.
106. Ibid., 123.
107. Moltmann, *GiC*, 10–12, 321–22 n. 8.

malignant nature, that it should not be possible to bring it to serve God joyfully, when He invites us by His liberality."[108]

It is from Calvin, as he is influenced by Aquinas, that the roots of mundane work versus *evangelical works* performed by Christians emerges in the British evangelical tradition via *vocatio Dei*. Only by submissive and worshipful acknowledgement of God in their lives can the impious receive a qualitatively and quantitatively enhanced measure of the Spirit for their work.

Vocatio Dei demonstrates Calvin's pervasive influence on all my interlocutors thus far. In fact, it would not be overstretching oneself to say that Calvin's doctrine of *vocatio Dei* is the governing principle in deciding whether good work has any value to God.

ASSESSING PECULIAR GRACE

Without doubt, Calvin's theology of peculiar grace has improved upon Schaeffer, Chalmers, and Baxter's accounts of the good work of the impious. By understanding that the impulse to work morally in the world is generated by the Holy Spirit, Calvin locates human good in God himself.

Further, Calvin understands that good work is manifest in the impious through natural gifts of the Spirit, but in order to properly differentiate the intensity of the presence of the Spirit among the pious and the impious, he rightly separates natural from supernatural gifts. This theological move allows Calvin to wisely account for the beneficence of the work of the impious without undercutting the sealing of the Spirit which pious men experience through justification and sanctification.

This pneumatological difference of intensity in the impious, which is an unsalvific presence of the Spirit, restricts the efficacy and scope of the empowerment of their work. Because the agents are impious, the measure of the Spirit endowed upon them could never be conceived in such a way as to convey any eternal implications from their work. In other words, even though the Holy Spirit is present through *peculiar grace* to empower good work, that work will only ever be counted as mundane, temporal work, not as *evangelical works* which pertain to eternity.

It is true to say that not all God's work is eternal in nature; some work has temporal ends. However, Calvin confines the work of the Spirit in the impious to temporal means because he could never deign to suggest they could offer anything which pertains to eternity. Indeed, how could the

---

108. Calvin, *Commentaries on Moses*, Deuteronomy 28.45; Torrance, *Calvin*, 34.

impious, who have been predestined to an eternal damnation, contribute any effort towards the kingdom of God in its fullness, Calvin asks?

Despite this, Calvin has understated the Spirit's empowerment in the impious; the supernatural gift of charity highlights this issue in particular. Calvin's claim that charity towards one's neighbour belongs exclusively to the supernatural gifts of the pious is a bizarre one. It is short-sighted to assert that the impious by their natural gifts cannot show compassionate charity, particularly in light of the narrative of the Good Samaritan (which is curiously absent in Calvin's discussion of gifts).

This biblical story is an exception to Calvin's understanding of what gifts belong to whom, for if the Good Samaritan was heterodox in belief, and so outwith God's own people (which excludes him from supernatural gifts according to Calvin), Calvin's claim is contravened. This unlikely Samaritan is Jesus' key exemplar of loving one's neighbor in accordance with God's love. John Baggett adds, "It did not matter that the Samaritan did not have a pure ancestry, or hold the "right" beliefs, or perform the "right" rituals in the "right" places. What mattered was that he treated another human being in need[.]" Indeed, "[h]e loved God by loving his neighbor in need, and the clear implication was that God approved."[109]

Combatting my view, John Matheson argues that Calvin only attributes acts of charity to supernatural gifts because what the "impious" *appear to do* when showing charity is not *true* charity. Drawing upon the theology of Reinhold Niebuhr, Matheson argues that impious agents lack "the dimension of depth" in their acts of charity and thus only practice "humanistic virtue" and "the virtue of pity." Matheson expands on this: "It is only when we love men in God that we love them truly. The humanitarian activity of our time is generous and self-sacrificing, yet much of it is superficial. It alleviates, but it fails to redeem."[110]

What Matheson claims is that for true acts of charity to be performed, a true love for God must be at its foundation. By this is meant that a subjective faith in Christ must be present and operative in the agent concerned. If acts of compassion are performed without the inspiration of Christian faith, Matheson says of Calvin, without *vocatio Dei* the act is second class and cannot be counted as actual neighborly love. The inability to surrender to *vocatio Dei* in their work renders the work of the impious qualitatively inferior and this is why Calvin provides an account of *both* the supernatural *and* natural gifts. In so doing, Calvin recognizes the periodic good of the

---

109. Baggett, *Seeing*, 133. Some interpreters may contend that this narrative was merely illustrative and not an actual situation that took place. Even so, Jesus uses an "impious" exemplar to make his point.

110. Matheson, "Calvin's Doctrine," 53.

work of the impious while ranking the inferior nature of these gifts below their supernatural equivalent.

Yet Calvin's rationale is still circumvented by the fact that Jesus undoes Calvin's distinction between natural/supernatural gifts as the Good Samaritan exemplifies. This impious foreigner shows compassion to his fellow man and is lauded by Jesus for his *true* love of the other.

This said, I am in agreement with all the other supernatural gifts Calvin attributes exclusively to the pious, but the rigidity with which Calvin applies the dichotomy between the supernatural and natural gifts weakens with the exception shown. This reveals the obduracy of Calvin's theological schema for gifts among the impious. Calvin's strict delineation of the pious and impious in the way shown is helpful, but the restriction of the efficacy of the Spirit's agency in the impious weakens and undermines his argument. To curb the potency of the Spirit's agency through these agents is both understandable given his theological schema, but is unnecessarily constraining of God the Spirit. To regulate the Spirit's work through the impious in this way is simply too presumptuous.

I will now begin to demonstrate Calvin's general conception of the eschatological duality between heaven and earth in view of the work of the impious in preparation of my analysis of his exegesis of the parable of the sheep and the goats.

WORK AND THE ESCHATON

Calvin has an extensive treatment of the parable of the sheep and the goats in his commentary on the synoptic gospels and from the outset he makes clear the purpose of this parable: "The sum of what is said is, that believers, ought to contemplate with the eyes of faith the heavenly life, which, though it is now concealed, will at length be manifested at the last coming of Christ."[111]

Calvin expresses this in light of the opening verse of the parable of the sheep and the goats which relates to what will take place at Christ's *parousia*. Indeed, there is no doubt whatsoever that this parable should evoke the reaction Calvin claims by those who take the Bible seriously. Moreover, Calvin goes on to explain that if Jesus' disciples become bored and forgetful by virtue of the delay of the *parousia*, the sheep and the goats provide the necessary jolt to ensure the pious live righteously in the interim.[112]

---

111. Calvin, *Commentary on a Harmony*, Matt 25:31.
112. Ibid., Matt 25:31.

Demonstrating his influence upon each chapter's interlocutor explored thus far, Calvin assumes the sheep of the parable are Jesus' disciples. His portrayal of the great judgment is then combined with his doctrine of the visibility and invisibility of the Church. Deriving such thinking from verse thirty-two, where the Son of Man separates the sheep from the goats, Calvin argues that "the wicked are now mixed with the good and holy, so that they live together in the same flock of God."[113] Calvin's assumption of the Christian identity of the sheep is confirmed by drawing upon Ezek 34:18, which he believes speaks of fierce enemy goats attacking the poor sheep of God's true flock. This interpretation is highly dubious. Nevertheless, using this passage as an Old Testament echo of the sheep and the goats, Calvin says, "therefore Christ's discourse amounts to this, that believers ought not to think their condition too hard, if they are now compelled to live with *the goats*, and even to sustain many serious attacks and annoyances from them . . . for the difference will one day appear."[114]

Calvin is correct here with regard to the difficulty of identifying the sheep and goats. This contextual reading, however, which is entirely informed by his ecclesiology and the context of Christendom, is a derivative of his doctrine of predestination, and is evident once more when discussing the opening words of verse thirty-four, 'Come, you that are blessed by my Father.' Calvin describes:

> We must remember Christ's design; for he bids his disciples rest satisfied now with hope, that they may with patience and tranquillity of mind look for the enjoyment of the heavenly kingdom; and next, he bids them strive earnestly, and not become wearied in the right course. To this latter clause he refers, when he promises the inheritance of the heavens to none but those who by good works aim at the prize of the heavenly calling. But before speaking of the reward of good works, he points out, in passing, that the commencement of salvation flows from a higher source; for by calling them *blessed of the Father*, he reminds them, that their salvation proceeded from the undeserved favor of God. Among the Hebrews the phrase *blessed of God* means one who is *dear to God*, or *beloved by God*. Besides, this form of expression was not only employed by believers to extol the grace of God towards men, but those who had degenerated from true godliness still held this principle. *Enter, thou blessed of God,* said Laban to Abraham's servant, (Gen 24:31). We see that nature suggested to them this expression, by which they ascribed to

113. Ibid., Matt 25:32.
114. Ibid. (original emphasis).

God the praise of all that they possessed. There can be no doubt, therefore, that Christ, in describing the salvation of the godly, begins with the undeserved love of God, by which those who, under the guidance of the Spirit in this life, aim at righteousness, were predestined to life.[115]

For Calvin, what Christ's words in verse thirty-four reveal is the Father's predestination of the elect and reprobate, and showing his anxiety about the fact that the sheep are saved solely by their works, Calvin wishes to avert his concern by harmonizing this with a Pauline doctrine of unmerited grace.

Calvin reads into the words "blessed of the Father" a predetermined designation of the pious in Christ, which in turn lessens the import of the reward for works of which Christ speaks. This reward is for continually fostering righteous *acts, evangelical works*, in light of the overarching and prior grace of Christ's atonement, for only this makes sense of such a contrary parable to the Apostle Paul's doctrine of justification. With these moves, the progenitor of Stott's understanding of the parable comes to bear.

These words are adjoined and confirmed, says Calvin, by the following clause "inherit the kingdom prepared for you from the foundation of the world." He says,

> For though the life of the godly be nothing else than a sad and wretched banishment, so that the earth scarcely bears them; though they groan under hard poverty, and reproaches, and other afflictions; yet, that they may with fortitude and cheerfulness surmount these obstacles, the Lord declares that a *kingdom* is elsewhere *prepared for them*. It is no slight persuasive to patience, when men are fully convinced that they do not run in vain; and therefore, lest our minds should be cast, down by the pride of the ungodly, in which they give themselves unrestrained indulgences—lest our hope should even be weakened by our own afflictions, let us always remember the inheritance which awaits us in heaven; for it depends on no uncertain event, but was *prepared for us* by God before we were born,—*prepared*, I say, for each of the elect, for the persons here addressed by Christ are the *blessed of the Father*.[116]

With this, it can be seen that Calvin understands the beginning of this parable to relate to his doctrine of divine foreknowledge and predestination which segregates those who will be saved and damned in an ultimate sense

115. Ibid., Matt 25:34.
116. Ibid.

before time. As such, the sheep *must* be viewed as the elect of God because they are those who will ultimately be saved in light of God's foreknowledge and predestination. The whole parable is then theologically colored by this opening interpretation which presses Calvin to remark that any interpretation which understands "that the reward was laid up with a view to their future merits" is very "easy to object" to.[117]

Progressing on to the two critical conjunctions "for" in verses 35 and 42 ("for I was hungry," etc.), Calvin claims that these do not communicate a works-salvation like that of the "Papists" because this would again infer "eternal life by good works." These conjunctions must have a different function, he reasons, because if this parable is to be read through (and thus subordinated to) the Apostle Paul's doctrine of justification by faith, they must operate somewhat alternatively. He states, "It is improper to conclude from his [Jesus'] words what is the value of the merits of works. With regard to the stress which they lay on the word *for*, as if it pointed out the *cause*, it is a weak argument; for we know that, when eternal life is promised to the righteous, the word *for* does not always denote a cause, but rather the order of procedure."[118]

In other words, in light of the predestination of God's elect by his grace from 'the foundation of the world' (v. 34), the conjunctions "for" in verses 35 and 42 speak of the ensuing reward of works *in light of* the overarching foreknowledge of God. Because Calvin has interpreted the sheep and goats in light of this predestinarian theology, the conjunctions "for" must surely refer to the order in which the judgment will be enacted, not following any form of causality of works to salvation. However, Calvin does admit that his interpretation of "for" is not the dominant understanding, leaving readers feeling as if he has altered its meaning simply to suit his own theology, and in the process doing violence to the text. Even though Calvin caveats that these conjunctions are not always understood as "the order of procedure," what if he has misapplied this alternative meaning? He does not anticipate any such eventuality.

Nevertheless, Calvin does concede the passage conveys a reward of works, but again hedges that this is contingent upon the understanding of a prior adoption of particular people by God. He bases this assertion upon 2 Tim 4:8 ("From now on there is reserved for me the crown of righteousness, which the Lord, the righteous judge, will give me on that day, and not only to me but also to all who have longed for his appearing") which he draws in for support, and where the Apostle Paul's confidence in following

117. Ibid.
118. Ibid., Matt 25:35.

Christ convinces him of his inheritance of the divine kingdom.[119] Calvin concludes,

> We must therefore hold these two principles, first, that believers are called to the possession of the kingdom of heaven, so far as relates to good works, not because they deserved them through the righteousness of works, or because their own minds prompted them to obtain that righteousness, but because God justifies those whom he previously elected (Rom 8:30). Secondly, although by the guidance of the Spirit they aim at the practice of righteousness, yet as they never fulfill the law of God, no reward is due to them, but the term *reward* is applied to that which is bestowed by grace.[120]

The reward does not come as a result of works performed, as Calvin evades the meaning of the parable to guard against human ostentation, but comes solely from God's grace. Refocusing on the sheep and goats, Calvin insists that Jesus is not intending to be exhaustive in his list of works which the sheep perform but this list should be understood as pertaining exclusively to "believers" and the hope of "a pious and holy life." Yet, according to Calvin, "the worship of God is more important than charity towards men," for, "[i]f a man were to take no thought about God, and were only to be beneficent towards men, such compassion would be of no avail to him for appeasing God, who had all the while been defrauded of his right."[121]

This is consistent with his doctrine of *vocation Dei* which I showed earlier, and with such a statement, Calvin's direct influence upon Schaeffer, Chalmers and Baxter becomes apparent. All human agency must be enacted in light of faith and worship of God, Calvin suggests, because this matter is of the upmost importance when compared with the works of faith. "Accordingly," Calvin claims, "Christ does not make the chief part of righteousness to consist in alms, but, by means of what may be called more evident signs, show what it is to live a holy and righteous life[.]" The primary focus of this parable, then, is the sheep's prior faith in Christ, according to Calvin, because to stray from this into warped questioning about works and acts would be to fall foul of the errors of the Roman Catholic Church. Nonetheless, Calvin still recommends "the exercise of charity, [which] does not exclude those duties which belong to the worship of God[.]"[122]

---

119. Ibid.
120. Ibid.
121. Ibid.
122. Ibid.

However, this is a description of *evangelical works* which excludes mundane work. Calvin's overall concern in the midst of all his equivocation is that man might go astray in his endeavors and end up disobeying divine commands if he were to be too work-focused. If man is left to seek "the Supreme Judge's" approval through their works, there is no way that he could stay aligned with God. Quoting Isa 1:12 ("When you come to appear before me, who asked this from your hand? Trample my courts no more"), Calvin believes that this is the appropriate divine denouncement against those who wish to earn their way to salvation.[123]

But what does Calvin make of the sheep's ignorance of their acts which are accepted by Christ? First of all, Calvin reasserts his certainty that the identity of the sheep is "the righteous"—those who have already subjectively received Christ. This is followed by his belief that the ignorance of the sheep proves the vulnerability and fickle nature of man, even pious man. That the righteous are unaware of the significance of their works reveals "what they know well"; in other words, they are uninformed of the potency of their acts, and Calvin believes this ignorance proves the flailing nature of man in view of God's grace. "[W]hat they know well" refers to man's ignorance and doubting, for this is all man is capable of. "But as this was not so deeply impressed on their minds as it ought to have been, he [Christ] holds out to them this lively representation."[124] Again, Calvin reveals that this parable has been given as a pedagogical warning to negligent Christians.

"[J]ust as you did it to one of the least of these my brothers, you did it to me" (v. 40). Calvin focuses upon the term "brothers" in this verse to explain that good works performed by the righteous should be aimed particularly towards the poor and unfortunate of *the Church*; that is the substance of the term "brothers" utilized here for Calvin:

> Believers only are expressly recommended to our notice; not that he bids us altogether despise others, but because the more nearly a man approaches to God, he ought to be the more highly esteemed by us; for though there is a common tie that binds all the children of Adam, there is a still more sacred union among the children of God. So then, as those, who belong to the household of faith ought to be preferred to strangers, Christ makes special mention of them . . . And certainly, by calling them *brethren*, he confers on them inestimable honor.[125]

---

123. Ibid.
124. Ibid., Matt 25:37.
125. Ibid., Matt 25:40.

Concerned about disingenuous church-goers, who are in fact predestined to an eternal hell, Calvin interprets the sheep and goats in such a way that motivates the righteous to focus their acts of compassion on one another, not prioritizing the impious poor. "He [Christ] will then order the wicked to *depart* from him, because many hypocrites are now mixed with the righteous, as if they were closely allied to Christ."[126] The "reprobate," then, when answering the Son of Man's indictment against them, disclose "vain excuses" about how they have "deceived themselves" by not having sought God in their lives. Indeed, such a reaction by the goats, according to Calvin, "will be of no avail to them at the last day."[127] Their end is certain for it has been foreseen since the 'foundation of the world.'

Furthermore, that the poor of the Church are to be "preferred" to strangers in compassionate acts is a shocking admission by Calvin, especially since he says with regard to Heb 13:2 ("Do not neglect to show hospitality to strangers, for by doing that some have entertained angels without knowing it"):

> And that he might commend this duty the more, he adds, that angels had sometimes been entertained by those who thought that they received only men. I doubt not but that this is to be understood of Abraham and Lot; for having been in the habit of showing hospitality, they without knowing and thinking of any such thing, entertained angels; thus their houses were in no common way honored. And doubtless God proved that hospitality was especially acceptable to him, when he rendered such a reward to Abraham and to Lot. Were any one to object and say, that this rarely happened; to this the obvious answer is,—That not mere angels are received, but Christ himself, when we receive the poor in his name.[128]

In conclusion, Calvin shows inconsistency when Heb 13:2 is compared with the sheep and the goats because of the inclusion of "brothers" in the latter which clearly isolates and favors the poor of the Church. In light of Heb 13:2, however, Calvin would have done better if had not restricted the "brothers" of the sheep and the goats to this usage for in so doing strangers would have been protected as Christ might be found to be mystically present among them.

---

126. Ibid., Matt 25:41.
127. Ibid., Matt 25:44.
128. Calvin, *Commentaries on Hebrews*, 13:2.

ANALYZING CALVIN'S INTERPRETATION

From the outset, Calvin problematically eisegetes his predestinarian theology into the parable of the sheep and goats which provides the perfect platform for him to analyze the binary nature of the final state of man. The text in no way suggests the predestinarian framing of the story which he claims, yet he ensures that it fits with his overall theological program laid out in his *Institutes*.

Were Calvin fair to the parable, the language "inherit the kingdom prepared for you from the foundation from the world" (v. 34) would mean that *anyone who chooses to act* under God's reign by unwittingly serving Christ among the needy is deserving of inheriting the kingdom. The kingdom has indeed been prepared from the genesis of the world but this should not force the reader to conclude that each and every person has been fatalistically foreordained to a particular destiny, as Calvin argues. What the parable actually teaches is that people do have a choice to love their poor neighbor and there is a genuine freedom to operate in such a kingdom manner.

In view of this libertarian choice to love the poor, the two conjunctions "for" in verses 35 and 42 ("for I was hungry . . .") are nothing to do with the "order of procedure," despite Calvin's wish to redefine the meaning of this straightforward conjunction; they are to do with the causality of behaving aright, even if this upsets Calvin's theological system. There is no way around this, but Calvin has produced an untenable redefinition in order to dampen the force of the parable's message, avoiding supporting the Roman Church's cause.

This leads to a further problem with Calvin's interpretation of the parable: the identity of the sheep and the goats. Calvin imposes the divine foreknowledge of the dual destinies of the pious and the impious (heavily influenced by later Pauline and Johannine theology), and concludes that the sheep must be the pious, those who have been elected into the kingdom from eternity past. However, if there is genuine openness and freedom to choose to love the poor, and if there is a direct causality between human behavior and a particular ultimate destiny, there cannot be, as Calvin postulates, any predetermination of the beast's identity in this parable in the strict manner he proposes because each person determines their own destiny.

Also, if the parable is not about the giving of alms but about pious worship, as Calvin relates in his interpretation, the parable no longer bears any resemblance to its original composition. The parable of the sheep and the goats has been deformed so much by Calvin that it no longer contains the goad explicit within it.

Finally, it is a weak argument to propose that the ignorance of the sheep somehow validates their identity as the pious. This is in no way persuasive and fits untidily into Calvin's overall scheme of predestined man. As I will show in the final chapter, an alternative reading of these verses should be adopted so as to give the parable its due.

CONCLUSION

When reflecting on the final state, Calvin's positivity about the beneficent actions of the impious disappears because he fears any narrative which promotes the meritorious works of man towards ultimate salvation. There is no great disjunction between Calvin's account of peculiar grace and his interpretation of the sheep and the goats because *peculiar grace* ultimately concludes that despite the inspiration and empowerment of the Holy Spirit, good work by the impious is only ever empowered by an unsalvific measure of the Spirit. Thus, their work can only ever be considered as mundane, temporal work. It is considered thus because of the agents it inspires: the impious. Precisely because the impious cannot be saved ultimately, reasons Calvin (due to their damnation from eternity past), there is only a secondary and inferior presence of the Spirit present among them.

This line of reasoning works retrospectively from Pauline and Johannine portrayals of the eschatological destination of the impious, and this is why he must create a lower tier of pneumatological presence and empowerment for them. Calvin must maintain this obstacle to the kingdom of God for the impious and he successfully does this with his inferior account of grace, and with his interpretation of the sheep and the goats.

Despite the fact that this is only a discussion of unsalvific grace, Calvin's understanding of natural gifts is particularly good, especially the fact that he understands and acknowledges them as pneumatologically empowered. With this move Calvin radically improves upon all the thinkers considered thus far, for he locates goodness in man through the presence of the Holy Spirit. This is something that it surprisingly underemphazised and overlooked by the previous interlocutors. Moreover, by dichotomizing gifts into supernatural/natural, Calvin is also able to differentiate between the special seal of grace by the Spirit in the pious and the reason for the impulse to do good work among the impious. This is an important distinction to maintain and one which British evangelicals have continually upheld. Notwithstanding his erudite account shown here, is it appropriate or theologically correct to insist upon the temporal or unsalvific nature of the Spirit's operations as Calvin does for the good work of the impious? Does this not undermine the divinity of the Holy Spirit? Should not all work by the divine be perceived as eternally efficacious, irrespective of the faith status of men? To justify his position, I have shown that Calvin appeals to scripture; his use of Old Testament pneumatology is generally more convincing than his use of the New Testament.

Calvin has indeed provided a helpful rationale in understanding the good work of the impious, but questions still remain. His account of the parable of the sheep and the goats is interpreted entirely in light of his predestinarian system outlined in his *Institutes*, and as a consequence, a true and honest reading of the parable is made obscure which then serves to prohibit any meaningful link between work and the eschaton.

Without doubt Calvin has done much to provide British evangelicals with an account of the good work of those who are not elect, however, the absence of the eschatological implications of his appeal to pneumatology as their divine empowerment leave it weakened.

In the following chapter, I will investigate John Wesley's account of the work of the heathen and the empowerment through which their work can be good. As Calvin has provided the most sophisticated account of good work by those who are not Christian thus far, Wesley has much to improve upon.

Furthermore, as I have shown in previous chapters, Wesley's interpretation of the parable of the sheep and the goats will be explored to ascertain whether he makes any connection between the good work of the heathen and the eschaton. This penultimate stage in my study will prepare the way for my repair and suggestions for the British evangelical tradition.

5

John Wesley (1703–91)
Co-operative Heathen Conscience with Prevenient Grace

CALVIN PROVIDED AN ACCOUNT of good work by the impious by identifying pneumatology as the key to work's empowerment, but in order to differentiate duly between the indwelling nature of the Spirit in the pious and the impious, he had to create a two-tier system of the Spirit. His understanding of natural and supernatural gifts provides an erudite conception of this, but it is bound by the eternal determination of his overarching doctrine of predestination. Calvin rightly views the Spirit empowering good work by the impious, and maintains a qualitative difference between this and the salvific indwelling and empowerment of the work of the pious. The former has no connection to the eschaton, however, and this is evident in the *Institutes* and in his interpretation of the sheep and the goats.

Even though he was sometimes falsely accused of advocating salvation *by* works,[1] I will evaluate afresh the nature of Wesley's understanding of good work by the heathen, for in Wesley's context the evangelical notion of *work* was of simultaneous import in both religious and secular settings.[2] I will employ Wesley's term *heathen* to describe those who are not Christian, and although he also employs the term *pagan* on occasion, I will use the former, as he makes more frequent use of it. Furthermore, the term *heathen* refers to those belonging to Christendom, for occasionally he distinguishes

---

1. Jackson, "Mr. Hill's Review," 10:379.
2. Walsh, "The Bane of Industry?," 233.

between the *heathen* and the *Mohametans* in discussion of those who are not Christian.

In connection with the point above, like Calvin before him, Wesley turns to grace to explain *how* good works take place. By viewing grace pneumatologically, Wesley is of automatic interest to my purpose here because this will contrast him with Calvin. As with Calvin, the eschatological implications of such an account of heathen work will be scrutinized through Wesley's understanding of the relationship between work and the eschaton in the parable of the sheep and the goats (Matt 25:31–45).

WESLEY'S CONTEXT

Wesley was an eighteenth-century Englishman living in a burgeoning industrialized world. John Cobb describes Wesley, like the magisterial Reformers, as a *social reformer*.[3] Wesley's social reform came in the form of hierarchical paternalism as Wesley resisted sharing the responsibility of his orphanages, schools and preaching circuits.[4] Nevertheless, Wesley's social influence is summed up well with the following words: "The Awakening which abolished the slave trade, pioneered popular education, humanized the prison system, established a world missionary movement, emancipate England's 'industrial slaves,' and raised up valiant leadership both in Trade Unionism and the Parliamentary Labor movement—that awakening inspired also the modern philanthropic and social-service movement."[5]

There are three striking elements of culture that were particularly pronounced in eighteenth-century British society: (1) Protestantism, (2) commerce, and (3) empire.[6] All three are prominent in the works of Wesley.

As Englishmen were forced from their homes by enclosing landlords to work in the brutish factories of the industrial world of the eighteenth century, an ever-increasing working class emerged. If indeed one happened to be a mill or factory owner or a land aristocrat during this time, a fortune was ready to be made. Sadly, workers' dignity was continually breached during this smoke-plumed, grime-smeared time of economic boom.[7] Many of the factory workers whom Wesley helped were the poor seeking sustenance who had drifted into towns and cities from outlying agricultural areas.

3. Cobb, *Grace*, 21.
4. Noll, *Rise of Evangelicalism*, 225.
5. Bready, *This Freedom*, 286–87. The term "Awakening" here refers to the eighteenth-century evangelical revival in Britain that Wesley was associated with.
6. Wahrman, *The Making of the Modern Self*, 199.
7. Henderson, *John Wesley's Class Meeting*, 17–18.

Preying upon their desperation, factory foremen often exploited them with pitiful pay and gruesome working conditions. As a result, the countryside was bereft of laborers, and cities were bursting with impoverished ones, many of whom were children as young as four or five years old.[8]

Being far from home, some of these isolated workers voluntarily joined and found solace in Wesley's organized groups of Christians, and here they discovered Christian discipline—Methodism.[9] These groups brought stability to life amid turbulence and forced displacement, and this provided a rare self-assurance to those laboring in demeaning workplaces.[10] This Christian rigor and practice corresponded to the rhythms of factory work; Methodism became a contextual form of mission which adapted to the minute and hour hands of the industrial clock.[11]

However, Wesley and his Methodists were not simply a religion for the working class, but also of "the industrial bourgeoisie."[12] To the latter, Wesley issued continuous warnings of obsessions with riches and pleasures the booming industry afforded. His sermon *The Use of Money* provided a Christian rationale for how to handle the lures of money that reveals his indebtedness to William Law's (1686–1761) *A Serious Call to a Devout and Holy Life*, even despite Wesley's revulsion to natural law. Law's treatise made an enormous impression upon Wesley (revealing Wesley's Anglican heritage), and helped him grasp the nexus of true religion.[13]

It was not all positive for Wesley however. The charge of inciting the spirit of the French Revolution among the English working class was brought to Wesley's door.[14] Rumors emerged, and false claims were made that Wesley and the Methodists were separatists or perhaps papists, and they were also accused of being allies of the rebellious Scottish Bonnie Prince Charlie who was planning to invade England to regain the English crown for the Stuart line.[15]

These false associations attached to Wesley and his Methodists were fabricated to ensure the maintenance of public order, but they showed an ability to alleviate and transform the social order because they were

---

8. Henderson, *John Wesley's*, 18–19.
9. Heitzenrater, *Wesley*, 127.
10. Moltmann, *Spirit*, 165–66.
11. Ibid., 166.
12. Thompson, *Making*, 391.
13. Noll, *Rise*, 66–67.
14. Outler, "Wesley in the Christian Tradition," 12.
15. Heitzenrater, *Wesley*, 133, 151, 160–61.

"untrammelled by the silken chains which bound the Establishment."[16] Such was the outworking of Methodism's non-conformist ecclesiology.

Politically, Wesley was a High Tory with a deep Anglican heritage, and was thus a staunch loyalist of the King which he relates when writing to John Mason concerning American resistance to Methodist doctrine:[17] "We are no republicans, and never intend to be."[18] Methodism was able to take up the social opportunities of the day in a manner which the Church of England could never have,[19] and yet, Wesley's death happened to coincide with the early fascination with the French Revolution.[20]

Furthermore, Wesley's ability to socially reform was shaped not only by his Anglican heritage but also by his deep-seated pietism.[21] This pietism was fomented through a cantankerous friendship with Zinzendorf and the Herrnhut community in Germany; the Fetter Lane Society in London; Rhineland spirituality as well as Arndt and Hallensian Pietism.[22] Wesley has also been perceived as a Christian mystic;[23] Roman Catholic;[24] an English Puritan;[25] proto-Barthian;[26] Eastern Orthodox;[27] and from the Holiness tradition.[28] Whichever of these is appealed to, an introduction to Wesley's conception of grace is now required to discover the nature of prevenient grace which aids heathen workers towards advantageous work.

THE CHARACTER OF GRACE

Before considering Wesley's theology of works it is critical to clarify the nature of grace that empowers heathen works. In other words, it is imperative to ask whether grace is uncreated or a substance that is brought into being

---

16. Tawney, *Religion*, 275.
17. Noll, *Rise*, 200.
18. Wesley, "Letter to John Mason—13th January 1790."
19. Tawney, *Religion*, 275.
20. Thompson, *Making*, 45.
21. Moltmann, *Spirit*, 164–71; O'Malley, "Pietistic Influence on John Wesley," 48–70; O'Malley, "'Pietist Influences in the Eschatological Thought," 127–39.
22. O'Malley, "Pietistic Influence on John Wesley," 48–70.
23. Orcibal, *Révue de l'Histoire*, 50–109.
24. Piette, *John Wesley*.
25. Monk, *John Wesley*.
26. Deschner, *Wesley's Christology*.
27. Maddox, *Responsible*.
28. Cox, *John Wesley's Concept*.

from God for creation? Is grace primarily a *pardon* for man or a *power* to enable ethical living?

Attending to the first question, Wesley, influenced by Eastern Orthodoxy, viewed grace as uncreated, and indeed, part of the divine energies immanently present in the Holy Spirit.[29] This is an undeserving gift that overflows from God's loving nature towards man, and vying for this Eastern approach, Wesley draws upon 2 Pet 1:4 for support: "become participants of the divine nature."[30] Commenting on this biblical injunction Wesley says, "Ye may become partakers of the divine nature—Being renewed in the image of God, and having communion with them, so as to dwell in God and God in you."[31]

Grace is thus divine power within man enabling his very existence.

With respect the second question, considering that grace has brought creation into being *ex nihilo* and continues to sustain it, Wesley emphasized grace as a form of *empowerment* for man more prominently than stressing *pardon*. Grace is the Holy Spirit's presence in the world and exists to inspire and cajole man benevolently towards good works. This is not enforced by the Spirit, but he persuades man to co-operate willingly, and this can take place frequently and regularly, prior to an acknowledgement and/or appreciation of the Giver of the gift of grace.[32] Grace comes to empower man, then, as a gift through His favor.[33] With this, Wesley's understanding of grace avoids any Pelagian connotations. But in order to flesh out the grace at work among men more fully, Wesley's understanding of the image of God must be examined.[34]

IMAGO DEI

Man was made in God's image (*imago Dei*) as a dependent being, and thus his very existence emanates from God's grace.[35] Grace is not simply an antidote for sin; it arrived prior to sin and gifted creation its life and existence. Wesley remarks, "All the blessings which God hath bestowed upon man are of his mere grace, bounty, or favor; his free, undeserved favor; favor alto-

---

29. Maddox, *Responsible*, 86; Stephanou, *Patristic*, 11:18–20.
30. Collins, *Wesley*, 13.
31. Wesley, *John Wesley's Notes*, I.4.
32. Outler, *John Wesley*, 33; Wynkoop, *A Theology of Love*, 155; Maddox, *Responsible*, 86.
33. Collins, *Wesley*, 13.
34. Outler, "Wesleyan Quadrilateral," 34.
35. Luby, *Perceptibility of Grace*, 52.

gether undeserved; man having no claim to the least of his mercies. It was free grace that 'formed man of the dust of the ground, and breathed into him a living soul,' and stamped on that soul the image of God, and "put all things under his feet."[36]

With man as *imago Dei*, a glimpse of God's nature is disclosed: "God is . . . said to be love; intimating that this is his darling, his reigning attribute, the attribute that sheds an amiable glory on all his other perfections."[37]

Thus, man was made with relational love at the epicenter of his being.[38] *Imago Dei* is further understood by Wesley to have been formed in a threefold manner: (1) naturally, (2) politically, and (3) morally. These three are unique but interrelate.[39] Wesley states,

> "And God," the three-one God, "said, Let us make man in our image, after our likeness. So God created man in his own image, in the image of God created he him:" (Gen. 1:26, 27:)—Not barely in his *natural image,* a picture of his own immortality; a spiritual being, endued with understanding, freedom of will, and various affections;—nor merely in his *political image,* the governor of this lower world, having "dominion over the fishes of the sea, and over all the earth;"—but chiefly in his *moral image;* which, according to the Apostle, is "righteousness and true holiness" (Eph. 4:24). In this image of God was man made. "God is love:" Accordingly, man at his creation was full of love; which was the sole principle of all his tempers, thoughts, words, and actions.[40]

(1) The natural image is made up of a "spiritual nature and immortality of the soul" in addition to the principle of self-motion which can be delineated into three further aspects: *understanding, will* and *liberty.*[41] *Understanding* is the faculty that can discern between good and evil, and this gives him the rational capability to weigh-up ethical situations with clarity. The *will* has "a power of directing his own affections and actions" and *liberty* or freewill makes available the possibility to choose either good or evil according to *understanding* and the *will*:[42] "Without this, both the will and the understanding would have been utterly useless. Indeed, without

36. Wesley, *Sermons*, 1.
37. Wesley, *John Wesley's Notes*, 4:8.
38. Collins, *Wesley*, 51.
39. Weber, *Politics*, 393.
40. Wesley, "New Birth," 1:1.
41. Collins, *Wesley*, 52.
42. Wesley, "On the Fall of Man."

liberty, man had been so far from being a *free agent*, that he could have been no *agent* at all. For every *unfree being* is purely passive; not active in any degree."[43]

(2) Man's political image coheres with the natural in Wesley's conception of *imago Dei*. It concerns the cultural mandate for man to govern God's creation, to rule and subdue the earth as God's representative, and as such, he is a mark of God's presence on the "lower earth." Wesley says of Adam, "As he has the government of the inferior creatures, he is as it were God's representative on earth. Yet his government of himself by the freedom of his will, has in it more of God's image, than his government of the creatures."[44]

(3) The final strand of *imago Dei* for Wesley is the moral image. This is the chief aspect of *imago Dei* because it plays a pivotal role in his theology as a whole, and as it promotes the holiness and love of God in man.[45] Yet this strand of *imago Dei* was completely destroyed by sin's entrance into the world. This devastating moment also injured the political image, and as a result, man now often rules immorally, ravishing and plundering creation irresponsibly, so that God's presence through him has effectively vanished from the earth.

I will focus my concentration on the often neglected political aspect of *imago Dei* in Wesley's theology as this pertains most directly to his theology of works.[46] Additionally, Wesley engages the political image only as it impinges upon the moral image, thus demonstrating the importance of cooperating with grace in work.[47] The lack of discussion of the political image in Wesleyan theology should not negate its relevance to Wesley's theology of works, but rather, necessitate its development.

As mentioned earlier, the political image has its focus on the fulfillment of the cultural mandate of Gen 1:28: "Be fruitful and multiply, and fill the earth and subdue it; and have dominion over the fish of the sea and over the birds of the air and over every living thing that moves upon the earth." Wesley comments, "Man was God's vice regent upon earth, the prince and governor of this lower world; and all the blessings of God flowed through him to the inferior creatures. Man was the channel of conveyance between his Creator and the whole brute creation."[48]

---

43. Wesley, "End of Christ's Coming," 1:4.
44. Wesley, *John Wesley's Notes*, 4.8; 1:28; 3:2.
45. Maddox, *Responsible*, 68.
46. Ibid., 68.
47. Weber, *Politics*, 410.
48. Wesley, "General Deliverence," 1:3.

There is a two-pronged and interrelated nature to Wesley's interpretation of the cultural mandate at work here:

(i) Responsibility—man is God's vice regent upon the earth. The political image ought to represent God's ultimate governance of the universe by enfleshing a responsible maintenance and shaping of the earth which reveals the second prong of political imaging:[49]

(ii) Stewardship. The responsibility that man had been entrusted with was *the care of creation*, and as Wesley's comment above demonstrates, man existed as a mediator between God and all non-human creation; the political image was intended to mirror God as creator to the rest of creation, albeit in a finite manner.[50] Collins rightly puts it, "Humanity, according to Wesley, is the great conduit, the chosen channel, of God's blessings for the rest of creation and is therefore in some sense responsible for the general state of the animal realm." This is not to be a dominion "over," but "with" and "for" the world.[51]

Postlapsarianly however, the political image became dysfunctional and like Calvin, Wesley affirms Augustine's doctrine of original sin: "It is certain that 'God made man upright'; perfectly holy and perfectly happy: But by rebelling against God, he destroyed himself, lost the favour and the image of God, and entailed sin, with its attendant, pain, on himself and all his posterity."[52]

Sin destroyed the chief aspect of *imago Dei*, that is, the moral image, but did not completely eliminate Wesley's three-fold understanding of it. The remaining aspects (the natural and the political strands) have not been entirely wiped out but have been severely damaged.[53] Wesley describes the consequences of sin taking hold of God's political image when recounting Adam and Eve in the first moments of sin: "She then 'gave to her husband, and he did eat.' And in that day, yea, that moment, he *died!* The life of God was extinguished in his soul. The glory departed from him. He lost the whole moral image of God,—righteousness and true holiness."[54]

---

49. Weber, *Politics*, 393.

50. Ibid. Verhey differentiates between "dominion" or "rule" and "stewardship." For him, "dominion" is a good gift from God to man. "Stewardship," on the other hand, is subject to God's authority, protecting God's agents from undue despotism of the earth, something which I believe is incorrectly attributed to the term "dominion." Verhey, *Nature*, 136–42.

51. Collins, *Wesley*, 54.

52. Wesley, "Mystery of Iniquity," 2.

53. Collins, *Wesley*, 63.

54. Wesley, "The End of Christ's Coming," 1:10.

So laborious toil, rather than liberating work, is man's subsequently imposed sentence.[55] The injured political image is further manifest in Wesley's remarks upon Luke 12:19 where a foolish businessmen says to himself: "soul, soul, you have ample goods laid up for many years; relax, eat, drink, be merry": "Thou no longer talkest of *thy* goods, or *thy* fruits, knowing they are not thine, but God's. The earth is the Lord's, and the fullness thereof: He is the Proprietor of heaven and earth. He cannot divest himself of his glory; he must be the Lord, the possessor, of all that is. Only he hath left a portion of his goods in thy hands, for such uses as he has specified."[56]

The rich fool is the perfect exemplar of heathen work because he believes his acquired possessions are *his*. Wesley's concept of God as Proprietor/Governor underlies his criticism of the fool because it gives man's dominion its limits; man is simply meant to steward that which is God's by right (*de jure*). Man does not *possess* non-human creation but is left with the responsibility of it until God calls him to account, and because the fool is not justified by faith, his political stewarding will oftentimes go awry. Sin skews the political image so man no longer knows how to work morally because he forgets the great Proprietor owns everything. Man should work in harmony with him in accordance with the moral law but is unable due to the loss of the moral image of God through sin. Wesley is clearly influenced by Baxter in his designation of God as "Proprietor." This also made its mark on Chalmers, as I have shown. On the other hand, man should exhibit God's presence and be a blessing to the rest of creation by virtue of the fact that he has been "crowned . . . with glory and honor" (Ps 8:5b).[57]

But if the political image has not been completely decimated, what is it capable of doing?

PREVENIENT GRACE FOR POLITICAL LIVING

"Although Wesley's writings have rarely been studied for its political significance, the political, social and economic implications of his life and ministry can scarcely be avoided."[58] In like manner with Calvin's peculiar grace, God graciously and continuously provides for man despite his sin so that he can gradually learn to act politically once again. Wesley says, "The same free grace continues to us, at this day, life, and breath, and all things. For there is nothing we are, or have, or do, which can deserve the least thing at God's

---

55. Collins, *Wesley*, 60.
56. Wesley, "On Wordly Folly," 2:4.
57. Collins, *Wesley*, 62.
58. Maddox, *Political Writings*, 37.

hand. 'All our works, Thou, O God, hast wrought in us.' These, therefore, are so many more instances of free mercy: and whatever righteousness may be found in man, this is also the gift of God."[59]

Whenever a good work is enacted, it is never without the helping hand of God because God himself is the fount of all good. As the psalmist says: "I have no good apart from you" (Ps 16:2). Wesley must account for this theologically rather than naturally. He describes: "For allowing that all the souls of men are dead in sin by *nature*, this excuses none, seeing there is no man that is in a state of mere nature; there is no man, unless he has quenched the Spirit, that is wholly void of the grace of God. No man living is entirely destitute of what is vulgarly called *natural conscience*. But this is not natural: It is more properly termed *preventing grace*."[60]

The term "preventing" (*praevenīre*) here is Latin's present infinitive ("prevenient" being the contemporary substitute) indicating something which precedes something else. This form of grace precedes the salvation of sinners and is itself unsalvific. Nevertheless it is the active moral empowerment of all men.

Notable in Wesley's quotation above is the mention of the Holy Spirit. Preventing grace refers to the agency of the Spirit in man and creation universally; as long as the Spirit has not been entirely resisted, agents can perform good works in and for the world through him. However, Wesley stresses that good works are impossible without the Spirit because man is completely depraved in his sin, thus all good which comes from him must surely stem from the Spirit's inspiration, not from his sinful nature.

Wesley is strikingly close to Calvin's notion of peculiar grace on this point. Although Wesley follows Augustine and sixteenth-century reformers in his interpretation of original sin, by appealing to the Eastern Fathers he significantly distances himself from them in his conception of grace.[61] He is quick to ensure that his account of original sin and total depravity is not left to Calvin's capricious account of predestination:

> Call it therefore by whatever name you please, election, preterition, predestination, or reprobation, it comes in the end to the same thing. The sense of all is plainly this,—by virtue of an eternal, unchangeable, irresistible decree of God, on part of mankind are infallibly saved, and the rest infallibly damned; it being impossible that any of the former should be damned, or that any of the latter should be saved. But if this be so, then is all

---

59. Wesley, "Salvation by Faith," 1.
60. Wesley, "On Working Out," 3:4.
61. Collins, *Wesley*, 73; Bundy, "Christian Virtue," 139.

preaching vain. It is needless to them that are elected; for they, whether with preaching or without, will infallibly be saved.[62]

Wesley draws upon John 1:9 ('The true light, which enlightens everyone, was coming into the world') as one of his mainstay biblical texts for prevenient grace. Here, Jesus is disclosed as the divine agent who graciously enables good work. He comments upon the Apostle John's logos-christology, "Everyone has some measure of that light, some faint glimmering ray, which, sooner or later, more or less, enlightens every man that cometh into the world."[63] Even though the effects of sin have devastated much of man's ability, because of Christ's ubiquitous light, depravity is no longer total. The restorative, enlightening Christ in man now empowers him by grace.[64] Wesley says in more detail,

> Every man has a greater or less measure of this [prevenient grace], which waiteth not for the call of man. Every one has, sooner or later, good desires; although the generality of men stifle them before they can strike deep root, or produce any considerable fruit. Everyone has some measure of that light, some faint glimmering ray, which, sooner or later, more or less, enlightens every man that cometh into the world. And every one, unless he be one of the small number whose conscience is seared as with a hot iron, feels more or less uneasy when he acts contrary to the light of his own conscience. So that no man sins because he has not grace, but because he does not use the grace which he hath.[65]

Note here the universality of grace which speaks of the divine desire to see all receive salvation. Moreover, Christ is a ubiquitous presence in all, an assertion based on John 1:9. This, too, reveals the influence of Justin Martyr (AD 103–6 5) upon Wesley, who says, "And those of the Stoic school—since, so far as their moral teaching went, they were admirable, as were also the poets in some particulars, on account of the seed of reason [the Logos] implanted in every race of men—were, we know, hated and put to death—Heraclitus for instance, and, among those of our own time, Musonius and others."[66]

---

62. Wesley, "Free Grace," 9, 10.
63. Wesley, "On Working Out," 3:4.
64. Collins, *Wesley*, 74.
65. Wesley, "On Working Out," 3:4.
66. Justin Martyr, "Second Apology," 8.

This Patristic influence in Welsey's thinking provokes him to say that Christ "is the Word whom the Father begat or spoke from eternity; by whom the Father speaking."[67] Christ extends his "light" to all men regardless of faith conviction and he does not indwell persons on merit; good works are both christologically illuminated and pneumatologically empowered. Both Christ and the Spirit work simultaneously, uniquely and harmoniously, to empower good works. For Wesley, there is no such thing as a "natural" person left wholly without some form of the presence of God. Umphrey Lee sums Wesley up well, "In this world, man exists as a natural man *plus* the prevenient grace of God."[68]

Prevenient grace then is both christological and pneumatological for Wesley, a commitment that Clark Pinnock (1937–2010), a protagonist of many Wesleyan distinctives, adopts.[69] Pinnock believes that Wesley is essentially advancing the third article of the Nicaean-Constantinopolitan creed through his notion of prevenient grace which reads: "we believe in the Holy Spirit, the Lord, and Giver of Life."[70] This creedal article bonds well with Wesley's theology of grace despite Wesley's lack of appeal to it in these discussions.

"The true light" which illuminates man is present in all to some degree; this logos christology takes place through the Holy Spirit. Prevenient grace is thus present by a matter of degree, which is why Wesley states that everyone has "*some measure* of that light, *some faith glimmering ray.*" Wesley says again, "For the effectual working of the Spirit of God goes through the whole creation; and that in the natural, as well as spiritual, world. For could mere matter act or move? Could it gravitate or attract? Just as much as it can think or speak."[71]

Consequently, man is able to collaborate occasionally or consistently with prevenient grace, albeit unwittingly and sporadically, just as it can be ignored and offended.

NARROW PREVENIENT GRACE

Albert Outler helpfully distinguishes between two uses of prevenient grace in Wesley's writings: (1) *narrow* prevenient grace, and (2) *broad* prevenient grace. Narrow prevenient grace has the salvation of man (*ordo salutis*) as its

67. Wesley, *John Wesley's Notes*, 1:1.
68. Lee, *John Wesley*, 124–25.
69. Olson, *Semper*, 23.
70. Pinnock, *Flame*, 239.
71. Wesley, *John Wesley's Notes*, 5:6.

focus which originates from the debate between Calvinists and Arminians in sixteenth- and seventeenth-century Holland and England.[72] This form of prevenient grace takes precedence in Wesley's writings[73] because man requires a right standing before God, his faculties repaired, and his morality restored through faith in Christ.[74] In fact, narrow prevenient grace is grounded entirely in Christ's crucifixion; thus it must be recognized that Wesley's account of prevenient grace is, in the main, the starting place for his soteriology, for grace is present in all by the Spirit with the specific purpose to woo all to Christ.[75]

> Some great truths, as the being and attributes of God, and the difference between moral good and evil, were known, in some measure, to the heathen world. The traces of them are to be found in all nations; So that, in some sense, it may be said to every child of man, "He hath showed thee, O man, what is good; even to do justly, to love mercy, and to walk humbly with thy God." With this truth he has, in some measure, "enlightened every one that cometh into the world."[76]

Narrow prevenient grace exists primarily among the heathen to sensitize and benevolently cajole them toward God the Father through Christ.[77] This reveals Wesley's reliance upon the Dutchman, Jacobus Arminius (1560-1609)[78], even though his reading of Arminius was not extensive.[79] Arminius says, for example, "Those individuals who *would*, through his preventing grace, *believe*, and, through his subsequent grace *would persevere*, according to the before described administration of those means which are suitable and proper for conversion and faith; and, by which foreknowledge, he likewise knew those who *would not believe and persevere*."[80]

The problem which Wesley toiled with was how to convey a restorative account of grace which did not *enforce* man's participation. Because grace is resistible in its prevenient form, it should not be mistaken for human freewill. But because this aspect of grace specifically focuses on the *ordo salutis*,

---

72. Collins, *Wesley*, 75.
73. Ibid., 76.
74. Maddox, *Responsible*, 83.
75. Dunning, *Grace*, 339; Wood, *Grace*, 209-22.
76. Wesley, "On Working Out," 2:1.
77. Langford, ""John Wesley's Doctrine," 59.
78. Gunter, ""John Wesley," 446-64.
79. Maddox, *Responsible*, 90.
80. Arminius, "Declaration of Sentiments," 247-48.

I will lay greater stress on the following aspect—broad prevenient grace for this discussion's purposes.[81]

BROAD PREVENIENT GRACE

Prevenient grace is broad in the sense that it enables virtuous living pan-anthropically and pan-historically,[82] even if there are those who find an absence of exegetical warrant for this.[83] It must be reiterated that such grace is unsalvific by nature despite its narrow equivalent wooing man to follow Christ. Concerning the universality of broad prevenient grace, Wesley states, "Certainly, whether this is natural or superadded by the grace of God, it is found, at least in some small degree, in every child of man. Something of this is found in every human heart, passing sentence concerning good and evil, not only in all Christians, but in all Mahometans, all Pagans, yea, the vilest of savages."[84]

Consequently, Socrates is appealed to by Wesley as an exemplar of a heathen working in the Spirit without any sign of Christian faith. Socrates was able to convey philosophical insight by virtue of the Spirit of truth working through him:[85]

> We may likewise reasonably suppose, that some traces of knowledge, both with regard to the invisible and the eternal world, were delivered down from Noah and his children, both to their immediate and remote descendants. And however these were obscured or disguised by the addition of numberless fables, yet something of truth was still mingled with them, and these streaks of light prevented utter darkness. Add to this, that God never, in any age or nation, "left himself" quite "without a witness" in the hearts of men; but while he "gave them rain and fruitful seasons," imparted some imperfect knowledge of the Giver. "He is the true Light that" still, in some degree, "enlighteneth every man that cometh into the world." But all these lights put together availed no farther than to produce a faint twilight. It gave them, even the most enlightened of them, no elegcos, no demonstration, no demonstrative conviction, either of the

---

81. Outler, "John Wesley: Folk Theologian," 153; Maddox, *Responsible*, 83; Dunning, *Grace*, 339.
82. Outler, "John Wesley's Interests," 105.
83. Witherington, *Problem*, 209.
84. Wesley, *Sermons*, 1:1.
85. Starkey, *Work of the Holy Spirit*, 40.

invisible or of the eternal world. Our philosophical poet justly terms Socrates, "The wisest of all moral men;" that is, of all that were not favoured with Divine Revelation.[86]

There is no one outwith the reach of the Spirit's broad prevenient grace then, not even other religious believers, protest or practical atheists. All have the potential of co-operating with prevenient grace, Wesley argues, albeit they are less likely to do so than the Christian.

In the Church of England's Thirty-Nine Articles which reveals a secondary origin of Wesley's conception of grace, broad prevenient grace is articulated: "The condition of Man after the fall of Adam is such, that he cannot turn and prepare himself, by his own natural strength and good works, to faith; and calling upon God. *Wherefore we have no power to do good works pleasant and acceptable to God, without the grace of God by Christ preventing us*, that we may have a good will, and working with us, when we have that good will."[87]

Christ, in his grace, ubiquitously comes to distorted men to enable them to reinvigorate their mandate to develop and cultivate the earth. Without Christ, man is only "natural" and thus unable to function morally at work, and the term "natural" here betrays Thomas Boston's (1676–1732) influence upon Wesley. Boston's *Human Nature in its Fourfold State* (a text which possibly became the most reprinted book in eighteenth-century Scotland) delineates sharply between man who has become 'natural' because of sin, and man who is in a state of grace.[88] Boston relates,

> Most men are so far from making God their chief end, in their natural and civil actions, that in these matters, God is not in all their thoughts. . . . And what are the unrenewed man's civil actions, such as buying, selling, working, &c., but fruit to himself? (Hos 10:1). . . . for they have no eye to God therein, to please Him; but all they had in view was to please themselves (Gen. 6:3). In opposition to their natural relative state, the state of corruption, there is a change made upon them in regeneration whereby their nature is changed.[89]

With Christ mysteriously inspiring man, good works can be performed by anyone: "While a man is in a mere natural state, before he is born of God, he has, in a spiritual sense, eyes and sees not; a thick impenetrable

---

86. Wesley, "Difference between Walking," 9–10.
87. "Articles of Religion" in *Book of Common Prayer*, X (my emphasis).
88. Noll, *Rise*, 53.
89. Boston, *Human Nature*, 126, 203.

veil lies upon them; he has ears, but hears not; he is utterly deaf to what he is most of all concerned to hear. His other spiritual senses are all locked up: He is in the same condition as if he had them not. . . . [T]herefore, though he is a living man, he is a dead Christian."[90]

The heathen are in a similar position to Christians in their works (except for the destruction of the moral image among them) because they cannot begin their progressive healing through prevenient grace except through justification and sanctification. This is so because Christians have a clear advantage over the heathen in works for they can morally discern with greater sensitivity to the Spirit's leading regarding what forms of work to undertake, where to work and how to work. After all, Christians "have the mind of Christ" (1 Cor 2:16b). This advantage is to have commenced the healing process through justification so as to do *evangelical works*, not simply mundane work.

Concerning the natural image, the heathen demonstrate nascent tendencies of affection and actions in the Spirit, and although they are bestowed with this potential, it would be false to claim that this is something of their *possession*. Rather, prevenient grace must be viewed as *God's activity* in their lives, for the depravity of men does not obliterate all human faculties but shuts off much of God's presence so as to be without his enabling power to live effectively.[91] Christ gives himself to men through the grace of the Spirit prior to salvation for their sake. Wesley describes the heathen's ability to work according to the good by God's grace:

> Can it be denied that something of this is found in every man born into the world? And does it not appear as soon as the understanding opens, as soon as reason begins to dawn? Does not every one then begin to know that there is a difference between good and evil; how imperfect soever the various circumstances of this sense of good and evil may be? Does not every man, for instance, know, unless blinded by the prejudices of education, (like the inhabitants of the Cape of Good Hope) that it is good to honour his parents? Do not all men, however uneducated or barbarous, allow, it is right to do to others as we would have them do to us?[92]

Wesley adopts two different analogies to describe how the heathen engage the world by prevenient grace (albeit in a limited sense). The first of these picks up the image of a newborn child where despite its infancy, its

90. Wesley, "The New Birth," 2:4.
91. Maddox, *Responsible*, 89–90.
92. Wesley, "On Conscience," 1:4.

senses are operational. However, these senses are by no means fully operational regardless of their acute sensitivity; they require continuous training towards maturity in order to interpret life aright: "Before a child is born into the world he has eyes, but sees not; he has ears, but does not hear. He has a very imperfect use of any other sense. He has no knowledge of any of the things of the world, or any natural understanding. To that manner of existence which he then has, we do not even give the name of life. It is then only when a man is born, that we say he begins to live."[93]

The second analogy Wesley draws upon is a toad trapped in a tree trunk; the tree is felled, cracks open, and the toad leaps out. Wesley speculates as to how long this toad has been inside the oak. Perhaps it has lived its entire life trapped inside the vertical organism. Assuming this, the toad has had limited fresh air to breathe and has never seen the light of day. Its perception of noises outside of the trunk have been muted and dulled at best, and its space to maneuver has been greatly restricted. In other words, its sensory perspective of the outside world is distorted and far from reality, and while these experiences are valid, they are far from a comprehensive and clear perspective of the world. Wesley draws some conclusions from such an analogy for the heathen:

> How exact a parallel may be drawn between this creature (hardly to be called an animal) and a man that is "without God in the world!" . . . Every one of these is in exactly such a situation with regard to the invisible as the toad was in respect to the visible world. That creature had undoubtedly a sort of life, such as it was. It certainly had all the internal and external parts that are essential to animal life; and, without question, it had suitable juices, which kept up a kind of circulation. This was a life indeed! And exactly such a life is that of the Atheist, the man "without God in the world." What a thick veil is between him and the invisible world, which, with regard to him, is as though it had no being! He has not the least perception of it; not the most distant idea. . . . In a word, he has no more intercourse with a knowledge of the spiritual world, than this poor creature had of the natural, while shut up in its dark enclosure.[94]

Wesley's use of "without God in the world" here is important because it originates in the Apostle Paul's letter to the Ephesians (2:12) where he discusses the meaning of works in light of grace. The immediate literary context of this phrase reveals that "even when we were dead in our trespasses, [God]

---

93. Wesley, "The New Birth," 2:4.
94. Wesley, "On Living Without God," 6, 8.

made us alive together with Christ" (2:5). Paul's statement here reveals that Christ has objectively enlivened man *prior* to faith in him. This is an actuality for heathen and Christians alike, and yet those who are "atheists in the world" live contrary to the liberation which Christ has wrought for them and so they remain "dead Christians."[95]

As Karl Barth would describe it two centuries later, the heathen walk blindly up the downward escalator of God's love and grace.[96] In light of the grace of the Christ, the Apostle Paul maintains that the cultural mandate (Gen 1:28; 2:15) is liberated and reinstated as one key goal for which the salvation of man is intended. He says, "For we are what he has made us, created in Christ Jesus for good works, which God prepared beforehand to be our way of life" (Eph 2:10).

Given this literary context of Eph 2, the goal of workers is made plain. Further, the heathen can progress towards the goal of working in tandem with the Father in the Spirit by surrendering to Christ's justification for them, and in the meantime, as Wesley conveys with his toad and tree analogy, the heathen do have some capability to work beneficently for the world despite their lack of "the powers of the world to come." However, even this inferior capability to work can be shut off from the heathen prior to justification as Wesley's sermon "On Living Without God" relates how incapacitated heathen man was when compared to the state of awakened faith:

> But the moment the Spirit of the Almighty strikes the heart of him that was till then without God in the world, it breaks the hardness of his heart, and creates all things new. The Sun of Righteousness appears, and shines upon his soul, showing him the light of the glory of God in the face of Jesus Christ. He is in a new world. All things round him are become new, such as it never before entered into his heart to conceive. He sees, so far as his newly-opened eyes can bear the sight . . . By the same gracious stroke, he that before had ears but heard not is now made capable of hearing. He hears the voice that raiseth the dead,—the voice of Him that is "the resurrection and the life." He is no longer deaf to his invitations or commands, to his promises or threatenings; but gladly hears every word that proceeds out of his mouth, and governs thereby all his thoughts, words, and actions.[97]

---

95. Ibid., 1.
96. Bettis, "Universalist," 430.
97. Wesley, "On Living Without God," 9–10.

It is curious why Wesley makes a robust case for broad prevenient grace among the heathen, and then so powerfully denies it in the next breath. However, as I will show from his sermon "On Conscience," Wesley does have an account of good works by the heathen which most likely reveals that the quotation above is an instance where Wesley is at pains to stress the depravity of man, and the necessity of being justified by Christ through faith.

Wesley nuances his polemic about the hopeless state of man outside of Christ by admitting that progressive growth is observable among the heathen, albeit minimal growth because of their lack of salvation: "But before this universal change there may be many partial changes in a natural man, which are frequently mistaken for it, whereby many say, 'Peace, peace!' to their souls, when there is no peace . . . that total change from the image of the earthly Adam into the image of the heavenly, from an earthly, sensual, devilish mind, into the mind that was in Christ."[98]

All this is to be couched, relates Wesley, within the sphere of divine love for creation, a perspective which is paramount in understanding the interplay between God and the heathen:

> Let it be observed, I purposely add, "to those that are under the Christian dispensation," because I have no authority from the Word of God "to judge those that are without." Nor do I conceive that any man living has a right to sentence all the heathen and Mahometan world to damnation. It is far better to leave them to him that made them, and who is "the Father of the spirits of all flesh;" who is the God of the Heathens as well as the Christians, and who hateth nothing that he hath made.[99]

Yet because man is depraved by nature, it is never man's sinful nature which inspires good work, but broad prevenient grace. It is only through this grace that human beings can produce good works, for when prevenient grace is resisted, the depravity of man is at work, keeping the benevolent Spirit of God at bay.[100] But by co-operating with the broad operations of prevenient grace, man crowns his work which Wesley reveals when writing to John Smith:[101] "I believe firmly, and that in the most literal sense, that 'without God we can do nothing'; that we cannot think, or speak, or move an hand or an eye without the concurrence of the divine energy; and that all

---

98. Ibid., 12.
99. Ibid., 14.
100. Cobb, *Grace*, 40.
101. Ibid., 40.

our natural faculties are God's gift, nor can the meanest be exerted without the assistance of His Spirit."[102]

What this means is that the Holy Spirit makes up a significant and constitutive part of man; men do not exist apart from God, only afterwards coming into relationship with him through faith. Instead, what must be understood is that without the grace of the Holy Spirit man does not even exist. This is apparent in creational scriptures such as: "then the LORD God formed man from the dust of the ground, and breathed into his nostrils the breath [*neshama*] of life; and the man became a living being" (Gen 2:7); "when you take away their breath [*ruach*], they die and return to the dust. When you send for your spirit [*ruach*], they are created; and you renew the face of the ground" (Ps 104:29b–30).

Twentieth- and twenty-first-century perspectives on these biblical texts remark that in the Genesis text the term *neshama* is used, a term which connotes Adam as a living soul, and *neshama* is a synonym of *ruach* which is commonly used to refer to the "breath of life" in human beings.[103] John Taylor in his famous text *The Go-Between God* also postulates, "*Ruach* is a different kind of power inherent in man, associated not so much with his being alive as with him being a person. We might call it the power of his personhood, the power of his separate otherness, the power by which he is recognized as himself."[104] Without the Spirit enlivening the dust of the earth then, men are non-existent according to the psalmist. Wesley's account is faithful to such creational, biblical manifestations of the Spirit's constitutive part of man, and as such, Ben Witherington III's attack on the absence of biblical foundations of prevenient grace, is unfounded.[105]

Pinnock pushes a little further by rightly asserting that the Spirit of God is ubiquitously present, working in every heart, working in every sphere of life at all times throughout history. The Spirit's form of influence is not merely domestic, noetic or ontic, but global, Pinnock asserts, for the whole of creation is groaning under the weight of sin's contradiction, all the while the Spirit empowers groaning prayers in light of a coming hope (Rom 8:22–27).[106]

---

102. Wesley, *Letters of John Wesley*, 7.
103. Kim, *Holy Spirit*, 11.
104. Taylor, *Go-Between*, 7.
105. Witherington, *Problem*, 209.
106. Pinnock, *Flame*, 200.

IMPLICATIONS OF PREVENIENT GRACE

What does prevenient grace enable heathen work to accomplish in society? Despite the sinful malfunction of the political image, the mandate to govern responsibly the earth is still binding, and this is so despite sin's influence in much that is done for the world through work. The binding role of stewardship even retains fragments of its analogy to God as creator, as it was prelapsarianly.[107]

However, the political image is no longer the direct conduit of God to the rest of creation due to the shattering of the moral image. Despite this, Theodore Weber helpfully suggests that the *constitution* of the political image is still intact somewhat, even if the *representational aspect* of it is lost and redirected to man's selfish agenda. Men can nevertheless govern the earth and its non-human creatures so that they might benefit the world consistently.[108]

Further, Wesley limited political responsibility to those who held political office. Because God elects governments, those in political office are the sole political agents under him (Rom 13): "They [those in political office] are all from God, who constituted all in general, and permits each in particular by his providence. The powers that be are appointed by God—It might be rendered, are subordinate to, or, orderly disposed under, God; implying, that they are God's deputies or vice regents and consequently, their authority being, in effect, his, demands our conscientious obedience."[109]

All remaining people belong under the descending conferral of authority by which they are to submit to those elected over them. This means, for Wesley, that all those outwith political office have no divine commission to care politically for creation. Weber, however, challenges Wesley's notion of the political image in light of prevenient grace because God's restoration of man to his political role through grace should no longer be restricted to elected politicians. "When humankind as a whole is defined essentially in a vocation of governance imaging God, it is no longer possible theologically to exclude the mass of humanity from the political process."[110]

Wesley's formula for the political image was: "*from God and therefore not from the people,*" but this must be reformed in light of the implications of the restoration of the political image to: "*from God and therefore through*

---

107. Weber, *Politics*, 395.
108. Ibid., 395.
109. Wesley, *John Wesley's Notes*, 13:1.
110. Weber, *Politics*, 399.

the people."¹¹¹ There should be no exclusion or exemption from working politically in the world because it is man's responsibility, regardless of competence. Instead, man should be viewed politically *because* he is created, not by way of office or political election as Wesley maintains.¹¹² The heathen are not excluded from this shared responsibility, and because the political image remains intact despite the savage molestation of sin, the heathen can be included in the participative task of shaping and re-shaping the earth. They, as is common to all men, are political by their commission and constituent nature.¹¹³

However, it is necessary for the fulfillment of the political image that (1) man accepts his responsibility for creation, and that (2) creation is indeed cared for rather than destroyed.¹¹⁴ For Wesley, man is political and can bring about his own success and fulfillment, unlike Aristotle's political animal (*zōon politikon*).

CONSCIENCE

Wesley describes the work of prevenient grace in most detail through the category *conscience*, a term he employs as a synonym of prevenient grace.¹¹⁵ First of all, a definition of conscience is in order as Wesley believes there exists four different meanings of the term. Conscience is (1) *a witness*—it testifies to "what we have done, in thought, or word, or action"; (2) *a judge*—"passing sentence on what we have done, that it is good or evil"; (3) the sentence of judgment stemming from "occasioning a degree of complacency in him that does well, and a degree of uneasiness in him that does evil";¹¹⁶ and (4) in the letter to the Hebrews Wesley adds a fourth aspect of conscience—man's "inmost soul."¹¹⁷ A blend of all four is required so that conscience can be defined as "that faculty whereby we are at once conscience of our own thoughts, words, and actions; and of their merit or demerit, of their being good or bad; and, consequently, deserving either praise or censure."¹¹⁸

---

111. Ibid.
112. Ibid., 399.
113. Ibid., 401.
114. Ibid., 400. For a good example of responsible political ethics see, Northcott, *A Moral Climate*, chapter 5.
115. Wesley, "On Working Out," 3:4.
116. Wesley, "On Conscience," 1:7.
117. Wesley, *John Wesley's Notes*, 9:14.
118. Wesley, "On Conscience," 1:3.

Conscience produces moral self-awareness, and is not a natural law at work in man, for there is nothing natural about prevenient grace, but rather, supernatural. Wesley insists that it is Christ who enlightens every person, so that one must say "He," not nature, "has told you, O mortal, what is good" (Mic 6:8a). This understanding of Christ's ubiquity is then worked out pneumatologically because apart from the Holy Spirit no one can enact a good work.[119]

Wesley identifies the narrative of Balak and Balaam as an example of conscience at work among the heathen. Balak, the king of Moab, summons Balaam to curse the Israelites as they make their way from Egypt to the promised land via Moab. Balaam, a diviner by trade, is visited by the God of Israel who commands him to "speak only what I tell you to speak" (Num 22:35; 23:26). As Balaam eventually explains to King Balak the reason why he did not complete his task, he confesses, "The word that God puts in my mouth, that is what I must say" (Num 22:38). This indeed is what comes to pass (Num 23:16). Wesley argues that Balaam (and perhaps also Balak) is the perfect example of inspiration by "divine impressions" via his conscience even though he is not a formal follower of YHWH:[120]

> This occasioned his consulting with, or asking counsel of, Balaam,—his proposing the question to which Balaam gives so full an answer: (Micah 6:5ff.:) "O my people," saith the Prophet in the name of God, "remember what Balak the King of Moab consulted," (it seems, in the fulness of his heart,) "and what Balaam the son of Beor answered him. Wherewith," saith he, "shall I come before the Lord, and Bow myself before the high God. Shall I come before him with calves of a year old? Will the Lord be pleased with thousands of rams, or with ten thousand rivers of oil? Shall I give my first-born for my transgression the fruit of my body for the sin of my soul" (This the kings of Moab had actually done, on occasions of deep distress; a remarkable account of which is recorded in the third chapter of the Second Book of Kings.) To this Balaam makes that noble reply, (being, doubtless, then taught of God,) "He hath showed thee, O man, what is good; and what doth the Lord require of thee, but to do justly, to love mercy, and to walk humbly with thy God."[121]

Using Mic 6:8, Wesley locates the source of heathen ability to do good, and in the case of Balaam, christologically. This use of scripture builds upon

---

119. Watkin-Jones, *The Holy Spirit*, 271.
120. Wesley, "On Conscience," 1:6.
121. Ibid.

and supports Wesley's understanding of John 1:9 (as the narrative of Balaam and Balak demonstrates) which reveals a degree of moral assessment for work among the heathen. The Apostle Paul's letter to the Romans reveals an explanation of how this takes place: "When the Gentiles, who do not possess the law, do instinctively what the law requires, these, though not having the law, are a law to themselves. They show what the law requires is written on their hearts, to which their own conscience also bears witness; and their conflicting thoughts will accuse [*katēgorountōn*] or perhaps excuse [*apologoumenōn*] them on the day (Rom 2:14–16a)."

Wesley observes in the Apostle Paul's epistles that the term "conscience" takes the form of "a faculty or power, implanted by God in every soul that comes into the world."[122] Further:

> God has made us thinking beings, capable of perceiving what is present, and of reflecting or looking back on what is past. In particular, we are capable of perceiving whatsoever passes in our own hearts or lives; of knowing whatsoever we feel or do; and that either while it passes, or when it is past. This we mean when we say, man is a conscious being: He hath a consciousness, or inward perception, both of things present and past, relating to himself, of his own tempers and outward behavior. But what we usually term conscience, implies somewhat more than this. It is not barely the knowledge of our present or the remembrance of our preceding life. To remember, to bear witness either of past or present things, is only one, and the least office of conscience: Its main business is to excuse or accuse, to approve or disapprove, to acquit or condemn.[123]

This matches Wesley's description of broad prevenient grace in man:

> For allowing that all the souls of men are dead in sin by nature, this excuses none, seeing there is no man that is in a state of mere nature; there is no man, unless he has quenched the Spirit, that is wholly void of the grace of God. No man living is entirely destitute of what is vulgarly called natural conscience. But this is not natural: It is more properly termed preventing grace. Every man has a greater or less measure of this [prevenient grace], which waiteth not for the call of man.[124]

This conscience among the heathen is nothing other than the "finger of God" in their midst: "But what is the rule whereby men are to judge of right

---

122. Wesley, "The Witness," 5.
123. Ibid., 4.
124. Wesley, "On Working Out," 3:4.

and wrong whereby their conscience is to be directed? The rule of Heathens, as the Apostle teaches elsewhere is 'the law written in their hearts;' by the finger of God; 'their conscience also bearing witness,' whether they walk by this rule or not, 'and their thoughts the mean while accusing, or even excusing,' acquitting, defending them; η και απολογουμενςν (Rom 2:14–15)."[125]

The works of the heathen could be eschatologically significant, according to the Apostle, either for reward (*apologoumenōn*) or punishment (*katēgorountōn*) depending on their adherence to the voice of conscience. With this, Wesley reveals that works are not simply for temporal life but correlate to the eschaton. The implication here, although left undeveloped by both the Apostle Paul and Wesley, is that some heathen will be approved by a judging Jesus at the eschaton because they acted upon their conscience in accordance with the moral law. This key point will be discussed later in my analysis of the sheep and the goats. Recollecting my opening chapter, Schaeffer also employs Rom 2 to evaluate the good work of non-Christians, and comes to similar conclusions but without any discussion of conscience.

Oswald Chambers postulates, in his considerable discussion of conscience, that conscience cannot be viewed as God's voice *universally* among men. This is problematic, Chambers insists, because God's voice would be universally audible to all men, and in his opinion, this is evidently not the case.[126] But if Maddox is correct in saying that prevenient grace is something that can be resisted or fostered, then God's Spirit at least prompts ubiquitously, while also resisted, quenched, and unrecognized.

Ray Dunning helpfully builds upon Maddox adding nuances which describe conscience as the "formal" work of the Spirit's prevenient grace in all even if "materially" the consequence of family upbringing, education, and experience has not been part of their formation.[127]

Biblically speaking, John 16:8–11 is key to grasping Wesley's understanding of "conscience." The Apostle John writes concerning the Holy Spirit's relationship with the heathen, "And when [the Comforter] comes, he will prove the world wrong about sin, righteousness and judgment: about sin, because they do not believe in me; about righteousness, because I am going to the Father and you will see me no longer; about judgment, because the ruler of this world has been condemned."

Dunning is correct to ascertain this teaching of Jesus in Wesley's notion of conscience, for this is precisely the emphasis which Wesley develops, albeit without alluding to this particular passage. Jesus' emphasis in this

---

125. Wesley, "The Witness," 6.
126. Chambers, *Philosophy*, 61.
127. Dunning, *Grace*, 433.

teaching is that the Holy Spirit gives man moral antennae to discern good from evil. But in what way is John referring to "the world" in verse 8? Does "the world" refer to those who put Jesus to a political dissident's death or does it refer to those *who will be* indwelt by the Holy Spirit through faith in Christ?[128] There is nothing to suggest that the Spirit's operations are limited to Christians from this monologue, rather, the opposite. The Spirit is at work among all men, seeking to get their attention prior to faith, and even though the Spirit especially indwells Christians, he is nonetheless present for the heathen also through their conscience.

This example implies three further ramifications about conscience: (1) workers can know themselves, their thoughts, and sometimes their intentions. "[T]his is not possible for [them] to do, without the assistance of the Spirit of God."[129] (2) Wesley assumes a cognizance of the moral law that can be learned but which requires an existing and active knowledge of scripture. Rather than a theological rule, this point manifests Wesley's method of imparting biblical knowledge to groups of workers during his missionary endeavors. (3) Conscience implies a knowledge that all one's work, words, and thoughts, are to come under the rule of the moral law of Christ. "If you say, 'Yes, there certainly may be a consciousness of having done right or wrong, without any reference to him;' I answer, This I cannot grant: I doubt whether the very words, right and wrong, according to the Christian system, do not imply, in the very idea of them, agreement and disagreement to the will and word of God."[130]

So a person must be wittingly and willingly able to acknowledge God because of the conscience of prevenient grace. This is somewhat unrealistic. Wesley makes his practical method for making disciples binding and universal for conscience, but this need not necessarily follow. Simply because Wesley insisted upon the rigorous discipline of biblical reading for those who joined his Methodist groups, it does not necessarily follow that conscience need be acknowledged for it to be operative in all men.

Yet through prevenient grace, despite sin's destruction of the moral image of God, heathen man is enabled to make moral judgments once more, and he is able to discern when things are or are not the way they ought to be. Wesley says elsewhere, "But it is not true, that either the *public* or the *moral sense* (both of which are included in the term conscience) is now natural to man. Whatever may have been the case at first, while man was in a state of

---

128. Ibid.
129. Wesley, "On Conscience," 1:11.
130. Ibid., 1:12.

innocence, both the one and the other is now a branch of that supernatural gift of God which we usually style, preventing grace."[131]

Lastly, as if to conclude his thoughts on the topic, Wesley says of conscience while quoting Luke 6:31 ("Do to others as you would have them do to you"), "Do not all men, however uneducated or barbarous, allow, it is right to do to others as we would have them do to us?"[132] But how does the heathen conscience actually co-operate with the Holy Spirit?

Although Chalmers succeeds Wesley's account of conscience historically, Wesley's delineation of the concept is far superior because he is able to ground the nature of conscience christologically and pneumatologically through the biblical narrative directly. Both accounts are adequately described, but only one is definitively rooted from scripture and Christian theology. Chalmers' notion of conscience is simply hampered by its transcendental categories of the Scottish enlightenment.

SYNERGISM

"Synergism," from the Greek *synergos* and the Latin *synergismus*, meaning "a working together," gives Wesley's prevenient grace its character. Man can decide to co-operate with divine grace in his works so that there can be said to be a "division of labour" between the Spirit and the human agent.[133] Typically, synergism is discussed in soteriological debates, and it was the claim of some Calvinists in Wesley's day that he advocated a faith *and* works-based salvation as a result of his commitments to synergism.[134] In contrast to synergism, "monergism" is understood to teach that God alone works through human agency irrespective of man's will. In other words, there is only one active agent—God.

The Apostle Paul's injunction to the Philippian church to 'work out [*katergazesthe*] your own salvation with fear and trembling; for it is God who is at work [*energōn*] in you, enabling you both to will and to work [*energein*] for his good pleasure' (Phil 2:12a–13) is appealed to by Wesley as a good example of why synergism is preferable to monergism as an account of the empowerment of work. "First, God works; therefore you *can* work. Secondly, God works, therefore you *must* work."[135] Furthermore, the middle voice of *katergazesthe* strongly indicates the synergy of both divine

131. Ibid., 1:9. "[A] state of innocence" is the language of Thomas Boston.
132. Ibid., 1:4.
133. Dunning, *Grace*, 429.
134. Outler, *John Wesley*, 350.
135. Wesley, "On Working Out," 3:2.

and human participation as the middle voice "is in meaning much closer to the Active than to the Passive [voice]."[136] Therefore this voice of the verb *ergon* (to work) conveys the distribution and joining together of human and divine wills in labor. Because God the Spirit is at work ubiquitously, man has therefore the inspiration to work and this can result in the heathen doing good, but without a pneumatological progenitor there can be no good work by man. Because of the prevenient grace of the Spirit, man is given the imperative to work, and because the Spirit is present to work in and with him, he has the virtuous faculties to do so.

Ostentatious work, also, is often covertly subverted by God's grace: "God worketh in you; therefore you can work: Otherwise it would be impossible. If he did not work it would be impossible for you to work out your own salvation. 'With man this is impossible,' saith our Lord, 'for a rich man to enter into the kingdom of heaven.' Yea, it is impossible for any man, for any that is born of a woman, unless God work in him."[137]

Seen here also is language that befits narrow prevenient grace; the impulse of the Spirit in wooing men to Christ.

Wesley's friend, William Tilly, and also Macarius of Egypt (300–391), both influences of Wesley's synergistic prevenient grace, stressed that men should put the grace of God to work. Wesley says of Tilly: "Dr. Tilly's sermons on Free Will are the best I ever saw. His text is, 'Work out your own salvation with fear and trembling.'"[138] Macarius also reveals the kind of thinking which Wesley attributes to Christians:

> 3. *Question:* Do they then not know that they are possessed of something which they had not before? *Answer:* They do: but still they look upon themselves to be of no esteem. Though with God they are precious, yet with themselves they are not so—but just as if they had known nothing at all.[139]

Wesley, though, put more of an emphasis upon *grace's empowerment* in man's works: "But rest not here. Let thy 'righteousness exceed the righteousness of the Scribes and Pharisees.' Be not thou content to 'keep the whole law, and offend in one point.' Hold thou fast all His commandments, and all 'false ways do thou utterly abhor.' Do all the things whatsoever He hath

---

136. Wenham, *Elements*, 92.
137. Wesley, "On Working Out," 3:1.
138. See Wesley's reliance upon Tilly in *The Letters of John Wesley*.
139. Macarius of Egypt, "Spiritual Homily XV."

commanded, and that with all thy might. Thou canst do all things through Christ strengthening thee; though without Him thou canst do nothing."[140]

But what form does man's part in synergism take? Wesley's comments concerning this oscillate considerably, and conclude that any discussion of human co-operation with God which accentuates quietism, unconditional election or limited atonement, is to be automatically rejected. This anti-Calvinist principle governs his notion of synergism, for although man is depraved because of sin, the imperative to work for good is always binding. In other words, Wesley continually stressed the infusion of the restoring powers of the grace of the Spirit for a depraved race: "This faculty seems to be what is usually meant by those who speak of natural conscience; an expression frequently found in some of our best authors, but yet not strictly just. For though in one sense it may be termed natural, because it is found in all men; yet, properly speaking, it is not natural, but a supernatural gift of God, above all his natural endowments."[141]

The ability to respond to prevenient grace does not originate in the conjured effort of man, but graciously begins its restoration because of the Christ event. Good work stems *entirely* from prevenient grace.[142] However, there is a genuine human contribution with the grace of the Spirit Wesley maintains, otherwise "we were mere machines, stocks, and stones."[143] But in case too much credit is given to man's works, Wesley hardly ever stresses man's part in this collaboration, but instead it is enough for him to explain the Spirit's inspiration in the work of the heathen.

Consequently, Wesley does not clearly develop a theology of *human participation* with the Spirit, but instead claims that synergistic participation takes the shape of passive openness to the Spirit's influence that highlights libertarian freedom (and thus a rejection of determinism).[144] But this account comes too close to man's passivity, almost to the negation of synergism.

More accurately, *co-operative* prevenient grace is imbedded in all men as God's *activity* because "[v]irtue assumes that the intellect and will are ordered to something external to the human person."[145] The good must continually be chosen by the heathen despite the temptation and freedom to do otherwise. Wesley gets it right on this occasion: "It may be farther observed,

140. Wesley, "Upon Our Lord's Sermon," 4:13.
141. Wesley, "On Conscience," 1:5.
142. Maddox, *Responsible*, 93.
143. Wesley, "Heavenly Treasure," 1:1.
144. Collins, *Wesley*, 15.
145. Long, *Moral*, 175.

(and it is an important observation,) that where there is no liberty, there can be no moral good or evil, no virtue or vice. The fire warms us; yet it is not capable of virtue: it burns us; yet this is no vice. There is no virtue, but where an intelligent being knows, loves, and chooses what is good."[146]

What is good can only be realized in the virtuous working life, for "Jesus' human performance is the renewal of the image of God in creatures."[147] God is to be credited with the influence of good work without forgetting to give human work its lesser due. This reveals a healthy divine/human ordering in Wesley; God takes priority but the agency of man does play a part, and man is always the junior partner in this co-operation for good works. This is the nature of synergism in Wesley's account of prevenient grace.[148]

ANALYSIS OF PREVENIENT GRACE

Where Wesley's theology of grace for heathen work differs from Calvin's account is that it seeks to explicate *how*, and to what degree, human and divine agency interrelate, whereas Calvin's account is more descriptive of the instances where grace empowers observable forms of work in society. Wesley's outlining of prevenient grace is almost entirely lacking Calvin's identifiable examples, and without doubt, Wesley would have benefited from Calvin's account of "natural" gifts as a way of articulating benevolent ability among the heathen. By appealing to *charismata*, Calvin is able to establish firmly his link between the impious and the Holy Spirit in a way that ensures the indwelling of the Holy Spirit among Christians has a greater degree of intensity. Nevertheless, Wesley's account of prevenient grace on the whole outdoes Calvin's equivalent because it bypasses Calvin's capricious conception of predestination that eventually suffocates his generally positive account.

Appalled by Calvin's doctrine of predestination, which ends up dominating all other doctrines in his system, Wesley's account of heathen conscience improves that which ends so negatively with Calvin. This gives the good work of the heathen the opportunity to shine without the tarnish of a determined eschatological destination.

As alluded to earlier, Wesley's account of synergism does much to support the Spirit of God as the progenitor of all that is good in human agency. This is laudable on his part. However, his account is considerably weakened by the absence of man's participation in synergism; after all, how synergistic is Wesley's account of prevenient grace if he refuses to say anything about

---

146. Wesley, "End of Christ's Coming," 1:6.
147. Long, *Moral*, 174.
148. Collins, *Wesley*, 76.

man's contribution in view of divine inspiration? Ensuring that Calvinistic determinism does not rule men, Wesley deems it unnecessary to make a huge case for man's part in synergism; it is enough for him to make a cursory comment that men are not inanimate objects, otherwise the trap of Calvin's doctrine of predestination rears its ugly head.

If Wesley had returned to his conception of the "natural" image of God in man, however, he would have been able to utilize his threefold notion that man still has some function in (1) *understanding*, (2) *will*, and (3) *liberty* despite the results of sin. This cluster of faculties would explain man's important, but inferior, part in synergism.

It is important that Wesley has provided a functional appropriation of *imago Dei* alongside his other two strands for to ignore the blatant revelation of this in scripture would be a great omission. However, it is disappointing that Wesley does not have an adequate or lengthy treatment of this. The moral image is his dominant stress and interest, thus the political image is squeezed out continually, and almost forgotten. Perhaps if he had concentrated more upon the political image, Wesley might not seem at first glance an unusual interlocutor for the modern subject of work. Theodore Weber's critique of not only Wesley's under-emphasis of the political image of God in man, but his notion of the descending conferral of authority in his political thinking though, frees Wesley up to grant all men the responsibility to act politically in view of the broad prevenient grace of God.

By identifying "conscience" as a key synonym of prevenient grace, Wesley makes significant strides into explicating the nature of this grace for all men. He oscillates at times between the heathen having no ability to do good and their modest capabilities, which is in actual fact his attempt to show that he remains deeply committed to the depravity of man prior to justification.

This can be frustrating reading given his positive estimation of the operation of conscience in other places; on these occasions he is intentionally hedging as he reacts to those who wish to criticize his practical theology. On the other hand, he positively acknowledges the broad prevenient grace of God among the heathen as he identifies the narrative of Balak and Balaam as a specific instance of it at work. This is the genius of developing the category of conscience: it forces Wesley to describe, as much as is possible, just *how* the Spirit is at work in the subconscious of men, and in this sense, his outlining of conscience is a general strength in his overall conception of broad prevenient grace among the heathen.

Given that Wesley placed a large degree of emphasis upon the importance of works performed, what did he make of the correlation between works and the eschaton in the parable of the sheep and the goats?

THE SHEEP AND THE GOATS

The true co-operation that takes place in synergism lends itself to discussing the parable of the sheep and the goats because there appears to be a causal link between man's mundane work and his eternal destiny, despite the evangelicals investigated here decrying such a notion. If good work partly exists for human perfection, as Wesley argues, this parable might end up supporting his theory of synergism further.

Wesley preached two sermons and made some comments in his *Notes on the New Testament* on the sheep and the goats, and I will now evaluate several of Wesley's pertinent thoughts from these sources.

Wesley seeks to explain the sheep and the goats by proposing that the means of grace is not limited to preaching and reception of scripture, Eucharist, or fasting and prayer (private and public); the means of grace must also include "works of piety." He explains,

> Surely there are works of mercy, as well as works of piety, which are real means of grace. They are more especially such to those that perform them with a single eye. And those that neglect them, do not receive the grace which otherwise they might. Yea, and they lose, by a continued neglect, the grace which they had received. Is it not hence that many who were once strong in faith are now weak and feeble-minded. And yet they are not sensible whence that weakness comes, as they neglect none of the ordinances of God. But they might see whence it comes, were they seriously to consider St. Paul's account of all true believers: "We are his workmanship, created anew in Christ Jesus unto good works, which God hath before prepared, that we might walk therein." (Eph 2:10)[149]

Because of the salvific nature of the works of the sheep they are considered "real" acts of grace, for except for grace how else could works count towards eternal bliss? Moreover, such works must also be considered ordinances of God, which Wesley supports by quoting the Apostle Paul's brief summation of the meaning of work in light of creation. Also, the identity of the sheep is revealed by Wesley as "true believers" producing good works or *evangelical works* in light of Christ, which remains a task solely for the saints. Because of the Christian identity of the sheep, Wesley interprets the parable as an explanation of the necessity of works that perfect the Christian toward their ultimate redemption:

---

149. Wesley, "On Visiting the Sick," 1:1.

The walking herein is essentially necessary, as to the continuance of that faith whereby we are already saved by grace, so to the attainment of everlasting salvation. Of this cannot doubt, if we seriously consider that these are the very words of the great Judge himself: "Come, ye blessed children of my Father, inherit the kingdom prepared for you from the foundation of the world. For I was hungry, and ye gave me meat: Thirsty, and ye gave me drink: I was a stranger, and ye took me in: Naked, and ye clothed me: I was sick, and ye visited me: I was in prison, and ye came unto me." (Matt 25:34, & c.) "Verily, I say unto you, Inasmuch as ye have done it to the least of these my brethren, ye have done it unto me." If this does not convince you that the continuance in works of mercy is necessary to salvation, consider what the Judge of all says to those on the left hand: "Depart, ye cursed, into everlasting fire, prepared for the devil and his angels: For I was hungry, and ye gave me no meat: Thirsty, and ye gave me no drink: I was a stranger, and ye took me not in: Naked, and ye clothed me not: Sick and in prison, and ye visited me not. Inasmuch as ye have not done it unto one of the least of these neither have ye done it unto me." You see, were it for this alone, they must "depart" from God "into everlasting punishment."[150]

With this interpretation, Wesley follows Baxter's conclusions regarding the interrelation between faith and works towards salvation. Baxter's writings were a huge influence in Wesley's spiritual pilgrimage,[151] and he was so moved by Baxter's *A Christian Directory*, that he had it reprinted five times for circulation throughout Britain.[152] Wesley's interpretation of this parable also challenged the antinomianism of the quietist Moravians (who subscribed to Luther's commentary on Galatians; a commentary which Wesley found "muddy, shallow, confused, and tinctured with mysticism"[153]), and Calvinists like George Whitefield (1714–70), who reacted with vehement rejoinders to Wesley's theological commitments.[154]

In the same vein as Baxter, Wesley approaches Matt 25:31–46 from the perspective of "plain duty, which all that are in health may practice in a higher or lower degree; and which, nevertheless, is almost universally neglected, even by those that profess to love God."[155]

150. Ibid., 2.
151. Bebbington, *Evangelicalism*, 35.
152. Maddox, *Responsible*, 252, 372 n. 153.
153. Heitzenrater, *Wesley*, 135.
154. Noll, *Rise*, 113.
155. Wesley, "On Visiting the Sick," 1:4.

In his sermon "On Visiting the Sick" Wesley appeals to certain French ladies as important exemplars of mercy which he wishes to instill in his listeners:

> In Paris, ladies of the first quality, yea, Princesses of the blood, of the Royal Family, constantly visit the sick, particularly the patients in the Grand Hospital. And they not only take care to relieve their wants, (if they need anything more than is provided for them,) but attend on their sick beds, dress their sores, and perform the meanest offices for them. Here is a pattern for the English, poor or rich, mean or honorable! For many years we have abundantly copied after the follies of the French; let us for once copy after their wisdom and virtue, worthy the imitation of the whole Christian world. Let not the gentlewomen, or even the countesses in England, be ashamed to imitate those Princesses of the blood! Here is a fashion that does honour to human nature. It began in France; but God forbid it should end there![156]

With this, Wesley should be lauded for placing a far greater stress upon empathy and Christian charity in his ethical program than all those revealed in the preceding chapters. Differing in some way with the preceding Calvinists of this study, a romantic mood pervades much of Wesley's theology which might be attributed to the Romantic movement in Wesley's lifetime.

Progressing from the implications of visiting the sick, Wesley goes on to outline *how* to go about performing such a task by compounding the fact that it is Christians who are divinely helped to perform this gravely significant work. By prescribing intentional prayer to "the Father of Lights" as a necessitating restraint against ostentation in such work, Wesley clearly assumes that the sheep of the parable are Christian. In this respect, Wesley follows Calvin's anxiety over possible human pretension in their work:

> I proceed to inquire, in the Second place, How are we to visit them? In what manner may this labour of love be most effectually performed? How may we do this most to the glory of God, and the benefit of our neighbour? But before ever you enter upon the work, you should be deeply convinced that you are by means sufficient for it; you have neither sufficient grace, nor sufficient understanding, to perform it in the most excellent manner. And this will convince you of the necessity of applying to the Strong for strength; and of flying to the Father of Lights, the Giver of every good gift, for wisdom; ever remembering, "there is a Spirit in man that giveth wisdom; and the inspiration of

---

156. Ibid.

the Holy One that giveth understanding." Whenever, therefore, you are about to enter upon the work, seek his help by earnest prayer. Cry to him for the whole spirit of humility, lest if pride steal into your heart, if you ascribe anything to yourself, while you strive to save others you destroy your own soul. Before, and through the work, from the beginning to the end, let your heart wait upon him for a continual supply of meekness and gentleness, of patience and longsuffering, that you may never be angry or discouraged at whatever treatment, rough or smooth, kind or unkind, you may meet with.[157]

Furthermore, Wesley reveals that those who should perform these works of mercy are those who "desire to 'inherit the kingdom' of their Father, which was 'prepared forth from the foundation of the world.'"[158] Cognizance of the threat of an eternal hell will also motivate those who wish to inherit the kingdom to act according to the works of the sheep: "It is equally incumbent on young and old, rich and poor, men and women, according to their ability. None are so young, if they desire to save their own souls, as to be excused from assisting their neighbours. None are so poor, (unless they want the necessaries of life,) but they are called to do something, more or less, at whatever time they can spare, for the relief and comfort of their afflicted fellow-sufferers."[159]

Then Wesley identifies the rich as the most able to fulfill these tasks because of the wealth of their resources, for he states, "But those 'who are rich in this world,' who have more than the conveniences of life, are peculiarly called of God to this blessed work, and pointed out to it by his gracious Providence."[160]

In missionary fashion, Wesley uses his prescription of how to visit the sick as a means to ensure each and every person served is also justified in God's sight through faith. He creates a catechism for the Church for good works, and the conversion of the heathen. Not that service itself is invaluable, although there is a sense in which Wesley, reminiscent of Chalmers, eventually relegates the importance of acts of mercy to justification by faith. Nevertheless, Wesley does still believe these acts are to be practiced and have some import in and of themselves:

> These little labours of love will pave your way to things greater importance. Having shown that you have a regard for their

157. Ibid., 2:1.
158. Ibid., 3:1.
159. Ibid., 3:2.
160. Ibid., 3:3.

> bodies, you may proceed to inquire concerning their souls. And here you have a large field before you; you have scope for exercising all the talents which God has given you. May you not begin with asking, "Have you ever considered, that God governs the world;—that his providence is over all, and over you in particular—Does any thing then befall you without his knowledge,—or without his designing it for your good He knows all you suffer; he knows all your pains; he sees all your wants. He sees not only your affliction in general, but every particular circumstance of it. Is he not looking down from heaven, and disposing all these things for your profit?" You may then inquire, whether he is acquainted with the general principles of religion.[161]

It is surprising, Wesley remarks, that the Son of Man does not provide spiritual reasons for why both the sheep and the goats are saved and damned respectively. Instead, the King provides reasons that pertain to actions performed or left undone, and because it appears odd to Wesley for scripture to argue this message, he attempts to soften the blow to his readers and listeners by providing an explanation for this:

> This institution unites together in one all the various acts of mercy. The several works of charity mentioned above are all contained in this. It comprises all corporeal (if I may so speak) and all spiritual benefits; all the instances of kindness which can be shown either to the bodies or souls of men. To show this beyond all contradiction, there needs no studied eloquence, no rhetorical colouring, but simply and nakedly to relate the thing as it is.[162]

> All these works of outward mercy suppose faith and love, and must needs be accompanied with works of spiritual mercy. But works of this kind the Judge could not mention in the same manner. He could not say, I was in error, and ye recalled me to the truth; I was in sin, and ye brought me to repentance. In prison—Prisoners need to be visited above all others, as they are commonly solitary and forsaken by the rest of the world.[163]

When considering the ignorance of the sheep's performed works and the goats' neglected works, Wesley distances himself from a literal interpretation, because without the ability to prepare in prayer before doing the works of service this parable negates the usefulness of its message for

---

161. Ibid., 2:4.
162. Wesley, "Reward of the Righteous," 3:1.
163. Wesley, *John Wesley's Notes*, 25:35.

Christian perfection. Because Wesley imposes upon the sheep the identity of Christians, meaning those who have already accepted Christ as savior, it troubles him as to why the sheep are unaware of the significance of their good works.

Whereas for Calvin, this ignorance supported his interpretation of the unmeritorious work of the saints, Wesley, on the other hand, makes an allegorical and hermeneutical move to bypass that which does not ratify his understanding of the parable:

> But in what sense are we to understand the words that follow "Lord, when saw we thee hungry, and gave thee meat or thirsty, and gave thee drink"? They cannot be literally understood; they cannot answer in these very words; because it is not possible they should be ignorant that God had really wrought by them. Is it not then manifest, that these words are to be taken in a figurative sense? And can they imply any more, than that all which they have done will appear as nothing to them; will, as it were, vanish away, in view of what God their Saviour had done and suffered for them.[164]

Wesley finds the parable does not suit his use of it, and despite the elevated significance that the Son of Man gives to good works, Wesley ignores this to focus on God's works instead. Almost as if he has no other place to turn, he reacts against what is an uncomfortable parable for his theological schema, leaving the reader wondering whether scripture or Wesley's theological system should dictate the parable's interpretation.

ANALYSIS OF WESLEY'S INTERPRETATION OF THE SHEEP AND THE GOATS

The real strength of Wesley's interpretation lies in his understanding that works play a contributing part towards the salvation of some. The sheep and the goats support Wesley's synergistic beliefs that man adds to that which leads to his ultimate redemption, albeit a greatly inferior work than God's. This was precisely the problem with Calvin's interpretation; he simply wished to explain away the plain meaning of good work's relationship to the eschaton. However, like Baxter before him, Wesley falls down when claiming these works must be understood in light of the faith of Christians, in other words, as *evangelical works*.

---

164. Wesley, "The Reward," 4.

Where Wesley's interpretation lacks credibility, however, is found firstly in his identification of the sheep as Christians, and secondly, with the lack of cognizance the sheep have of their works. In fact, the latter point in one sense controls his assumption of the former. Because Wesley wishes to use the parable as a catechism of how works combine with the faith of the saints towards their perfection, he objects to the sheep's ignorance of the importance of their works. For Wesley, these works are prepared with prior meditation in order to enact mercy with the utmost effectiveness, however, he changes hermeneutical tack once the ignorance of the sheep's work causes him applicatory problems, which is wholly unsatisfying.

The sheep are erroneously identified as Christians by Wesley because he assumes a prior faith among the sheep, even though there is no indication of the Christian identity of the sheep in the parable itself. Wesley, like all the theological figures of this project, assumes and transposes the many other New Testament visions of the final state for the saints on to the identity of the sheep. He may indeed be correct about general New Testament teaching concerning the eternal destination of the Church, but this should not necessarily dictate his conclusions about the identity of the sheep in this parable, particularly when the sheep are clueless to the import of their work.

CONCLUSION

In this chapter I have shown how Wesley's conception of prevenient grace functions as it synergistically co-operates with the heathen conscience. It is through this universally permeating grace that they are capable of good works. This grace stems from both Christ and the Holy Spirit, and as such, workers cannot claim any good of themselves but must credit the divine Son and Spirit. These works can be enacted by Christian and heathen alike, but the former is far advanced in co-operating with the Spirit's promptings.

It is Wesley's detailed unfolding of *how* this takes place that outshines Calvin's important account. Calvin argues that the Spirit inspires the good work of the impious, but Wesley goes much further by describing *the nature of the synergistic co-operation* of the heathen with broad prevenient grace. Further, he solidifies this with numerous biblical examples of this participation in good work.

Without doubt, Wesley is indebted to Calvin's account of *peculiar grace*, but Wesley advances past him because of his reliance upon the Greek Fathers' notion of grace's empowerment of man. This grounds Wesley in the Eastern Church tradition rather than Calvin's reliance upon the Latin tradition of Aquinas.

Together with this thesis' other theological figures, the significance of the good work of the heathen has only temporal ends. Without justification by faith, they argue, heathen work is not taken seriously by God, hence their mundane work is viewed as temporal. This is further compounded by the common interpretation that the sheep are understood exclusively as Christians, already justified by faith in Christ.

Now that each century of British evangelical theology has been thoroughly evaluated with respect of the good work of non-Christians, in the following chapter I will provide an alternative interpretation of the sheep's identity, and why they are oblivious to the works they have done. This will demonstrate the causal link between the good work of non-Christians and the eschaton. Moreover, in contention against Calvin and Wesley's creation of two-tiers of the agency of the Holy Spirit in benevolent human work, I will argue that these tiers need not exist, and that dissolving such will provide an adequate pneumatological explanation for the connection between good work performed by non-Christians and the eschaton.

6

An Evangelical Re-reading of the Sheep and the Goats

The Grace-Empowered and Eternal Efficacy of Good Work by Non-Christians

IN LIGHT OF THE theologies of good work by non-Christians seen thus far in the British evangelical tradition, I will now attempt to repair the lacuna, as I see it, between the pneumatological empowerment of good work by some non-Christians, shown by Wesley in particular, and the final state of the new creation.

By providing a fresh and innovative reading of the parable of the sheep and the goats (a parable with which each of my selected British evangelicals have engaged), the hiatus between the work of some non-Christians and the eschaton can be bridged.

It will be argued that Wesley's theology of broad prevenient grace provides the best rationale for *how* good work by some non-Christians will be accepted into the final state. This will be argued, however, by contending against Wesley's assumption of the temporality of work performed by broad prevenient grace. By stressing the empowerment of good work of non-Christians as pneumatological in nature, it will be asserted that the cumulative effects of said work grants these workers entry into the new creation; this is the essential corollary of any work of the Spirit, regardless of the agents concerned. Such a conclusion will be ventured because the divinity of the Spirit's agency is eternally efficacious like all of God's work.[1]

NON-CHRISTIAN WORK AND THE ESCHATON

Having shown that some non-Christian work is empowered by the Holy Spirit, according to Calvin and Wesley, I will now show that such work is worthy of Christ's welcome into the eschaton by virtue of its divine co-agency and empowerment. I will do this by focusing on the parable of the sheep and goats, a parable almost all contemporary theologies of work ignore. This is due to two important factors that I have alluded to at different junctures: (1) the actions of both the sheep and the goats are consistently interpreted in evangelical theologies as *evangelical works*, and not work *qua* work. In other words, the compassion of the sheep is always interpreted as demonstrative of *Christian* agency or *evangelical works* as a consequence of faith in Christ. Thus, the term *evangelical works* has been interpreted as a superior form of Christian agency.[2] As a result, British evangelical interpretations of the parable have intentionally cordoned off the parable of the sheep and the goats from the theology of work, and hence its absence from contemporary literature.

Lester DeKoster proffers the only substantive account that considers the sheep and the goats as critical to a modern theology of work.[3] However, he does not recognize that the sheep could ever be identified as non-Christians. Except for this, there is no other detailed contemporary exposition or adoption of this parable in theologies of work which is due in no

---

1. In light of the under-appreciated link between work and the eschaton in the parable of the sheep and goats, I will not attempt to pacify the force of this by synthesizing it with the Apostle Paul's "anti-works" theology, as this would necessitate a far larger thesis. Indeed, the *sensus plenior* of scripture should be sought after with regard to the eschatological implications of human work, but this must remain for a future project. However, I will maintain a strict focus upon the sheep and goats (combining periodically two related Synoptic teachings of Jesus which convey the same message) with regards the direct link between work and the final state. Even though my strict adherence to the sheep and the goats will appear as a works-salvation, apart from justification by faith, I will venture that this parable reveals the eternal significance of good work performed by some non-Christians. The isolated reading that I will offer here is essential to allow the force of the parable's theology have its full impact. Only then can the deeper meaning of how the sheep and goats factor as part of a broader biblical soteriology be investigated.

2. Holl, "History," 126–27.

3. Stevens has a two page discussion of the sheep and the goats in: *Doing God's Business*, 214–15.

small way to the sheer lack of eschatologically minded theologies of work; the vast majority of theologies of work are protologically orientated.[4]

Therefore, when British evangelicals interpret this parable, it is notable that the actions of both the sheep and goats are limited to social relief initiatives, or *evangelical works*, enacted through faith. But this definition ought not to be so tightly constrained. Clothing, feeding, visiting, welcoming, caring for the sick, and providing drink for the thirsty, are all services regularly applied to those who need it in various forms of ordinary work today.[5]

This is not a random list, but rather the identification of fundamental human necessities which wider cultural services provide. "I was hungry and you gave me food" could refer to work relating to agriculture, wholesale or retail foods, kitchens or restaurants, transportation of food, manufacturing implements used for cooking and agriculture, and many support services which make and distribute food.

"I was thirsty and you gave me something to drink" could refer to municipal and private water services, water purification, water exploration and desalination, well-drilling, pipe-laying, plumbing installation or maintenance, manufacturing or servicing water-related equipment, and working in water-related goods and services.

"I was a stranger and you welcomed me" (v. 35) must be a chief part of the Church's missional remit. "I was naked and you gave me clothing" could refer to the textile industry, clothes designers, retail outlets for clothing, cotton picking, and the farming of sheep and cashmere wool.

"I was sick and you took care of me" could refer to NHS and private medical care, counseling, visiting, healing, the manufacturing and sale of medicines, and medical research.

"I was in prison and you visited me" (v. 36) could refer to social services, the legal system, politics and government, and human rehabilitation initiatives.[6] In light of this I will assume the actions of the sheep to include both acts of compassionate service *and* ordinary work.

(2) Until Miroslav Volf[7] and Darrell Cosden,[8] no evangelical theology of work had identified any corollary between meaningful work and the eschaton, and yet, this parable in a very direct manner discloses just this connection. The reason why such a suggestion is so novel is because evangelical

---

4. For an entry point into this debate, see: Preece, *Viability*; Volf, "Eschaton," 130–43; Schuurman, "Creation," 144–58; O'Donovan, *Resurrection*, 53–58.

5. Stevens and Ung, *Taking Your Soul*, 73.

6. DeKoster, *Work*, 13.

7. Volf, *Work*.

8. Cosden has shown the essential ontological link between work and its workers: *Work*; *Heavenly*.

theology, as I have shown, has always maintained an *eschatological duality* between earthly and heavenly life. Heavenly life does not correspond to the earth in any way. The separation of earth from heaven ensures that earthly work has nothing to do with the life to come, particularly when it comes to the subject of non-Christians. I have shown in all the previous chapters that the work of non-Christians is especially restricted to temporal ends, precisely because of their faith status.

Furthermore, I have demonstrated in previous chapters that British evangelicals have consistently handed down a particular interpretation of the parable of the sheep and goats, where the sheep are understood as Christians who have subjectively accepted Christ by faith, and the goats are those who have no faith in Christ at all.

Hermeneutically, the move which is made is to canonically transpose onto this parable that which Pauline and Apocalyptic biblical theology later teaches about the respective eternal destinies of Christians and non-Christians. For example, the Apostle Paul says in the Thessalonian correspondence, "When the Lord Jesus is revealed from heaven with his mighty angels in flaming fire, inflicting vengeance on those who do not know God and on those who do not obey the gospel of our Lord Jesus. These will suffer the punishment of eternal destruction, separated from the presence of the Lord and from the glory of his might, when he comes to be glorified by his saints . . ." (2 Thess 1:7b–10a).

In Revelation, the Apostle John shares similar thoughts: "Then I saw a new heaven and a new earth; for the first heaven and the first earth had passed away, and the sea was no more. And I saw the holy city, the new Jerusalem, coming down out of heaven from God, prepared as a bride adorned for her husband. . . . But as for the cowardly, the idolaters, and all liars, their place will be in the lake that burns with fire and sulfur, which is the second death" (Rev 21:1–2, 8).

Evangelicals argue that because only the saints are those who will end up in everlasting bliss, according to the above quoted passages, they must be identified as the sheep of the parable discussed in this thesis. The goats, on the other hand, are viewed as non-Christians because they are destined for an indubitably punitive afterlife, the very destiny of non-Christians (Gk. *apiston*—Rev 21:8) in the above quoted passages. Because of these episodes in the biblical narrative, evangelical theologies have imposed the identities of both the sheep and the goats upon the parable, thus I will attempt to reinterpret it differently. I will come to this shortly.

IDENTIFYING GAPS AND OVERSIGHTS

Several gaps present themselves in the interpretations shown in this thesis that pertain to contemporary matters for a theology of the good work of non-Christians. First of all, it becomes apparent that the work of non-Christians (goats) according to my evangelical interlocutors, has a definite moral and eschatological status. In other words, what they commit to, or resist doing, has moral implications, that raises a connected issue: whether work should be conceived ontologically consociate to its worker, particularly if (1) work should be considered in a meta-social manner, for example: whether the total sum of working projects should predominate over the sum of individual contributions, and (2) whether it is justifiable to focus on the products of work themselves to determine whether particular work is granted entry into eternal life by the Son of Man, rather than focusing on the morality of the agents.

In order to make strides towards answering these questions, I will now provide my own interpretation of the sheep and the goats as a necessary corrective to British evangelical theologies of non-Christian work. This will not only be immediately pertinent to non-Christian workers and their work, but to their work as it pertains to the eschaton.

A READING OF THE SHEEP AND THE GOATS

At the end of chapter 24 of Matthew's Gospel there is an apocalyptic narrative about devoted and evil servants (24:45–51), followed by three parables in chapter twenty-five about the end of the earthly age (25:1–13; 14–30; 31–46). The first of these opens with the words, "Then the kingdom of heaven will be like this" (25:1), which serves as an opening line to the subject of all three stories in chapter twenty-five. Indeed, Matthew twenty-four and twenty-five are referred to as "the eschatological discourse" in the gospel of Matthew.[9] By the end of the parable concerned here, and the beginning of chapter 26, the subject matter shifts again as Jesus turns to Jerusalem in anticipation of his redemptive work on the cross and resurrection.

As I have shown in the previous chapters, contrary to much evangelical speculation, neither the sheep nor the goats have any cognizance that they have or have not served the Son of Man with their work. This is highly significant on several levels. For instance, to the untrained eye, the

---

9. Burridge, *Imitating Jesus*, 201. France has argued that of the three parables of Matthew 25, the sheep and the goats is the only one which is in reference to the final judgment. France, *The Challenge*, 177–78.

difference between sheep and goats in second Temple Palestine was opaque. Clean sheep were noticeably different from goats, as sheep were normally white, whereas goats were mainly brown and black. However, while grazing on the hillside, from a distance the sheep looked dark with large patches of brown and black caused by the dusty ground, so only an experienced shepherd knew the difference between the two beasts. The parable simile, then, is intended to convey just this difficulty in discerning which beast is which.[10]

In light of this, the parable suggests that the difference between those who serve Christ, and those who do not, is obscure, and impossible for anyone other than the Son of Man to discern. So in one sense, the evangelicals scrutinized in this thesis are too hasty in attributing the identity of the sheep to Christians, yet I will also attempt to loosely identify the sheep of the parable, but on a different basis than British evangelical theology has done until now.

My contention with British evangelical interpretations of the sheep lies with their insistence that, unless the sheep are definitively understood as Christians, it is impossible to avoid acknowledging that the parable conveys a different soteriology from the Pauline notion of justification by faith. I have shown how unsatisfying the contortions evangelical exegetes have had to stoop to in order to avoid this conclusion. Rather, by taking the risk of letting the parable speak for itself, and subsequently working hard to perceive its meaning in light of the *sensus plenior* of scripture, is a considerably preferable hermeneutical approach.

Those deemed to be sheep say to their divine judge when granted the gift of "the kingdom prepared for" them: "Lord, when was it that we saw you hungry and gave you food, or thirsty and gave you something to drink? And when was it that we saw you a stranger and welcomed you, or naked and gave you clothing? And when was it that we saw you sick or in prison and visited you?" (Matt 25:37–39).

The goats answer the judge in the same manner, although in the negative in view of their condemnation to "eternal punishment" (25:44–46). What is to be made of this? One conclusion might be advanced: that the sheep cannot be Christians who have subjectively received the grace offered through Christ because surely Christians have the discernment of faith to understand the poignant *cognizance* of serving those in need. Would Christians be so unaware of their mysteriously hidden Lord so as to fail to recognize the import of performing such acts unto him? This is feasible, despite the fact that the Johannine Jesus states that "the sheep follow him because they know his voice. They will not follow a stranger" (John 10:4b–5a).

---

10. France, "On Being Ready," 190.

Yet it is clear that the sheep of the Matthean parable under consideration do not know Christ's voice among the poor and needy. The sheep, the parable tells the reader, are mystified by the pronouncement that their work has served the Son of Man. This strongly indicates their uninformed perspective, which in turn reveals that their acts were performed unto the Son of Man, unwitting of his identity among the needy.

Perhaps, however, both the sheep *and* the goats should be understood as Christians, as they both respond to the Son of Man's judgment by naming him "Lord" (vv. 27, 44); might this not indicate their intimate relationship with the divine King? Not necessarily. For even the obstinate Pharisee Saul, who put the early Church to the sword for belief in Jesus, cries out "Who are you, Lord?" when confronted by the very person he disbelieved (Acts 9:5).

However, there is the possibility that the sheep could be undiscerning Christians who, as Chalmers proposes, in the outworking of their faith, happen to have unwittingly grasped the opportune moment to act aright. Might it not be preferable, though, to conclude that indicated by the sheer level of their shock, these workers are a collection of non-Christians who have been caught unawares by the rewarding Christ? This might well be the case given their cluelessness to the importance of their work for the poor. Included among the sheep in this reading could also be Chalmers' undiscerning Christians.

Following interpretations like those in my previous chapters, the twenty-first-century evangelical exegete Craig Blomberg contends that the sheep could never be identified as non-Christians unwittingly serving Christ through their work, for this would undermine what, in his mind, is Christianity's dominant interpretation of the sheep and the goats.[11]

The sheep should always be viewed as Christians, argues Blomberg, because of two key phrases in the parable: "the least of these brothers and sisters of mine" (25:40), and "the least of these" (25:45).[12] First of all, Blomberg contends that the term "brothers" (Gk. *Adelphōn*) refers to both familial *and* spiritual kin in Matthean usage; this term is never used, he reasons, with respect to the brother/sisterhood of humanity generally.

Moreover, "the least" in verses 40 and 45 demonstrate the superlative of the adjective "little"; this, too, is a term used solely of Jesus' true devotees, claims Blomberg. He links "the least" with the "little ones" of Matt 18:6, 10, 14 and concludes that "unless major problems result in applying

---

11. Blomberg, *Preaching*, 206–7.

12. These verses are the apex of the parable, according to Dodd, *Parables*, 65 n. 5.

this understanding to the parable of the sheep and the goats, we should try to interpret the terms 'brothers' and 'least' as referring exclusively to Christians."[13]

Despite his exerted efforts, Blomberg's interpretation of these terms is forced, for he simply cannot accept the possibility that some of the sheep are non-Christians because he must exclude a works-salvation, particularly with respect to those without a relationship with God the Father. But it is telling that Blomberg feels the need to mitigate against the sheep being understood as non-Christians, a consideration never acknowledged by my previous interlocutors. This is interesting, because for Blomberg it must appear that the parable could be read in this way. That he admits this gives slight warrant to my reading in that it is a feasible reading of the text. In the main, Blomberg must draw in external factors to impinge upon this passage so as to move him away from the interpretation proposed in this thesis.

The issue of "the least of these" and "the little ones" in Blomberg's interpretation butts up against two problems. First, "the little ones" of Matthew eighteen refers to the children who Jesus played with (18:1–5); Jesus' whole discourse is in reference to them. So to claim that the term "brothers" is restricted to Jesus' spiritual kin (the gathered disciples), thus linking these brothers to 'the least of these' from the sheep and the goats, grossly overlooks the fact that little children *generally* are included in the kingdom by default, simply by being children (18:3). This is a point Jesus also stresses for "the poor in spirit" (Matt 5:3), not for those who have subjectively and positively responded to Christ by faith necessarily.[14] Moreover, Ulrich Luz relates that "brothers" here means *anyone* who does the Father's will, therefore Blomberg's linkage with the "little ones" of Matthew eighteen is untenable because the children refers to children and humanity generally.[15]

Second, that the needy who require help are limited to the *Christian* needy of the world is also an untenable interpretation to maintain.[16] Granted, "little ones" does appear in Matt 10:40–2 in the context of hospitality being shown to Jesus' disciples whilst the gospel message is simultaneously accepted by strangers. But when Blomberg's interpretation of "brothers" and "the least of these" as synonyms of "little ones" is eliminated (for by no means are they synonymous despite their loose grammatical relationship) there is no place for the identity fabrication of the sheep's work obstructing

---

13. Blomberg, *Preaching*, 208.

14. Moltmann supports such a connection between the poor and the sheep of the parable. Moltmann, *Way*, 101–2.

15. Luz, *Matthew 21–28*, 279.

16. Jones, *Gospel of Matthew*, 154.

a theology of the good work of non-Christians (or as they might be more accurately described), clandestine kingdom workers). This would then be true of the goats also as they had no idea what they had neglected to do. Furthermore, to employ the terms *Christian/non-Christian* at all here is anachronistic because the first of these terms only came into existence after Pentecost (Acts 11:26).

The parable of the sheep and the goats requires an improved interpretation of the identities of the recipients of "eternal life" or "eternal fire," and must allow the parable to speak on its own Matthean terms. To aid this, it might be helpful if evangelical readers attempt to interpret the sheep and the goats as belonging to the primitive churches of the ancient world, and imagine interpreting this parable as the only account of Jesus in their possession. Otherwise, the theologians I have investigated in this thesis will dilute the thrust of the parable's meaning by synthesizing it with alternative visions of the eschaton in scripture. Only after this move should it be considered with other eschatological pictures from scripture.

If it is viable to understand the sheep as clandestine kingdom workers by virtue of their bewilderment at working according to kingdom values, then what this parable portrays is the salvation of those who unwittingly serve the Son of Man in and through their work, both formally Christian and not. "For what is said here is that those who will find life are those who have performed acts of kindness to people in distress, whereas those destined for the fire are those who have ignored people's needs."[17] The people aiding those requiring assistance (and in so doing serving their ultimate Judge and king as he is mystically and covertly present among them) are saved to "eternal life" (25:41). This is made all the more apparent by the two conjunctions "for" (Gk. *gar*) in verses 35 and 42.[18] These conjunctions reinforce the intrinsic connection between work performed (and unperformed), and the subsequent eternal destination of each worker. It might be said then, as Burridge does, that "Matthew argues for ethical behaviour because of the consequences" which lie ahead (5:12, 21–23, 46; 6:1–6, 16–18; 7:1–2, 23; 10:15, 41–42; 11:22, 24; 12:36, 41–2; 13:42, 50; 22:13; 23:33; 24:51).[19] For if the Son of Man is served by superlative work, judgment day will reveal these agents inheriting eternal life.

Such a line of reasoning establishes that clandestine kingdom workers will be saved for heaven, not hell, because of how they work and live in this

---

17. France, "On Being Ready," 191.
18. Ibid., 191.
19. Burridge, *Imitating*, 202.

life.[20] That these agents are unwitting of the Son of Man they have served is a more accurate interpretation than the standard evangelical understanding which seems to underplay this point.

Because the sheep did not act ethically with the expectation of a heavenly reward, by virtue of not being subjectively under the Son of Man's lordship, the self-conscious search for salvation through merit, which the Protestant Reformation vociferously reacted against, is rendered inapplicable because of the lack of salvific yearning.[21] Reformation and evangelical theologies are often neurotic on this point, seeing meritorious intention in the work of non-Christians where there is none.

These unwitting workers of good, then, can be understood as clandestine kingdom workers due to their sheer surprise at the Son of Man's generous adjudication of their labors. It is also fair to label these workers, *secret saints*, those who do the will of the Father without any cognizance of doing this work for Him or being this kind of saint. Tom Greggs concurs when he relates: "The surprise of those on the side of the sheep may well indicate that there are some (perhaps many) whose actions of grace arise from God's graciousness without an overt recognition of this[.]"[22]

Earlier in Matthew's Gospel there is a precursor to the parable of the sheep and the goats that stresses there are those who claim to be Christ's, but who in reality are not so, as shown in chapter 2 of this book. The inverse is also true; there are those who Jesus claims as his own *simply because of the work they demonstrate*. For example, he says, "Not everyone who says to me, 'Lord, Lord,' will enter the kingdom of heaven, *but only the one who does the will of my Father in heaven*. On that day many will say to me, 'Lord, Lord, did we not prophesy in your name, and cast out demons in your name, and do many deeds of power in your name?' Then I will declare to them, 'I never knew you; go away from me, you evildoers'" (Matt 7:21–23; my emphasis).

The will of the Father here could easily refer to ordinary everyday work. In her contribution to the theology of work, Esther Reed responds to Matthew 7:21–23 by saying that these "terrifying words suggest that there are false vocations and that we shall not know definitively until the day of judgement whether we have understood our vocation aright."[23] Reed dis-

---

20. Although some my language here is similar to Rahner's "anonymous Christianity" thesis, his project has in fact quite a different trajectory and purpose to mine, not least because he argues his case using Thomist theology. Rahner's project advocates a particular version of Christian universalism whereas I am seeking to provide a theology of the work of "non-Christians," not a Christian universalism.

21. Davies, *Matthew*, 174.

22. Greggs, *New Perspectives*, 160.

23. Reed, *Crucible*, 20.

cusses this assuming a Christian readership, and her alarm here should also alert would-be followers of Christ to a dictum of the Lukan Jesus: "Why do you call me 'Lord, Lord,' and do not do what I tell you?" (Luke 6:46). The Synoptic Jesus is forthright on this point: correct piety and faith is meaningless unless it is demonstrative, enfleshed, and in line with the will of the Father.

Therefore, when the sheep and goats is linked with Matt 7:21–3 and Luke 6:46, Jesus is unmistakably frank when he states that some of those who reckon themselves as belonging to his inner brigade will ultimately be denied by Him because of particular work left undone. Likewise, there will be those (perhaps many) who have no obvious outward connection with Jesus, but work according to the Father's will, and in so doing serve Jesus' "purposes in the world."[24] This service will result in their ultimate inclusion in the fulness of the kingdom of God. What is starkly incontestable, is that both groups in the parable of the sheep and goats are excluded, and included respectively, according to that which they *do* in this life.

Apart from creating serious paranoia among formal followers of Jesus, the sheep and the goats scythes through false piety and practice, embracing those who have through work truly loved their neighbor, and by extension, Christ. Stanley Hauerwas aptly puts it: "All people, whether they are Christians or not, know all they need to know to care for 'the least of these.' The difference between followers of Jesus and those who do not know Jesus is that those who have seen Jesus no longer have any excuse to avoid 'the least of these.'"[25]

Do all people know they need to work in this way, as Hauerwas claims? Indeed, all people have the potential to co-operate with broad prevenient grace, but not all people are open to the Spirit who compels them to help those in need, for they have closed themselves off from being likely to participate with the Spirit. In this way, Chalmers' Aristotelian account of ethical/unethical momentum or habit might be helpful to draw in. Thus, it can be concluded, that some people do not instinctively *know* they are responsible for those in need in society. Nevertheless, Hauerwas rightly conveys the grave responsibility which humanity has for one another.

For the sheep, the eschatological judgment day will consist of two divine injunctions: (1) "Come" and (2) "inherit." Both of these stem from the Son of Man, a figure starkly reminiscent of the Danielic figure (a son of man who "comes with clouds of heaven" and is granted "dominion and glory and kingship, that all peoples, nations, and languages should serve him" (Dan

---

24. Volf, *A Public Faith*, 34.
25. Hauerwas, *Matthew*, 211.

7:14) who is divine judge over all humankind, elevating the divine/human Son's authority and rank. Readers of this parable are left in no doubt of the magnitude of this judging "king" (Matt 25:34). He has the ultimate say in what work is worth His notice, and resultantly, workers' final salvation.

Equally distinguished, but only making a fleeting appearance in the parable, is God the Father; "my Father" as the Son calls him (Matt 25:34). What the sheep discover is that the Son's righteous judgment of their work will result in their "inheritance" (Gk. *Klēronomēsate*) of the kingdom. More accurate, is that the sheep are compelled to take up this offer of inheritance as the Son's aorist imperative mood suggests; in the punctiliar moment in which the divine Son strongly exhorts them to inherit all that is now duly theirs, they must do so in that singular instance.

Furthermore, God the Father has adopted a preparatory role in the background of world history as He anticipates those who do His will on earth as in heaven. Because the sheep have enacted God the Father's will on earth, the sheep are "blessed," and this blessing takes the form of reaping the spoils of the kingdom of "eternal life." God the Father's preparations of the kingdom in all its fulness have been ongoing since the "foundation of the world"; a work of serious duration. Thus not only are the sheep confronted by God the Father and God the Son on judgment day (a daunting enough experience!), but they are subsequently compelled to receive a well-honed Fatherly work arranged for them because of the poignancy of their earthly work.

The appearance of both the Father and the Son in the parable raises the question of the Holy Spirit, and the apparent incomplete picture of God's triunity. The empowerment of the work of clandestine kingdom workers by the Spirit complements that which this parable discloses about the triune life of God. I will suggest that John Wesley's theology of broad prevenient grace should be enlisted in partnership with my reading of the sheep and the goats as a rationale for *how* some of those who are not the Son of Man's formal followers are enabled to work in such a manner which prompts their generous reward to "eternal life." I will relate more of this later.

Having said all this, my biblical hermeneutics may be objected to on the basis that parables from the Gospel genre of the New Testament are not to be exegeted in such an analytical manner. Some might argue that attempting to be so precise undoes the opaque intention of Jesus. To defend my hermeneutical approach, I have taken the hermeneutical and exegetical lead of my evangelical partners but have come to a different conclusion than they have. Indeed, my conclusion contends for a more uncertain outcome about the identities of the sheep and goats, the very demand that might be made against this hermeneutical approach in the first instance. Perhaps my conclusions will pacify somewhat those who dislike my hermeneutical method.

AUGMENTING BRITISH EVANGELICAL THEOLOGY

There are two main areas that demand attention in light of my contemporary reading of the sheep and the goats: (1) should work not be considered exclusively because of the work performed instead of via the faith status of the agent? This question also necessitates two adjoining questions: (*a*) can work be understood with regard the beneficence and virtue of its products without an exclusive focus on the agents concerned? If it can, (*b*) should the work of non-Christians not have a critical place in Christian ethics, as *God the Spirit himself* inspires and grants power for particular work to be performed? This would elevate the significance of good work by non-Christians. (2) Should not the good work of non-Christians, and the agents themselves, be understood more holistically than is currently the case in the British evangelical tradition through a *social perspective* on work?

Identifying the Holy Spirit as the origin of all good in human agency, as I showed in Wesley, is to acknowledge that the good work of non-Christians is never done apart from God's grace. Good work need not solely stem from Christian agents, as clearly this is not always the case, but because good can be enacted potentially by anyone, this must be seen as the Holy Spirit's clandestine influence in human lives. As Volf says, "For whether we believe in God or not, God may be at work in the hearts of the people and in the providential leading of the world."[26] This is why it is essential that the good work of non-Christians be included in explorations of Christian theology and ethics.

Wesley ably demonstrates how the moral, intellectual, interpersonal and affections are stirred by the Spirit in some work by non-Christians which takes place through their conscience, a concept that is biblically grounded, and not transcendental in nature like Chalmers' account. Furthermore, Wesley demonstrates that when the Spirit is engaged with, this is done *freely*. His account of synergism is critical to this, where "a working together" gives prevenient grace its character. Human agents decide to co-operate with the Holy Spirit in their work and thus there is a "division of labour" between the

---

26. Volf, *Against the Tide*, 16–17.

Spirit and the human agent.[27] Consequently, it can be said that there is an actual freedom for conscientious non-Christians to interact with the Spirit in their work, albeit they are not cognizant of co-operating with the Spirit.

A small, but important aspect of Calvin's account should be incorporated into Wesley's account of broad prevenient grace: Calvin's designation of "natural gifts." The Spirit is the progenitor of good work by non-Christians through inferior gifts of the Spirit, which are spiritually distinct from the *charismata* allotted to Christians. Problematically, however, Calvin's theology is hamstrung by his predestinarian schema, thus only this vignette is worth mentioning for my purposes here.

All work by non-Christians is deemed temporal and solely for this earthly age, according to Wesley's schema, and thus there is the need to repair his account of prevenient grace because of the disjunction between the co-agency of the Holy Spirit in work by non-Christians, and work's limitation to this age. What is necessary is an account that portrays the corollary of pneumatologically inspired work with the new creation, otherwise there is an oversight of the efficacy of the Spirit's eschatological work to complete creation.

SIGNIFICANT WORK DESPITE THE *ORDO SALUTIS*

What the previous chapters have shown is that British evangelical theologians view *good* work as contingent upon faith in Christ in the agents concerned. Without Christian faith, work is in opposition to God because it is performed without a heart of gratitude to Him, and thus is not enacted deliberately toward worship of the divine. This emphasis is partly misplaced by British evangelicals because of the restriction of the theology of work to justification by faith. Thus, when they fleshed out their theologies of work in their respective contexts, they were inevitably formed around the overarching locus of all Protestant reflection—*sola fide*. Because of the all-absorbing British evangelical obsession of *sola fide* governing theological reflections on work, it never occurred to evangelicals to locate work around an alternative and more appropriate locus.

(a) The Benefits of Work's Products

How is that, which is unwittingly done unto Christ, determined when considering the parable of the sheep and the goats? If Christ is served by certain

27. Dunning, *Grace*, 429.

projects performed by those of different faiths, no faith, and Christian faith, might *the projects themselves* become the basis by which particular work is judged, and not the faith status of agents? In other words, is it the *form* or *type* of work which has positive effects on the world which is of import to Christ, rather than the faith of its agents? Regardless of the agents' relationship to the triune God, if their embodied actions reflect the kingdom, perhaps it is *these actions* which are worth the Son of Man's eschatological judgment of humanity at the close of world history.

What is certain here is that this is the case because of the *charity* of these works. Werner Jeanrond correctly attests in this regard: "God's love is not to be funneled into human souls, but human beings are invited to become responsible agents of love in the network of loving relationships."[28] In this sense, work manifested through charity has salvific consequences for the eschaton because "God's permanent invitation to participation in his new creation . . . includes the humanization of mankind."[29]

The inconsequence of the agent's faith status for the work itself is certainly demonstrated as the scripture in this chapter discloses: "just as you did it to one of the least of these who are members of my family, you did it to me" (Matt 25:40). Further, "Not everyone who says to me, 'Lord, Lord,' will enter the kingdom of heaven, but only the one who does the will of my Father in heaven" (Matt 7:21); "'Why do you call me 'Lord, Lord,' and do not do what I tell you?" (Luke 6:46). This suggests that the development of the earth is hugely significant to Christ, because if the work itself is a key focus, the will of God the Father to make his kingdom come on earth as it is in heaven becomes paramount. That this aim includes workers who harmonize with projects towards this end (witting or unwitting though they might be) should amount to more than simply the faith status of each agent before Christ.

However, given that all workers do not and have not *consistently* worked in harmony with a kingdom future, how will the Son of Man determine who are sheep, and who are goats? There are times and seasons (and perhaps not even blocks of time, but isolated occasions) when workers serve the kingdom's purposes, and other times when workers cantankerously work against it.[30] In light of this vacillating reality, which of these occasions or phases of people's lives does the Son of Man select to judge humanity by? Is humanity's judgment based upon those agents who have amassed a greater

---

28. Jeanrond, *Theology of Love*, 248.
29. Newlands, *Theology*, 169.
30. For some, I am being far too generous to humanity here.

accumulation of good work than others, and with greater frequency? If this is so, what quota must humanity attain in order to make salvation's grade?

Without doubt, if this line of reasoning is on-track, it would propel those cognizant of this parable to determine to work more consistently with kingdom principles. However, recalling that the parable manifests neither the sheep nor the goats being cognizant of the ultimate ramifications of their work towards the needy, makes it impossible to determine which work the Son of Man will select in making his eternal judgment. Ultimately, the just nature of this judge will simply have to be trusted.

Cognizance of the eschatological consequences, according to the parable, is not present among the sheep or goats, but their *active participation* is. This is absolutely critical to their ultimate destiny. Eventually this parable reinforces that each worker will be dealt with *personally* by the Son of Man. In this sense, evangelical theologies are not amiss in emphasizing the *personal* ramifications of this parable. In other words, work's products must not be entirely disassociated from the responsibilities and ethics of workers.

(b) Pneumatologically Empowered Work

It will have been evident throughout chapters 4 and 5 that I believe the alternative doctrinal locus around which a theology of non-Christian work should circumnavigate is *pneumatology*. Over the course of the twentieth century, pneumatology has been a relatively neglected doctrine, yet this no doubt will begin to change as a result of the explosion of growth in the Pentecostal church worldwide, and arguably, such a change in the doctrinal shift of gravity is already beginning.

Kathryn Tanner has argued that contemporary pneumatologies typically orbit around an instant, direct, and unmediated notion of the Holy Spirit's operations "in exceptional events, rather than in the ordinary run of human affairs[.]" However, the identification of pneumatology in the ordinary run of human affairs is a complementary emphasis of the Spirit's operations intimately involved with "historical process, mediation, publicity, [and] surprise within the course of the commonplace[.]"[31] Even though Tanner does not advance this towards a theology of the work of non-Christians, as I am doing here, it is this latter emphasis which is critical to a pneumatology of the work of non-Christians. Lester DeKoster sums this up well:

---

31. Tanner, *Work of the Spirit*, 87. Tanner has provided her own account of divine and human agency in *Economy of Grace*.

"As seed multiplies into a harvest under the wings of the Holy Spirit, so work multiplies into a civilization under the intricate hand of that same Spirit."[32]

As I have shown in Wesley's theology of broad prevenient grace, it is the Holy Spirit who is the ground of all good work by non-Christians; it is the Spirit who is the progenitor of desire to produce good work, and who provides empowerment to perform such. Hence, pneumatology is a preferable locus for theologies of work to encircle than *sola fide* because beneficent conservation, and the insightful development of creation through work, is by no means exclusive to Christians.

My contention in this thesis is that whenever the Spirit is synergistically at work in human agents, such work manifests the type of work exemplified by the sheep of the parable. In other words, without God's grace instigating and enabling such work, it would never be performed. The Son of Man grants entry into the fulness of the kingdom because of work enacted by that which the Spirit initially and preveniently inspired. Oliver O'Donovan states in this regard, "Human deeds become what they are not in themselves, the story of God's gracious purposes."[33]

This locus of empowerment which enables Christ to be served through kingdom work is not related in the sheep and the goats. However, if Wesley's theology of broad prevenient grace is understood as a complimentary, and subsidiary account, of empowerment to the moral agency of the sheep, a theology of good work by non-Christians begins to emerge. Moreover, this augmentation of British evangelical theology through Wesley serves to complete the picture of God's triunity in this parable. Prevenient grace provides the reason why particular workers can unwittingly serve Christ.

Those who participate with this grace for work are those who serve the needy, and by extension, serve Christ; those who refuse to serve in this manner are those who refused co-operation with prevenient grace, and thus end up condemned to "eternal fire" (Matt 25:41). This is a conclusion, however, that neither Wesley nor the other thinkers in this thesis have gone so far to state, because this form of grace is meant to solely serve temporal matters as broad prevenient grace relates to non-Christians alone.

However, what British evangelicals have noted when discussing the Holy Spirit is the eternal efficacy of His work in the sense of its continuance into the new creation. This has only been the case, however, with respect to the sanctification of persons by the Spirit as ontologically separated from all their corporeal work (the salvation of wooed persons to Christ is a clear exception to this). Consistently ruled out is human work empowered and

32. DeKoster, *Work*, 2.
33. O'Donovan, *Resurrection*, 264.

inspired by the Spirit which extends past that of the salvation of souls to other forms of benevolent work for the earth.[34] But in order to identify how the Spirit's work is eternally efficacious in the work of the sheep, three classical attributes of the Holy Spirit must be acknowledged.

(A) ESCHATOLOGICAL AND CLASSICAL PNEUMATOLOGY

1. By understanding the Spirit as *omnipotent*, God's relationship to the world comes to the fore, and speaks of the world being cajoled to its completion by the Spirit. By identifying the omnipotence of God, it can be said that the Spirit has power to fulfill God the Father's will for creation through his creatures. The Holy Spirit has the authority to complete that which he has brought into being in the first instance (Rom 8:18–23).[35]

As both Calvin and Wesley have shown, the Spirit dispenses gifts to all humanity, even to secret saints, and through this bestowal humanity live and move and have their being (Acts 17:28). Humanity possesses the Spirit of God as a *gift* from Christ, and through these spiritual gifts given for everyday work in the power of the Spirit, God's purpose for creation is not ultimately thwarted (despite many set-backs), but eventually comes to pass in the way intended. For when the Spirit co-works with moral human endeavor, not only is his identity as Creator Spirit periodically apparent through benevolent *human shaping*, but his eschatological influence is also operative. The Spirit's eschatological trajectory acknowledges good and moral work to the extent that the Son of Man will grant its workers entry into the fulness of the kingdom. This reveals the orthodox Protestant doctrine of the kingdom of nature or things outside of the Church (*regnum naturæ*), and the kingdom of grace or those things part of the Church (*regnum gratiæ*) being fulfilled in the kingdom of glory (*regnum gloriæ*). The Father draws both nature and grace towards the kingdom of glory through the Holy Spirit.[36]

2. The Spirit's omnipotence is directly related to His *omniscience*, because both attributes of the Spirit are eschatological in focus. Because the Spirit is fully *cognizant* that God the Son will renew creation *de facto* (Col 1:15–20; Rev 21:1–3), it is His intent to actualize this through His power (Rom 8:18–23). In other words, because the Spirit knows all things, His

---

34. Mouw has shown that there will be an eschatological continuation of some work by secret saints into the new creation through his exegesis of Isaiah 60: *When the Kings*, 20–37. His account, however, is not a pneumatological one.

35. Lewis, *Evangelical Dictionary*, 498.

36. Moltmann, *Trinity*, 209.

omniscience informs His omnipotence to perfect creation. As the Spirit works within time, a task partially undertaken through witting and unwitting human agents, He morally guides humanity to prepare creation as much as possible prior to Christ's return for Christ to complete it.

To conserve and steward creation according to kingdom principles is to ensure that at Christ's *parousia* there is less for Him to redeem and transform. Such a claim is not semi or fully Pelagian because the inclination to conserve creation is generated by the inspiration of the Spirit in the first instance. Any work that takes responsibility for creation is performed in the Spirit because it falls in line with God's primordial, commanding mandate. In this sense then, creation's conservation proleptically anticipates its future transformation (*transformatio mundi*).

3. The Apostle Paul declares in his letter to the Ephesian church that God "accomplishes all things according to his counsel and will" (Eph 1:11). This omnipotent will is enacted because the Holy Spirit is *omnipresent*; continuously working on creation towards it fulfillment. There is no one that is outwith the Spirit's ubiquitous purview towards this goal.

As the Spirit of God inspires, influences, cajoles, and empowers humanity in their work through omnipresent conscience, such co-agency of the Spirit is efficacious, because nothing that He is involved in will go astray or fall by the wayside, for all His work is, and will turn out to be, ultimately and eternally successful. If the grace of the Spirit inspires such work, and if co-operated with, the Son of Man will grant eternal life to the spiritual work of clandestine kingdom workers. For when assessing the tension between God's providence, and human responsibility, both the Spirit's independent working, and his co-operative empowerment of human agency are viewed as equally potent for creation. A theology of the Word of God demonstrates how this takes place.

(B) THE ETERNAL EFFICACY OF THE SPIRIT'S CO-WORKING WITH HUMANITY

In the Old Testament the prophets were illuminated, and inspired to speak on God's behalf by the prompting of His Spirit so that it could be said, in Isaiah for example, that God's spoken and commanding Word was the means by which God's power accomplished its goal. God describes this potency to His creatures using the analogy of water, and the work of a farmer: "For as the rain and the snow come down from heaven, and do not return there until they have watered the earth, making it bring forth and sprout, giving seed to the sower and bread to the eater, so shall my word be that goes out from my mouth; it shall not return to me empty, but it shall accomplish that which I purpose, and succeed in the thing for which I sent it" (Isa 55:11).

When God commanded creation into being ("Let there be . . ."), such words were efficacious, and creation was. When He promised never to flood the earth again as in the days of Noah, His Word was binding. When He promised that He would send a Messiah to deliver Israel, it came to pass. When God utters His will, it is not vacuous, but sincere and intentional. Hence, when God said that He will make a new heavens and a new earth, He fully intends to make good on His promise.

This view of the new creation understands that the triune God will transform *this current creation* (*transformatio mundi*), rather than annihilate it. Helpful to note is the distinction between the two New Testament meanings of the term 'new' with respect the new creation. *Kainós* denotes something that is new in nature, something that has been improved or bettered.[37] *Néos*, however, denotes newness as something that has never before existed, something that is new in time. This second term is almost never used of the new creation in the New Testament (the one exception being Col 2:10). So when the Apostle Paul says, "So if anyone is in Christ, there is a new (*kainē*) creation" (2 Cor 5:17a), he is referring to a renewed nature in a follower of Christ. However, this is not a newness which speaks of a complete change, but a transformation of the existing state of a person. In the same way, creation as a whole will be renovated and transformed, for *kainós* indicates the current creation's renovation into a renewed condition: "Then I saw a new (*kainon*) heaven and a new (*kainēn*) earth" (Rev 21:1).

With this in mind, it is important to acknowledge the *eternality* of God's Word. By "eternality" here I am not wishing to debate whether God or creation is eternal; instead, I want to establish the *eternal efficacy* of God's Word, for when God speaks and desires something, it comes to pass. Isaiah expresses: that God's Word "shall not return to [Him] empty, but it shall accomplish that which [He] purpose[d], and succeed[ed] in the thing for which [He] sent it" (Isa 55:11). Such a command has concrete, and eternally lasting value, because the very thing God wishes becomes an actuality through his Word.

The durability of God's agency is portrayed again effectively by Qoheleth when he says, "I know that whatever God does endures forever" (Eccl 3:14a). Jesus son of Sirach says in like manner: "[T]he Lord will never give up his mercy, or cause any of his works to perish" (Sir 47:22). Such

---

37. Behm, *Theological Dictionary*, 388.

announcements of God's commitment, and faithfulness, to his own work indicates "that God will not allow any of His words to fall (unfruitfully) to the ground."[38] His Word will last for eternity. It will not fade or falter.

The Word of God in this sense refers to the power of God to create and uphold His creation (Gen 1:3; Pss 33:6; 147:17, 18; 148:8; Rom 4:17; Heb 1:3; 11:3), and by such a commitment, God utters His voice so as to effect necessary goads and improvements to it for its perfection. Moreover, good work by some non-Christians, or indeed the work of some of the sheep, is also of great importance to God because it too is sometimes the work of His hands by virtue of the Spirit's co-agency and inspiration.[39] Just as God's Word accomplishes its intended task and purpose, so when the Holy Spirit empowers work by broad prevenient grace such human agency is eternally efficacious.

The co-agency of the Spirit in clandestine kingdom work operates in like manner to a theology of the Word, not least because the Word operates in the power of the Spirit in the first instance. As the psalmist relates, "By the word of the *Lord* the heavens were made, and all their host by the breath [*ruach*] of his mouth" (Ps 33:6).

Jürgen Moltmann correctly describes in this respect, "If the Spirit of God is understood as the quickening breath of God, then no Word goes out from God other than in the vibrancies and the keynote of his Spirit."[40] When the Spirit co-operates with clandestine kingdom work for the earth's benefit (even by what is incorrectly viewed as an *inferior* prevenient power of the Holy Spirit), this inspiration in aiding human projects is the ground and basis of this work. If the Spirit is *God* the Spirit, then the same theologic operates a pneumatology of work, as does a theology of the Word, for if the Word of God comes to pass and is eternally efficacious as a result of the divine command, the Spirit's enabling of human work is equally effective, precisely because of the Spirit's divinity.

But does not the different intensity and form of the Holy Spirit's indwelling in non-Christians negate the possibility of pneumatological work interrelating with the new creation? Calvin and Wesley felt compelled to discuss the different measure of the Spirit's presence in non-Christians and Christians, which consequently resulted in their eschatological dualizing between the temporality and eternality of the nature of the Spirit's operations in each group respectively.

---

38. Bertram, "ἔργον, ἐργάζομαι," 634.
39. Ibid.
40. Moltmann, *Way*, 289.

I do not object to this differentiation of pneumatological intensity between Christian/non-Christian. However, the degree of the Spirit's presence in non-Christians (as a result of not formally devoting themselves to Christ through faith) should not amount to the dismissal of non-Christian work as merely temporal. This was deemed necessary to relegate work by non-Christians who have no faith in Christ; if non-Christians are not destined for "eternal life," like the sheep, then there *must be* a temporal measure of the Holy Spirit at work among them to do good in the interim. In short, pneumatology was ordered into two tiers due to the theological locus of *sola fide*, around which all doctrines were judged.

Due to anxiety over conceding too much to non-Christian agency, the Spirit's efficacy is interpreted as being constrained to temporality in Wesley. Was this move justifiable? If Wesley's broad prevenient grace is understood *in light of* the parable of the sheep and the goats, and if the sheep are understood as some non-Christians, then the Spirit can be understood as He who fuels the good work of non-Christians to *eschatological* ends. The parable of the sheep and the goats, partnered with this alteration to Wesley's broad prevenient grace, undermines the evangelical tendency to eschatologically dualize mundane work so that it can only ever be temporal in nature.

A Social Perspective of the Pneumatology of Clandestine Kingdom Workers

Much of what I have related in the theology of the work of non-Christians has been individualistic, following the cues of evangelical thinkers. That is, each worker is assessed as an *individuum* or atom according to whether they have faith or not, and in which way they have co-operated with the Spirit in doing God's work for the earth. This can be recalled in the condemnation of the goats because of work neglected. But the question of a social perspective on the work of clandestine kingdom work must be seriously considered, for if it is plausible that anyone can work in tandem with the Spirit in their everyday work, the *whole of society's work* must be considered in light of the eschatological consequences of the sheep and the goats.

In one sense I have already being drawing attention to this by providing an account of how those outwith the Church can participate with the Holy Spirit in their everyday work.[41] In this way, all humanity can plausibly be involved wittingly or unwittingly in God's kingdom purposes for the earth. This thesis has already made the point that some non-Christians work

41. Most contemporary theologies of work, however, restrict their accounts of work to those who are formally part of the Church.

unconsciously for ultimate purposes in their earthly projects. This partially answers how *the whole of society* might occasionally participate together towards the New Jerusalem (especially when considered in connection with Church-focused theologies of work).

In speaking of work in this way, the nomenclature *non-Christian* work becomes clumsy because both *non-Christian* and *Christian* work is melded together in a complicated manner which cannot be crudely spliced apart. What is required instead is a view of work that comprehends participation with the Holy Spirit, regardless of the faith or persuasion of the workers involved, because any work which co-operates with the Spirit must be deemed worthy of redemption. Ultimately, God will have the complex task of partially saving some human culture and projects as they cohere with His purposes for the earth, and where there is genuine participation with the Holy Spirit, there is no doubt about the eternal efficacy and potency of his co-agency.

Furthermore, the aggregate results of society's work is disclosed from even a brief glance at the parable of the sheep and the goats. The Son of Man judges "all the nations" (25:32), and thus imposes a social context and meaning to the parable, even if Christian interpretations of the identity of the sheep and goats appear to venture into individualistic territory.

Because the outcome of this interpretation of the parable which I have advocated here is so disconcerting to the British evangelical tradition, they find it necessary to interpret the parable in the ways shown in the preceding chapters. This also highlights a theological determination to discover who is *in* and who is *out*, a dominant sectarian habit in the quest of the beasts' identities.

I do not wish to deny the reality that many countries, ethnic groups, tribes, companies, collectives, and projects, at different times work contrary to the principles of the kingdom of God. The reality is, however, that if some non-Christians sometimes work according to the good, it is more likely that many partake in projects that, although flawed, have *some* good intentions. Showing compassion through charities to those in great need, both domestically and abroad, exemplifies well-intentioned projects that reveal a glimpse of the kingdom. Often, however, these projects are unintelligently constructed.

A social perspective on the work of clandestine kingdom workers must also consider work that builds upon the projects of those who have gone before, and by whom they could not have added their own contribution. Academic work is most obviously of this nature, as each scholar weighs up and assesses the thinking of those who have gone before, so as to add to, advance past, or dispense with that which has been inherited.

Once again, what is of significance from the perspective of human agency is the value of the work done, that may stem from the Spirit of broad prevenient grace, for whenever a good work is enacted it is never without the helping hand of God, because God himself is the fount of all good. This social perspective is therefore historically linked as each generation learns from those who have gone before them.

There are those who birth new ideas which are good for the world, that might benefit those in need, and yet they are often frustrated by circumstances and sin. Consequently, these ideas seemingly disappear from the face of history. Occasionally, these ideas are rediscovered by others who catch the spirit of the original idea, or who appear to come up with the very same idea of their own accord, and are able to advance the idea, and bring it to its fruition. This could be understood as the Spirit pressing and inspiring particular projects throughout history. Even though sin resists many Spirit-inspired ideas for work, the Spirit will eventually ensure that certain moral endeavors are enacted for the world. Only the new creation will illuminate whether these rediscovered works were Spirit-empowered and infused.

Closely related to this are those works that have been arduously worked at but which do not come to fruition or satisfaction to the worker(s) concerned during his/her lifetime. There can be an enormous amount of effort and striving which goes into this type of scenario, and yet the worker runs out of years or motivation to see certain plans to their conclusion. Those who follow up and continue on things that have not quite been fulfilled or completed in the original worker's lifetime can push it over the line. In such cases, it is essential to see work as that which builds upon each generation's efforts as family businesses manifest. There can also be an overlap of good work as one worker passes on their skills to the next, and where the younger generation finishes projects that the older generation began. Once again, only the new creation will reveal whether these trans-generational works were empowered by the Holy Spirit of prevenient grace in clandestine kingdom workers.

Moreover, any good work by clandestine kingdom workers must also be attributed to the fact that human beings are communal beings. Thus any worker who contributes something good to society cannot be entirely "self-made." S/he has a mother and father, siblings, friends, teachers, mentors, institutions, and traditions that have shaped her/him into the worker s/he now is. Not only is such a worker formed by community, s/he is a worker *for* the community. Every good work produced, too, will affect neighbors, colleagues, clients, fellow citizens, locale, and possibly be globally significant.[42]

In light of all these factors, the work of the sheep, the good work of clandestine kingdom workers, will be eternally significant to the Son of Man as the Spirit inspires and enables it, for "unless the Lord builds the house, those who build it labor in vain" (Ps 127:1a).

THE INTENDED OUTCOME OF MY ARGUMENT

It is my hope that British evangelical theologies might consider softening the identities of the sheep and the goats in their interpretation of this parable. The fixed nature of current British evangelical understandings of the identities of the sheep and the goats does much to alleviate anxieties, but in the process it blunts the sharpness of Jesus' teaching. I am not contending against the obvious binary outcome at the eschaton, but I am imploring British evangelicals to consider an alternative interpretation of this parable for an eschatologically orientated theology of work. In so doing I believe that not only is this parable's goad restored, but also that the burgeoning literature on the theology of work is enriched.

Allowing for the potential that clandestine kingdom workers might not always be formally identifiable Christians, Jesus' message that neither the sheep nor the goats were cognizant of what they had enacted, is given the elevated importance intended. This should give much credence to the position that clandestine kingdom workers, those who do not officially belong to the Church, might end up being included in the Father's kingdom as a result of their work. It is not to say that *all* those who are not Christian will be ultimately saved for the kingdom, but I have argued that there should be more fluidity as to who might be included. Jesus is deliberately ambiguous on this matter. Indeed, in both Matthew and Luke, Jesus also points out that those who believe they do belong to God's kingdom *might* be in for a shock. Only right and true actions will determine this. This language might be viewed as encroaching upon inclusivist soteriological debates, but I have not come to this by operating within the locus of this discussion.[43] Rather, the implication of the parable of the sheep and the goats is drawn into these debates. However, the inclusivist soteriology debate never arrives at my conclusions via a theology of work.

One objection to my argument might be, "why become a Christian if those other than Christians will be saved ultimately?" It is imperative

42. Volf, *Public*, 33.

43. See: Sanders, *No Other Name*.

that submitting to Christ's lordship is the primary form of relationship for humankind, because being deliberately formed into Christ's image to be known, and know Him, is that which God intends for us. The Apostle Paul remarks that it is by seeing the glory of the Lord through a mirror that humans "are being transformed into the same image from one degree of glory to another" (2 Cor 3:18). Indeed, *eternal life* is that which the Apostle John designates as *knowing* the Father and the Son, the same two divine persons revealed in the sheep and the goats (John 17:3). Thus, to intentionally know, love, and follow Christ here and now, is imperative for humankind. I do not wish to suggest anything other than this.

I have simply sought to develop an eschatologically orientated theology of work about those who are not Christian, and it so happens that through theological investigation of the sheep and the goats, perhaps some of those who do not follow Christ could possibly end up being saved ultimately because of their good work. My intention in offering this to the field of the theology of work is to show how a strict designation of the outcome of the eschaton according to human agency should have a degree of fluidity to it.

What my argument necessitates is the eventual dissolution of the *mundane work* versus *evangelical works* dichotomy. For if those who work in accordance with the Son of Man, albeit unwittingly, include those who are not Christian, and are seen as only working in a mundane manner, the significance of *evangelical works* loses its perceived importance. It is noteworthy that both John Stott and Craig Blomberg recognized that the parable of the sheep and the goats could be interpreted in the way I have argued here. It is disappointing they felt this jarring parable required explaining away rather than accepting its challenge. But this is due to the accepted evangelical hermeneutic that if one passage of scripture conflicts with another, one passage must bow under a different interpretation so as to promote harmony in the *sensus plenior* of scripture. The sheep and the goats *has to* bow to the Apostle Paul's doctrine of justification by faith because otherwise justification by faith appears to be undermined by Jesus. Clearly, this is something all Protestants wish to avoid. Consequently, I hope that my thesis is a heuristic for British evangelical theologies in being brave enough to speak honestly about what we read in scripture, even if it seems to upset settled evangelical systems of thought.

Overall, and more importantly, my thesis has offered a detailed investigation of the eschatological implications of good work performed by non-Christians, or better still, clandestine kingdom workers as an extension of Miroslav Volf's initial sketch. Identifying the parable of the sheep and the goats has been critical to this theological development as it identifies the link between human agency and the eschaton. This establishes the correct insight of Volf's original thought.

Building latterly upon Calvin, then Wesley, this thesis is rooted in Protestant and British evangelical pneumatologies, albeit via my repair of them. Drawing pneumatology into an eschatologically orientated theology of work was important because it explains *how* the work of clandestine kingdom workers can be good, and thus count for heaven.

Accordingly, my argument has dissolved the hollow wall erected originally by Aquinas between the efficacy of the Spirit's agency for the work of Christians, and the Spirit's apparently inferior empowerment for clandestine kingdom workers. By doing away with this pneumatological differentiation the empowerment to work for good towards ultimate purposes and destiny is straightforward for those who are not Christian. Again, the parable of the sheep and the goats points us towards this eschatological conclusion.

This project remedies from a British evangelical standpoint the under-investigated gap of the temporal and eschatological implications of good work by those who do not know Christ.

Bibliography

Alexander, Ralph H. *Ezekiel*. Edited by Frank E. Gaebelein. The Expositor's Bible Commentary 6. Grand Rapids: Zondervan, 1986.
Allender, Dan B. *Sabbath*. Nashville: Thomas Nelson, 2009.
Allison, C. Fitzsimmons. *The Rise of Moralism: The Proclamation of the Gospel from Hooker to Baxter*. Wilton, CT: Morehouse Barlow, 1966.
Ames, William. *The Marrow of Sacred Divinity, Drawne out of the holy scriptures, and the interpreters thereof, and brought into Method*. London, 1641.
Anderson, John. *Reminiscences of Dr Chalmers*. The notes of a newspaper reporter, 1851.
Anonymous. "Richard Baxter's 'End of Controversy.'" *Bibliotheca Sacra* 12 (April 1855) 348–85.
Aquinas, Thomas. *The Summa Theologica*. Translated by Fathers of the English Dominican Province. http://www.newadvent.org/summa/.
Arendt, Hannah. *The Human Condition*. Chicago: University of Chicago Press, 1958.
Aristotle. *Nicomachean Ethics*. Translated by J. A. K. Thomson. London: Penguin, 2004.
———. *Politics*. Translated by Ernest Barker. Oxford: Oxford University Press, 2009.
Arminius, Jacobus. "Declaration of Sentiments." In *The Writings of James Arminius*, edited by James Nichols. vol. 1. Grand Rapids: Baker, 1977. http://wesley.nnu.edu/arminianism/the-works-of-james-arminius/volume-1/arminius-theological-sentiments/.
Atherton, John. *Transfiguring Capitalism: An Enquiry into Religion and Global Change*. London: SCM, 2008.
Augustine of Hippo. *City of God and Christian Doctrine*. Edited by Philip Schaff. Translated by Marcus Dods. Nicene and Post-Nicene Fathers of the Christian Church 2. Edinburgh: T. & T. Clark, 1886.
———. *The Confessions*. Translated by Philip Burton. London: Everyman's Library, 2001.
———. "Exposition on Psalm 131." Edited by Philip Schaff. Translated by J. E. Tweed. Nicene and Post-Nicene Fathers 8. Buffalo: Christian Literature, 1888.
———. "Harmony of the Gospels." Edited by Philip Schaff. Translated William Findlay. Nicene and Post-Nicene Fathers, First Series 6. New York: Christian Literature, 1886.
———. "Homilies on the Gospel of John." Edited by Philip Schaff. Translated by John Gibb and James Innes. Nicene and Post-Nicene Fathers of the Christian Church 7. Edinburgh: T. & T. Clark, 1888.

———. "Of the Morals of the Catholic Church." Edited by Philip Schaff. Translated by Richard Stothert. Nicene and Post-Nicene Fathers 4. Buffalo: Christian Literature, 1887.

———. "On Rebuke and Grace." Edited by Philip Schaff. Translated by Peter Holmes and Robert Ernest Wallis. Nicene and Post-Nicene Fathers, First Series 5. Buffalo: Christian Literature, 1887.

———. "Our Lord's Sermon on the Mount: Book 1." Edited by Philip Schaff. Translated by William Findlay. Nicene and Post-Nicene Fathers: First Series 6. New York: Christian Literature, 1886.

———. "Sermons on Selected Lessons of the New Testament: Sermon LXIII." Edited by Philip Schaff. Translated by William Findlay. Nicene and Post-Nicene Fathers: Series 1. New York: Christian Literature, 1886.

Bacote, Vincent E. *The Spirit in Public Theology: Appropriating the Legacy of Abraham Kuyper*. Grand Rapids: Baker Academic, 2005.

Badcock, Gary D. *Light of Truth and Fire of Love: A Theology of the Holy Spirit*. Grand Rapids: Eerdmans, 1997.

———. *The Way of Life: A Theology of Christian Vocation*. Grand Rapids: Eerdmans, 1998.

Baggett, John. *Seeing Through the Eyes of Jesus: His Revolutionary View of Reality and His Transcendent Significance for Faith*. Grand Rapids: Eerdmans, 2008.

Balthasar, Hans Urs von. *Man in History: A Theological Study*. London: Sheed & Ward, 1968.

Barrs, Jerram. "Francis Schaeffer: His Legacy and His Influence on Evangelicalism." In *Francis Schaeffer: A Mind and Heart for God*, edited by Bruce A. Little, 75–87. Phillipsburg, NJ: P&R, 2010.

———. "Francis Schaeffer: The Man and His Message." *Reformation 21: The Online Magazine of the Alliance of Confessing Evangelicals* (2006) 1–15.

Barth, Karl. *Church Dogmatics III/4: The Doctrine of Creation*. Translated by Geoffrey W. Bromiley and T. F. Torrance. Edinburgh: T. & T. Clark, 1961.

———. *Witness to the Word: A Commentary on John 1; Lectures at Münster in 1925 and at Bonn in 1933*. Translated by Geoffrey W. Bromiley. Grand Rapids: Eerdmans, 1986.

Barton, Stephen C. "Johannine Dualism and Contemporary Pluralism." In *The Gospel of John and Christian Theology*, edited by Richard Bauckham et al., 3–18. Grand Rapids: Eerdmans, 2008.

———. "Wisdom and Spirituality in Biblical Perspective." In *The Bible and the Business of Life: Essays in Honor of Robert J. Bank's Sixty-Fifth Birthday*, edited by Simon Holt et al., 15–29. Adelaide: ATF, 2004.

Basil the Great. "De Spiritu Sancto." Edited by Philip Schaff et al. Translated by Blomfield Jackson. Nicene and Post-Nicene Fathers, Second Series 8. Buffalo: Christian Literature, 1895.

Bauckham, Richard J. *The Theology of the Book of Revelation*. Cambridge: Cambridge University Press, 2001.

Bauman, Zygmunt. *Liquid Modernity*. Cambridge: Polity, 2000.

Baxter, Richard. *Aphorismes of Justification, With their Explication annexed. Wherein also is opened the nature of the Covenants, Satisfaction, Righteousnesse, Faith, Works, &c.* London, 1649.

———. *A Call to the Unconverted to Turn and Live*. York: Wilson, Spence & Mawman, 1657.

———. *Catholick Theologie: Plain, Pure, Peaceable; For Pacification of the Dogmatical Word-Warriors*. Part 2. London: Robert White, 1675.

———. *A Christian Directory or, A Sum of Practical Theology or Cases of Conscience*. London: George Virtue, 1846.

———. *An End of Doctrinal Controversies: which have lately troubled the churches by reconciling explication without much disputing*. John Salusbury, 1691.

———. *The Glorious Kingdom of Christ: Described and Clearly Vindicated*. London: T. Snowden–The Bible & Three Crowns, 1691.

———. *The Holy Commonwealth: Or Political Aphorisms*. London: Thomas Underhill & Francis Tyton, 1659.

———. *Methodus Theologiae Christianae*. Part 3. London: Typis M. White et T. Snowden, et prostant venales apud Nevil Simmons, 1681.

———. *Of the Imputation of Christ's Righteousness to Believers: In what sence sound Protestants hold it; And, Of the false devised sence, by which Libertines subvert the Gospel. With an Answer to some common Objections, especially of Dr. Thomas Tully, whose Justif. Paulina occasioneth the publication of this*. London, 1675.

———. *Reliquiæ Baxterianæ: or Mr. Richard Baxter's Narrative of the most memorable Passages of his Life and Times*. London: T. Parkhurst, J. Robinson, F. Lawrence and F. Dunton, 1696.

———. *Rich: Baxter's Confession [sic] of his Faith, Especially concerning the Interest of Repentance and sincere Obedience to Christ, in our Justification & Salvation*. London, 1655.

———. *The Saints' Everlasting Rest*. Abridged by Benjamin Fawcett. New York: American Tract Society, n.d.

———. *The Saints Everlasting Rest: Containing the Proofs of the Truth and Certain Futurity of Our Rest: And that the Scripture Promising that Rest to us, is the Perfect & Infallible Word and Law of God*. Part 1. London: Printed for Thomas Underhill and Francis Tyton, 1654.

———. *The Saints' Everlasting Rest: or a Treatise on the Blessed State of the Saints in their Enjoyment of God in Heaven*. Edinburgh: Waugh and Innes, 1824.

———. *Two Disputations of Original Sin*. London: Robert Gibbs, 1675.

Bebbington, David. *Evangelicalism in Modern Britain: A History from the 1730s to the 1980s*. Grand Rapids: Baker Academic, 1992.

Begbie, Jeremy. "Christ and the Cultures: Christianity and the Arts." In *The Cambridge Companion to Christian Doctrine*, edited by Colin E. Gunton, 101–18. Cambridge: Cambridge University Press, 2004.

Behm, J., III. "Καινός." In *Theological Dictionary of the New Testament*, edited by Gerhard Kittel et al., 1:389–90. Translated by Geoffrey W. Bromiley. Grand Rapids: Eerdmans, 2003.

Bellah, Robert N., et al. *The Good Society*. New York: Knopf, 1991.

Benington, John. *Culture, Class & Christian Beliefs*. London: Scripture Union, 1973.

Benne, Robert. *The Ethic of Democratic Capitalism: A Moral Reassessment*. Philadelphia: Fortress, 1981.

Bergmann, Sigurd. *Creation Set Free: The Spirit as Liberator of Nature*. Grand Rapids: Eerdmans, 2005.

Berkhof, Hendrikus. *Christian Faith: An Introduction to the Study of the Faith.* Grand Rapids: Eerdmans, 1979.

———. *The Doctrine of the Holy Spirit.* The Annie Kinkead Warfield Lectures, 1963–1964. London: Epworth, 1965.

Bertram, G. "ἔργον, ἐργάζομαι." In *Theological Dictionary of the New Testament,* edited by Gerhard Kittel, 2:635–55. Translated by Geoffrey W. Bromiley. Grand Rapids: Eerdmans, 1964.

Best, Harold M. "Schaeffer on Art and Music." In *Reflections on Francis Schaeffer,* edited by Ronald W. Ruegsegger, 131–72. Grand Rapids: Academie, 1986.

Bettis, J. D. "Is Karl Barth a Universalist?" *Scottish Journal of Theology* 20 (1967) 423–36.

Biéler, Andre. *Calvin's Economic and Social Thought.* Edited by Edward Dommen. Translated by James Greig. Geneva: WCC, 2005.

Blaikie, W. G. *Thomas Chalmers.* Edinburgh: Oliphant, Anderson and Ferrier, n.d.

Blair, Philip. *What on Earth? The Church in the World and the Call of Christ.* Cambridge: Lutterworth, 1993.

Blenkinsopp, Joseph. *Ezekiel.* Interpretation. Louisville: John Knox, 1990.

Blomberg, Craig L. *Preaching the Parables: From Responsible Interpretation to Powerful Proclamation.* Grand Rapids: Baker Academic, 2004.

Bockmuehl, Klaus. *The Challenge of Marxism: A Christian Response.* Leicester: InterVarsity, 1980.

Boersma, Hans. *A Hot Pepper Corn: Richard Baxter's Doctrine of Justification in Its Seventeenth-Century Context of Controversy.* Vancouver, BC: Regent College Publishing, 2004.

Borgen, Ole Edward. *John Wesley on the Sacraments: A Theological Study.* Nashville: Abingdon, 1972.

Boston, Thomas. *Human Nature in Its Fourfold State of Primitive Integrity, Entire Depravity, Begun Recovery and Consummate Happiness or Misery.* London: Banner of Truth Trust, 1964.

Bowling, A. "Lebanon." In vol. 3 of *The Zondervan Pictorial Encyclopedia of the Bible,* edited by Merrill C. Tenney et al., 903. Grand Rapids: Zondervan, 1978.

Bready, J. Wesley. *This Freedom—Whence?* New York: American Tract Society, 1944.

Breen Timothy H., and Stephen Foster. "The Puritans' Greatest Achievement: A Study of Social Cohesion in Seventeenth-Century Massachusetts." In *Puritan New England: Essays on Religion, Society, and Culture,* edited by Alden T. Vaughan and Francis J. Bremer, 110–27. New York: St. Martin's, 1977.

Brock, Brian. *Christian Ethics in a Technological Age.* Grand Rapids: Eerdmans, 2010.

———. Review of *A Theology of Work* and *The Heavenly Good of Earthly Work* by Brian Brock. *European Journal of Theology* 17 (2008) 93–94.

Brockway, Allan R. *The Secular Saint.* New York: Doubleday, 1968.

Brown, David. Review of *Work in the Spirit* by Miroslav Volf. *Studies in Christian Ethics* 6 (1993) 76–77.

Brown, Malcolm. "Work: A Spiritual Activity?" *Crucible: The Christian Journal of Social Ethics* (January–March 2011) 3–5.

Brown, Malcolm, and Paul Ballard. *The Church and Economic Life: A Documentary Study; 1945 to the Present.* London: Epworth, 2006.

Brown, Stewart J. *Thomas Chalmers and the Godly Commonwealth.* Oxford: Oxford University Press, 1982.

Brunner, Emil. *The Divine Imperative: A Study in Christian Ethics*. Translated by Olive Wyon. London: Lutterworth, 1937.
Brunner, Emil, and Karl, Barth. *Natural Theology: Comprising "Nature and Grace" by Emil Brunner and the Reply "No!" by Karl Barth*. Translated by Peter Fraenkel. London: G. Bles, Centenary, 1946.
Budziszewski, J. *Evangelicals in the Public Square: Four Formative Voices on Political Thought and Action*. Grand Rapids: Baker Academic, 2006.
Bundy, David. "Christian Virtue: John Wesley and the Alexandrian Tradition." *Wesleyan Theological Journal* 26 (1991) 139–63.
Burgalassi, Silvano. "Towards a Theology of Man as Worker." In *Work and Religion*, edited by Gregory Baum, 103–16. Concilium 131. Edinburgh: T. & T. Clark, 1980.
Burke, Edmund. *Reflections on the Revolution in France*. Oxford: Oxford University Press, 1993.
Burridge, Richard A. *Imitating Jesus: An Inclusive Approach to New Testament Ethics*. Grand Rapids: Eerdmans, 2007.
Butler, Joseph. *The Analogy of Religion, Natural and Revealed, to the Constitution and Course of Nature. To which are added two brief dissertations: I. Of Personal Identity. II. Of the Nature of Virtue*. London: printed for James, John and Paul Knapton, at the Crown in Ludgate Street, 1736.
Buxton, Graham. *Celebrating Life: Beyond the Sacred-Secular Divide*. Milton Keynes: Authentic Media, 2007.
———. *The Trinity, Creation and Pastoral Ministry: Imaging the Perichoretic God*. Milton Keynes: Paternoster, 2005.
Calhoun, Robert L. "Work and Vocation in Christian History." In *Work and Vocation: A Christian Discussion*, edited by John Oliver Nelson, 82–115. New York: Harper, 1954.
Callahan, J. P. "John R. W. Stott." In *Evangelical Dictionary of Theology*, edited by Walter A. Elwell, 1151–52. Grand Rapids: Baker Academic, 2009.
Calvin, John. *The Catechism of the Church of Geneva by the Rev. John Calvin*. Translated by Elijah Waterman. Hartford: Sheldon & Goodwin, 1815.
———. *Commentaries on the Epistle of Paul the Apostle to the Hebrews*. Translated by John Owen. Grand Rapids: Christian Classics Ethereal Library, 1853.
———. *Commentaries on the Epistle of Paul the Apostle to the Romans*. Translated by John Owen. Grand Rapids: Christian Classics Ethereal Library, n.d.
———. *Commentaries on the Epistles of Paul the Apostle to the Corinthians*. Vol. 1. Translated by William Pringle. Grand Rapids: Christian Classics Ethereal Library, 1848.
———. *Commentaries on the Epistles of Paul to the Galatians and Ephesians*. Translated by William Pringle. Grand Rapids: Christian Classics Ethereal Library, 1854.
———. *Commentaries on the First Book of Moses Called Genesis*. Vol. 1. Translated by John King. Grand Rapids: Baker, 1996.
———. *Commentaries on the Four Last Books of Moses Arranged in the Form of a Harmony*. Vol. 3. Translated by Charles William Bingham. Grand Rapids: Christian Classics Ethereal Library, n.d.
———. *Commentaries on the Twelve Minor Prophets*. Vol. 1. Translated by John Owen. Grand Rapids: Christian Classics Ethereal Library, 1846.

———. *Commentaries on the Twelve Minor Prophets–Zechariah and Malachi*. Vol. 5. Translated by John Owen. Grand Rapids: Christian Classics Ethereal Library, 1849.

———. *Commentary on the Book of Psalms*. Vol. 1. Translated by James Anderson. Grand Rapids: Christian Classics Ethereal Library, 1845.

———. *Commentary on the Book of Psalms*. Vol. 5. Translated by James Anderson. Grand Rapids: Christian Classics Ethereal Library, 1849.

———. *Commentary on the Book of the Prophet Isaiah*. Vol. 2. Translated by William Pringle. Grand Rapids: Christian Classics Ethereal Library, 1847.

———. *Commentary on the Book of the Prophet of Isaiah*. Vol. 3. Translated by William Pringle. Grand Rapids: Christian Classics Ethereal Library, 1850.

———. *Commentary on the Gospel According to John*. Vol. 1. Translated by William Pringle. Grand Rapids: Christian Classics Ethereal Library, 1847.

———. *Commentary on a Harmony of the Evangelists, Matthew, Mark, and Luke*. Vol. 3. Translated by William Pringle. Grand Rapids: Christian Classics Ethereal Library, n.d.

———. *Institutes of the Christian Religion*. Edited by John T. McNeill. Translated by Ford Lewis Battles. Philadelphia: Westminster, 1960.

The Canons and Decrees of the Council of Trent: with a supplement, containing the condemnations of the early reformers, and other matters relating to the council by Council of Trent (1545–1563). Translated by Theodore Alois Buckley. London: George Routledge, 1851.

Catherwood, Christopher. *Five Evangelical Leaders*. London: Hodder & Stoughton, 1984.

Chalmers, Thomas. *The Application of Christianity to the Commercial and Ordinary Affairs of Life*. Glasgow: Chalmers & Collins, 1820.

———. "A Course of Lectures on Butler's 'Analogy of Religion.'" In *Posthumous Works of the Rev. Thomas Chalmers*, edited by William Hanna, 9:46–78. Edinburgh: Thomas Constable, 1852.

———. "The Influence of Christianity in Aiding and Augmenting the Mercantile Virtues." In *Discourses on the Application of Christianity to the Commercial and Ordinary Affairs of Life: Chalmers's Works*. Edinburgh: Published for T. Constable by Sutherland and Knox, 1850.

———. "Lectures on the Epistle of Paul the Apostle to the Romans." Lecture 83. In vol. 25 of *The Works of Thomas Chlamers*. Glasgow: William Collins, 1836–42.

———. *Memoirs of Dr Chalmers: The Christian's Great Interest*. Glasgow: n.p., 1952.

———. *Memoirs of the Life and Writings of Thomas Chalmers*. Edited by William Hanna. Edinburgh: Thomas Constable, 1849.

———. "Morrells' *Modern Philosophy*." *North British Review* 6 (1846–47) 311.

———. "On the Advantage of Christian Knowledge to the Lower Orders of Society." In *Discourses on the Application of Christianity to the Commercial and Ordinary Affairs of Life: Chalmers's Works*. Edinburgh: Sutherland and Knox, 1850.

———. "On the Christian Education of the People." In *Political Economy in Connexion with the Moral State and Prospects of Society Vol. 2: Chalmers's Works*. Edinburgh: Thomas Constable, 1854.

———. "On the Mercantile Virtues Which May Exist without the Influence of Christianity." In *Discourses on the Application of Christianity to the Commercial and Ordinary Affairs of Life: Chalmers's Works*. Edinburgh: Sutherland and Knox, 1850.

———. "On the Moral Influence of Fidelity." In *Discourses on the Application of Christianity to the Commercial and Ordinary Affairs of Life: Chalmers's Works*. Edinburgh: Sutherland and Knox, 1850.

———. *On the Power Wisdom and Goodness of God Manifested in the Adaption of External Nature to the Moral and Intellectual Constitution of Man*. London: Henry Bohn, 1833.

———. "On the Supremacy of Conscience." In *Natural Theology Vol. 1: Chalmers's Works*. Edinburgh: Sutherland and Knox, 1850.

———. "On the Universality of the Gospel Offer." In vol. 10 of *The Works of Thomas Chalmers*. Glasgow: William Collins, 1836–42.

———. *Posthumous Works of the Rev. Thomas Chalmers*. Vol. 4. Edited by William Hanna. Edinburgh: Published for T. Constable by Sutherland and Knox, 1863.

———. "The Power and Operation of Habit." In *Natural Theology Vol. 1: Chalmers's Works*. Edinburgh: Sutherland and Knox, 1850.

———. *Select Works of Thomas Chalmers Comprising his Miscellanies; Lectures on Romans; Astronomical, Commercial, Congregational, and Posthumous Sermons in Four Volumes*. Vol. 2, *Romans*. New York: Robert Carter, 1850.

———. "Speech Delivered on the 24th May 1822, before the General Assembly of the Church of Scotland, explanatory of the measures which have been successfully pursued in St. John's Parish, Glasgow for the extinction of its compulsory pauperism." Printed as an appendix to his *Christian and Economic Polity of a Nation with Special Reference to Large Towns*, London, 1856.

Chambers, Oswald. *The Philosophy of Sin*. London: Simpkins and Marshall, 1949.

Chenu, Marie-Dominique. *The Theology of Work: An Exploration*. Chicago: Henry Regnery, 1966.

Chester, Tim. *Mission and the Coming of God: Eschatology, the Trinity and Mission in the Theology of Jürgen Moltmann and Contemporary Evangelicalism*. Milton Keynes: Paternoster, 2006.

Clapp, Rodney. "The Theology of Consumption and the Consumption of Theology: Toward a Christian Response to Consumerism." In *Border Crossings: Christian Trespasses on Popular Culture and Public Affairs*, 126–56. Grand Rapids: Brazos, 2000.

Clark, Dennis. *Work and the Human Spirit*. New York: Sheed & Ward, 1967.

Clarke, Paul Barry. "Work." In *Dictionary of Ethics, Theology and Society*, edited by Paul Barry Clarke et al., 889–93. London: Routledge, 1996.

Cliffe, J. T. *The Puritan Gentry: The Great Puritan Families of Early Stuart England*. London: Routledge & Kegan Paul, 1984.

Cobb, John B., Jr. *Grace and Responsibility: A Wesleyan Theology for Today*. Abingdon: Nashville, 1995.

———. "The Holy Spirit and the Present Age." In *The Lord and Giver of Life: Perspectives on Constructive Pneumatology*, edited by David H. Jensen, 147–61. Louisville: Westminster John Knox, 2008.

Cockburn, Henry. *Journal 1831–1854*. Vol. 2. Edinburgh: Edmonston and Douglas, 1874.

Coffey, John. "Puritan Legacies." In *Cambridge Companion to Puritanism*, edited by John Coffey, 327–46. Cambridge: Cambridge University Press, 2008.

Collins, Kenneth J. *The Theology of John Wesley: Holy Love and the Shape of Grace.* Nashville: Abingdon, 2007.

Comrie, Lee. "Work and Salvation." In *Work and Religion*, edited by Gregory Baum, 129–36. Concilium 131. Edinburgh: T. & T. Clark, 1980.

Congar, Yves. *I Believe in the Holy Spirit.* Vol. 3, *The River of Life Flows in the East and in the West.* London: Chapman, 1983.

Coppedge, Allan. *John Wesley in Theological Debate.* Wilmore, KY: Wesley Heritage, 1988.

Cosden, Darrell. "Eschatology Goes to Work." In *What Are We Waiting For? Christian Hope and Contemporary Culture*, edited by Stephen Holmes et al., 175–85. Carlisle: Paternoster, 2008.

———. *The Heavenly Good of Earthly Work.* Peabody, MA: Hendrickson, 2006.

———. *A Theology of Work: Work and the New Creation.* Carlisle: Paternoster, 2004.

Costa, Ruy. "The Weekend: Labor and Leisure in America." In *Sunday, Sabbath, and the Weekend: Managing Time in a Global Culture*, edited by Edward O'Flaherty et al., 139–54. Grand Rapids: Eerdmans, 2010.

Cox, Harvey G., Jr. "Make Way for the Spirit." In *God's Life in Trinity*, edited by Miroslav Volf et al., 93–100. Minneapolis: Fortress, 2006.

———. *The Secular City: Secularization and Urbanization in Theological Perspective.* Harmondsworth: Penguin, 1968.

Cox, Leo G. *John Wesley's Concept of Perfection.* Kansas City: Beacon Hill, 1964.

Cragg, Gerald R. *The Church and the Age of Reason, 1648–1789.* Harmondsworth: Penguin, 1970.

Crandon, John. *Mr. Baxters Aphorisms exorcized and anthorized. Or an examination of and answer to a book written by Mr. Ri: Baxter teacher of the church at Kederminster in Worcester-shire, entituled, Aphorisms of justification.* Part 2. London: Printed by M. S. and are to be sold by T: Brewster at the three Bibles in Pauls Church-yard: and L. Chapman at the Crowne in Popes-head Alley, 1654.

Crow, Earl P. "John Wesley's Conflict with Antinomianism in Relation to the Moravians and Calvinists." PhD diss., University of Manchester, 1964.

Daane, James. "A Review of 'How Should We Then Live? The Rise and Decline of Western Thought and Culture.'" *Christian Century* 94 (October 12, 1977) 923.

Dabney, D. Lyle. "The Nature of the Spirit: Creation as a Premonition of God." In *The Work of the Spirit: Pneumatology and Pentecostalism*, edited by Michael Welker, 71–86. Grand Rapids: Eerdmans, 2006.

Davey, Andrew. *Urban Christianity and Global Order: Theological Resources for an Urban Future.* London: SPCK, 2001.

Davies, Margaret. *Matthew.* Sheffield: JSOT, 1993.

Dawn, Marva J. *Keeping the Sabbath Wholly: Ceasing, Resting, Embracing, Feasting.* Grand Rapids: Eerdmans, 1989.

———. *The Sense of the Call: A Sabbath Way of Life for Those Who Serve God, the Church, and the World.* Grand Rapids: Eerdmans, 2006.

De Botton, Alain. *The Pleasures and the Sorrows of Work.* London: Hamish Hamilton, 2009.

DeKoster, Lester. *Work: The Meaning of Your Life; A Christian Perspective.* Grand Rapids: Christian's Library, 2010.

Demant, V. A. *Religion and the Decline of Capitalism: The Holland Lectures for 1949.* London: Faber & Faber, 1952.

Deschner, John. *Wesley's Christology: An Interpretation*. Dallas: Southern Methodist University Press, 1960.
Dodd, C. H. *The Parables of the Kingdom*. London: Fontana, 1961.
Dodds, James. *Thomas Chalmers: A Biographical Study*. Edinburgh: William Oliphant, 1879.
Duchrow, Ulrich. "Calvin's Understanding of Society and Economy." *Theologies and Cultures* 6 (2009) 58–97.
Dudley-Smith, Timothy. *John Stott: A Global Ministry*. Leicester: InterVarsity, 2001.
Duncan, Henry. *Edinburgh Christian Instructor*. June 23, 1824.
Dunn, James D. G. *Jesus and the Spirit: A Study of the Religious and Charismatic Experience of Jesus and the First Christians as Reflected in the New Testament*. London: SCM, 1983.
Dunning, H. Ray. *Grace, Faith, and Holiness: A Wesleyan Systematic Theology*. Kansas City: Beacon Hill, 1988.
Duriez, Colin. *Francis Schaeffer: An Authentic Life*. Nottingham: Crossway, 2008.
Edwards, David L., and John R. W. Stott. *Essentials: A Liberal-Evangelical Dialogue*. London: Hodder & Stoughton, 1988.
Eichrodt, Walther. *Ezekiel: A Commentary*. Translated by Cosslett Quin. London: SCM, 1986.
———. *Theology of the Old Testament*. Vol 1. Translated by John Baker. London: SCM, 1978.
Elliot, Mark. "Human Beings in Action: Understanding Anthropology through Work and Society." In *The Dynamics of Human Life*, edited by Mark Elliot, 196–221. Carlisle: Paternoster, 2001.
Ellul, Jacques. *The Meaning of the City*. Translated by Dennis Pardee. Grand Rapids: Eerdmans, 1993.
———. *Reason for Being: A Meditation on Ecclesiastes*. Translated by Joyce Main Hanks. Grand Rapids: Eerdmans, 1990.
———. *The Technological Society*. Translated by John Wilkinson. New York: Vintage, 1964.
———. "Work and Calling." *Katallagete* 4 (1972) 8–16.
Erickson, Millard. *Christian Theology*. Vol. 2. Grand Rapids: Baker, 1984.
Evans, Stephen C. *Kierkegaard's "Fragments" and "Postscript": The Religious Philosophy of Johannes Climacus*. Atlantic Highlands, NJ: Humanities, 1983.
Fee, Gordon D. *Empowering Presence: The Holy Spirit in the Letters of Paul*. Peabody, MA: Hendrickson, 1994.
Fergusson, David A. S. *The Cosmos and the Creator: An Introduction to the Theology of Creation*. London: SPCK, 1998.
———. "Divine Providence and Action." In *God's Life in Trinity*, edited by Miroslav Volf et al., 153–65. Minneapolis: Fortress, 2006.
———. "Eschatology." In *The Cambridge Companion to Christian Doctrine*, edited by Colin E. Gunton, 226–44. Cambridge: Cambridge University Press, 2004.
Fergusson, David A. S., and Marcel Sarot. *The Future as God's Gift: Explorations in Christian Eschatology*. Edinburgh: T. & T. Clark, 2000.
Fisher, George P. "The Theology of Richard Baxter." *Biblioteca Sacra* 9 (1852) 135–69.
———. "The Writings of Richard Baxter." *Biblioteca Sacra* 9 (1852) 300–328.
Fletcher, Christine. "Restoring the Sense of Divine Vocation to Work." *Crucible: The Christian Journal of Social Ethics* (January–March 2011) 25–32.

Ford, David F. *Christian Wisdom: Desiring God and Learning in Love.* Cambridge: Cambridge University Press, 2007.
Fox, Matthew. *The Reinvention of Work: A New Vision of Livelihood for Our Time.* San Francisco: Harper Collins, 1994.
France, Richard T. "On Being Ready (Matthew 25:31–46)." In *The Challenge of Jesus' Parables,* edited by Richard N. Longenecker, 177–96. Grand Rapids: Eerdmans, 2000.
France, Richard T., and A. E. McGrath. *Evangelical Anglicans: Their Role and Influence in the Church Today.* London: SPCK, 1993.
Fuller, Thomas. *The Church History of Britain: From the Birth of Christ until This Year MDCXLVIII.* Vol. 2. Oxford: Oxford University Press, 1875.
Gay, Craig M. *The Way of the (Modern) World: Or, Why It's Tempting to Live as if God Doesn't Exist.* Grand Rapids: Eerdmans, 1998.
Georgi, Dieter. *The City in the Valley: Biblical Interpretation and Urban Theology.* Studies in Biblical Literature. Atlanta: SBL, 2005.
Giacumakis, George, Jr., and Gerald C. Tiffin. "Francis Schaeffer's New Intellectual Enterprise: Some Friendly Criticisms." *Fides et Historia* 9 (1977) 52–58.
Gillet, R. W. *The Human Enterprise: A Christian Perspective on Work.* Kansas City: Leaven, 1985.
Gladwin, John. *God's People in God's World.* Leicester: InterVarsity, 1979.
Gordon, Bruce. *Calvin.* New Haven: Yale University Press 2011.
Gorringe, Timothy J. *Capital and Kingdom: Theological Ethics and the Economic Order.* Maryknoll, NY: Orbis, 1994.
———. *The Common Good and the Global Emergency: God and the Built Environment.* Cambridge: Cambridge University Press, 2011.
———. *Discerning Spirit: A Theology of Revelation.* London: SCM, 1990.
———. *Furthering Humanity: A Theology of Culture.* Aldershot, UK: Ashgate, 2004.
———. *A Theology of the Built Environment: Justice, Empowerment, Redemption.* Cambridge: Cambridge University Press, 2007.
Gouge, Thomas. *Principles of Christian Religion: Proved by Scripture, propounded by questions and answers: short for memory, plain for the meanest capacity, and profitable for all. Imprimatur Charles Herle.* London: printed by R. L. for Samuel Man at the Swan in Paul's Church Yard, 1645.
Graham, Elaine. "Being, Making and Imagining: Toward a Practical Theology of Technology." *Culture and Religion* 10 (2010) 221–36.
Green, Michael. *I Believe in the Holy Spirit.* London: Hodder & Stoughton, 1997.
Green, R. H. *Labour, Employment and Unemployment: An Ecumenical Reappraisal.* Geneva: WCC, 1987.
Greenhill, William. *An Exposition of the Prophet Ezekiel with Useful Observations Thereupon.* London: Samuel Holdsworth, Amen Corner, Paternoster Row, 1839.
Greggs, Tom. "Beyond the Binary: Forming Evangelical Eschatology." In *New Perspectives for Evangelical Theology: Engaging with God, Scripture and the World,* edited by Tom Greggs, 153–67. London: Routledge, 2010.
Gregory of Nyssa. "On the Holy Spirit, Against the Macedonians." Edited by Philip Schaff et al. Translated by William Moore and Henry Austin Wilson. Nicene and Post-Nicene Fathers, Second Series 5. Buffalo: Christian Literature, 1893.
Grenholm, Carl-Henric. *Protestant Work Ethics: A Study of Work Ethical Theories in Contemporary Protestant Theology.* Uppsala: Graphic Systems, AB, 1993.

Grenz, Stanley J. *Renewing the Center: Evangelical Theology in a Post-Theological Era.* Grand Rapids: Baker Academic, 2000.
———. *Theology for the Community of God.* Grand Rapids: Eerdmans, 2000.
Grenz, Stanley J., and John R. Franke. *Beyond Foundationalism: Shaping Theology in a Postmodern Context.* Louisville: Westminster John Knox, 2001.
Gribble, R. F. "Tarshish." In *The Zondervan Pictorial Encyclopedia of the Bible*, edited by Merrill C. Tenney et al., 5:597–98. Grand Rapids: Zondervan, 1978.
Grogan, Geoffrey W. *The Faith Once Entrusted to the Saints? Engaging Issues and Trends in Evangelical Theology.* Nottingham: InterVarsity, 2010.
Grotius, Hugo. *Annotationes in the Novum Testamentum.* Groningae: Zuidema, 1826–34.
Gunter, W. Stephen. "John Wesley, a Faithful Representative of Jacobus Arminius." *Wesleyan Theological Journal* 42 (2007) 446–64.
Gunton, Colin E. "Creation: (1) Creation and Mediation in the Theology of Robert W. Jenson. An Encounter of Convergence." In *Father, Son and Holy Spirit: Toward a Fully Trinitarian Theology*, 93–106. London: T. & T. Clark, 2003.
———. "Creation: (2) The Spirit Moved Over the Face of the Waters. The Holy Spirit and the Created Order." In *Father, Son and Holy Spirit: Toward a Fully Trinitarian Theology*, 107–12. London: T. & T. Clark, 2003.
———. "The Doctrine of Creation." In *The Cambridge Companion to Christian Doctrine*, edited by Colin E. Gunton, 141–57. Cambridge: Cambridge University Press, 2004.
———. *The Promise of Trinitarian Theology.* London: T. & T. Clark, 2003.
———. *The Triune Creator: A Historical and Systematic Study.* Edinburgh Studies in Constructive Theology. Edinburgh: Edinburgh University Press, 1998.
Hall, R. H. *Dimensions of Work.* Beverly Hills: Sage, 1986.
Hardman Moore, Susan. "Calvinism and the Arts." *Theology in Scotland* 16 (2009) 75–92.
Hardy, Lee. *The Fabric of This World: Inquiries into Calling, Career Choice, and the Design of Human Work.* Grand Rapids: Eerdmans, 1990.
———. Review of *Work in the Spirit* by Miroslav Volf. *Calvin Theological Journal* 28 (1993) 191–96.
Harper, Kenneth C. "Francis A. Schaeffer: An Evaluation." *Bibliotecha Sacra* 133 (1976) 130–42.
Hart, Ian. "Genesis 1.1—2.3 as a Prologue to the Book of Genesis." *Tyndale Bulletin* 46 (1995) 315–36.
———. "The Teaching of Luther and Calvin about Ordinary Work: 1. Martin Luther (1483–1546)." *Evangelical Quarterly* 67 (1995) 35–52.
———. "The Teaching of Luther and Calvin about Ordinary Work: 2. John Calvin (1509–64)." *Evangelical Quarterly* 67 (1995) 121–35.
———. "The Teachings of the Puritans about Ordinary Work." *Evangelical Quarterly* 67 (1995) 195–209.
Hart, Trevor. "Eschatology and Imagination." In *What Are We Waiting For? Christian Hope and Contemporary Culture*, edited by Stephen Holmes et al., 127–37. Milton Keynes: Paternoster, 2008.
Hastings, Adrian. *A History of British Christianity, 1920-1984.* London: Collins, 1986.
Hauerwas, Stanley. *Matthew.* Theological Commentary on the Bible. Grand Rapids: Brazos, 2006.

———. "A Trinitarian Theology of the Chief End of All Flesh." In *In Good Company: The Church as Polis*, 185–98. Notre Dame: University of Notre Dame Press, 1995.

———. *With the Grain of the Universe: The Church's Witness and Natural Theology*. London: SCM, 2002.

———. "Work as Co-Creation: A Critique of a Remarkably Bad Idea." In *In Good Company: The Church as Polis*, 109–24. Notre Dame: University of Notre Dame Press, 1995.

Hays, Richard B. *First Corinthians*. Interpretation. Louisville: John Knox, 1997.

Healy, J. D. "Natural Rights." In *New Dictionary of Christian Ethics and Pastoral Care*, edited by David J. Atkinson et al., 621–22. Leicester: InterVarsity, 1995.

Hefner, Philip. *The Human Factor: Evolution, Culture, and Religion*. Minneapolis: Fortress, 1993.

Heitzenrater, Richard P. *Wesley and the People Called Methodists*. Nashville: Abingdon, 1995.

Helm, Paul. *John Calvin's Ideas*. Oxford: Oxford University Press, 2004.

Henderson, D. Michael. *John Wesley's Class Meeting: A Model for Making Disciples*. Nappanee, IN: Francis Asbury, 1997.

Hendry, George S. *The Holy Spirit in Christian Theology*. London: SCM, 1965.

Henry, Carl F. H. *Aspects of Christian Social Ethics*. Grand Rapids: Eerdmans, 1964.

———. *The Christian Mindset in a Secular Society*. Portland, OR: Multonomah, 1984.

———. *Christian Personal Ethics*. Grand Rapids: Eerdmans. 1957.

———. *Frontiers in Modern Theology: A Critique of Current Theological Trends*. Chicago: Moody, 1964.

———. *God, Revelation and Authority*. Waco, TX: Word, 1976–83.

———. *The God Who Shows Himself*. Waco, TX: Word, 1966.

———. *A Plea for Evangelical Demonstration*. Grand Rapids: Baker 1971.

———. *The Uneasy Conscience of Modern Fundamentalism*. Grand Rapids: Eerdmans, 1947.

Heron, Alasdair I. C. *The Holy Spirit: The Holy Spirit in the Bible, the History of Christian Thought, and Recent Theology*. Philadelphia: Westminster, 1983.

Heslam, Peter S. *Creating a Christian Worldview: Abraham Kuyper's Lectures on Calvinism*. Grand Rapids: Eerdmans, 1998.

———. *Globalization: Unravelling the New Capitalism*. Cambridge: Grove, 2003.

———. *Transforming Capitalism: Entrepreneurship and the Renewal of Thrift*. Cambridge: Grove, 2010.

Higginson, Richard. *Called to Account: Adding Value in God's World; Integrating Christianity and Business Effectively*. Guilford: Eagle, 1993.

———. *Questions of Business Life: Exploring Workplace Issues from a Christian Perspective*. Carlisle: Authentic Media, 2002.

———. "Work in the Spirit: Book Review." *Journal of Theological Studies* 44 (1993) 475–76.

Hill, Christopher. *Puritanism and Revolution: Studies in Interpretation of the English Revolution of the Seventeenth Century*. Cambridge. MA: Harvard University Press, 1958.

Hillman, Robert J. "Grace in the Preaching of Calvin and Wesley." In *Dig or Die: Papers Given at the World Methodist Historical Society Conference, 10–15 August, 1980*, edited by J. Udy and Eric G. Clancy, 279–89. Sydney: World Methodist Historical Society, 1981.

Hilton, Boyd. *The Age of Atonement: The Influence of Evangelicalism on Social and Economic Thought, 1795–1865.* Oxford: Clarendon, 1988.

———. "Chalmers as a Political Economist." In *The Practical and the Pious: Essays on Thomas Chalmers (1780–1847),* edited by A. C. Cheyne, 141–56. Edinburgh: The Saint Andrew Press, 1985.

Hoeksema, Herman. *The Protestant Reformed Churches in America: Their Origin, Early History and Doctrine.* Grand Rapids: First Protestant Reformed Church, 1936.

Holl, Karl. "The History of the Word Vocation (Beruf)." Translated by Heber F. Peacock. *Review and Expositor* 55 (1958) 126–54.

Howard, Sue, and David Welbourn. *The Spirit at Work Phenomenon.* London: Azure, 2004.

Hughes, John. *The End of Work: Theological Critiques of Capitalism.* Oxford: Blackwell, 2007.

———. "Work, Prayer and Leisure in the Christian Tradition." *Crucible: The Christian Journal of Social Ethics* (January–March 2011) 7–15.

Hughes, John, and Andrew Morton. *Work, Worth and Community: Responding to the Crisis of Work.* Occasional Paper No. 37. Edinburgh: CTPI, 1996.

Hughes, Philip Edgcumbe. *Theology of the English Reformers.* London: Hodder & Stoughton, 1965.

Hurst, John Fletcher. *John Wesley the Methodist: A Plain Account of his Life and Work by a Methodist Preacher.* New York: The Methodist Book Concern, 1903.

Inglis, John. *The Grounds of Christian Hope in the Universal Prevalence of the Gospel.* N.p.: SSPCK, 1818.

Ingram, Douglas. *Ambiguity in Ecclesiastes.* London: T. & T. Clark, 2006.

Innes, Keith. "Towards an Ecological Eschatology: Continuity and Discontinuity." *Evangelical Quarterly* 81 (2009) 126–44.

Jackson, Thomas. "Mr. Hill's 'Review of all the Doctrines Taught by Mr. John Wesley.'" In *The Works of John Wesley,* 10:395–96 . Grand Rapids: Zondervan, 1958.

Jeanrond, Werner G. *A Theology of Love.* London: T. & T. Clark, 2010.

Jencks, Maggie Keswick. "A View From the Front Line." 1995. https://www.maggiescentres.org/media/uploads/file_upload_plugin/view-from-the-front-line/view-from-the-front-line_1.pdf.

Jensen, David H. *Responsive Labor: A Theology of Work.* Louisville: Westminster John Knox, 2006.

John Paul II. *Laborem Exercens (On Human Work).* London: Catholic Truth Society, 1981.

Johnson, P. G. *Grace: God's Work Ethic; Making Connections Between the Gospel and Weekday Work.* Valley Forge, PA: Judson, 1985.

Johnson, Todd E., and Dale Savidge. *Performing the Sacred: Theology and Theatre in Dialogue.* Grand Rapids: Baker Academic, 2009.

Johnston, Robert K. *Reel Spirituality: Theology and Film in Dialogue.* Grand Rapids: Baker Academic, 2006.

Jones, Ivor H. *The Gospel of Matthew.* London: Epworth, 1994.

Jorgenson, Allen. "Crux et Vocatio." *Scottish Journal of Theology* 62 (2009) 282–98.

Justin Martyr. "Second Apology." In *Ante-Nicene Fathers 1,* edited by Alexander Roberts et al. Translated by Marcus Dods and George Reith. http://www.newadvent.org/fathers/0127.htm. Buffalo: Christian Literature, 1885.

Kaiser, E. G. "Theology of Work." In *New Catholic Encyclopedia*, 14:1015–17. New York: McGraw-Hill, 1967.
Kärkkäinen, Veli-Matti. *Pneumatology: The Holy Spirit in Ecumenical, International, and Contextual Perspective*. Grand Rapids: Baker Academic, 2005.
Kauppi, Lynn Allan. *Foreign but Familiar Gods: Greco-Romans Read Religion in Acts*. London: T. & T. Clark, 2006.
Keeble, N. H. *Richard Baxter: Puritan Man of Letters*. Oxford: Clarendon, 1982.
Kelly, J. N. D. *Early Christian Doctrines*. London: A. & C. Black, 1993.
Kelsey, David H. *The Uses of Scripture in Recent Theology*. Philadelphia: Fortress, 1975.
Kendall, R. T. *Calvin and English Calvinism to 1649*. Oxford: Oxford University Press, 1979.
Kevin, Ernest F. *The Grace of Law: A Study in Puritan Theology*. London: Carey Kingsgate, 1964.
Kim, Kirsteen. *The Holy Spirit in the World: A Global Conversation*. London: SPCK, 2008.
Kolden, Marc. "Work and Meaning: Some Theological Reflections." *Interpretation* 48 (1994) 262–71.
Kuiper, Herman. *Calvin on Common Grace*. Goes, Netherlands: Oosterbaan & Le Cointre, 1928.
Kuyper, Abraham. *Calvinism: Six Stone Lectures*. Edinburgh: T. & T. Clark, 1898.
———. *The Work of the Holy Spirit*. Translated by Henri de Vries. New York: Cosimo, 2007.
Kuzmič, Peter. "Eschatology and Ethics: Evangelical Views and Attitudes." In *Mission and Transformation: A Theology of the Whole Gospel*, edited by Vinay Samuel et al., 134–65. Carlisle: Regnum 1999.
———. "History and Eschatology: Evangelical Views." In *In Word and Deed: Evangelism and Social Responsibility*, edited by Bruce J. Nicholls, 135–64. Exeter: Paternoster 1985.
Lamont, William. *Puritanism and Historical Controversy*. Montreal: McGill-Queen's University Press, 1996.
Lampe, G. *God as Spirit*. London: SCM, 1983.
Langford, Thomas Anderson. "John Wesley's Doctrine of Justification by Faith." *Bulletin of the United Church of Canada Committee on Archives and History* 29 (1980) 47–62.
Larive, Armand. *After Sunday: A Theology of Work*. New York: Continuum, 2004.
Lausanne Occasional Paper 21. "Evangelism and Social Responsibility: An Evangelical Commitment." http://www.lausanne.org/grand-rapids-1982/lop-21.html#7.
Laylor, J. *Money and Morals: A Book for the Times*. London: John Chapman, 1852.
Lederle, H. I. *Treasures Old and New: Interpretations of Spirit-Baptism in the Charismatic Renewal Movement*. Peabody, MA: Hendrickson, 1988.
Lee, Umphrey. *John Wesley and Modern Religion*. Nashville: Cokesbury, 1936.
Lehmann, Hartmut. "Ascetic Protestantism and Economic Rationalism: Max Weber Revisited after Two Generations." *Harvard Theological Review* 80 (1987) 307–20.
———. "The Rise of Capitalism: Weber versus Sombart." In *Weber's Protestant Ethic: Origins, Evidence, Contexts*, edited by Hartmut Lehmann et al., 195–209. Cambridge: Cambridge University Press, 1993.
Leo XIII. *Rerum Novarum*. 1891. http://www.vatican.va/holy_father/leo_xiii/encyclicals/documents/hf_l-xiii_enc_15051891_rerum-novarum_en.html.

Lewis, C. S. *The Problem of Pain*. Glasgow: William Collins, 1983.
Lewis, Gordon R. "Attributes of God." In *Evangelical Dictionary of Theology*, edited by Walter A. Elwell, 492–500. Grand Rapids: Baker Academic, 2001.
Lindström, Harald. *Wesley and Sanctification*. Wilmore, KY: Francis Asbury, 1996.
Lloyd Thomas, J. M. *The Autobiography of Richard Baxter (Reliquiae Baxterianae)*. London: Everyman's Library, 1831.
Loane, Marcus L. *Makers of Religious Freedom in the Seventeenth Century: Henderson, Rutherford, Bunyan, Baxter*. London: InterVarsity, 1960.
Long, D. Stephen. *John Wesley's Moral Theology: The Quest for God and Goodness*. Nashville: Kingswood, 2005.
Luby, Daniel Joseph. "The Perceptibility of Grace in the Theology of John Wesley: A Roman Catholic Consideration." PhD diss., Pontificia Studiorum Universitas A. S. Thomas Aquinas in Urbe, 1984.
Luther, Martin. *A Treatise on Good Works*. Translated by M. Reu. Grand Rapids: Christian Classics Ethereal Library, n.d.
Luz, Ulrich. *Matthew 21–28: A Commentary*. Translated by James E. Crouch. Minneapolis: Fortress, 2005.
Lynch, Kevin. *The Image of the City*. Cambridge, MA: MIT Press, 1960.
Lyon, David. *Karl Marx: A Christian Appreciation of His Life and Thought*. Tring, UK: Lion, 1979.
Macarius of Egypt. "Spiritual Homily XV: Concerning the Worth and Condition of the Christian." Translated by D. R. Jennings. *Monachos.net*. http://www.monachos.net/content/patristics/patristictexts/181.
Macaulay, Ranald. "Francis Schaeffer in the Twenty-First Century." In *Francis Schaeffer: A Mind and Heart for God*, edited by Bruce A. Little, 51–74. Phillipsburg, NJ: P&R, 2010.
———. "The Great Commissions." In *Christianity in a Changing World: Biblical Insights on Contemporary Issues*, edited by Michael Schluter, 39–50. London: Marshall Pickering, 2000.
MacLeod, Donald. "Covenant Theology." In *Dictionary of Scottish Church History and Theology*, edited by Nigel M. de S. Cameron et al., 214–18. Edinburgh: T. & T. Clark, 1993.
Maddox, Graham. *Political Writings of John Wesley*. Bristol: Thoemmes, 1998.
Maddox, Randy L. *Responsible Grace: John Wesley's Practical Theology*. Nashville: Kingswood, 1994.
Malthus, Thomas. *An Essay on the Principles of Population*. Edited by Antony Flew. Harmondsworth: Penguin, 1978.
Marchant, G. J. C. Review of *He is There and He is Not Silent* by Francis A. Schaeffer. *The Churchman* 88 (1974) 63.
Marquardt, Manfred. *John Wesley's Social Ethics: Praxis and Principles*. Translated by John E. Steely and W. Stephen Gunter. Nashville: Abingdon, 1992.
Marshall, I. Howard. "Culture and the New Testament." In *Down to Earth: Studies in Christianity and Culture; The Papers of the Lausanne Consultation on Gospel and Culture*, edited by John R. W. Stott et al., 17–32. London: Hodder & Stoughton, 1981.
———. "Eschatology at the Heart of New Testament Theology." In *What Are We Waiting For? Christian Hope and Contemporary Culture*, edited by Stephen Holmes et al., 35–47. Milton Keynes: Paternoster, 2008.

Marshall, Paul. *Calling, Work and Rest.* Potchefstroom: PU for CHE, Institute for Reformational Studies, 1991.

———. *The Kind of Life Imposed on Man: Vocation and Social Order from Tyndale to Locke.* Toronto: University of Toronto Press, 1996.

Martin, Hugh. *Puritanism and Richard Baxter.* London: SCM, 1954.

Marx, Karl. *Capital: A Critique of Political Economy.* Translated by Eden Paul and Cedar Paul. London: J. M. Dent, 1930.

Matheson, J. G. "Calvin's Doctrine of the Christian Life." *Scottish Journal of Theology* 2 (1949) 48–56.

Mawson, Michael. "Understandings of Nature and Grace in John Milbank and Thomas Aquinas." *Scottish Journal of Theology* 65 (2009) 347–61.

McCabe, Herbert. *God Matters.* London: Geoffrey Chapman, 1987.

McCaffrey, John. "The Life of Thomas Chalmers." In *The Practical and the Pious: Essays on Thomas Chalmers (1780–1847)*, edited by A. C. Cheyne, 31–64. Edinburgh: Saint Andrew Press, 1985.

McConville, Gordon. "Berith." In *New International Dictionary of Old Testament Theology and Exegesis*, edited by Willem A. VanGemeren, 1:747. Carlisle: Paternoster, 1997.

———. "The Old Testament and the Enjoyment of Wealth." In *Christ and Consumerism: A Critical Analysis of the Spirit of the Age*, edited by Craig Bartholomew et al., 34–53. Carlisle: Paternoster, 2001.

McDonald, H. D. *The Christian View of Man.* London: Marshall, Morgan & Scott, 1981.

McDonough, William, and Michael Braungart. *Cradle to Cradle: Remaking the Way We Make Things.* New York: North Point, 2002.

McFadyen, Alistair. *Bound to Sin: Abuse, Holocaust and the Christian Doctrine of Sin.* Cambridge: Cambridge University Press, 2000.

———. "Trinity and Human Individuality: The Conditions for Relevance." *Theology* 95 (1992) 10–18.

McGrath, Gavin J. *Grace and Duty in Puritan Spirituality.* Nottingham: Grove, 1991.

McIntyre, John. Review of *God in Creation*, by Jürgen Moltmann. *Scottish Journal of Theology* 41 (1988) 267–73.

———. *The Shape of Pneumatology: Studies in the Doctrine of the Holy Spirit.* Edinburgh: T. & T. Clark, 1997.

Meeks, M. Douglas. *God the Economist: The Doctrine of God and Political Economy.* Minneapolis: Fortress, 1989.

———. "The Social Trinity and Property." In *God's Life in Trinity*, edited by Miroslav Volf et al., 13–21. Minneapolis: Fortress, 2006.

Meilaender, Gilbert. *The Freedom of a Christian: Grace, Vocation, and the Meaning of Our Humanity.* Grand Rapids: Brazos, 2007.

———, ed. *Working: Its Meaning and its Limits.* Notre Dame: University of Notre Dame Press, 2000.

Middleton, J. Richard. "Is Creation Theology Inherently Conservative? A Dialogue with Walter Brueggemann." *Harvard Theological Review* 87 (1994) 257–77.

———. *The Liberating Image: The Imago Dei in Genesis 1.* Grand Rapids: Brazos, 2005.

Milbank, John. *Theology and Social Theory: Beyond Secular Reason.* Oxford: Blackwell, 2006.

Miller, Alexander. *The Christian Significance of Karl Marx.* London: SCM, 1947.

Miller, David W. *God at Work: The History and Promise of the Faith at Work Movement.* Oxford: Oxford University Press, 2007.
Miner, Robert. *Truth in the Making: Creative Knowledge in Theology and Philosophy.* London: Routledge, 2004.
Misina, Tija. Review of *A Theology of Work* by Darrell Cosden. *Scottish Journal of Theology* 62 (2009) 364–67.
Moe-Lobeda, Cynthia. "Offering Resistance to Globalization: Insights from Luther." In *Globalization and the Good*, edited by Peter Heslam, 95–104. London: SPCK, 2004.
Moltmann, Jürgen. *The Coming of God: Christian Eschatology.* Translated by Margaret Kohl. SCM: London, 1996.
———. *Creating a Just Future: The Politics of Peace and the Ethics of Creation in a Threatened World.* London: SCM, 1989.
———. *The Future of Creation: Translated Essays.* Translated by Margaret Kohl. Philadelphia: Fortress, 1979.
———. *God for a Secular Society: The Public Relevance of Theology.* Translated by Margaret Kohl. London: SCM, 1999.
———. *God in Creation: An Ecological Doctrine of Creation.* Translated by Margaret Kohl. SCM: London, 1997.
———. "The Right to Meaningful Work." In *On Human Dignity: Political Theology and Ethics*, translated by M. Douglas Meeks, 37–54. London: SCM, 1984.
———. *The Source of Life: The Holy Spirit and the Theology of Life.* Translated by Margaret Kohl. London: SCM, 1997.
———. *The Spirit of Life: A Universal Affirmation.* Translated by Margaret Kohl. SCM: London, 1992.
———. *Theology and Joy.* Translated by R. Ulrich. London: SCM, 1973.
———. *The Way of Jesus Christ: Christology in Messianic Dimensions.* Translated by Margaret Kohl. London: SCM, 1990.
Monk, Robert C. *John Wesley, His Puritan Heritage.* Nashville: Abingdon, 1966.
Moore, Thomas. *A Life at Work: The Joy of Discovering What You Were Born to Do.* London: Piatkus, 2009.
Morris, Leon. *Luke.* Tyndale New Testament Commentaries. Leicester: InterVarsity, 1984.
Morris, Thomas V. *Francis Schaeffer's Apologetics: A Critique.* Chicago: Moody, 1978.
Moule, C. F. D. *The Holy Spirit.* London: Continuum, 2000.
Mouw, Richard J. *He Shines in All That's Fair: Culture and Common Grace.* Grand Rapids: Eerdmans, 2001.
———. *When the Kings Come Marching In: Isaiah and the New Jerusalem.* Rev. ed. Grand Rapids: Eerdmans, 2002.
Mouw, Richard J., and Sander Griffioen. *Pluralisms and Horizons: An Essay in Christian Public Philosophy.* Grand Rapids: Eerdmans, 1994.
Murray, John. *Collected Writings of John Murray.* Vol. 2, *Selected Lectures in Systematic Theology.* Edinburgh: Banner of Truth Trust, 1977.
———. *Principles of Conduct: Aspects of Biblical Ethics.* London: Tyndale, 1957.
Nasar, Jack L. *Environmental Æsthetics: Theory, Research and Applications.* Cambridge: Cambridge University Press, 1992.
Nash, Elizabeth J. "A New Model for a Theology of Work." *Modern Churchman* 29 (1986–87) 23–27.

Needham, N. R. *Common Grace and the Work of the Christian Institute.* Newcastle-upon-Tyne: The Christian Institute, 2008.
Neff, W. S. *Work and Human Behavior.* Chicago: Aldine, 1977.
Newbigin, Lesslie. *Honest Religion for Secular Man.* London: SCM, 1969.
Newlands, George M. *Theology of the Love of God.* London: Collins, 1980.
Nicol, Iain G. "Vocation and the People of God." *Scottish Journal of Theology* 33 (1980) 361–73.
Niebuhr, H. Richard. *Christ and Culture.* New York: Harper Colophon, 1975.
Niebuhr, Reinhold. *The Children of Light and the Children of Darkness: A Vindication of Democracy and a Critique of Its Traditional Defenders.* London: Nisbet, 1944.
———. *Love and Justice: Selections from the Shorter Writings of Reinhold Niebuhr.* Louisville: Westminster John Knox, 1992.
———. *Moral Man and Immoral Society.* London: Continuum, 2005.
Nixon, Leroy. *John Calvin's Teachings on Human Reason.* New York: Exposition, 1963.
Noble, David F. *The Religion of Technology: The Divinity of Man and the Spirit of Invention.* London: Penguin, 1999.
Noll, Mark A. "Introduction to Modern Protestantism." In *The Teachings of Modern Christianity: On Law, Politics, and Human Nature,* edited by John Witte Jr. and Frank S. Alexander, 1:261–87. New York: Columbia University Press, 2006.
———. *The Rise of Evangelicalism: The Age of Edwards, Whitefield and the Wesleys.* Downers Grove, IL: InterVarsity, 2004.
Northcott, Michael S. "BP, the Blowout and the Bible Belt: Why Conservative Christianity Does Not Conserve Creation." *The Expository Times* 122 (2010) 117–26.
———. "Concept Art, Clones, and Co-Creators: The Theology of Making." *Modern Theology* 21 (2005) 219–36.
———. "The Market, the Multitude and Metaphysics: Ronald Preston's Middle Way and the Theological Critique of Economic Reason." *Studies in Christian Ethics* 14 (2004) 12–34.
———. *A Moral Climate: The Ethics of Global Warming.* London: Darton, Longman & Todd, 2007.
———. "The Parable of the Talents and the Economy of the Gift." *Theology* 107 (2004) 241–49.
Oden, Thomas C. *The Transforming Power of Grace.* Nashville: Abingdon, 1993.
O'Donnell, John. "Exploring the Human: Theology in Dialogue." *Gregorianum* 67 (1986) 125–32.
O'Donovan, Oliver. *Begotten or Made?* Oxford: Clarendon, 1998.
———. "The Natural Ethic." In *Essays in Evangelical Social Ethics,* edited by David F. Wright, 19–35. Exeter: Paternoster, 1978.
———. *Resurrection and the Moral Order: An Outline for Evangelical Ethics.* Leicester: Apollos, 1996.
———. "Towards an Interpretation of Biblical Ethics: The Tyndale Biblical Theology Lecture 1975." *Tyndale Bulletin* 27 (1976) 54–78.
———. *The Ways of Judgement.* The Bampton Lectures 2003. Grand Rapids: Eerdmans, 2005.
Oliver, David. *Work: Prison or Place of Destiny?* Milton Keynes: World, 2000.

Olson, Roger E. "Postconservative Evangelical Theology and the Theological Pilgrimage of Clark Pinnock." In *Semper Reformandum: Studies in Honor of Clark H. Pinnock*, edited by Stanley E. Porter et al., 16–37. Carlisle: Paternoster, 2003.

O'Malley, J. Steven. "Pietist Influences in the Eschatological Thought of John Wesley and Jürgen Moltmann." *Wesleyan Theological Journal* 29 (1994) 127–39.

———. "Pietistic Influence on John Wesley: Wesley and Gerhard Tersteegen." *Wesleyan Theological Journal* 31 (1996) 48–70.

Orcibal, Jean. "Les Spirituels Français et Espagnols Chez John Wesley et ses Contemporains." *Révue de l'Histoire des Religions* 139 (1951) 50–109.

Oslington, Paul. "Divine Action, Providence and Adam Smith's Invisible Hand." In *Adam Smith as Theologian*, edited by Paul Oslington, 61–75. New York: Routledge, 2011.

Osterhaven, M. E. "Works." In *Evangelical Dictionary of Theology*, edited by Walter A. Elwell, 1295–97. Grand Rapids: Baker Academic, 2009.

Outler, Albert C. *John Wesley*. New York: Oxford University Press, 1964.

———. "John Wesley: Folk Theologian." *Theology Today* 34 (1977) 150–60.

———. "John Wesley's Interests in the Early Fathers of the Church." In *The Wesleyan Theological Heritage: Essays of Albert C. Outler*, edited by Thomas C. Oden et al., 97–110. Grand Rapids: Zondervan, 1991.

———. "Wesley in the Christian Tradition." In *The Place of Wesley in the Christian Tradition: Essays Delivered at Drew University in Celebration of the Commencement of the Publication of the Oxford Edition of the Works of John Wesley*, edited by Kenneth E. Rowe, 11–38. Metuchen, NJ: Scarecrow, 1976.

———. "The Wesleyan Quadrilateral in John Wesley." In *The Wesleyan Theological Heritage: Essays of Albert C. Outler*, edited by Thomas C. Oden et al., 145–58. Grand Rapids: Zondervan, 1991.

Owen, John. *The Holy Spirit*. Edinburgh: Banner of Truth Trust, 1998.

"Oxford Declaration on Christian Faith and Economics." www.calvin.edu/~pribeiro/DCM.../Economics-1.doc.

Packer, J. I. *A Man for All Ministries: Richard Baxter 1615–1691*. London: Needham's, 1991.

———. *Richard Baxter: The Redemption and Restoration of Man in the Thought of Richard Baxter; A Study in Puritan Theology*. Carlisle: Paternoster, 2003.

Padilla, René. "How Evangelicals Endorsed Social Responsibility 1966–1983." *Transformation: An International Dialogue of Evangelical Social Ethics* 2 (1985) 27–33.

Parker, S. *The Future of Work and Leisure*. New York: Praeger, 1971.

Paton, David. *The Clergy and the Clearances: The Church and the Highland Crisis 1790–1850*. Edinburgh: John Donald, 2006.

Paul, Robert S. *The Atonement and Sacraments*. Nashville: Abingdon, 1960.

Perkins, William. "A Treatise of the Vocations or Callings of Men: With the Sorts and Kinds of Them and the Right Use Thereof." In *The Works of William Perkins*, edited by Ian Breward, 3:747–79. Appleford, UK: Sutton Courtenay, 1970.

Pieper, Josef. *Leisure, the Basis of Culture*. Translated by Alexander Dru. London: Faber & Faber, 1958.

Pierard, Richard V. "Schaeffer on History." In *Reflections on Francis Schaeffer*, edited by Ronald W. Ruegsegger, 197–220. Grand Rapids: Academie Books, 1986.

Piette, Maximin. *John Wesley in the Evolution of Protestantism.* London: Sheed and Ward, 1937.
Pinnock, Clark H. *The Flame of Love: A Theology of the Holy Spirit.* Downers Grove, IL: InterVarsity, 1996.
Plant, Raymond. "Conservative Capitalism: Theological and Moral Challenges." In *Theology in the City: A Theological Response to "Faith in the City,"* edited by Anthony Harvey, 68–97. London: SPCK, 1989.
Plato. *Protagoras.* Translated by Benjamin Jowett. http://www.fullbooks.com/Protagoras.html.
———. *Republic.* Translated by Robin Waterfield. Oxford: Oxford University Press, 1998.
Poole, Eve. *The Church on Capitalism: Theology and the Market.* London: Palgrave Macmillan, 2010.
———. "Management as Sacred Trust." *Crucible: The Christian Journal of Social Ethics* (January–March 2011) 33–44.
Preece, Gordon. "Vocation in a Post-vocational World: Meaning, De-meaning and Re-meaning of Work." In *The Bible and the Business of Life: Essays in Honor of Robert J. Banks's Sixty-Fifth Birthday,* edited by Simon Holt and Gordon Preece, 192–215. Adelaide: ATF, 2004.
Quistorp, Heinrich. *Calvin's Doctrine of the Last Things.* Translated by Harold Knight. London: Lutterworth, 1955.
Ramsey, Paul. "A Theory of Virtue According to the Principles of the Reformation." *The Journal of Religion* 27/3 (1947) 181.
Reed, Esther. *Christian Ethics in the Workplace.* London: Darton, Longman & Todd, 2010.
Reid, W. S. "John Calvin." In *Evangelical Dictionary of Theology,* edited by Walter A. Elwell, 200–203. Grand Rapids: Baker Academic, 2001.
———. "John Knox, Pastor of Souls." *Westminster Theological Journal* 40 (1977) 1–21.
———. "Work." In *Evangelical Dictionary of Theology,* edited by Walter A. Elwell, 1295. Grand Rapids: Baker Academic, 2009.
Rémy, Jean. "Work and Self-Awareness." In *Work and Religion,* edited by Gregory Baum, 3–11. Concilium 131. Edinburgh: T. & T. Clark, 1980.
Ricardo, David. "On the Principles of Political Economy and Taxation." In *Works and Correspondence of David Ricardo,* edited by Piero Sraffa, 1:1–413. Cambridge: Cambridge University Press, 1973.
Rice, Daniel F. "Natural Theology and the Scottish Philosophy in the Thought of Thomas Chalmers." *Scottish Journal of Theology* 24 (1971) 23–46.
Richardson, Alan. *The Biblical Doctrine of Work.* London: SCM, 1954.
Robinson, D. S. *The Story of Scottish Philosophy.* New York: Exposition, 1961.
Rogers, Eugene F., Jr. *After the Spirit: A Constructive Pneumatology from Resources Outside the Modern West.* London: SCM, 2006.
Rogers, Jack. "Francis Schaeffer: The Promise and the Problem." *Reformed Journal* 27/5 (1977) 12–15; *Reformed Journal* 27/6 (1977) 15–19.
Rolston, Holmes, III. "Responsible Man in Reformed Theology: Calvin Versus the Westminster Confession." *Scottish Journal of Theology* 23 (1970) 129–56.
Rookmaaker, Hans. *Gauguin and Nineteenth-Century Art Theory: The Complete Works of Hans R. Rookmaaker.* Vol. 1. Carlisle: Piquant, 2002.

———. *Synthetist Art Theories: Genesis and Nature of the Ideas on Art of Gauguin and His Circle*. Amsterdam: Swets & Zeitlinger, 1959.

Roos, L. "On a Theology and Ethics of Work." *Communio* 11 (1984) 100–119.

Rosato, Philip J. "Spirit-Christology as Access to Trinitarian Theology." In *God's Life in Trinity*, edited by Miroslav Volf et al., 166–76. Minneapolis: Fortress, 2006.

Roxborogh, John. "Chalmers' Theology of Mission." In *The Practical and the Pious: Essays on Thomas Chalmers (1780-1847)*, edited by A. C. Cheyne, 74–85. Edinburgh: The Saint Andrew Press, 1985.

———. *Thomas Chalmers: Enthusiast for Mission; The Christian Good of Scotland and the Rise of the Missionary Movement*. Carlisle: Paternoster, 1999.

Ruegsegger, Ronald W. "Francis Schaeffer on Philosophy." In *Reflections on Francis Schaeffer*, edited by Ronald W. Ruegsegger, 107–30. Grand Rapids: Academie Books 1986.

———. "Schaeffer's System of Thought." In *Reflections on Francis Schaeffer*, edited by Ronald W. Ruegsegger, 25–43. Grand Rapids: Academie Books, 1986.

Rundle, Steve, and Tom Steffen. *Great Commission Companies: The Emerging Role of Business in Missions*. Downers Grove, IL: InterVarsity, 2003.

Runyon, Theodore. "The New Creation: The Wesleyan Distinctive." *The Wesleyan Theological Journal* 31 (1996) 5–19.

Ruskin, John. *The Crown of Wild Olive: Four Lectures on Work, Traffic, War, and the Future of England*. New York: Thomas Y. Crowell, n.d.

———. *Unto This Last*. N.p.: Filiquarian, 2007.

Ryken, Leyland. *Worldly Saints: The Puritans as They Really Were*. Grand Rapids: Zondervan, 1990.

Samuel, Vinay, and Chris Sugden. "Toward a Theology of Social Change." In *Evangelicals and Development: Towards a Theology of Social Change*, edited by Ronald J. Sider, 45–68. Exeter: Paternoster, 1981.

Sayers, Dorothy L. *Why Work?* London: Methuen, 1942.

Schaeffer, Edith. *L'Abri*. Worthing, UK: Norfolk and Henry E. Walter, 1969.

———. *The Tapestry*. Waco, TX: Word, 1981.

Schaeffer, Francis A. *Death in the City: The Relevance of the Message of the Bible to the Twentieth Century World*. London: InterVarsity, 1970.

———. *Genesis in Space and Time: The Flow of Biblical History*. London: Hodder & Stoughton, 1973.

———. *The God Who Is There*. Francis A. Schaeffer Trilogy: The Three Essential Books in One Volume. Leicester: InterVarsity, 1990.

———. *How Should We Then Live?* Complete Works of Francis A. Schaeffer 5. Wheaton, IL: Crossway, 1994.

———. *Pollution and the Death of Man*. The Complete Works of Francis A. Schaeffer: 5. Wheaton, IL: Crossway, 1994.

———. "A Review of a Review." *The Bible Today* 42 (1948) 7–9.

Scharen, Christian A. B. *Faith as a Way of Life: A Vision for Pastoral Leadership*. Grand Rapids: Eerdmans, 2008.

Schenk, Richard. "Work: The Corruption or Perfection of the Human Being?" *Nova et Vetera* 2/1 (2004) 129–45.

Schumacher, E. F. *Good Work*. New York: Harper & Row, 1979.

———. *Small Is Beautiful: A Study of Economics as if People Mattered*. London: Blond & Briggs, 1973.

Schüssler Fiorenza, Francis. "Religious Beliefs and Praxis: Reflections on Catholic Theological Views of Work." In *Work and Religion*, edited by Gregory Baum, 92–102. Concilium 131. Edinburgh: T. & T. Clark, 1980.

Schuurman, Douglas J. "Creation, Eschaton, and Social Ethics: A Response to Volf." *Calvin Theological Journal* 30 (1995) 144–58.

Schweiker, William. "The Spirit of Life and the Reverence for Life." In *God's Life in Trinity*, edited by Miroslav Volf et al., 22–32. Minneapolis: Fortress, 2006.

Schweizer, Eduard. "σάρξ, σαρκικός, σάρκινος." In *Theological Dictionary of the New Testament*, translated by Geoffrey W. Bromiley, 7:124–31. Grand Rapids: Eerdmans, 1995.

———. "ψυχικὸς." In *Theological Dictionary of the New Testamtent*, edited by Gerhard Kittel et al., 9:661–63. Translated by Geoffrey W. Bromiley. Grand Rapids: Eerdmans, 1995.

Schweitzer, Albert. *The Philosophy of Civilization*. Translated by C. T. Campion. New York: Prometheus, 1987.

Sennett, Richard. *The Corrosion of Character: The Personal Consequences of Work in the New Capitalism*. New York: Norton, 1998.

———. *The Craftsman*. New Haven: Yale University Press, 2008.

Shelley, J. A. *Not Just a Job: Serving Christ in Your Work*. Downers Grove, IL: InterVarsity, 1985.

Sheppard, David. *Built as a City: God and the Urban World Today*. London: Hodder & Stoughton, 1974.

Sherman, Doug, and William Hendricks. *Your Work Matters to God*. Colorado Springs: Navpress, 1987.

Siebert, Rudolf. "Work and Religion in Hegel's Thought." In *Work and Religion*, edited by Gregory Baum, 117–28. Concilium 131. Edinburgh: T. & T. Clark, 1980.

Silvas, Anna M. *The Asketikon of St Basil the Great*. Oxford: Oxford University Press, 2005.

Simmons, Laura K. "Dorothy L. Sayers' Theology of Work and Vocation in Everyday Life." In *The Bible and the Business of Life: Essays in Honor of Robert J. Banks's Sixty-Fifth Birthday*, edited by Simon Holt et al., 192–215. Adelaide: ATF, 2004.

Simon, Y. R. *Work, Society and Culture*. New York: Fordham University Press, 1971.

Smail, Thomas A. "The Cross and the Spirit: Towards a Theology of Renewal." In *Charismatic Renewal: The Search for a Theology*, edited by Tom Smail et al., 49–70. London: SPCK, 1995.

———. *The Giving Gift: The Holy Spirit in Person*. London: Hodder & Stoughton, 1988.

———. "In Spirit and in Truth: Reflections." In *Charismatic Renewal: The Search for a Theology*, edited by Tom Smail et al., 109–16. London: SPCK, 1995.

———. *Like Father, Like Son: The Trinity Imaged in Our Humanity*. Milton Keynes: Paternoster, 2005.

———. "A Renewal Recalled." In *Charismatic Renewal: The Search for a Theology*, edited by Tom Smail et al., 7–21. London: SPCK, 1995.

Smith, David W. *Transforming the World? The Social Impact of British Evangelicalism*. Carlisle: Paternoster, 1998.

Sölle, Dorothee, with Shirley A. Cloyes. *To Work and Love: A Theology of Creation*. Philadelphia: Fortress, 1986.

Soskice, Janet Martin. "Creation and Relation." *Theology* 94 (1991) 31–39.

Stackhouse, Ian. *The Gospel-Driven Church: Retrieving Classical Ministries for Contemporary Revivalism.* Milton Keynes: Paternoster, 2005.

Stackhouse, Max L. "Business, Economics and Christian Ethics." In *The Cambridge Companion to Christian Ethics*, edited by Robin Gill, 228–42. Cambridge: Cambridge University Press, 2003.

Stackhouse, Max L., et al. *On Moral Business: Classical and Contemporary Resources for Ethics in Economic Life.* Grand Rapids: Eerdmans, 1995.

Starkey, Lycurgus M. *The Work of the Holy Spirit in the Theology of John Wesley.* New York: Columbia University Press, 1953.

Stephanou, Eusebius. "The Church Fathers on Divine Indwelling and the Theology of Grace." *Patristic and Byzantine Review* 11 (1992) 18–20.

Stevens, R. Paul. "All Are Called: The Universal Vocation of the People of God." In *The Bible and the Business of Life: Essays in Honor of Robert J. Banks's Sixty-Fifth Birthday*, edited by Simon Holt et al., 101–18. Adelaide: ATF, 2004.

———. *Doing God's Business: Meaning and Motivation for the Marketplace.* Grand Rapids: Eerdmans, 2006.

———. *The Other Six Days: Vocation, Work, and Ministry in Biblical Perspective.* Grand Rapids: Eerdmans, 2000.

Stevens, R. Paul, and Alvin Ung. *Taking Your Soul to Work: Overcoming the Nine Deadly Sins of the Workplace.* Grand Rapids: Eerdmans, 2010.

Stob, Henry. "Observations on the Concept of the Antithesis." In *Perspectives on the Christian Reformed Church: Studies in Its History, Theology, and Ecumenicity*, edited by Peter de Klerk et al., 241–56. Grand Rapids: Baker, 1983.

Storkey, Alan. *A Christian Social Perspective.* Leicester: InterVarsity, 1979.

———. *Transforming Economics: A Christian Way to Employment.* London: SPCK, 1986.

Stott, John R. W. *Christian Mission in the Modern World.* Downers Grove, IL: InterVarsity, 2008.

———. *The Cross of Christ.* Leicester: InterVarsity, 1999.

———. "Epilogue: The Task Which Now Awaits Us." In *Essays in Evangelical Social Ethics*, edited by David F. Wright, 179–83. Exeter: Paternoster, 1978.

———. *Issues Facing Christians Today: New Perspectives on Social and Moral Dilemmas.* Grand Rapids: Zondervan, 2006.

———. "Evangelism and Social Responsibility: An Evangelical Commitment." Lausanne Occasional Paper 21. http://www.lausanne.org/all-documents/lop-21.html.

Stott, John R. W., and Robert T. Coote. *Down to Earth: Studies in Christianity and Culture; The Papers of the Lausanne Consultation on Gospel and Culture.* London: Hodder and Stoughton, 1981.

Sugden, Chris, and Oliver Barclay. *Kingdom and Creation in Social Ethics.* Nottingham: Grove, 1990.

Tanner, Kathryn. *The Economy of Grace.* Minneapolis: Fortress, 2005.

———. "Workings of the Spirit: Simplicity or Complexity?" In *The Work of the Spirit: Pneumatology and Pentecostalism*, edited by Michael Welker, 87–105. Grand Rapids: Eerdmans, 2006.

Tawney, R. H. *Religion and the Rise of Capitalism.* West Drayton: Penguin, 1948.

Taylor, Charles. *A Secular Age.* Cambridge, MA: Belknap, 2007.

Taylor, John V. *The Go-Between God: The Holy Spirit and the Christian Mission.* London: SCM, 1976.
Telford, John. "From the Death of Whitefield to the Death of Charles Wesley." In *The Life of John Wesley by John Telford*, 18. New York: Hunt & Eaton, 1924.
Temple, William. *Christianity and the Social Order.* London: Penguin, 1942.
The Thirty-Nine Articles of the Faith of the Church of England. http://anglicansonline.org/basics/thirty-nine_articles.html.
Thomas, Carolyn E. "Sports." In *Spirituality and the Secular Quest*, edited by Peter H. Van Ness, 498–529. New York: Crossroad, 1996.
Thomas, Keith, ed. *The Oxford Book of Work.* Oxford: Oxford University Press, 1999.
Thompson, E. P. *The Making of the English Working Class.* London: Penguin, 1991.
Tidball, Derek J. *Contemporary Evangelical Social Thinking—A Review.* Nottingham: A Shaftesbury Project, 1977.
———. *Who Are the Evangelicals? Tracing the Roots of Today's Movement.* London: Marshall Pickering, 1994.
Torrance, James B. "Strengths and Weaknesses of the Westminster Theology." In *The Westminster Confession in the Church Today: Papers Prepared for the Church of Scotland Panel on Doctrine*, edited by Alasdair I. C. Heron, 40–53. Edinburgh: The Saint Andrew Press, 1982.
Torrance, T. F. *Calvin's Doctrine of Man.* London: Lutterworth, 1949.
———. *Scottish Theology: From John Knox to John McLeod Campbell.* Edinburgh: T. & T. Clark, 1996.
Troeltsch, Ernst. *The Social Teaching of the Christian Churches.* Vol. 2. Translated by Olive Wyon. London: George Allen & Unwin, 1931.
Trueman, Carl R. "A Small Step towards Rationalism: The Impact of the Metaphysics of Tommaso Campanella on the Theology of Richard Baxter." In *Protestant Scholasticism: Essays in Reassessment*, edited by Carl R. Trueman et al., 181–95. Carlisle: Paternoster, 1999.
Tulloch, John. *English Puritanism and Its Leaders: Cromwell, Milton, Baxter, Bunyan.* Edinburgh: William Blackwood, 1861.
Turnau, Theodore A. "Reflecting Theologically on Popular Culture as Meaningful: The Role of Sin, Grace, and General Revelation." *Calvin Theological Journal* 37 (2002) 270–96.
Turner, Max. *Power from on High: The Spirit in Israel's Restoration and Witness in Luke-Acts.* Sheffield: Sheffield Academic Press, 2000.
Van Ruler, Arnold A. *Calvinist Trinitarianism and Theocentric Politics: Essays Toward a Public Theology.* Lewiston, NY: Edwin Mellen, 1989.
Van Til, Cornelius. *Common Grace and the Gospel.* Phillipsburg, NJ: Presbyterian & Reformed, 1972.
———. *The Defense of the Faith.* Philadelphia: Presbyterian & Reformed, 1972.
Van Til, Henry R. *The Calvinistic Concept of Culture.* Grand Rapids: Eerdmans, 2001.
Venolia, Carol. *Healing Environments.* Berkeley, CA: Celestial Arts, 1988.
Verhey, Allen. *Nature and Altering It.* Grand Rapids: Eerdmans, 2010.
Voges, Friedhelm. "Chalmers' Thinking Habits: Some Lessons from His Theology." In *The Practical and the Pious: Essays on Thomas Chalmers (1780–1847)*, edited by A. C. Cheyne, 157–65. Edinburgh: The Saint Andrew Press, 1985.
Volf, Miroslav. *Against the Tide: Love in a Time of Petty Dreams and Persisting Enemies.* Grand Rapids: Eerdmans, 2010.

———. "Eschaton, Creation, and Social Ethics." *Calvin Theological Journal* 30 (1995) 130–43.

———. "In the Cage of Vanities: Christian Faith and the Dynamics of Economic Progress." In *Rethinking Materialism: Perspectives on the Spiritual Dimension of Economic Behavior*, edited by Robert Wuthnow, 169–91. Grand Rapids: Eerdmans, 1995.

———. "Materiality of Salvation: An Investigation in the Soteriologies of Liberation and Pentecostal Theologies." *Journal of Ecumenical Studies* 26 (1989) 447–67.

———. "On Human Work: An Evaluation of the Key Ideas of the Encyclical *Laborem Exercens*." *Scottish Journal of Theology* 37 (1984) 67–79.

———. "On Loving with Hope: Eschatology and Social Responsibility." *Transformation* 7 (1990) 28–31.

———. *A Public Faith: How Followers of Christ Should Serve the Common Good*. Grand Rapids: Brazos, 2011.

———. "Redeeming the Past?" *Christian Century* 119 (2002) 44.

———. "Theology for a Way of Life." In *Practicing Theology: Beliefs and Practices in Christian Life*, edited by Miroslav Volf and Dorothy C. Bass, 245–63. Grand Rapids: Eerdmans, 2002.

———. *Work in the Spirit: Toward a Theology of Work*. Eugene, OR: Wipf & Stock, 2001.

———. *Zukunft der Arbeit–Arbeit der Zukunft: Der Arbeitsbegrif bei Karl Marx und seine theologische Wertung*. Munich: Kaiser, 1988.

Volf, Miroslav, and Gordon Preece. "Work." In *The Oxford Companion to Christian Thought*, edited by Adrian Hastings et al., 759–61. Oxford: Oxford University Press, 2000.

Vos, Arvin. *Aquinas, Calvin and Contemporary Protestant Thought: A Critique of Protestant Views on the Thought of Thomas Aquinas*. Grand Rapids: Eerdmans, 1985.

Vos, Geerhardus. *Biblical Theology: Old and New Testaments*. Grand Rapids: Eerdmans, 1948.

Wahrman, Dror. *The Making of the Modern Self: Identity and Culture in Eighteenth-Century England*. New Haven: Yale University Press, 2004.

Wainwright, Geoffrey. "The Holy Spirit." In *The Cambridge Companion to Christian Doctrine*, edited by Colin E. Gunton, 273–96. Cambridge: Cambridge University Press, 2004.

Walsh, John. "'The Bane of Industry'? Popular Evangelicalism and Work in the Eighteenth Century." In *The Use and Abuse of Time in Christian History: Papers Read at the 1999 Summer Meeting and the 2000 Winter Meeting of the Ecclesiastical History Society*, edited by R. N. Swanson, 223–41. Suffolk, UK: Published for the Ecclesiastical History Society by the Boydell Press, 2002.

Walzer, Michael. *The Revolution of the Saints: A Study in the Origins of Radical Politics*. London: Weidenfeld & Nicolson, 1966.

Watkin-Jones, Howard. *The Holy Spirit from Arminius to Wesley: A Study of Christian Teaching Concerning the Holy Spirit and His Place in the Trinity in the Seventeenth and Eighteenth Centuries*. London: Epworth, 1929.

Watts, John D. W. *Isaiah 34–66*. Word Biblical Commentary 25. Waco, TX: Word, 1987.

Weber, Max. *The Protestant Ethic and the Spirit of Capitalism*. Translated by Talcott Parsons. London: Routledge, 2007.

Weber, Otto. *Foundations of Dogmatics*. Vol. 1. Translated by Darrell L. Guder. Grand Rapids: Eerdmans, 1981.

Weber, Theodore R. *Politics in the Order of Salvation: Transforming Wesleyan Political Ethics*. Nashville: Kingswood, 2001.

Weir, Stuart. "Unwitting Workers of Grace." *Crucible: The Christian Journal of Social Ethics* (January–March 2011) 41–48.

Welker, Michael, *Creation and Reality*. Translated by John F. Hoffmeyer. Minneapolis: Fortress, 1999.

———. *God the Spirit*. Translated by John F. Hoffmeyer. Minneapolis: Fortress, 1994.

Wenham, J. W. *The Elements of New Testament Greek*. Cambridge: Cambridge University Press, 1976.

Wesley, John. "The Difference between Walking by Sight, and Walking by Faith" (Sermon 113). In *The Sermons of John Wesley*, edited by Thomas Jackson. Nampa, ID: Northwest Nazarene University, 1872.

———. "The End of Christ's Coming" (Sermon 62). In *The Sermons of John Wesley*, edited by Thomas Jackson. Nampa, ID: Northwest Nazarene University, 1872.

———. "Free Grace" (Sermon 128). In *The Sermons of John Wesley*, edited by Thomas Jackson. Nampa, ID: Northwest Nazarene University, 1872.

———. "The General Deliverance" (Sermon 60). In *The Sermons of John Wesley*, edited by Thomas Jackson. Nampa, ID: Northwest Nazarene University, 1872.

———. "The Heavenly Treasure in Earthly Vessels" (Sermon 124). In *The Sermons of John Wesley*, edited by Thomas Jackson. Nampa, ID: Northwest Nazarene University, 1872.

———. "Justification by Faith" (Sermon 5). In *The Sermons of John Wesley*, edited by Thomas Jackson. Nampa, ID: Northwest Nazarene University, 1872.

———. "Letter to John Robson—September 30th 1735." In *The Letters of John Wesley*, edited by John Telford. London: Epworth, 1931.

———. "Letter to Thomas Church—2nd February 1745." In *The Letters of John Wesley*, edited by John Telford. London: Epworth, 1931.

———. "Letter to John Smith—25th June 1746." In *The Letters of John Wesley*, edited by John Telford. London: Epworth, 1931.

———. "Letter to Charles Wesley—3rd August 1771." In *The Letters of John Wesley*, edited by John Telford. London: Epworth, 1931.

———. "Letter to John Mason—21st November 1776." In *The Letters of John Wesley*, edited by John Telford. London: Epworth, 1931.

———. "Letter to John Mason—13th January 1790." In *The Letters of John Wesley*, edited by John Telford. London: Epworth, 1931.

———. "Letter to John Smith—25th June 1746." In *The Letters of John Wesley*, edited by John Telford. London: Epworth, 1931.

———. "Letter to Charles Wesley—3rd August 1771." In *The Letters of John Wesley*, edited by John Telford. London: Epworth, 1931.

———. "Letter to John Mason—21st November 1776." In *The Letters of John Wesley*, edited by John Telford. London: Epworth, 1931.

———. "Letter to John Mason—13th January 1790." In *The Letters of John Wesley*, edited by John Telford. London: Epworth, 1931.

———. "The More Excellent Way" (Sermon 89). In *The Sermons of John Wesley*, edited by Thomas Jackson. Nampa, ID: Northwest Nazarene University, 1872.

———. "The Mystery of Iniquity" (Sermon 61). In *The Sermons of John Wesley*, edited by Thomas Jackson. Nampa, ID: Northwest Nazarene University, 1872.

———. "New Birth" (Sermon 45). In *The Sermons of John Wesley*, edited by Thomas Jackson. Nampa, ID: Northwest Nazarene University, 1872.

———. "The New Creation" (Sermon 64). In *The Sermons of John Wesley*, edited by Thomas Jackson. Nampa, ID: Northwest Nazarene University, 1872.

———. "Notes on the Epistle to the Hebrews." In *John Wesley's Notes on the Bible*, edited by Thomas Jackson. Nampa, ID: Northwest Nazarene University, 1872.

———. "Notes on the First Book of Moses called Genesis." In *John Wesley's Notes on the Bible*, edited by Thomas Jackson. Nampa, ID: Northwest Nazarene University, 1872.

———. "Notes on the First Epistle of John." In *John Wesley's Notes on the Bible*, edited by Thomas Jackson. Nampa, ID: Northwest Nazarene University, 1872.

———. "Notes on the Gospel According to Matthew." In *John Wesley's Notes on the Bible*, edited by Thomas Jackson. Nampa, ID: Northwest Nazarene University, 1872.

———. "Notes on the Gospel According to St. John." In *John Wesley's Notes on the Bible*, edited by Thomas Jackson. Nampa, ID: Northwest Nazarene University, 1872.

———. "Notes on Paul's Epistle to the Ephesians." In *John Wesley's Notes on the Bible*, edited by Thomas Jackson. Nampa, ID: Northwest Nazarene University, 1872.

———. "Notes on the Revelation of Jesus Christ." In *John Wesley's Notes on the Bible*, edited by Thomas Jackson. Nampa, ID: Northwest Nazarene University, 1872.

———. "Notes on the Second Epistle General of Peter." In *John Wesley's Notes on the Bible*, edited by Thomas Jackson. Nampa, ID: Northwest Nazarene University, 1872.

———. "Notes on St. Paul's Epistle to the Romans." In *John Wesley's Notes on the Bible*, edited by Thomas Jackson. Nampa, ID: Northwest Nazarene University, 1872.

———. "Notes on St. Paul's First Epistle to the Corinthians." In *John Wesley's Notes on the Bible*, edited by Thomas Jackson. Nampa, ID: Northwest Nazarene University, 1872.

———. "On Conscience" (Sermon 105). In *The Sermons of John Wesley*, edited by Thomas Jackson. Nampa, ID: Northwest Nazarene University, 1872

———. "On Living Without God" (Sermon 125). In *The Sermons of John Wesley*, edited by Thomas Jackson. Nampa, ID: Northwest Nazarene University, 1872.

———. "On the Fall of Man" (Sermon 57). In *The Sermons of John Wesley*, edited by Thomas Jackson. Northwest Nazarene University: Nampa, ID, 1872.

———. "On the Wedding Garment" (Sermon 120). In *The Sermons of John Wesley*, edited by Thomas Jackson. Nampa, ID: Northwest Nazarene University, 1872.

———. "On Visiting the Sick" (Sermon 98). In *The Sermons of John Wesley*, edited by Thomas Jackson. Nampa, ID: Northwest Nazarene University, 1872.

———. "On Working Out Your Own Salvation" (Sermon 85). In *The Sermons of John Wesley*, edited by Thomas Jackson. Nampa, ID: Northwest Nazarene University, 1872.

———. "On Worldy Folly" (Sermon 119). In *The Sermons of John Wesley*, edited by Thomas Jackson. Nampa, ID: Northwest Nazarene University, 1872.

———. "The Origin, Nature, Properties, and Use of the Law" (Sermon 34). In *The Sermons of John Wesley*, edited by Thomas Jackson. Nampa, ID: Northwest Nazarene University, 1872.

———. "The Repentance of Believers" (Sermon 14). In *The Sermons of John Wesley*, edited by Thomas Jackson. Nampa, ID: Northwest Nazarene University, 1872.

———. "The Reward of the Righteous" (Sermon 99). In *The Sermons of John Wesley*, edited by Thomas Jackson. Nampa, ID: Northwest Nazarene University, 1872.

———. "The Righteousness of Faith" (Sermon 6). In *The Sermons of John Wesley*, edited by Thomas Jackson. Nampa, ID: Northwest Nazarene University, 1872.

———. "Salvation by Faith" (Sermon 1). In *The Sermons of John Wesley*, edited by Thomas Jackson. Nampa, ID: Northwest Nazarene University, 1872.

———. "Upon Our Lord's Sermon on the Mount: Discourse Five" (Sermon 25). In *The Sermons of John Wesley*, edited by Thomas Jackson. Nampa, ID: Northwest Nazarene University, 1872.

———. "The Witness of Our Own Spirit" (Sermon 12). In *The Sermons of John Wesley*, edited by Thomas Jackson. Nampa, ID: Northwest Nazarene University, 1872.

West, Philip. "Cruciform Labour? The Cross in Two Recent Theologies of Work." *Modern Churchman* 28 (1985–86) 9–15.

———. "Karl Barth's Theology of Work: A Resource for the Late 80s." *Modern Churchman* 30 (1988–89) 13–19.

Westermann, Claus. "Work, Civilisation and Culture in the Bible." In *Work and Religion*, edited by Gregory Baum, 81–91. Concilium 131. Edinburgh: T. & T. Clark, 1980.

Whybray, R. N. *Isaiah 40–66*. Grand Rapids: Eerdmans, 1975.

Wickham, E. R. *Church and People in an Industrial City*. London: Lutterworth, 1962.

Williams, Rowan. *On Christian Theology*. Oxford: Blackwell, 2000.

Willmer, Haddon. "Images of the City and the Shaping of Humanity." In *Theology in the City: A Theological Response to "Faith in the City,"* edited by Anthony Harvey, 32–46. London: SPCK, 1989.

Wilson, Leonard G. *Sir Charles Lyell's Scientific Journals on the Species Question*. New Haven: Yale University Press, 1970.

Wingren, Gustaf. *The Christian's Calling: Luther on Vocation*. Edinburgh: Oliver & Boyd, 1958.

Witherington, Ben, III. *The Problem with Evangelical Theology: Testing the Exegetical Foundations of Calvinism, Dispensationalism and Wesleyanism*. Waco, TX: Baylor University Press, 2005.

———. *Work: A Kingdom Perspective on Labor*. Grand Rapids: Eerdmans, 2011.

Witten, Marsha G. "'Where Your Treasure Is': Popular Evangelical Views of Work, Money, and Materialism" In *Rethinking Materialism: Perspectives on the Spiritual Dimension of Economic Behavior*, edited by Robert Wuthnow, 117–41. Grand Rapids: Eerdmans, 1995.

Wogaman, J. Philip. "The Economic Encyclicals of Pope John Paul II." In *The Making of an Economic Vision*, edited by J. M. Houck et al., 44–66. Lanham, MD: University Press of America, 1991.

Wogaman, P. C. *Economics and Ethics: A Christian Inquiry*. Philadelphia: Fortress, 1986.

Wolterstorff, Nicholas. *Art in Action: Toward a Christian Æsthetic*. Grand Rapids: Eerdmans, 1980.

———. "The Bible and Economics: The Hermeneutical Issues." *Transformation* 4 (1987) 11–9.

———. "Has the Cloak Become a Cage? Charity, Justice, and Economic Activity." In *Rethinking Materialism: Perspectives on the Spiritual Dimension of Economic Behavior*, edited by Robert Wuthnow, 145–68. Grand Rapids: Eerdmans, 1995.

Wood, Arthur Skevington. "The Contribution of John Wesley to the Theology of Grace." In *Grace Unlimited*, edited by Clark H. Pinnock, 209–22. Minneapolis: Bethany Fellowship, 1975.

Wright, Christopher J. H. *The Mission of God: Unlocking the Bible's Grand Narrative*. Downers Grove, IL: InterVarsity Academic, 2006

Wright, D. F. "John Calvin." In *Biographical Dictionary of Evangelicals*, edited by Timothy Larsen et al., 111–12. Leicester: InterVarsity, 2003.

Wright, N. T. *The New Testament and the People of God: Christian Origins and the Question of God*. Vol. 1. London: SPCK, 1992.

Wynkoop, Midred Bangs. *A Theology of Love: The Dynamic of Wesleyanism*. Kansas City: Beacon Hill, 1972.

Yang, Shun-Chung. "Alternative Ways of Life in Response to Economic Recession—A Theological Stand." *Asia Journal of Theology* 24 (2010) 204–18

Yong, Amos. *The Spirit Poured Out on All Flesh: Pentecostalism and the Possibility of Global Theology*. Grand Rapids: Baker Academic, 2005.

Yule, George. *Puritans in Politics: The Religious Legislation of the Long Parliament 1640–1647*. Appleford: Sutton Courtenay, 1981.

www.ingramcontent.com/pod-product-compliance
Lightning Source LLC
Chambersburg PA
CBHW071247230426
43668CB00011B/1631